WAR AND DIPLOMACY
IN THE NAPOLEONIC ERA

WAR AND DIPLOMACY IN THE NAPOLEONIC ERA

Sir Charles Stewart, Castlereagh and the Balance of Power in Europe

Reider Payne

BLOOMSBURY ACADEMIC
LONDON • NEW YORK • OXFORD • NEW DELHI • SYDNEY

BLOOMSBURY ACADEMIC
Bloomsbury Publishing Plc
50 Bedford Square, London, WC1B 3DP, UK
1385 Broadway, New York, NY 10018, USA

BLOOMSBURY, BLOOMSBURY ACADEMIC and the Diana logo are trademarks of
Bloomsbury Publishing Plc

First published in Great Britain 2019

Cover design: Graham Robert Ward
Cover image: Sir Charles William Stewart (later 3rd Marquess of Londonderry)
by Sir Thomas Lawrence © National Portrait Gallery

A catalogue record for this book is available from the British Library.

A catalog record for this book is available from the Library of Congress.

ISBN: HB: 978-1-7883-1512-8
ePDF: 978-1-7867-3567-6
eBook: 978-1-7867-2567-7

Series: International Library of Historical Studies

Typeset by Newgen KnowledgeWorks Pvt. Ltd., Chennai, India
Printed and bound in Great Britain

To find out more about our authors and books visit www.bloomsbury.com
and sign up for our newsletters.

CONTENTS

PLATES

1. Robert Stewart, 2nd Marquess of Londonderry, by Sir Thomas Lawrence. Exhibited at the Royal Academy in 1821, Lawrence's portrait shows Britain's foreign secretary at the height of his influence and fame. Lauded throughout Europe by his courtesy title of Viscount Castlereagh, the foreign secretary was one of the architects of the Congress System and of Britain's pre-eminent position amongst the great European powers
   Mount Stewart Londonderry Loan
   Photo © Trustees of the Londonderry Estate/Bryan Rutledge

2. Charles William Stewart, 1st Lord Stewart (later 3rd Marquess of Londonderry), by Sir Thomas Lawrence. The artist began work on this painting in 1818. By this time Castlereagh's younger brother was a key figure in Britain's diplomatic networks. Sir Archibald Alison wrote of the relationship between the two brothers: 'Though their characters were thus different, the tenderest friendship existed between them, which continued with the most eminent advantage to both through the whole of life.'
   Mount Stewart Londonderry Loan
   Photo © Trustees of the Londonderry Estate/Bryan Rutledge

3. Lady Catherine Stewart as Saint Cecilia and her son, Frederick Stewart, later 4th Marquess of Londonderry, by Sir Thomas Lawrence
   Mount Stewart Londonderry Loan
   Photo © Trustees of the Londonderry Estate/Bryan Rutledge

4. Amelia Anne Stewart, Marchioness of Londonderry, by Richard James Lane
   At the Congress of Vienna, Lord and Lady Castlereagh were spied on as they looked at boutiques and shops
   © National Portrait Gallery

5. Sir John Moore by Charles Turner after Sir Thomas Lawrence (published 1809)
   © Yale Center for British Art, Paul Mellon Collection

6. Arthur Wellesley, 1st Duke of Wellington, by William Say after Thomas Phillips; mezzotint published 8 November 1814
   © National Portrait Gallery

7. King George IV after Sir Thomas Lawrence (based on an earlier painting of 1815). Prince Regent from 1811 due to George III's incapacity. After the limitations on the Regency ended in 1812,

ACKNOWLEDGEMENTS

This book is very much a labour of love about two individuals who have long fascinated me. There are many whom I would like to thank since I began work on this project. First and foremost, my thanks are due to Dr Kathleen Walker-Meikle, who has read countless drafts and has cheerfully immersed herself into the world of nineteenth-century European diplomacy. I would also like to particularly thank Professor Stephen Conway, who has been generous with his time and encouragement, and Professor Dominic Lieven, for sharing his expertise on Alexander I and the Russian Empire.

I also want to thank Professor Grayson Ditchfield, Dr Andrew Hanham (and my thanks also to Dr Clive Cheesman for introducing me to Dr Hanham's work) and Professor Nanora Sweet.

My thanks are also due to my editor, Joanna Godfrey, and to her colleagues at I.B. Tauris and Bloomsbury.

This book would not have been possible without the generous assistance received from various archive offices over the course of the past several years. In this respect, I would very much like to thank the staff of the British Library, The National Archives, the Public Record Office of Northern Ireland, Devon Archives and Local Studies, Durham County Record Office and Kent History and Library Centre.

I am also grateful to those who helped with my requests for images. My thanks are due to the National Portrait Gallery, the National Trust images team, the National Trust at Mount Stewart, the Marquess of Londonderry and the Trustees of the Londonderry Estate, the Châteaux de Versailles et de Trianon, the Réunion des Musées Nationaux Grand Palais, the O. W. Klinckowström Art Collection, Finnish National Gallery/Sinebrychoff Art Museum, the Rijksmuseum, and the Yale Center for British Art, Paul Mellon Collection.

Quotations from archives are by the kind permission of the British Library, The National Archives, the Deputy Keeper of the Records, Public Record Office of Northern Ireland, the Earl of Clanwilliam, Devon Archives and Local Studies Service, Durham County Record Office and by courtesy of the Kent History and Library Centre, Maidstone.

Images are reproduced by the kind permission of the National Portrait Gallery, the National Trust, the Marquess of Londonderry and the Trustees of the Londonderry Estate, the Châteaux de Versailles et de Trianon, the Réunion des Musées Nationaux Grand Palais, the O. W. Klinckowström Art Collection, Finnish National Gallery/Sinebrychoff Art Museum, the Rijksmuseum and the Yale Center for British Art, Paul Mellon Collection. I am particularly grateful to the Marquess of Londonderry and the Trustees of the Londonderry Estate for permission to reproduce the paintings of Charles William Stewart, later 3rd Marquess of Londonderry (1778–1854), by Sir Thomas Lawrence PRA, and Frances Anne Emily Vane-Tempest, later Marchioness of Londonderry (1800–1865), by Sir Thomas Lawrence PRA.

Publication of this work has been made possible with the generous assistance of a grant from the Isobel Thornley Bequest, University of London, and by a grant from the Scouloudi Foundation in association with the Institute of Historical Research.

NOTE ON STYLE

The names of most European sovereigns have been anglicized: for example, Ferdinand VII, King of Spain, rather than Fernando VII; and Francis I, Emperor of Austria, rather than Franz I. As is customary, Napoléon's name is anglicized to Napoleon. There are three imperial sovereigns who feature heavily in the book: Alexander I, Emperor of Russia; Francis I, Emperor of Austria; and Napoleon I, Emperor of the French. To avoid confusion at certain points in the text, the Russian Emperor is usually styled as the Tsar, although contemporaries would have referred to him as Emperor.

French titles are given with the rank in lower case and are not anglicized. For example, the duc de Dalberg rather than the Duke of Dalberg. Similarly, Spanish titles are not anglicized, so that Wellington becomes Duque de Ciudad Rodrigo rather than Duke of Ciudad Rodrigo. Marshals of the French Empire are referred to simply by their names, so, for example, Marshal Ney is not referred to as prince de la Moskowa.

Following the death of the first Marquess of Londonderry in 1821, Lord Castlereagh succeeded as second Marquess. However, he is referred to throughout as Castlereagh. It also avoids any confusion to his younger brother who succeeded as third Marquess of Londonderry in 1822 (and after this date, Frederick Stewart, the future fourth Marquess, is referred to as Viscount Castlereagh).

The spelling from quoted archive materials and printed primary sources is mostly reproduced as per the original. However, in some cases individual words have been modernized.

As this book is not intended as an exhaustive history of the period 1808–22, some events outside of the direct narrative are either omitted or briefly noted – for example, the British naval campaigns against France, or the war between Britain and the United States, which broke out in 1812 and was formally concluded by the 1814 Treaty of Ghent.

Map 1 Europe in late 1812

Finland

St Petersburg

Stockholm

Baltic
Sea

R U S S I A N   E M P I R E

Moscow

PRUSSIA

Vistula

Warta

Warsaw

Katzbach

DUCHY OF
WARSAW

Reichenbach

A U S T R I A N

Vienna   Buda   Pest

E M P I R E

Dnieper

Pruth

O T T O M A N

Danube

Balkans

Black Sea

Constantinople

E M P I R E

Provinces

Adriatic Sea

LES

Aegean Sea

Ionian Islands

Mediterranean Sea

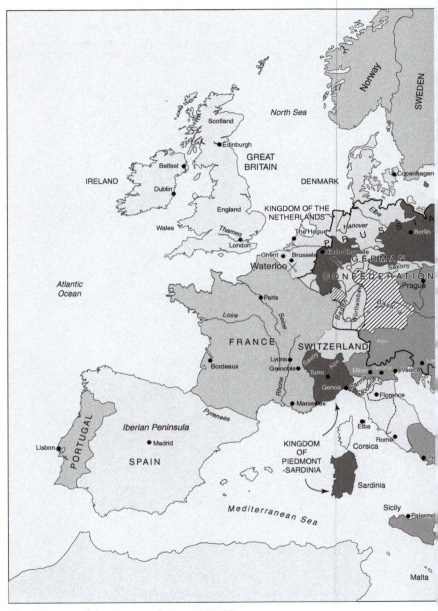

Map 2 Europe of the Congress System 1815–22

Finland

St Petersburg

Stockholm

R U S S I A N   E M P I R E

Moscow

Batlic
Sea

Vistula

Warsaw

C O N G R E S S
P O L A N D

Oder

Troppau

Kraków

A U S T R I A N

Vienna

Buda ● Pest

E M P I R E

Pruth

Crimea

Georgia

Danube

Black Sea

Dinaric Alps

Balkans

O T T O M A N

Mt. Rila   Rhodope

Adriatic Sea

aples

Constantinople

E M P I R E

Pindus

Ionian Islands

Aegean Sea

KINGDOM OF
THE TWO SICILIES
(1816)

Mediterranean Sea

INTRODUCTION: THE DRAGON'S CREST

History has not been kind to Sir Charles Stewart – ennobled in 1814 as Lord Stewart for services in war and diplomacy, and from 1822, the third Marquess of Londonderry. Stewart was often his own worst enemy, but he can also thank the Duke of Wellington for the harsh judgement of posterity. Wellington famously dismissed Stewart as an intriguer and 'mischief maker' who 'used to harass the cavalry to death by constant patrols and reconnaissances'. The Duke recalled threatening his subordinate with arrest, at which the penitent officer 'burst out crying, and begged my pardon, and hoped I would excuse his intemperance'. This criticism, published in the Croker Papers, continued with Wellington's critique of Stewart's relationship with his elder brother, Lord Castlereagh:

> It is wonderful what influence he had over him, and not only influence, for that might be produced by brotherly love, but Castlereagh had a real respect for Charles's understanding, and a high opinion of his good sense and discretion. This seems incomprehensible to us, who know the two men, but the fact was so.[1]

Wellington had shared much with Stewart, both on the battlefield and in the complex diplomatic networks of Congress Europe. The political actions of the then third Marquess of Londonderry after 1822 led to a sharp deterioration in their relations so much so that the Duke ceased to hold any real regard for Castlereagh's younger brother – even though he owed him more than he ever suspected, beyond his trusted horse, Copenhagen.[2]

After the third Marquess's death in 1854, it was left to his second wife, Frances Anne, to commission a biography. She alighted on the lawyer and historian Sir Archibald Alison as an appropriate author. The family recognized that the two brothers had been inseparable in public life. They would now be inseparable as subjects of history. Frances Anne rapidly took charge of her late husband's affairs, including his volumes of correspondence.[3] It was not until October 1861 that the work was finished. Published as a three-volume set rather than the planned two, it had its share of flaws and inaccuracies. It was one of a series of public and private tributes commissioned by Lady Londonderry. Another, in the City of Durham, was one of the more public. The larger-than-life equestrian statue of the third Marquess as a military man, by Raffaelle Monti, was unveiled in the Market Place in Durham on 2 December 1861. As for Alison's work, *Lives of Lord Castlereagh and Sir Charles Stewart*, the author's aim was to 'bring out the character of both the eminent men to whom it relates and establish the importance of their public acts on an imperishable basis'.[4] Unfortunately by the time the volumes appeared, there were very few who remembered the great partnership between the two brothers, only ended by Castlereagh's tragic death in 1822.

Frances Anne's efforts did not stand the test of time.[5] The great twentieth-century historian of British diplomacy, Sir Charles Webster, argued that Castlereagh's 'affection' for his brother 'survived all Stewart's faults and blunders. These were many.' Webster added for good measure, 'Nor had he too many brains, though he was not without a certain shrewdness which enabled him to find out the shady side of Metternich's character.' At least his supposed lack of intelligence was offset by 'energy and a complete devotion to his duties'.[6] Stewart has also appeared in publications centred on his second wife, Frances Anne, as well as in accounts of the Londonderry family by H. Montgomery Hyde.[7] However, his life is usually brought to the public's attention through biographies of his brother, Lord Castlereagh.[8] Recently, John Bew's *Castlereagh: Enlightenment War and Tyranny* (2011) noted that Castlereagh 'valued his brother's unfailing loyalty'.[9] Other modern historians of the period, including Rory Muir, Adam Zamoyski, Michael V. Leggiere, Dominic Lieven and Mark Jarrett, have illustrated Stewart's career in international affairs, particularly as an ambassador.[10]

However, this book examines the origins of the partnership between Stewart and Castlereagh, forged during the Peninsular War. It then traces the increasing importance of that partnership through the German campaign of 1813–14, which ended with the allies marching to the very gates of Paris. Stewart was then centre stage at the Congress of Vienna, not just for picking fights with the local population, but as the foreign secretary's trusted lieutenant. Finally, the book looks at Stewart's career as a peacetime ambassador, a cornerstone of the Anglo-Austrian alliance, who put the Vienna embassy at the heart of Britain's diplomatic networks. By so doing, Stewart became the inseparable and valued partner of his formidable elder brother, Lord Castlereagh.

At many times in his career, Stewart would deprecate his own talents and abilities, and there is no doubt that he did very well out of the Hanoverian patronage system. However, to ascribe this to mere brotherly love is to do a disservice to both Stewart and Castlereagh. The limits of the patronage system would certainly have been strained to near breaking point by placing somebody not up to the job into two sensitive diplomatic posts. The fact that Stewart acquitted himself with honour as a diplomat, ultimately providing a link between Castlereagh and Prince Metternich for almost ten years, shows that he was far from being a nonentity promoted beyond his abilities. Castlereagh was undoubtedly exasperated by his brother's mania for the battlefield at inopportune moments, or by his spending habits and unrealistic ambitions, but his confidence in Stewart's abilities was never shaken.

From Ulster gentry to Irish peerage

Charles Stewart was born in Dublin on 18 May 1778, the second child and eldest son of Robert Stewart's second marriage to Lady Frances Pratt. Stewart was part of a prominent northern Irish family which had risen in social status. As with many Ulster families, the Stewarts had originally come from Scotland and had emigrated to Ireland during the reign of James I. Stewart was very proud of his family ancestry and would describe his forebears in grand terms.[11] The Stewarts acquired the estate of Ballylawn in County Donegal, and over the course of 'several generations' they 'gradually enriched' themselves, 'partly by ability and prudence, partly by fortunate marriages'. In the eighteenth century the Stewarts would rise further. The first step was taken by Alexander Stewart, born in 1700, at Stewart's Court in Ballylawn. Alexander married the heiress Mary Cowan in 1737, and by so doing was able to push the family into the ranks of the Ulster gentry. Their son, Robert Stewart, born on 27 September 1739, would go one step further and take the family into the Irish aristocracy.[12]

In the 1740s, the Stewarts' social position was further consolidated by the purchase of the Newtownards Estate on the shores of Strangford Lough. Here Alexander's son, Robert Stewart, would oversee the building of Mount Stewart. Robert Stewart took another huge step for the family in 1766, when he married Lady Sarah Seymour-Conway, the daughter of the first Earl of Hertford. This was by any accounts a spectacular match. Hertford was lord lieutenant of Ireland, and a very well connected politician who would go on to hold the court position of lord chamberlain.[13] It was also an important religious step as Sarah was a member of the Church of England. Anglicanism was the established religion not only in England and Wales, but also in Ireland. Although the majority of the population in Ireland had remained Roman Catholic, the Church of Ireland was an integral element of the Ascendancy. The Stewarts shared the Presbyterianism of many of their Ulster neighbours, but Anglicanism was the religion of the British and Irish political establishments.

The eldest son from this marriage died young, but their second child, Robert Stewart, was born in Dublin on 18 June 1769. Lady Sarah Stewart died in childbirth only a year later. Robert Stewart senior would marry again in 1775. His second wife, Lady Frances Pratt, was the daughter of the first Earl Camden. A pillar of the legal profession, Camden had risen to the peak of the law to become lord chancellor, a post he relinquished in 1770. The result of this marriage was eight children, the first a daughter named Frances Anne, born in 1777. After Charles's arrival in 1778, Frances gave birth to six more daughters: Caroline (b.1781), Georgiana (b.1785), Selina (b.1786), Matilda Charlotte (b.1787), Emily Jane (b.1789) and Catherine Octavia (b.1792).[14] Although there was almost a ten-year age difference between Robert and Charles, the two half-brothers would form a close attachment, and 'though their characters were thus different, the tenderest friendship existed between them, which continued with the most eminent advantage to both through the whole of life'.[15]

Charles Stewart was packed off to Eton by his grandfather Lord Camden, who took a great interest in his upbringing.[16] Charles's brother, Robert Stewart, had been carefully brought up in Anglican establishments, first at Armagh Royal School, before going up to St John's College, Cambridge. Charles Stewart was also to be educated at a staunchly Anglican school. As with Robert's education, this showed the family was taking care to secure its future as a dynasty which could take its place among the British and Irish ruling elites. As part of the Stewarts' increasing prominence, Robert Stewart senior was elected to the Irish House of Commons in 1771. The Irish parliament, which met in Dublin, consisted, like Westminster, of a House of Commons and a House of Lords. In reality, the major decisions were made in London and in Dublin Castle, the seat of the Crown's representative, the lord lieutenant of Ireland.[17]

Robert Stewart senior served as an MP in the Irish House of Commons until 1783; his growing stature was further recognized when he was sworn of the Irish Privy Council. In 1789, more honours came his way when he was raised to a barony in the Irish peerage. Robert senior took the title of Baron Londonderry, giving the family a seat in the Irish House of Lords. Great things were also expected of Robert Stewart, who early on showed that he had his full share of abilities. In 1790, aged 21, he was elected MP for County Down. Although the costs of this election delayed the completion of Mount Stewart, it was an essential start of any political apprenticeship.

Soldier and courtier

By the time Charles Stewart left Eton in 1794, Britain and France had been at war for over a year.[18] This was a France transformed by its revolution of 1789. Despite the optimism of the French Revolution's early years, moderate politics eventually collapsed. By spring 1792, France was at war with Austria and Prussia. In September, French political life was transformed by the deposition of the King. The new French Republic, soon gripped by the Terror, put Louis XVI on trial for high crimes and treason. The King was found guilty and guillotined in Paris on 21 January 1793. Although Britain was shaken by the news, it was more alarmed by the expansionist rhetoric of the French government, and by events in the Austrian Netherlands (modern-day Belgium) which was completely overrun by French forces. This left the Dutch Republic very exposed. British foreign policy in the Low Countries revolved around keeping the French out of Dutch affairs, and maintaining the regime of the Stadtholder, Willem V, Prince of Orange. British policy also centred on the status of the Scheldt Estuary, which was closed to free navigation. The French opened up the estuary in November 1792. The British government regarded this as a direct threat to its security, as it would allow Antwerp, so close to Britain and now occupied by the French, to thrive as a great port. The Dutch Republic was also now clearly threatened. War between Britain and France was inevitable. The French government made the first move, declaring war on both Britain and the Dutch Republic on 1 February 1793.

Charles Stewart did not have to wait long before setting off to war. In October 1794, aged 16, he was commissioned as an ensign and joined the Earl of Moira's expedition to the Low Countries. Moira was sent to provide reinforcement to Britain's first major land campaign of the French Revolutionary Wars, commanded by George III's second son, Frederick, Duke of York. The British and their allies attempted to halt the French advance but were ultimately unsuccessful.

The Habsburgs lost the Austrian Netherlands and the Dutch Republic lost its independence. Stewart was soon involved in another military campaign, this time in the west of France, part of British efforts to bolster the remnants of the French Royalist uprising in the Vendée. Arriving at Quiberon Bay in June 1795, Stewart, appointed as assistant-deputy quartermaster general, found himself with the occupying forces on the Isle-Dieu, off the coast of France. The result was another military setback for Britain.[19]

Stewart was not deterred by these early experiences. Having quickly reached the rank of major, he felt confident enough to map out his ambitions to his father, Lord Londonderry. Writing after landing at Plymouth in September 1795, the young and well-connected officer wrote, 'The more I see of the profession I have chosen, the more I am persuaded it is more adapted to my inclination in actual service than any other I could have followed.' If peace was to break out he would go to Cambridge, although Stewart conceded, 'I might not exactly there perhaps gain many acquirements for the profession I am on (& which I ever mean to adhere to) yet I am sure I sh[oul]d gain there that mind of knowledge which I see military men in general so defective in.'

Stewart told his father that there were two expeditions in the offing, one to the West Indies and one to the Cape of Good Hope. General Doyle, likely to assume a home command, had 'urged' Major Stewart to 'remain to tally with him'. Stewart though was anxious to go to the West Indies or the Cape, 'To get something by my own exertions . . . for you must recollect I am a Major in the Army without ever having done anything to merit it.'[20] It was not to be the West Indies or the Cape, but mainland Europe again. Under the command of Colonel Charles Craufurd, Stewart was attached to the Austrian armies in the campaigns of 1795 and 1796.[21] The French were on the offensive again, determined to 'push the Austrians out of Germany and Italy and force Vienna to terms'.[22]

Major Charles Stewart was in the thick of the action during this campaign. In August 1796, the 18-year-old Stewart was severely wounded at Donauwörth when a musket ball 'entered his face under the eye, went through his nose, and was extracted on the opposite side'. Stewart was wounded 'whilst charging with some heavy Austrian cavalry that were driven back by the French hussars'. Major Stewart, 'in a senseless state . . . was carried back to the village of Donauwert [*sic*], where he was put into a cart with some wounded Austrians, and in this condition conveyed to the rear'.[23] Stewart made a full recovery, returned home and was appointed as an aide-de-camp (ADC) to his uncle, the lord lieutenant of Ireland, John Jeffreys Pratt, second Earl Camden. In a society where patronage connections and ties of family were vital to careers, Camden's mark of favour was an important step for an ambitious officer. Stewart was appointed lieutenant colonel in the 5th Dragoons on 1 January 1797.

While Charles Stewart was making his reputation as a gallant and headstrong officer, his brother continued to rise politically. Having allied himself to the government of William Pitt the Younger, Robert Stewart had assumed a prominent part in Irish politics, a state of affairs reinforced by Lord Camden's appointment as lord lieutenant. His ambitions also turned to a British career: an outlook which would greatly influence his younger brother's future prospects. When Pitt offered Robert Stewart a Cornish constituency for the Westminster Parliament in 1794, he took this opportunity to make his mark on British political life. Two years later he was brought in at Orford thanks to his uncle, the second Marquess of Hertford.

On 8 August 1796, Lord Londonderry was promoted two steps in the Irish peerage to an earldom, becoming the first Earl of Londonderry. In consequence of this promotion, his heir, Robert Stewart, assumed the courtesy title of Viscount Castlereagh. However, Lord Castlereagh's growing importance to his step-uncle, Lord Camden, meant his British ambitions were temporarily put on hold. In June 1797, Camden gave Castlereagh a sinecure post as Keeper of the Privy Seal which meant giving up the seat at Orford, although Castlereagh retained his seat in the Irish House of Commons. As a loyal supporter of government, Castlereagh was active in the campaign against the United Irishmen, especially as acting chief secretary for Ireland during the rebellion of 1798.[24] Camden though was on borrowed time; widely blamed for having lost control of the country, he was replaced by Lord Cornwallis in June. In October 1798, Castlereagh was confirmed as chief secretary. It was from this office that he would be one of the main architects for promoting the Act of Union between Britain and Ireland.

Colonel Charles Stewart remained with his regiment throughout 1798. The 5th Dragoons had been regarded as 'in point of discipline . . . one of the worst regiments in the service', but by Stewart's 'exertions' had been transformed 'to a very high state of discipline and efficiency'.[25] This was not enough to save the regiment from being disbanded the following year, as Lord Camden advised his nephew on 11 January 1799.[26] A new regiment was found in the shape of the 18th Light Dragoons. Stewart's 'activity and success in completing and rendering efficient the corps' brought further recognition of his military talents.[27]

In 1799, Colonel Stewart accompanied the 18th Light Dragoons to the former Dutch Republic, now the Batavian Republic. The allies were determined to wrest control of the country from France. Command of the campaign was entrusted to the Duke of York, who was unfortunate to oversee another disastrous military expedition in the Low Countries – as with the previous campaign, sometimes due to circumstances beyond his control. Stewart was in action 'incessantly on horseback, and with the outposts, which were almost entirely formed of the troopers under his regiment'.[28] Stewart suffered another serious injury on 10 October when he was 'wounded in the head, at the out-posts near Schagenbrug [Schagerbrug] . . . by a musket-ball: the ball struck the glass he was looking through, which it broke, and was stopped by the brass tubes of the glass, or it would have proved fatal'.[29] This was to be Stewart's last military campaign of the French Revolutionary Wars. The time had come for him to put up his sword, and in March 1800 he was elected for the seat of Thomastown in the Irish House of Commons. A few months later, Stewart transferred to one of the seats for County Londonderry, which he would retain in the Westminster Parliament after the Act of Union with Ireland.

Debates on the proposed Act of Union between Britain and Ireland had dominated business in the Irish Parliament throughout 1799, with Castlereagh to the fore for the government. On 5 February 1800, Castlereagh delivered a key speech for the Union.[30] The bill was passed on 7 June. The Irish Parliament met for the last time on 2 August 1800 and the Act of Union came into effect on 1 January 1801, creating the United Kingdom of Great Britain and Ireland.[31] However, any joy that Castlereagh felt over steering the bill through the Irish Parliament quickly 'evaporated' in London. Although 'no explicit promises' had been made on securing Catholic Emancipation during the debates, 'the subtext was absolutely clear'.[32] The issue would be decided at Westminster, and it was widely known that Pitt was in favour of the measure, as were other leading ministers. George III though was implacably opposed. In this battle of wills, the King was the winner. Pitt offered his resignation, which the King accepted on 5 February. A recurrence of George III's illness, which had last affected the King in 1788–9, delayed the resignation until March. Castlereagh felt honour-bound to resign and left office in May 1801. A year later, the new prime minister, Henry Addington, secured peace with France with the signing of the Treaty of Amiens on 25 March 1802.

The France of 1802 was a very different country from that of 1793. Since a coup of 1799, one man had become undisputed ruler: Napoleon Bonaparte. Born in Corsica to minor nobility in 1769, Bonaparte had risen rapidly in the armies of the new French Republic thanks to powerful political patrons. The most influential was Paul Barras, the head of the Directory, a liberal republican regime, which had come to power in November 1795.[33] With the Directory's support, General Bonaparte received command of the Army of Italy. The Italian campaign saw the overthrow of ancient states and new pro-French republics created. The conquests of 1796–7 were followed by the military setback of the Egyptian campaign of 1798–9. Taking the decision to escape from this 'catastrophic invasion', Bonaparte would play a central role in the coup to seize power from the Directory once he had returned to Paris.[34] A number of disaffected politicians wanted a new kind of government, and regarded Bonaparte as 'a "safe" general'.[35] The politicians were proved wrong. The seizure of power was achieved peacefully in the 'Coup of Brumaire' on 9–10 November 1799. A new government, the Consulate, was installed. Napoleon (as he will now be called) became First Consul, and effective ruler of France.[36] Although the war continued after the coup, the combatants were increasingly weary. It was against this background that peace was agreed, but in reality the Treaty of Amiens proved to be only a breathing space for the warring powers.[37]

In July 1802, Castlereagh returned to government under Henry Addington as president of the Board of Control. Less than a year later the Addington government would be leading the country in a renewed war effort. The formal breakdown of peace in May 1803 heralded the start of the Napoleonic Wars, and the formation of the Third Coalition against France.[38] It also spelt the end for Addington's government. In May 1804, Pitt the Younger returned to office as prime minister. That same month, Napoleon was declared Emperor of the French. In December, at a magnificent coronation held in Paris, Napoleon crowned himself as emperor. A year later Napoleon was crowned as King of Italy in Milan Cathedral. France had come a long way since the Revolution. The Consulate had now been buried among the splendours of the French Empire.

There was to be no active posting for Stewart after the renewed outbreak of war. Castlereagh's appointment to high office undoubtedly boosted his brother's standing, and on 25 September 1803 Stewart was made an ADC to King George III and promoted to full colonel. In August 1804, he married Lady Catherine Bligh, daughter of the Earl and Countess of Darnley. Their son, Frederick Stewart, was born in July 1805. This event was significant for the future of the Londonderry title and the Stewart estates. After ten years of marriage, Castlereagh and his wife Amelia (Emily) had no children – and it seemed very likely that Frederick would eventually succeed to Lord Londonderry's honours. That same month, Castlereagh was appointed as war and colonial secretary.

In 1805, Charles Stewart published a work on army reform, *Suggestions for the Improvement of the Military Force of the British Empire*, in which he was listed as a brigadier general. This publication included proposals to divide regular army enlistments into three different periods, a reduction in the age of eligibility to receive military training, and the creation of a new rank (cadet or sub-ensign) to train non-commissioned officers earmarked for promotion. These ideas were reviewed in *The Annual Review and History of Literature* for 1805 which argued that the 'suggestions deserve the attention of government: a great revolution is become necessary in our armed establishment: we have not the removable force which the mere protection and preservation of our widely-scattered empire requires'.[39]

The death of Castlereagh's political patron, Pitt the Younger, in January 1806 proved a temporary setback to the careers of both Stewarts. Castlereagh did not serve in Lord Grenville's 'Ministry of All the Talents' but a year later returned to the War and Colonial Office under a new prime minister, the third Duke of Portland. Stewart also found a place in Portland's government, being appointed as undersecretary for war and the colonies in March 1807. Castlereagh and Stewart were now at the heart of British efforts against Napoleon.

It was not the best of times to be at the heart of that war effort. If Britain was paramount at sea, it had little to show in mainland Europe.[40] In particular, George III's Electorate of Hanover was always vulnerable, being occupied by the French early in the war. In December 1805, Britain's allies, Austria and Russia, were defeated at the Battle of Austerlitz, and the following July Napoleon revolutionized the political shape of Germany by creating the Confederation of the Rhine. In August 1806, the Holy Roman Empire was dissolved. The French were seemingly unstoppable. Prussia soon felt the invincibility of French arms. Despite the French victory over the Third Coalition, Prussia declared war against France, only to see its armies defeated at Jena and Auerstädt in October 1806.

Stewart's appointment to government in 1807 meant he was responsible for ensuring the efficient execution of Castlereagh's instructions. In early 1808, he was heavily involved in preparations for Sir John Moore's expedition to the Baltic. During April and May 1808, he was in regular contact with Moore and was not afraid to remind the general that he was speaking with Castlereagh's authority.[41] Stewart was diligent in his duty, and his letters followed Moore who found he could not escape the War Office easily.[42]

Moore's campaign was to be another setback in Britain's efforts, but with the French Empire seemingly at its zenith in Europe, armed revolts in Portugal and Spain would allow Britain's armies the chance to inflict a series of military defeats on France. Political office had already placed Stewart in an exalted domestic position. Events in mainland Europe would change his outlook, and set Charles Stewart on the road to becoming a leading international figure in the military and civilian worlds, and a trusted partner for his brother Lord Castlereagh. It all began in the Iberian Peninsula, where Stewart's four years of fighting, from 1808 to 1812, would be the opening act in a unique and meteoric career. From the Peninsular War, he would go on to serve as minister to Prussia and then ambassador to Austria, spending a decade at the heart of European diplomacy and politics. The coming decades would certainly prove to contemporaries the truth of the Stewart family's motto, *Metuenda corolla draconis*, 'The dragon's crest is to be feared.'[43]

Chapter 1

PORTUGAL AND SPAIN

Charles Stewart could look at his career in the summer of 1808 with some satisfaction. Enjoying a very privileged position in the military hierarchy, he was serving directly under Castlereagh at the War Office. In a role far removed from most other officers, Stewart was free to offer advice on military commitments, and on the deployment of Britain's meagre land forces, which paled into insignificance when compared to the military machine of the French Empire. These land forces would soon have their chance. Napoleon was determined to project his power into the heart of the Iberian Peninsula and enforce his Continental System on the whole of mainland Europe. This represented nothing less than a trade blockade against Britain, and an ultimately vain attempt to strangle the British economy. Napoleon now turned his attention towards the Kingdom of Portugal. The kingdom was Britain's oldest ally, with Portugal's friendship dating back to an alliance signed with England in the fourteenth century. As if Napoleon's attention was not bad enough for the Portuguese, trouble would also come from its neighbour, Spain. The government of Charles IV, allied to France despite the disaster of Trafalgar in October 1805, saw an opportunity for territorial aggrandizement. The result was an agreement with Napoleonic France to carve up Portugal between them in the event of an invasion.

The government of Dom João, the Prince Regent of Portugal, was faced with having to make an unpalatable choice between its oldest ally and the military might of France. The Portuguese attempted to conciliate both, but Napoleon was already concerned about future British assistance and decided to invade anyway. The French forces crossed into Portugal in November 1807 and occupied Lisbon the following month. The Portuguese royal family, now declared as deposed by the French, had no intention of allowing themselves to become prisoners. Dom João had received an assurance that British assistance would be forthcoming if the royal family had to leave the country for Brazil, the jewel in the Portuguese empire. In a remarkable move, this is precisely what happened: on 29 November the entire Portuguese royal family, together with many members of the landed and political elites, set sail from Portugal and were met by a waiting squadron of British warships. This huge convoy of sailing ships, which also contained the Portuguese treasury, arrived safely in Rio de Janeiro. Leaving behind a Regency Council, the legitimate Portuguese government had thwarted Napoleon's plans.

Spain itself was about to undergo huge turmoil. The weak government of Charles IV was overthrown in March 1808 when the King was forced to abdicate in favour of his son Ferdinand, Prince of Asturias. The new King, Ferdinand VII, was welcomed by the Spanish people. Unfortunately for Spain, Ferdinand deluded himself into believing that he could rely on Napoleon's friendship, a scheme which would be cemented by a marriage alliance with the Bonaparte dynasty. Napoleon had been singularly unimpressed with his Spanish allies and decided to remove the Bourbons completely from power. This was achieved with relative ease. Ferdinand and Charles were both duped into travelling to France, and once on French soil, Napoleon forced Ferdinand VII to abdicate on 6 May. The now vacant Spanish throne was given to Joseph Bonaparte, and to back up this new regime, France would occupy the country. The majority of the Spanish people wanted Ferdinand to return; the King though would be doomed to remain in French custody until 1814.

Tensions in Madrid were already at fever pitch, the flames fanned by bitter internal political rivalry. The spark that would set off the Spanish struggle against the French was the determination by Marshal Joachim Murat, the commander of the occupying forces, to remove Francisco de Paula, the youngest son of Charles IV, from Madrid. On 2 May a large crowd gathered outside the royal palace, determined that this symbolic male representative of the Spanish dynasty should not be removed from the capital city. The French fired on the crowd to disperse them, but the unrest rapidly spread throughout Madrid. What followed was the famous Dos de Mayo, two days of bloody fighting over the course of 2 and 3 May, between French troops and Spanish civilians. The French put the uprising down brutally, and followed their victory up with wholesale executions, a savage reprisal that would be immortalized by Goya. On 20 May, it was announced to the Spanish people that Ferdinand VII had abdicated. The announcement was met with a series of further uprisings in many Spanish provinces, so that by early June 'large parts of Spain were in a state of open rebellion.' However, Spain could not hope to defeat the French on its own.[1]

Spanish delegations were sent to London to request British aid in the struggle, and the government of the Duke of Portland became enthusiastic about some kind of military assistance. There was a renewed feeling of optimism that Britain could intercede militarily and come to the aid of both Portugal and Spain. However, at this stage there was no demand for British troops in Spain, so it was agreed that an army would be sent to Portugal, where resistance to the French occupation had also broken out. Once the idea of a military campaign had been agreed to, it remained to choose the commander. In the government's opinion there was really only one man: Lieutenant General Sir Arthur Wellesley.

Wellesley, born in Dublin in 1769, was the younger son of an Irish peer, Garret Wesley, first Earl of Mornington. The family name had long since been changed, and Wellesley was currently a loyal MP who held the key post of chief secretary for Ireland. Just as importantly, he was on very cordial terms with Lord Castlereagh at the War Office. Wellesley had served in the Low Countries in the early stages of the Revolutionary Wars, but he had earned his spurs and knighthood through service in India. Having been sent to India with his regiment, his prospects were transformed by the appointment in 1797 of his eldest brother, Richard Colley Wellesley, second Earl of Mornington, as the East India Company's governor general. The well-connected Arthur Wellesley was sent to campaign against Tipu Sultan, seen as a dangerous and determined enemy of British rule. After Tipu's defeat and death at Seringapatam in 1799, Wellesley was appointed governor of Mysore. Wellesley was then chosen to command the forces sent to fight the Maratha Confederacy, acquiring more military fame. By the time Wellesley returned to Britain in 1805, his service in India had earned him a formidable military reputation. Two years later he was selected to take a leading role in the Copenhagen campaign. Politically, Sir Arthur Wellesley was still linked to his eldest brother who had done much to help his career. Richard Wellesley, who had been created first Marquess Wellesley in 1799, had returned home from India in 1806. Although he was currently out of office, the Marquess was still regarded as potentially a major political operator. With government favour at his back, Sir Arthur Wellesley was now to lead the army destined for the Peninsula.

Wellesley's force, currently being assembled at Cork, had originally been intended for South America, but the government simply changed the orders and sent the army to Portugal. Although Wellesley left Ireland on 12 July 1808, there was a fundamental problem. Wellesley's army was to be reinforced, which would mean that a more senior officer would have to be appointed to overall command. There was simply no way that the Horse Guards and especially King George III, who had a strict sense of military hierarchy, would allow a substantial British military intervention to be commanded by a man who had only recently been promoted to lieutenant general. There were others more senior on the list, and two of these more senior figures were now selected. One was Sir Harry Burrard, but the overall command was given to Sir Hew Dalrymple, the governor of Gibraltar. Wellesley would only be in command until these two officers arrived, and Castlereagh must have hoped that the government's favoured general would be victorious before he could be superseded.

Charles Stewart was caught up in this feverish atmosphere of optimism, and was soon writing to his brother on possible areas of operations in Portugal and the best landing place for Wellesley, while also busily passing on the opinions of a number of military figures who pressed for quick and determined action in the Peninsula. Undoubtedly these officers saw Stewart as a useful conduit to offer opinions. Stewart himself was very keen on military action in Portugal, and urged his brother to have the necessary arrangements cleared by the Horse Guards as quickly as possible.[2] However, Stewart may have under-appreciated the delicacy of his brother's position as the Horse Guards was led by George III's second and favourite son, Frederick, Duke of York, the commander-in-chief of the army. Frederick, although a capable administrator and reformer, could be expected to hold similar views to the King on matters of hierarchy.

Castlereagh obviously appreciated his brother's insights, and Stewart was not shy of offering his very detailed opinions, as illustrated by an excited, and at times rather rambling, letter of 15 July 1808. Sir John Moore, a Whig-inclined general and one not trusted by the government, was somewhat denigrated in this letter, while Stewart was all for Sir Arthur Wellesley, who really was the man of the moment. As Stewart enthused, 'The Country are all with us as to Wellesley's Appointment . . . there is policy in taking advantage of the popularity attach'd to the character of a Commander to furnish him with more than common powers to accomplish a great object.' Stewart, echoing his brother's desire to leave the job to Wellesley, argued that the superseding generals would need time to embark:

> As a question of time therefore both with Ld C[hatham]. & the D of York You might have a fair plea for plan[nin]g the whole 19000 men for the dash at Lisbon under Wellesl[e]y. If He fails with such a force You have done Your Duty by giving him such ample means if He fails with his present Corps for want of numbers & you have 10 000 men airing on Shore after being in Transports for some weeks in the Baltic, What will the Country Say? or How will it be excused? Wellesl[e]y has the charge of the Lisbon operation, – Do not take it from him, But take advantage of the present circumstances & make it possible <u>Securance</u>.[3]

This was all sound advice, but Stewart, with his customary air of self-doubt, added, 'Forgive all this Brother of mine But I know you are good enough to listen to my Ideas, whenever I bore You with them however little they have in them.'[4]

Strategy was about to give way to action, as Stewart would soon relinquish his desk in the very heart of the military establishment. Undoubtedly to his very great delight, Stewart was ordered out to the Peninsula himself in August 1808. As a mark of high favour, he would have George III's grandson as one of his ADCs, in the person of George FitzClarence, the eldest illegitimate son of William, Duke of Clarence, the King's third son. Stewart was to earn the Duke of Clarence's warm affection for his 'kind attention and protection to George; he cannot have been with a better officer than yourself'.[5] Stewart's connections and reliability are apparent from this appointment, and FitzClarence's military education would not be entrusted to just anybody.

Sir John Moore was to be sent out with further reinforcements, and Stewart was given the temporary rank of brigadier general and assigned to the command of Moore's hussar brigades. Stewart though arrived too late to take part in the first major engagement of the Peninsular War. On 21 August, Wellesley's Anglo-Portuguese army met and defeated a French force under General Junot at the Battle of Vimeiro, temporarily putting paid to French ambitions. Unfortunately for Wellesley, Sir Harry Burrard also arrived to take temporary overall command. Although Burrard had the good sense not to interfere at Vimeiro, he soon interfered with Wellesley's overall plans. Sir Arthur wanted to take advantage of Junot's defeat to pursue the French, and deal them a more decisive blow. Burrard, a rather timid man, refused the request, and an opportunity to strike hard at the French was allowed to pass. Even more disappointing for Wellesley was the arrival of General Sir Hew Dalrymple, who now assumed overall command of British forces.

Once in the Peninsula, Stewart had been sent ahead by Sir John Moore on 19 August to announce his arrival to the other commanders. Now on the spot, he could also perform an invaluable service to his brother by reporting on events first-hand. It was a role that Charles Stewart would perform in various theatres for the next fourteen years. Stewart was quick to praise Wellesley, 'that Gallant fellow', and could assure the war secretary that 'British Troops conducted as Wellesl[e]y has led them will ever be invincible', while ruefully adding, 'I arrived here Yesterday unfortunately for me 2 days after the glorious day of the 21st'.[6] Unknown to General Stewart, he was also about to find himself in the middle of a military scandal, and so positioned would be uniquely well placed to pass on vital facts to Castlereagh.

After assuming command, Sir Hew Dalrymple had decided to accept proposals for a truce and entered into negotiations with the French, represented by General Kellerman. The French announced that they were prepared to evacuate Portugal, but only on certain conditions. The French were not to be treated as prisoners of war, the troops were to be transported with all their property (and loot) back home, and would be free to serve their emperor again in the Peninsula. As if this were not enough, the French further demanded that any pro-French Portuguese should not be persecuted and should be allowed to leave, and that Lisbon be recognized as a neutral port. This last point would allow the Russian fleet currently anchored there to leave unharmed. The Russian forces were far from neutral since Russia had been allied with Napoleon since the 1807 Treaty of Tilsit. Finally, all of the French horses were to be transported back to France. These terms might have been rather more palatable had the French actually repulsed the allies at Vimeiro. Stewart later recalled that when rumours of these terms became more widely known and news spread 'that they had been conditionally agreed to, the indignation of all ranks and classes in the army became unbounded'.[7]

The reports were not mere rumours, and Dalrymple agreed to the French proposals in their entirety. Dalrymple, a very competent governor of Gibraltar, was no fool, but his decision was a catastrophic mistake. The deal was formally concluded by the signing of the Convention of Cintra on 30 August. Even more worrying for the government back home, Sir Arthur Wellesley, had actually signed the convention, even though the initiative for the agreement lay firmly at Dalrymple's door. Dalrymple perhaps felt that the chance to rid Portugal of French troops should not be missed, but the terms appalled the Portuguese, especially as they would now witness the French escape with loot ransacked from their country. As a final insult to Portuguese sensibilities, the French were to be transported safely in Royal Navy ships.

When the terms became known in London there was uproar. Sir Arthur Wellesley, ably assisted by other members of his politically important family, would have to marshal all of his resources to ensure that he was not blamed and disgraced. Luckily for the Wellesleys, Lord Castlereagh was always likely to be predisposed to listen favourably to any defence. The Wellesleys were also fortunate in having a friendly witness on the spot in the shape of Charles Stewart, who could prepare the ground for Sir Arthur's defence. Writing on 1 September, the day after the convention's signing, Stewart made it clear to his brother that it was all Dalrymple's fault, and that Sir Hew would seek to pin all of the blame on Wellesley:

I think it very likely now this creditable Convention has been closed by Sir Hew Dalrymple that He will send his own Accounts to England & take good care to jockey all other Communications. I therefore avail myself of Sir Robert Wilson's going to Oporto to send You a few lines, although we are much in the dark at this place as to the State of things at present . . .

Believe me this Arrangement will neither be lik'd by our Army or the Portuguese, nor can I think it will be approved of at home, in whatever Language it is painted in, As all Idea of Hostilities are now over, I wonder Wellesl[e]y was not sent for to be at hand at the conclusion of the Arrangements, for his Able Advice & Assistance, But the fact is He was a Clog at Hd Qr. which it was found agreeable to shake off . . . I do not think W. seems inclin'd to go to England which I press'd him to do on the conclusion of the Convention because I thought it would be very advantageous that You should hear & know all he thinks, But He imagines it would either seem as if He was a party to all the Arrangements Sir Hew is now making, or as If He was unwilling to serve here no longer having himself the Chief Command these reasons evidently detain him although He feels his situation very uncomfortable.[8]

Accounts have concentrated on the rearguard action performed by the Wellesley family to ensure that Sir Arthur was not condemned for the Convention of Cintra, but Stewart's part in sending home the important news on the convention to his brother should not be overlooked.[9] The government would listen to Wellesley, but a more 'neutral' observation from Stewart would arm Castlereagh further. This would be all the more necessary, as Stewart's prediction that the convention would be disliked at home was a great understatement. The news of the victory of Vimeiro, coming to a country which had been starved of military success, had been followed rapidly by the news of this seemingly craven capitulation to French demands.

In the Peninsula, Charles Stewart did not hesitate to pass on further news. On 3 September, in a lengthy letter home, he again assured his brother of Wellesley's innocence in the affair, while complaining of 'mismanagement' in the campaign and taking the opportunity to rubbish both the Convention of Cintra in general and Sir Hew Dalrymple in particular. More worryingly he also warned his brother about the anger of Britain's Portuguese allies, 'I am satisfied that in the mode the Embarkation of the French Troops is to be effected You will never satisfy the British Nation much less will you satisfy the Portuguese that the plunder of their unfortunate Country is not carried off.' The time spent in the War Office certainly gave Stewart a good long-term perspective on issues, and even after the Convention of Cintra he looked ahead to future operations, and advised his brother on the best way to proceed:

From the State of the Portuguese Troops, & the mind of the Natives, (although I fear by recent mismanagement both have been much dissatisfied) I can not but think that 5 or 6000 men, with an Intelligent Commander and an able Diplomatist at Lisbon would be sufficient to put things here on a most respectable footing – The next point to look to would be the advance into Spain from hence of a . . . Corps of 12 or 15000 Men with the Cavalry and this I would send under Wellesl[e]y to act in conjunction with Cardanos [*sic*] from such a force on the Spot & from the influence of a man who would be so much look'd up to in Spain as Wellesl[e]y would now be You would always have a preponderating decision on the operations to be undertaken.[10]

Stewart, like his brother, wanted to see the armies commanded by Sir Arthur Wellesley: it was perhaps of little surprise that poor General Stewart was subjected to Dalrymple's 'extreme coolness', news of which was also helpfully passed on to London.[11] However, for the time being it was not to be. The disappointment and anger felt in Britain was such that the government felt obliged to order Wellesley, Dalrymple and Burrard back to face a formal Board of Inquiry, leaving the command in the hands of Sir John Moore. The Portland government had been forced into this action, and a board was established by the Duke of York to look into the details. Wellesley would be stuck at home, waiting to see if his career would be brought to a premature close. In the Peninsula, Charles Stewart now found himself working for a new commanding officer who was far from enjoying the confidence of the government. The closeness of General Stewart to the war secretary must have been particularly irritating to Moore, who labelled Stewart 'a very silly fellow'.[12] This was pure pique, as Stewart was far from being silly, whatever self-doubts he always harboured of his abilities.

Sir John Moore's irritation with Stewart would have increased had he read the opinions that his subordinate was transmitting home. Stewart had received confidential news from his brother on how the convention would be dealt with in London, noting 'although the Arrangement is not publickly declared there can be no doubt of its giving most general Satisfaction and under the Circumstances is the wisest that could have taken place'. Stewart believed that Wellesley would agree, and turning to his current commander argued, 'If I mistake not Moore highly prizes W[ellesley]' Abilities. He knows he is a quicker and a Cleverer Man than himself & will give his opinions their due Weight.' Still, Stewart did not underestimate Moore, who had 'steadiness & firmness to execute' and enjoyed a degree of popularity in the army only surpassed by Sir Arthur Wellesley.[13]

In London, the inquiry into the Convention of Cintra opened at the Royal Hospital, Chelsea, on 27 November 1808. The board, composed of a cross-selection of senior officers, did not condemn any individual for the convention. However, the limitations of both Dalrymple and Burrard had been publicly aired, and neither would ever be offered a field command again. The government was relieved that Wellesley's career was not irreparably damaged, which allowed for a return to the field of their favoured commander at some point in the future. At this moment Britain's hopes in the Peninsula lay not with Wellesley, but with Sir John Moore, who would face a renewed French onslaught. Throughout these events, General Charles Stewart would witness at first hand the elation of an offensive campaign as well as the horrors and disappointment of a retreat in the face of an overwhelmingly powerful French army.

Under Sir John Moore's command

Sir John Moore received the news that he had been appointed commander of the British forces on 6 October 1808. Moore had first seen active service in the American War of Independence. Since the outbreak of hostilities with France he had been in action in theatres across the world, including Corsica, the West Indies and Sweden. He had acquired a well-earned reputation as one of the country's most brilliant and courageous officers. However, Moore had one major disadvantage: he was mistrusted by the ministers of the Portland government, and especially by the war secretary, Lord Castlereagh. Moore had been close to William Pitt the Younger, but still had the reputation of being rather too 'Whiggish' for some. All of this put Charles Stewart in an awkward position. Stewart's presence was undoubtedly of great help to his brother Castlereagh, who did not regard Moore as 'his' general. Moore was aware of the administration's antipathy towards him, and it would be natural for Stewart, a man with a direct line of communication back to the government, to be tainted by association.

Leaving aside these political differences, there was still a war to be fought. As Portugal had been cleared of the French, Moore was ordered to advance into Spain to offer assistance to that country's military forces. Stewart, in command of the hussar brigades, was sent to the town of Villa Viçosa, to the east of Lisbon, in preparation for the advance. Arriving on 24 October, the hussars soon succumbed to dysentery, a situation not helped by the appalling weather conditions. Moore was marching onto Salamanca, where the British forces were to concentrate. However, the artillery column and cavalry, under the command of Lieutenant General John Hope, was to pass on to Salamanca by way of Madrid, the capital city having been evacuated by the French in August. This road was the only one deemed passable enough to take the weight of the guns.[14] Stewart was assigned to Hope's command, and on 5 November the hussars, having recuperated, crossed the Spanish border. Stewart now caught his first glimpse of Spain, and later recalled how the British were received by the Spanish 'with a degree of indifference', in marked contrast to the warmth of the Portuguese. Stewart though could not help but admire the Spanish people.[15]

As the British advanced into Spain, substantial French reinforcements were pouring into the country. Moore had been ordered to provide what military assistance he could, and clearly time was of the essence. Stewart's brigades had reached Merida by 8 November, and from there the route to Madrid was straightforward. On his arrival in the Spanish capital, Stewart paid his respects to Lord William Bentinck, the official British resident. Bentinck painted a gloomy picture of the Spanish administration, and its incapacity to deal with the crises with which it was faced. This was perhaps a little unfair on the Spanish political classes, who had suddenly been confronted with the deposition of the ruling house. Progress had at least been tentatively made, as those pro-French elements who had welcomed Joseph Bonaparte as king had been swept aside, and a Central Junta formed in September. This in turn would be replaced in 1810 by 'the new council of regency selected in its death throes by the Junta Central'.[16]

Napoleon had also not been idle, and the French Emperor was determined to stamp his authority on Spain. Napoleon had been rather indifferent to events in the Peninsula, but even he had become convinced that things could not go on as they were, and now led the new French invasion force in person. In Madrid, Stewart had been told by Bentinck that 'he was totally in the dark, and he believed others were equally so, touching the amount and situation of the French army'.[17] This was especially alarming as the French proceeded to defeat each Spanish army in its way, and Napoleon's thoughts inexorably turned to the reoccupation of Madrid and the reinstatement of Joseph Bonaparte as king. Not surprisingly, the Central Junta was anxious that the French should not retake the capital, and was keen for General Hope's troops to be detached from Moore's main force in order to defend Madrid.

General Hope was having none of this, as his orders were to stay in Madrid only long enough to collect his forces and then march on towards Salamanca. Moore had reached Salamanca on 14 November and would need all the British forces with him if he was to carry out his orders. Moore soon received news of the Spanish defeats; but for now the French were intent on destroying Spain's military forces and were not interested in the British. Back in Madrid, with his stragglers collected, Hope marched out. By 27 November his troops had passed the Guadarrama Mountains to the north of the capital, on their way to link up with Moore. In London, Castlereagh was more than aware of Hope's movements, thanks to the detailed report relayed to him by his brother.[18] The following day, Hope's forces received the dreadful intelligence that a substantial French army was nearing Valladolid, within marching distance of Salamanca itself. As if this were not bad enough, news was also received of the major Spanish defeat at the Battle of Tudela, fought on 23 November, which left Madrid open to French attack. The Central Junta was forced to flee to Seville.

In the face of French threats, Hope decided to change his route of march. All the while Stewart was busy sending out 'various enquiries as to the nature and strength of the French troops which had shown themselves in that quarter'.[19] Fortunately for Hope's force, with the exception of a minor skirmish on 29 November, his troops were left unmolested. Stewart himself reached Salamanca safely on 4 December. The day before, Stewart found the time to write to his brother, perhaps rather predictably to disparage Spain's military efforts, but interestingly he had seen enough of the Spanish people, and had been sufficiently cheered by the warm reception the British had received in Madrid, to make an accurate long-term assessment of the French occupation. Stewart would be proved right when he noted, 'I still am of opinion that whatever temporary triumphs Bonaparte may gain, He never will keep this Country.'[20]

Stewart had been sent on ahead by Hope with letters for Sir John Moore, whose headquarters had been established in Salamanca. Moore had received nothing but catastrophic news, as Spanish armies had been no match for the seasoned French troops, whose morale was sky-high with Napoleon in overall command. Moore's orders had been to offer assistance to the Spanish military; the run of defeats had made that a pointless exercise. Moore decided to retreat to Portugal. This news was certainly not to Stewart's taste, and perhaps wisely deciding to leave Salamanca the next day for the outposts, he sat down to complain to his brother in the most extraordinarily vociferous terms, detailing his open disagreement with Moore over strategy.[21] Clearly Moore had been anxious to take Castlereagh's brother into his confidence, a wise course of realpolitik. Retreat seemed incomprehensible to Stewart, but Moore did not want to see his army destroyed; British losses, unlike the French, could not easily be replaced. Moore also resisted all overtures to assist with the defence of Madrid, which soon capitulated to Napoleon. Although the order to retreat was soon countermanded, years later Stewart showed that he did not really understand his commanding officer, and accordingly judged Moore rather harshly.[22]

There was to be no retreat. Stewart was certainly elated at the news that the orders were countermanded. The reasoning was simple: Moore now knew what the French were about. A French messenger had been ambushed and killed by Spanish partisans near Segovia. The contents of the messenger's papers were acquired by Captain John Waters, one of Stewart's ADCs, and returned to British headquarters.[23] The intercepted documents not only revealed enemy troop movements but also showed that the French believed that all British forces had retreated to Portugal. Moore's determination was reinforced by Colonel Thomas Graham, who would gain a formidable reputation in the war. Graham not only brought definitive news of the capitulation of Madrid but was able to advise headquarters that Spanish resistance had not been crushed. It became apparent to Moore that his troops could still cause serious disruption to the enemy's communications with France, and with a degree of optimism the British marched out of Salamanca on 11 December.

Stewart's hussars were soon in action. On 12 December, at the village of Rueda, General Stewart came across a detachment of French cavalry, supported by a body of infantry. The desire to fight was too much, and that evening a warm engagement ensued, as Stewart recalled, 'The greater number were sabred on the spot, many were taken, and only a few escaped to inform General Franceschi, who occupied Valladolid . . . that the British army had not retreated.'[24] Stewart had been rather rash, and now the French knew that the British had not fled in headlong retreat to Portugal. Stewart made amends on 14 December, when he received intercepted French dispatches on the current movements of the troops under Marshal Soult, which were immediately sent on to headquarters. On their receipt, Moore decided to attack Soult, and hoped to have the assistance of Spanish troops under the command of the Marqués de la Romana. It had always been Moore's intention to cooperate with Romana, who still believed that the British were retreating to Portugal. Romana now agreed to retrace his march and to join his British allies.[25]

Despite the advance on Soult, Stewart still harboured doubts about his commanding officer, doubts he penned on 19 December for his brother Castlereagh in London:

Moores mind from the Conversation I have had with him looks with a gloomy and not with a Sanguine aspect on the future & I fear the Actions of a general, however meritorious & brave He may be, may be influenced by this turn of Character He will be always very cautious of risking that Reputation he has gain'd as a General of Division, & His Temper will not lead him to soar with energy & Activity over partial Difficulties that arise, as another friend of mine would do . . . It is perhaps quite wrong in me to state all this, But you know: I conceal nothing from You & seeing what I do, I must communicate confidentially or not at all, – A Breath of Censure in publick here will never (Be assur'd) pass my Lips – I love Moore as an Individual, He treats me so kindly, No man more brave, more fit to act, when His Line is chalk'd for him, But I question Whether He will not disappoint You now Although You had little other alternative in fixing Your Command & his Appt. embraces the least Difficulties – He is still strongly impress'd with the necessity of a Retreat (if made) being directed on the Portuguese Frontier.[26]

The advance continued, despite the deteriorating Spanish weather, now battering the troops with snowfalls and strong winds. The weather was taking its toll on Stewart, who wrote to his brother on 22 December, 'I have lost 2 of my best Horses, I broke the Leg of one in a rut in the Snow, you may remember him . . . If there is an opportunity send me for Gods sake 2 good Horses.'[27] British headquarters was moved forward to Sahagún, where two days earlier the British cavalry under Lord Paget had earned an overwhelming victory over the French. With this news still fresh in their minds, the glorious expectations of the troops can only be imagined as they made preparations on 22 December to attack Soult.

That same day, the Spanish relayed the news that Napoleon was preparing to bring his troops to bear on the British. Napoleon had learned two days previously of the British plan, and he was determined to put an end to it. The attack was abandoned. Moore decided that the best course of action was to withdraw to the north-west coast, assisted by Romana's troops. The Spanish fought rearguard actions for their allies, until they were comprehensively defeated at the Battle of Mansilla. At least the retreat witnessed one of Charles Stewart's great moments of glory. The British had reached Benavente in the north-west of Spain on 27 December, and the cavalry under Paget was again involved in fighting with the French. Once all of the troops had crossed the River Esla into Benavente, the bridge was to be destroyed by explosives. The final works were being overseen by the engineers, covered by troops, including those of the King's German Legion, under the command of a certain Brigadier General Charles Stewart. When the bridge was blown up, the British at Esla found that they had attracted the attention of French cavalry. This included the Chasseurs à cheval of the Imperial Guard, commanded by General comte Lefebvre-Desnouettes, a personal favourite of Napoleon. The French crossed the Esla, but the British cavalry, led by Lord Paget and General Stewart, won the day, taking a number of prisoners in the process, including Lefebvre-Desnouettes. Stewart recalled, 'It was said Napoleon himself was an eye-witness of this rencontre, from the opposite heights.'[28]

This glorious and successful action could not hide the fact that discipline in the British army was beginning to crumble, always a danger for a body of military men in retreat, with drunkenness and absenteeism increasing in steady measure. The troops reached the town of Villafranca on 2 January 1809, and here Moore was greeted by the sight of his own supplies ransacked by British troops. Everyone was now getting near their breaking point, and none more so than Stewart with the cavalry in the rearguard, responsible for repelling any French attacks and for ensuring that stragglers were not left behind. The full horrors of the retreat were taking their toll on Stewart, who witnessed the fate of the less fortunate stragglers who had simply frozen to death; his state of mind can be seen in this letter to his brother written from Villafranca:

> I have in vain endeavord before today to get an opportunity of writing you a few lines, But I have been so harrass'd, on horseback night & Day and scarcely without rest that it has been wholly out of my power, – You will I am sure enter into those feelings of satisfaction I derive from believing that my conduct has met with the approbation of the Army & with the Assistance & Gallantry of my Lads I have been so fortunate as to beat the best Corps of Cavalry in the French Service taking their General (Le Fevre).[29]

Just as alarmingly, the following day the British were once again attacked by advancing French troops, who since the engagement at Benavente had been keeping their distance. From Villafranca, the cavalry were sent on ahead to Lugo, followed by the rest of the army on 6 January. Moore remained determined to give battle to Soult's advancing troops if the opportunity arose, but battle was not joined, and the army was ordered to La Coruña. The leading troops arrived in the town on 11 January.

The expected Royal Navy fleet appeared on 14 January and now the military operation was one of holding back the French while the troops could embark on the waiting ships for home. One of the first to embark for home was Charles Stewart. As a later account noted, Moore determined to send Stewart home 'in order to report upon the progress of events'. Moore was reported as stating 'that Brigadier-general Stewart is a man in whose honour I have the most perfect reliance; he is incapable of stating anything but the truth'.[30] Moore also showed political astuteness in entrusting Stewart with the official dispatches for Castlereagh's attention in London.

There were outbreaks of skirmishing on 15 January, as Marshal Soult's forces had witnessed the arrival of the British ships but were not yet in a position to attack fully. The decisive battle came on 16 January. The French were intent on destroying the British army, but thanks to Moore this ambition was completely thwarted. The British successfully fought off the French, but only at the cost of their commander's life. Moore's heroic death was not in vain, and although fatally wounded, Sir John lived long enough to know that the French attacks had failed.

This brought the first British campaign in the Peninsula to an end. The army had been saved from destruction at the hands of the French Empire, and Britain's precious and limited land resources remained intact to fight another day. Stewart came home with his reputation as a cavalry commander substantially increased, and 'won for him the most flattering reception from all ranks', including a warm letter of praise from the Prince of Wales.[31] Stewart was not to settle into life at home for long. The British government was determined to return to the Peninsula. Although he had been damaged by the Convention of Cintra, there was really only one man that the government trusted to lead this new effort against Napoleon's armies. That man was Sir Arthur Wellesley. Charles Stewart would also play a leading role in the coming campaign, which would see France's invincible reputation tested through a war of dreadful attrition.

Chapter 2

TO WAR WITH WELLESLEY

The French still tried to exert control over Spain, but Portugal had not been overrun. Britain's old ally would need urgent help, and the Portland government was determined to send another force to the Peninsula with their favourite general, Sir Arthur Wellesley, in command. A place in this new campaign was found for Stewart. With typical understatement, in March 1809, Wellesley invited Charles Stewart to resume his military career: 'I hope that I shall have your assistance in the arduous concern which I am about to undertake.' Stewart's name had been mentioned as a suitable officer to undertake the duties of adjutant general, and Wellesley's invitation added the hope that Stewart would accept this offer.[1]

Stewart, always the man of action, did not leap at the chance, as the post of adjutant general involved a great deal of administrative work; his ambition was to carve a career for himself as a cavalry commander. Lord Castlereagh had other opinions, and he felt that this appointment would be the making of his brother, as he wrote on 25 March, 'I don't think any step promises to place you so much in the way of general military reputation as being close to Wellesley's person and at the head of his staff.' Castlereagh added, 'I don't know any school in which I would prefer to study, or which is likely to obtain the public confidence in an equal degree.'[2] Stewart, always ready to follow his brother's advice, accepted Wellesley's offer. Stewart's position on the staff would put him at the centre of Britain's new land campaign, and his rank of brigadier general was made substantive. The simple, even heartfelt, invitation from Wellesley to 'My Dear Charles' shows a warm relationship had emerged between the two men. For Stewart, a return to war meant the chance to acquire fresh laurels and to achieve fame as a general officer.[3] Stewart had been apart from his wife Catherine and his son Frederick during the previous campaign, and his reunion with both was brief. Stewart left Britain with Wellesley on 16 April.

Arriving in Portugal on 22 April, Stewart began life as Wellesley's adjutant general. The post was no sinecure. The two departments of the adjutant general and quartermaster general were responsible for most of the staff work. Stewart's department oversaw such vital needs as equipment, army discipline and intelligence, but perhaps with hindsight this post was not right for a man of Stewart's temperament, as he 'would have much preferred the command of a brigade of cavalry'. Most of the time was spent in 'endless pernickety paperwork', which in the long run was to sour Stewart's opinion of the role.[4] This was in the future, and it was with a sense of excitement at being back on an active military campaign that Stewart was soon writing home to his brother to tell him of army arrangements and the latest news on the French. As war secretary, Castlereagh undoubtedly made use of his brother's correspondence as a source of news and information, a trend which would continue in the years ahead. Stewart's political instincts, however, did not lie dormant, and he made clear to his brother that he had been following debates in the House of Commons and was keen to be kept abreast of news.[5]

The French commanders had been ordered by Napoleon to overrun Portugal, and Sir Arthur Wellesley was soon in action. Wellesley, appointed to the rank of marshal general in the Portuguese army, decided on an offensive, and headed for Oporto, Portugal's second city. The city had recently fallen to the French after much bloodshed, on 29 March. Wellesley reviewed the troops at Coimbra, and the campaign got underway. The bulk of the Portuguese forces set off first, with orders to cut the French off from Spain. This army was commanded by William Carr Beresford, the eldest illegitimate son of the Marquess of Waterford. Beresford was a British general and marshal of Portugal, who would come to work wonders with the training of his Portuguese troops, and would in turn be one of Wellesley's most trusted lieutenants.[6] Sir Arthur set off on 7 May with his British force, augmented by Portuguese soldiers. In the face of this a French army retreated in front of Wellesley. The following day, Stewart was involved in a sharp action, as reported by George FitzClarence: 'Our guns were brought up to bear upon them in their retreat, and Brig.-Gen. Stewart put himself at the head of two squadrons, and trotted after the enemy, who withdrew their troops with astonishing rapidity.'[7]

The allies had a skirmish with the French on 10 May, but on the following day at Grijo, south of Oporto, Stewart had a chance to exercise command. Leading two squadrons of the 16th and 20th Dragoons, he came across a strong French force. He ordered Major Blake of the 20th Dragoons to charge, and although the French managed to fire a volley, they broke and escaped, with the British dragoons in pursuit. The resulting carnage is memorably described in the diary of one of the officers present, William Tomkinson, who suffered serious injuries in the charge and blamed Stewart for what he regarded as a mistake:

> General Stewart was more to be condemned than any for sending the orders he did; but for this there was perhaps some reason, and not perhaps the most liberal . . .
>
> Had this affair occurred later in the war, no cavalry officer would have made the attack without representing the enemy's position.[8]

However, to all intents and purposes the action was a success. Many of the retreating French were ridden down by the cavalry and, in total, over a hundred prisoners were taken. The great historian of the Peninsular War, Sir Charles Oman, certainly saw nothing to censure in this charge even though Stewart was not to his taste as a senior officer; indeed Oman memorably described Stewart as 'one of those cavalry officers who thoroughly believe in their arm, and think that it can go anywhere and do anything'.[9]

The French retired beyond the River Douro, destroying the crossing, undoubtedly thinking this would seriously hinder the British offensive. Wellesley arrived at the Douro on 12 May and started sending his troops in barges across the river. Fortunately for Wellesley, the French completely failed to stop the troops crossing, and the fight for Oporto was at hand. The French were soon forced to retire, and their commander, Marshal Soult, turned his thoughts to the evacuation of the city. The French evacuation disintegrated into a disorderly retreat, and the troops fled in front of a British force commanded by John Murray. However, Murray made no attempt to engage the French, fearing, probably rightly, that they might turn and do his troops serious injury. This apparent holding back was noticed by Stewart, who could not bear to see the French get away. He now assumed command of the 14th Light Dragoons, part of Murray's force. A witness writing in 1810 recalled the 'severe' engagement. The troops received Sir Arthur's thanks, but one of the participants added a severe criticism of General Stewart's action to his account:

> On the merits of our charge, the comment of the French General ought not to be omitted: he sent for our men (who had been his prisoners, and afterwards escaped), and declared to them, that, in his opinion, 'we must have been all drunk, or mad; as the brigade we had attacked was nearly two thousand strong.'[10]

Stewart himself noted, 'The slaughter was great, for a panic had evidently arisen; and as we followed them a considerable way, repeated opportunities of charging to advantage were furnished.' Writing of this event, the soldier and historian Sir William Napier did not criticize Stewart's actions, noting, 'If general Murray had then fallen boldly in upon the disordered crowds, their discomfiture would have been complete.' Napier added that Stewart, along with another officer, Major Hervey, was 'impatient of this timidity'. Oman also saw nothing to criticize Stewart for in this escapade, but he too censured Murray, believing that Soult's entire force might have been cut off had he showed Stewart's initiative.[11]

Oporto was safely in British and Portuguese hands. Sir Arthur had shown that he was more than capable of conducting a successful offensive campaign. The government was keen to reinforce his position, while the general also received practical political support in the shape of his eldest brother Lord Wellesley, who was to be British ambassador to Spain. As one senior officer wrote to Stewart, tacitly acknowledging his superb connections, 'The Marquis Wellesl[e]y will be worth his weight in Gold!! I wish you could give me a letter of introduction to him.'[12]

In London, the Peninsula was not currently uppermost in the minds of the ministers. They had been following events in central Europe where war had erupted again following the decision of the Austrian Empire to re-enter the fight. Vienna had become increasingly alarmed by Napoleon's unstoppable rise and felt the time was right to check the French. The British had responded by sending troops to Walcheren in the Netherlands under the command of the Earl of Chatham. The result of this new campaign was a disaster for Britain and Austria. It was unfortunate that the joyous news of Oporto's capture reached London the same day as the government received intelligence of Austria's surrender to the French. Although the Austrian army had fought well, Vienna had been occupied, and after a bloody battle at Wagram, the Habsburgs had no choice but to sue for peace. The British troops at Walcheren were also withdrawn, but only after a substantial part of the force had been decimated by fever.

Back in Portugal, Wellesley's pursuit of Soult ended in disappointment, and he eventually had to abandon the chase. At least Soult had been driven clean out of Portugal, and naturally Wellesley's thoughts turned to active cooperation with the Spanish Junta. Stewart wrote home to his brother Castlereagh on 8 June, noting that as soon as the British were able to join with General Gregorio Garcia de la Cuesta, the commander of the Army of Extremadura, the allies would be 'capable of acting offensively against what force may be between this & the Ebro'. Stewart, using his very privileged position, did not hesitate to supply his brother with a shopping list of demands and, more importantly, up-to-date information on the army, quite possibly dictated by Sir Arthur himself:

> But I should like more Cavalry & 10,000 more Inf[antr]y. Before I saw the British fully committed in a Campaign in Spain again. As I shall keep you in constant Information of our Effectives & our Numbers I shall not allow you to be led away by paper numbers. You talk in your last of our having 30,000 men when the L[igh]t Brigade Appurtenances & Artillery arrive, – I fear we shall fall very short of that number.[13]

Stewart did not believe British forces would reach thirty thousand but realized that his brother the politician would need to make the case to increase the troop numbers. Stewart, having heard of Austria's war with France, but not yet of the result, appreciated that much of Castlereagh's time would be taken up with events in that theatre. He presumed that a British force would be sent into Germany, quite possibly to secure the liberation of Hanover, a course which 'will call loudly for Troops in that Quarter'. Stewart, pleading on behalf of Wellesley, was keen that Portugal and Spain remain at the forefront of the cabinet's thoughts. Stewart need not have worried, although his predictions of reaching the French border were somewhat premature, as was his postscript to his brother hoping that the government would give Wellesley a peerage.[14] Wellesley's coronet would have to wait, and it would be some years before British troops were at the Pyrenees.

The British government gave their assent for Wellesley to take his troops into Spain, where a force of 250,000 French was to be found. Moving south from Oporto, Wellesley halted at Abrantes, and detached the Portuguese to defend the kingdom's border. This pause also allowed the British troops to rest. While at Abrantes, Wellesley entered into communication with General Cuesta. Stewart found the time to write after arriving at Abrantes, thanking Lord Castlereagh for his continuing kindnesses to his wife. For Catherine Stewart, her husband's absence was part and parcel of military life, but this did not make it any easier. A few days later Stewart wrote to Castlereagh on official business, echoing Wellesley's disparagement of the misconduct of British troops; he was also engaged in sending Wellesley's dispatches to Cuesta, entrusting this duty to his ADC, George FitzClarence.[15]

After having rested his men, and in receipt of further funds from London, Wellesley left Abrantes on 27 June and proceeded on his march towards Spain. Stewart kept his brother informed of progress and warned of the deteriorating condition of the army. In this case, Stewart was again reinforcing and agreeing with a letter sent by Wellesley, and it is hard not to see Stewart being used by Sir Arthur as a useful means of repeating his message to the government. It could almost be Wellesley's pen, when the adjutant general advised his brother, 'I very much apprehend on our entry into Spain our numbers will diminish rather than encrease [*sic*], at least if I am to judge from what I have hitherto seen.'[16]

The British army crossed the border into Spain on 3 July, and having reached the town of Plasencia on 8 July, Sir Arthur wisely halted his troops and rode on to meet Cuesta in person. Stewart, as a staff officer, rode too in attendance on his chief. Things did not go well, and the British officers ended up arriving at night. Like many of his peers Stewart held a low opinion of General Cuesta on first sight.[17] On the Spanish side, Cuesta undoubtedly viewed Wellesley as a threat to his military position. In spite of this shaky start, a plan of action was agreed between the two commanders. Wellesley marched his troops out of Plasencia on 17 July and headed towards Talavera. After some brief fighting the allied troops entered Talavera itself. Although the French had evacuated the town, their commander, Marshal Victor, was determined to hold his position on the River Alberche. The French would have to be removed from their line of defence. Again Wellesley and Cuesta discussed battle tactics into the evening of 22 July. For whatever reason, there was no decisive attack on Victor's position the next day as the Spanish army made no attempt to move. The cautious Victor decided to withdraw that evening and headed for the relative safety of Toledo. Now Cuesta chose to act and followed Victor, but rashly he went without the British army. Wellesley refused to cooperate, although some British cavalry were sent forward, among whom was General Stewart.

Unknown to Cuesta, Victor's army would soon increase in size, swelled by the forces commanded by General Sebastiani and by Napoleon's brother, Joseph, King of Spain. At this point, Stewart and two squadrons of cavalry remained with the Spanish army and engaged the rearguard of the French.[18] Fortunately for the allied cause, Cuesta discovered that there was a substantial French army in front of him. The French, now numbering perhaps as many as fifty thousand men, turned to attack, but, assisted by General Sherbrooke's division, there was no Spanish rout. Cuesta was able to head back for Talavera on 26 July. The stage was prepared for one of the great set-piece battles in the Peninsular War under Sir Arthur Wellesley. The French armies, now under the overall command of Marshal Soult, had been ordered by Napoleon to put an end to this affront to France's power. Soult himself would not arrive in time for the Battle of Talavera, and it was left to Victor to win the laurels. Wellesley had different ideas, and he had no intention of being driven from the field.

The Battle of Talavera began with French attacks on British and Spanish positions on 27 July. Some Spanish troops broke and then fled, under Wellesley's line of sight. Sir Arthur's thoughts on this behaviour are not hard to guess, but more importantly it would do nothing to change his opinion of the Spanish military. The French attacks did not break the allied position, and the British settled down for the night 'upon our arms in momentary expectation of an attack, the cavalry resting beside their horses and the infantry upon the ground which they had occupied during the day; but no attack was made'.[19] The respite was brief. At the crack of dawn on 28 July the French attacked again, beginning with artillery fire. The fighting continued uninterrupted for over three hours, and as Stewart wrote, 'The slaughter on both sides was extensive, but the enemy's loss in killed and wounded vastly exceeded ours; and, what was not less flattering, his troops appeared dispirited and dismayed'.[20] The hottest action had been directed against the divisions of General Rowland Hill, who would become one of the war's most outstanding commanders, as well as towards the ranks of the King's German Legion, those staunch loyal Hanoverian troops. The defeat of the French attack caused a temporary truce in the fighting.

The truce lasted until the early afternoon, when the French guns again opened up on Wellesley's position. This was followed by the infantry, not only French but also composed of soldiers from Napoleon's German allies in the Confederation of the Rhine. The British waited until the last to fire their volleys into the enemy ranks, and a 'conflict now ensued, more desperate – because more completely hand to hand – than possibly the annals of modern warfare record'.[21] The British lines held, but some troops, impelled by the adrenalin of such desperate fighting, chased after the French; fortunately for Wellesley the subsequent enemy counter-advance was stopped in its tracks. There was then another French attack, which resulted in heavy British cavalry losses. This was not enough to change the course of the battle, and the French, badly shaken, retreated behind the River Alberche. As Rory Muir has written, 'Talavera was the bloodiest battle fought by the British army for at least fifty years, and possibly the greatest since the days of Marlborough'.[22] Stewart managed to find an active role for himself in the fighting, as FitzClarence recalled:

Gen. Stewart the Adjutant-General, who happened to be on the spot, persuaded their officers to follow their retreat along the fine Madrid road, which was one hundred and fifty yards wide. The enemy were overtaken retiring in two small columns, and to the attack of one gen. Stewart led the Spanish cavalry. The result, as indeed all we saw on this day of our allies, was a proof of their total want, not only of discipline, but of courage. On this and two succeeding attempts, (to which the English general headed them,) on receiving the enemy's fire, when the principal danger was past, they pulled up and fled in every direction; yet in Cuesta's account of this affair, he called it an 'intrepid charge'.[23]

On 31 July, Charles Stewart wrote a detailed account of the battle to his brother, with high and handsome praise for Sir Arthur Wellesley: 'who has resisted with effect, with 19000 men, the repeated & impetuous attacks of a French Army of not less than 45000 – of their best disciplined Troops.'[24] The government was very pleased with its favourite general and now raised him to the peerage. Wellesley became Viscount Wellington of Talavera, news which reached the commanding general in September.

Unfortunately for the British and their allies, there would be no opportunity to follow up this great victory, as Stewart himself realized when writing to his brother. Sir Robert Wilson, a brilliant and unorthodox general, had succeeded in harassing the French through 'a Campaign by themselves in the Mountains' and had even threatened Madrid with his two thousand men.[25] However, a Spanish army, under the command of General Francisco Javier Venegas, had been defeated by a smaller French force, and any opportunity to take the Spanish capital was lost. Thanks to the Spanish, the British also received intelligence that the French had an army of forty-five thousand men in the field under Marshal Soult. General Cuesta wanted to stand and fight, but the British realized that they could not afford another costly battle, especially as the troops were now suffering from lack of supplies. Just as importantly, the British did not rate the abilities of their Spanish allies that highly either.

This was certainly Stewart's view. Realizing that a withdrawal to Portugal was now very likely, Stewart rushed to defend Wellesley to his brother, assuring the war secretary that 'the measure of falling back; had become one of imperious necessity to tell the whole truth & the Army to a Man feel how little Assistance we have received.' Stewart knew that there would be criticisms at home of the military campaign and that 'Reports may also be spread that He is retiring from other Causes than wants of provisions', but belief in his commanding officer remained.[26] The government's confidence in Wellesley was hardly shattered by the retreat to Portugal, but this channel of information from Stewart was undoubtedly of assistance to Castlereagh, as it had been over the Convention of Cintra.

Despite his personal loyalty to the British commander, Stewart was becoming unhappy with his lot in the war. He complained to his wife Catherine in a series of letters, which had been passed on to Castlereagh. Stewart was forced to justify himself to his brother, and it is possible that the writer may have been suffering from a bout of depression, an affliction which would come to hinder his actions at other key times in his career. Stewart knew that 'little vexations' arose in public life, but as a man of action, felt that setbacks 'are most difficult for Tempers like mine to submit to in Silence & unconcern'. However, he was anxious to tell his brother that his unhappiness did not arise from 'a Love of Change . . . from Caprice, from a discontented Mind, or from a Total want of all solid Reasons'. At the heart of the matter was dissatisfaction with Wellesley's system of commanding the army. Stewart's unhappiness was increased by Wellesley's refusing his request for a field command. Stewart reassured his brother that he would not leave his military duties: 'With regard to relinquishing my Post or Seceding from the Army so long as it is Actively employ'd, I hope You know me well enough to be convinced I would sooner lose my Head, Nor have I ever expressd Dissatisfaction at not commanding a Brigade in the field.'[27]

The British continued to withdraw in the face of the French, and reached Badajoz on 3 September 1809. Stewart had advised his brother that the retreat would not go well with Lord Wellesley, the ambassador to Spain. This proved to be the case, and so a number of British troops were left on Spanish soil. General Stewart now received a remarkable offer. Marshal Beresford, writing from Lisbon, offered Stewart the command of the Portuguese cavalry in terms of the most fulsome praise: 'I would have been glad to have Persons in that situation of whose talents as Officers I have a very impressive opinion to what since I have known you in that Character I have of yours.' The appointment would come with promotion to major general, and Beresford wrote, 'I can only repeat how delighted I should be to have you as Commr. of this Cavalry. Circumstanced as you are with Wellesley, you will be aware I could not make any Proposal to him, to give me His Adjt. Genl. but that if you still wish to come to this Service you will be able to manage.'[28] Stewart turned to his brother for advice, but by the time he had the benefit of Castlereagh's opinion, news was received of political turmoil at home which had led to the collapse of the Duke of Portland's government, and marked the start of Stewart's visceral hatred of one of Britain's leading politicians, George Canning.

Duplicity and ambition

The Duke of Portland's government had been in decline. The *coup de grâce* was the extraordinary spectacle of the foreign and war secretaries taking potshots at each other. The political crisis originated with the foreign secretary, George Canning, who felt that the government needed a change of personnel. Canning and Lord Castlereagh increasingly disagreed over the conduct of the war. Canning wanted Castlereagh removed from office and replaced by his political ally, Lord Wellesley. The prime minister, the Duke of Portland, reluctantly agreed, as Canning threatened to resign from the government. Unfortunately, neither Portland, nor Castlereagh's uncle, Lord Camden, who had been let into these political machinations, had got round to actually telling Castlereagh of his impending removal from the War Office.[29]

When Castlereagh found out, he was understandably furious. Laying the blame firmly with the foreign secretary, he challenged Canning to a duel. The two men met on Putney Heath on 21 September 1809. The contest was rather uneven: Canning had never fired a pistol before whereas Castlereagh was considered a superb shot. Both men missed with their first shots. On the second, Castlereagh shot his opponent in the thigh.[30] London society was shocked at the idea of two senior politicians intent on shooting each other, and poor Portland, whose health had been deteriorating for some time, left office shortly afterwards. With Castlereagh and Canning now out of the government, George III turned to Spencer Perceval, the chancellor of the exchequer, to form a new administration. The news reached Charles Stewart the following month, and he was as furious as his brother at this insult to the family.

Stewart, quartered near Lisbon, had been taken sick, 'labouring under malaria fever'.[31] The chance to relax in good quarters was doing wonders, and by 20 October Stewart wrote, 'I begin to feel myself strong on my Legs, I have been on Horseback & I entertain no doubt of my rapid & perfect recovery'. Recognizing that little was likely to happen in the way of action, Stewart's thoughts turned to taking a leave of absence to fully recover. This desire was undoubtedly heightened by news of the duel at home, and Stewart had lost no time in putting his thoughts on paper. His first reaction had been to write to Lord Camden, which the gallant general admitted was 'a bad one, not that it expresses too strongly my feelings, – but in many parts I have been confus'd and <u>unintelligible</u>'. Stewart sounded out Lord Wellington, as Wellesley had become, and was annoyed that his commanding officer 'had by no means that warmth of feeling on the subject that I shd. have imagin'd from a Man so circumstanc'd as He is with regard to You'. Wellington laid the blame more with Portland than with Canning, which undoubtedly caused more irritation. Stewart pressed the issue:

> There was one point Ld W[ellingto]n let out to me which seem'd to stick a little with him, He stated in talking of Canning, on my urging the extraordinary Instances He had given of Duplicity & ambition – 'That it certainly was the case, for He had Documents to prove that it had been agreed by all the Cabinet that they wd. continue to act in their Situations, under Lord Wellesl[e]y He being placed in the Duke of P[ortland]s Shoes with the Single Exception of Mr C[annin]g. who positively declin'd it, And He added that Canning . . . seem'd evidently . . . to get his friend Ld Wellesl[e]y into a situation which would assist him in his views of becoming Prime Minister, which He got you out of his way, who was his principal hindrance in the H of Commons, as Perceval might be provided for.[32]

The episode left Stewart not only with a loathing of George Canning, it also lodged in his mind a mistrust of the Wellesley family, to the extent that he warned his brother: 'The Ws. will keep clear of him and <u>mark me</u> If they do not play their own Game.'[33]

Although Stewart's brother no longer held political office, this would not stop the flow of letters on official business between the two men. Stewart's thoughts also turned to his military career, and on the same day that he warned his brother about the Wellesleys, he wrote to Beresford, turning down the offer to command the Portuguese cavalry. Stewart told Beresford, 'The Opinions I have received home on the Subject, added to those of friends in this Country has induced me to relinquish, what my natural Inclinations would lead me perhaps to embrace, for my love for the Cavalry service is very deep rooted, and cannot be shaken.' Stewart, left to his own devices, would have jumped at the opportunity, but other counsel, likely both Castlereagh and Wellington, had advised him against acceptance. As Stewart commented, 'I am not so much at liberty as to think only of myself, or my own gratification – I have others depending on my Fate, and holding the situation I do now in this Army; I question whether it would be fair or just towards them to relinquish it.' At the back of Stewart's mind may have been a moment of doubt over the current campaign, telling Beresford that the cavalry command would be 'an uncertainty, or at least . . . a Post, the Stability of which, under the Actual State of Europe can not be said to be certain'.[34]

Portugal could and most certainly would be held, and Wellington was determined that the French would never get a chance to re-enter Lisbon as conquerors. The defeat of the Spanish at two major encounters, at Ocaña and at Alba de Tormes, on 19 November and 28–29 November respectively meant that any joint operations were out of the question, and that a retreat to Portugal was the only prudent option. In December, Wellington ordered his army to evacuate Spain. For now, large parts of Spain would in theory remain in French hands. Wellington's troops would occupy strong defensive positions in Portugal, and the time could be used to train the Portuguese military up to the highest standards, to render it an effective military force. It would mean months of defensive operations, much to the annoyance of a number of senior British officers. Stewart later wrote that this period allowed the troops to recover from their campaign and for sick soldiers to return to duty, all helped by being stationed in an area 'as salubrious as any in the Peninsula'.[35] However, Stewart was not one of those restive senior officers, as he had returned to Britain on sick leave.

Stewart embarked from Lisbon on 26 October, docking at Portsmouth on 3 November. This period of leave allowed Stewart to immerse himself briefly in domestic politics and to continue his campaign of castigating the Wellesley family in general to his brother.[36] At least Stewart could render assistance to Lord Wellington by reporting on Peninsula affairs in person to the government. The administration was somewhat different to the one in place when Stewart had gone off to war in the spring. The Duke of Portland had resigned, and at the head of the administration was Spencer Perceval. Castlereagh was no longer at the War Office; in his place was Robert Banks Jenkinson, second Earl of Liverpool. A protégé of Pitt the Younger, Liverpool had proved himself a steady and reliable minister, having served already at the Foreign and Home Offices. With Canning also gone, Lord Wellesley was earmarked for the post of foreign secretary. Wellington's elder brother would receive the seals of office in December.

Alison claimed that Stewart's conferences with the ministers went 'far to dispel the gloomy anticipations which the retreat of the British army had spread in the cabinet, as well as the country, and inspire them on solid grounds with a portion of the Commander-in-Chief'.[37] Whatever the truth of this assertion, Stewart certainly received material rewards for his labours in the field and for his representations to the cabinet. On 2 February 1810, Stewart, MP for County Londonderry, received in person the thanks of the House of Commons. On 5 February, the Speaker of the House, Charles Abbot, described Stewart in grandiloquent and heroic terms. Stewart modestly thanked the House for 'an honour far exceeding any little services I may have rendered'.[38]

Stewart was being kept up to date on events by Lord Wellington himself, who implored his adjutant general to remain in Britain and to 'not think of coming out' until he was fully recovered:

The Portuguese Army is certainly very much improved, & the Desertion is I believe nearly at an end. How it will be on Service I cannot tell. They are now sickly, owing to want of the Common comforts to preserve them from the Weather; but I hope that they will be healthy before we shall be attacked.

There is no doubt that the Task which I have undertaken is Herculean, particularly now that the Spanish Armies are all annihilated; & that there is nothing in the shape of an Army in the field but ourselves. I think that I am in such a situation that I can retire or embark when I please & if that be the case I cannot but feel that the longer I stay the better for the cause, & the more Honourable to the Country. Whether I shall be able to hold my ground at last, must of course depend upon the numbers & the Means by which I shall be attacked . . . The necessity of keeping my rear open to the Tagus is a difficulty; and I should be able to effect my object with great ease, if I was not under the necessity of effecting every thing not only without loss, but without risk, or even the appearance of risk, in order to please the good people . . . in England.[39]

Wellington further passed on his gratitude for Castlereagh's 'very fine speech upon the vote of Thanks, which is another Instance of his kindness to me of which I am very sensible'. At the forefront of Wellington's mind was a concern about the stability of the Perceval administration: 'It is impossible that the Govt. can last as now constituted. I was always certain of it; but they did right to try the experiment.'[40] This was undoubtedly a topic of conversation between Castlereagh and Stewart in London.

Stewart, who had already received the sinecure post of governor of Fort Charles in Jamaica, was becoming a national figure. The loss of his brother as patron at the War Office could have dealt a blow to his career. Certainly if he had still been in civilian office, Stewart would have felt duty-bound to resign. It was fortunate that he could continue close to Wellington, and having recovered his health, Stewart returned to Portugal in March 1810. Not long after his arrival, Stewart received a further reward for his services, when he was promoted to the rank of major general in July.

Stewart's optimism to the cabinet had been more than justified. In Portugal, unknown to the French, and to much of the British army, Wellington had been busily seeing to the country's defence. Wellington had ordered construction of the Lines of Torres Vedras, a series of defensive measures, which utilized natural as well as man-made defences. Once completed, the Lines would ensure the safety of Lisbon, and allow the British and Portuguese to withstand any future French invasion. Although the Lines would not come into their own until late 1810, the Portuguese Regency Council in Lisbon could feel some assurance that they were not going to be abandoned. Relations with the Regency were also now proceeding more smoothly, especially as they were now entrusted to a capable young diplomat, Charles Stuart.[41] Wellington had also used this time to train the Portuguese army, which had been brought up to exemplary standards thanks to the exertions of Marshal Beresford.

The British army, behind its defensive lines, had recovered from the previous campaign. Added to this, fresh reinforcements had been sent to Wellington, who now commanded a formidable Anglo-Portuguese army, numbering over fifty thousand men in total. Its first major encounter would be a test of the reforms which had been conducted in the Portuguese military. Without a reliable Portugal, there was little chance of Wellington's being able to fight in Spain, and ultimately no realistic chance of victory in the Peninsular War. The French meanwhile were far from passive, and their forces, now commanded by Marshal Masséna, were determined to defeat the British once and for all. As a preliminary to this new invasion, French thoughts turned to the Spanish fortress city of Ciudad Rodrigo, close to the Portuguese border. The siege began in late April, but the Spanish garrison was determined in its defence, holding out until July, when Marshal Ney's cannon breached the city's walls. Rather than risk the horrors of a full French assault, the Spanish capitulated. Wellington had made the tactical decision not to relieve the siege, but the bravery of the Spanish garrison had delayed the coming French onslaught. With the fall of Ciudad Rodrigo, the French now marched on the Portuguese frontier fortress of Almeida.

The French army clashed with the British advanced posts at the Côa on 24 July. The British light division, commanded by the impetuous Brigadier General Robert Craufurd, were ordered not to engage the French with the River Côa behind them. Craufurd could not resist the chance to fight, and rather than cross the river as directed by Wellington, he chose to stand his ground. What followed was a sharp skirmish, with the French suffering unduly heavy casualties thanks to Marshal Ney's tactical errors. Craufurd extricated his men from the battle, and the light division survived the day.[42] Masséna could now turn on Almeida. Wellington must have hoped that the garrison at Almeida would delay the French advance. The troops were well prepared and were commanded by an able British officer in the Portuguese service, Brigadier General William Cox. However, things went terribly wrong for the garrison, which was using the cathedral, the strongest building in the city, as a magazine. As the siege got underway, a damaged powder keg had left a trail of gunpowder back to this makeshift magazine. During the bombardment, a stray French shell ignited the powder and destroyed the cathedral, killing a number of the Portuguese defenders; a disappointed Wellington advised Stewart that the 'magazine & half the Town was blown up'.[43] Although Cox was willing to extract terms from the French in order to buy time, the garrison refused to follow his lead. Almeida surrendered shortly afterwards.

Masséna could now advance on Portugal, and marched along the northern Almeida to Coimbra road. As the French advanced they were harried by the traditional Portuguese militia, the Ordenanças, ready to launch surprise attacks on the French camps. French stragglers were always liable to be tortured and killed, although occasionally prisoners would be sent on to Wellington's headquarters. In response, Masséna ordered that anyone caught under arms but not in uniform was to be executed out of hand. Wellington was determined to deal a blow to the French advance, and the chance arose when the allied army came into contact with the French at Mortagua on 24 September. Masséna now continued to follow the allied troops further in the direction of Coimbra, Portugal's third city.

Wellington was waiting for Masséna on the Coimbra road. By 26 September Wellington had assembled his Anglo-Portuguese army on the ridge of Buçaco, preventing any French attempt to advance along this road. The French had no choice but to attempt to dislodge the fifty thousand British and Portuguese troops. The position was impressive, consisting 'of one huge mountain'.[44] Skirmishing took place between the two forces, in which one of Stewart's ADCs, Lieutenant Hoey, who, 'always in the post of danger, was with the rearguard – was killed at his General's side by a cannon shot'.[45]

Hostilities opened at daybreak on 27 September. Facing Wellington were three French corps, commanded by Marshal Ney and Generals Junot and Reynier. Notwithstanding the strong allied position, the French made every effort to attack Wellington, the armies hampered by the heavy fog which did not dissipate until later in the morning. Despite the gallantry of the French, they were eventually repulsed with heavy losses: 'French soldiers never fought more courageously . . . but their commanders had assigned them impossible tasks.'[46] Just as encouraging from the British point of view was the professionalism of many of the Portuguese troops, which was a tribute to the work of Marshal Beresford. Stewart was involved in some of the heaviest fighting, close to Wellington.[47] In his dispatch of the battle, Wellington made a point of praising 'the greatest assistance from the general and staff officers', singling out the adjutant and quartermaster generals to whom he was 'particularly indebted'.[48] Masséna made no further attempt at a frontal assault, which would only result in more French casualties. The Marshal decided on the following day to try and move to the right of the allied position, in order to flank Wellington's army.

Once the French had discovered that there was indeed an alternative route, Wellington had no choice but to retreat to the Lines of Torres Vedras, which saw 'morale in the Allied army plummet'.[49] The Anglo-Portuguese army left Buçaco under cover of night on 28 September, the French deceived by the camp fires which had been left by the troops. The French advanced on Coimbra and sacked the city. Masséna was not to have everything his own way. Leaving behind his wounded in Coimbra, he continued his advance on the allied position. Coimbra was then attacked by Portuguese cavalry and militia, led by the highly regarded Colonel Nicholas Trant. The city was recaptured on 7 October, and several thousand French prisoners were taken in the process, who were then marched to Oporto.

The allies began entering the Lines of Torres Vedras on 8 October, just as the Portuguese rains began. The French were not far behind, but Masséna had no idea about the Lines and was about to receive a rude awakening. The Portuguese civilians were also ordered behind the Lines and to leave nothing which could be used by the French. Things had ended rather unfortunately for Wellington, but there was to be no retreat from Portugal. Work on the Lines of Torres Vedras had been progressing over the course of the past year, and now they saved Portugal. They would protect Lisbon from French attack, and would thwart Napoleon's oft-quoted desire to drive the British back into the sea. Stewart himself 'rode along its entire extant almost every day for the next two months', and would remain by Lord Wellington's side.[50] Aside from the French, Wellington would have other problems to deal with at this time, including the maintenance of good relations with the Portuguese Regency.[51]

The Lines were manned by secondary troops, mostly Portuguese militia, as well as with Spanish and British troops. The front-line troops were safely to the rear, allowing them to rest and recover, while Wellington could also look forward to the arrival of reinforcements.[52] Apart from a sharp engagement on 14 October, the French made no attempt to breach the allied positions. Masséna instead decided to halt in front of the Lines, which was a dangerous move.[53] This stalemate continued for a month. On the night of 14 November, the French withdrew from their positions. Wellington believed that Masséna's intention was to cross the River Tagus and attempt to make contact with other French forces in the Peninsula. The French retired as far as Santarém, to the north-east of Lisbon, which proved to be a disastrous choice, as Wellington was still able to contain Masséna's army. The French were also hindered by the Portuguese-controlled fortress of Abrantes, which was unassailable, while allied forces, including the Ordenanças, made life unpleasant. In response, Masséna attempted to live off the land using 'a combination of energy, enterprise and sheer terror' to sustain his army. Some cheer was given by the arrival of nine thousand reinforcements under the command of General Drouet on 29 December, but even with these extra troops, there was little that Masséna could do. Attempts to break out all proved futile.[54]

This was probably the wrong time for Stewart to request a leave of absence, which he did on 5 January 1811, on personal grounds owing to 'the unhappy state of my family' and specifically concerns about his wife's health, 'which ever so short a period of my presence might relieve'. Stewart's biographer makes no mention of this request for leave, merely writing: 'In these glorious and most momentous operations . . . Stewart bore the whole share, excepting the French retreat, when he was confined to bed by fever.'[55] Wellington certainly had more pressing thoughts on his mind, as Masséna's army was deteriorating. The French commander had received orders from Napoleon to maintain his positions, but by February 1811 his army was beginning to fall apart.

Despite French threats and violence, there was no more food to be had from the unfortunate inhabitants. The French marshal bowed to the inevitable and ordered a retreat on 5 March. All the while, Wellington's forces were growing, and sooner or later the allies would launch an attack on the French. Masséna's order to retreat back to Spain was the only logical course of action, and it was one marked by atrocities committed against Portuguese civilians. In reprisal, any French stragglers who did not die by the roadside were likely to be tortured and then murdered by the local population.

Away from these horrific scenes, in Britain great political events were unfolding. The old King, George III, had succumbed to illness towards the end of 1810; an illness which had last afflicted him in 1804. The political world waited to see if he would recover, but it soon became apparent that Spencer Perceval's government would need to bring in a Regency Bill. The bill was passed, and on 5 February

1811, George, Prince of Wales, became Prince Regent. The Prince had once been the boon companion of the Whig leader, Charles James Fox, and years earlier would have brought his friends into power. That was a long time ago, and Fox had died in 1806. The Prince Regent was not close to the new generation of opposition Whig leaders, who were often lukewarm towards the war efforts. The Regent was especially distant from the main opposition leader, Charles, second Earl Grey: a personal consideration which would have international consequences. However, even thoughts of a change in ministry could have a destabilizing effect. Castlereagh kept his brother informed of political news, and in turn Stewart passed this on to Wellington. Lord Wellington remained quietly confident that the Whigs were not about to get their hands on power, telling his adjutant general, 'I think the circumstances of the Country, the state of Parties, the conduct & time of Life of the Prince are very different from what they were in 1788.'[56]

In the Peninsula, the French retreat was not total, and Masséna would make one last futile attempt to change his tactics. This was doomed to failure; the game was up. The latest Napoleonic invasion of Portugal had not succeeded, and Masséna's army continued to disintegrate as a military force. Wellington was now in pursuit of the French and was ready to give battle. Portugal had been saved, and another chink in Napoleon's military invincibility had been revealed to the governments of Europe. The allies could now think about the long and arduous task of driving the French from Spain, where Joseph Bonaparte's hold on power was still somewhat precarious. Wellington needed the full support of the British government to bring this about. Although he grumbled regularly about Perceval's government, and was in the habit of complaining to Lord Liverpool, the administration had continued to support his efforts. Wellington may have been optimistic about the likelihood of the Whigs remaining excluded from power, but there would naturally be concern in a number of quarters, as any change of government at this time might prove disastrous.

Chapter 3

GREAT GALLANTRY

The French had failed in their attempt to invade Portugal. On 29 March 1811, Marshal Masséna finally ordered his troops to cross the border. Following rapidly on his heels was Wellington's Anglo-Portuguese army. However, Masséna was reluctant to completely abandon Portugal, and instead of heading straight for Spain, he changed course and assumed a defensive position. The inevitable consequence was to invite a battle with Wellington, and on 3 April, this is precisely what he got. At Sabugal, close to the border with Spain, Masséna's army was attacked by the allies. In appalling weather conditions, the French fought bravely, with General Reynier's soldiers distinguishing themselves. This did not affect the outcome, and soon Masséna's troops were in full retreat, their discipline continuing to disintegrate. This victory ended the third Portuguese campaign. However, wresting Spain from Napoleon's control was another matter. Although the advance of the French Empire had been checked, an offensive to liberate Spain would be a huge undertaking. The course of the coming campaign would show that victory in the Peninsular War was still far from Wellington's grasp.

One outpost in Portugal remained in French hands: the fortress of Almeida. Lord Wellington's thoughts were also focused on the Spanish frontier fortress of Badajoz. The fortress had recently capitulated to the French, even though Sir William Beresford had been sent with eighteen thousand troops to lift the siege. With this vital strategic post under their control, the French remained in a very strong position to hamper any allied offensive. Beresford would have a tough job on his hands to dislodge Napoleon's soldiers. While Beresford was tasked with taking Badajoz, Wellington would deal with Almeida; General Charles Stewart, as adjutant general, remained with Wellington, and would soon be 'in the battle wherever danger was greatest'.[1]

The French had sent a relieving force to Almeida. The allied army was ready for a fight and had taken up a superb position around Fuentes de Oñoro. Once more, Wellington and Marshal Masséna would oppose each other across a battlefield. The battle began on 3 May, in savage fighting described by Stewart:

> Though checked in their first advance, the enemy repeatedly renewed their attack, bringing up fresh troops: and on every occasion they were driven back with a heroism which has never been surpassed. The French fought, however,

with great gallantry, and more than once stood to be bayoneted in the main street of the village; but their success, whenever obtained, lasted but a moment – and they were instantly swept away by a desperate charge from the men whom they believed beaten.[2]

Charles Stewart was 'beside the 71st in the desperate bayonet-fighting'. The next day brought a respite in hostilities as Masséna scouted Wellington's position and decided on an attempt to flank his opponent. In the early hours of 5 May, the French attacked again. Wellington's cavalry was soon involved in the battle, 'but were immediately charged in the low ground by the enemy's horse'. Fortunately, the French were 'driven back by the leading squadron of the British horse' commanded by Stewart 'who made Colonel La Motte, of the 13th Chasseurs, prisoner in single combat'. Stewart's reputation for courage, already becoming widely known, was certainly enhanced by this affair which 'attracted universal notice'.[3]

The French had threatened Wellington's position, but Masséna had been outmatched and outfought; even when Wellington's Seventh Division was in danger, the British commander had been able to send the Light Division under General Robert Craufurd to its aid. Once the danger passed, the French lost the battle. Masséna, anticipating Napoleon's reaction to another defeat, decided to throw more troops into the attack. The French again fought heroically but they could not break the allied line. Eventually, Masséna decided enough was enough. Much to Wellington's annoyance, the French garrison at Almeida managed to escape on the night of 10 May, after setting light to fuses to destroy the walls of the fortress, causing severe damage to the fortifications.

Stewart used his highly privileged position with Wellington to keep Castlereagh informed of progress with the campaign. On 14 May, a few days after Almeida's fall, Stewart sent a letter to his brother from allied headquarters at Villa Formosa. Stewart ensured that Castlereagh continued to have the most up-to-date news:

> Two of the Battalions are nearly entire, the mines under them having seemingly fail'd, I do not believe it is Lord Wellington's Intention to do any thing to Almeida untill [sic] He hears the wish & opinion of the Portuguese Government upon it. And what sum of money they will be dispos'd to lay out on it.
>
> Since the fall of Almeida Lord Wellington's Chief Attention is fix'd on the Southward, I can not positively say what his Motions may be, He is inclin'd to allow Beresford to go on with the Siege of Badajos [sic] . . . at the same time he is prepar[e]d to move there himself & to reinforce that part of the Army if necessary.[4]

The value of Stewart's correspondence home cannot be overestimated. Castlereagh was still out of office, but such a state of affairs could only be temporary. In the meantime, he was being kept apprised of Lord Wellington's actions.

With Almeida in allied hands, Wellington marched on to Badajoz in order to aid Beresford. On 22 May, Charles Stewart wrote of this latest advance to his brother.[5] Matters were of the utmost urgency. Masséna had paid the price for his string of defeats. Napoleon had dismissed him from the command of the Army of Portugal, meaning that Wellington had a new opponent: Marshal Marmont, who was determined to raise the siege of Badajoz. In the middle of this drama, Stewart found time to write to his brother in the early hours of 30 May, 'In front' of Badajoz, passing on his news and opinions of Sir William Beresford. Stewart rated Beresford as a commander and praised him as 'a very clever Man & as Generals go, one of the best we have as I always told you', but this was tempered, as 'it is said in Critical Moments he loses himself, & is not himself.' Mixing military news with domestic matters, Stewart's thoughts turned to Lord Castlereagh's farm, perhaps as a relief from the expected fighting to come, advising his brother, 'I have got You 2 capital Boars at least so they tell me, the finest comes fm. the noted plains of Talavera, & is so call'd, also six particular Sows, I am looking out for more Stock for your farm.'[6]

Stewart's thoughts of pig-farming were to be rudely interrupted by the French. On 1 June, Marmont's troops were on the march, and as they advanced, Lord Wellington realized that he had no choice but to raise the siege of Badajoz. The French were not going to risk a battle, and Wellington was able to retire in good order unmolested. Wellington had been alert to the probability of a strong counterattack, as the French were well aware of Badajoz's importance. Wellington had gambled on taking the fortress before the enemy arrived, but this was not to be, despite some heavy fighting and notable heroics. If Wellington needed reminding, the strength of French arms showed once more that the allies were a long way from driving Napoleon's forces across the Pyrenees.

The French were exhausted and still in no mood for a major battle. Wellington's troops were also shattered. Both armies had exerted themselves to the full in the blazing heat of a Portuguese summer, and by late June Lord Wellington decided that he would rest his troops. For General Stewart, this afforded an excellent opportunity to join his brother officers in a spot of fox hunting as well as in other diversions, as he wrote home to Catherine on 10 July:

> At headquarters we have become fortunate enough to become possessed of an excellent pack, which affords us much amusement . . . no man enters more heartily than our leader . . . In our quarters, too, we live gaily and well. A spirit of hospitality and good-fellowship everywhere prevails, and in the midst of war, both private theatricals and agreeable parties are of continual recurrence.[7]

Lord Wellington had other things on his mind than just hunting foxes: 'Nothing less than the reduction of Ciudad Rodrigo, an essential preliminary to offensive operations in Spain.'[8] The summer was not to be spent in restful diversions, and the blockade of Ciudad Rodrigo began on 11 August. Wellington ordered up his siege guns from Lisbon, but as with so much of the campaign in 1811, the whole business was to end in frustration and disappointment. On 22 September, a large French relieving force appeared; having made Ciudad Rodrigo safe, they now turned on the allies, and on 24 September, Wellington had another fight on his hands.

The French threw in their cavalry to attack the allied positions, charging 'in gallant style, cheering in the usual manner . . . and making directly for the guns'. The allied troops, with bayonets fixed, met the cavalry attack head-on. Charles Stewart, as always the dashing cavalryman, as well as a staff officer, was in the hottest of the fighting. The French launched assaults on the allied cavalry led by one of the foremost Hanoverian commanders, General Charles Alten, who was 'assisted with his usual gallantry' by General Stewart to meet this danger. The cavalry 'manfully stood their ground against the squadrons, four times more numerous, of Montbrun's dragoons'.[9] Attack after attack was launched on Alten's cavalry, which included the 1st Hussars of the King's German Legion and the 11th Light Dragoons. While these attacks were being fought off, the French moved up a column to surround Wellington's position. Luckily for the allies, one of Stewart's junior officers, Captain Dashwood, discovered this French plan and a retreat was ordered.[10]

The allied position was dangerous, but Wellington's troops were formed into squares and repelled the French cavalry attacks. The allied army continued its retreat to Fuenteguinaldo, and Wellington again assumed a defensive position. The evening of 25 September 'was spent as it is customary for soldiers to spend a night before they expect a battle; officers lay down in their cloaks upon the floors of the houses – the men slept on their arms, round fires which blazed along the range of the position'.[11] Stewart, along with the rest of Wellington's senior officers, was waiting for the next French onslaught; it never came. As Stewart wrote, 'But, instead of indulging our troops as they expected, Marmont contented himself with making an exhibition of his force, and executing a variety of manoeuvres in our presence, and it must be confessed that a spectacle more striking has rarely been seen.' Wellington could muster fifteen thousand men to stop the French, who probably had ten thousand more troops. To Stewart, the allies' 'numerical inferiority' was simply 'fearful'.[12] If Marmont had attacked, the consequences could have been serious, but the French commander would not risk tackling Wellington's defensive position. Wellington had a lucky escape and the allies were able to withdraw, again without having to fight their way against a strong French force.

On 29 September, Wellington's army retired into cantonments. This concluded Lord Wellington's frustrating campaign: it had begun with the French abandoning attempts to conquer Portugal but ended with the allied forces checked on the Spanish border. Stewart recalled that during this 'dreary and monotonous interval' Wellington 'ceased not for a moment to devise plans for the future'.[13] This lull in the fighting also gave Stewart the time to think about his own future. Having obviously been stung by some paternal advice, Stewart wrote a long and emotional letter to his father, Lord Londonderry, on 11 October. The very real sacrifices that the war had imposed on his young family had become intolerable, but Stewart had at least been able to rely on his brother Castlereagh, who, when 'Difficulty arises', was 'an Anchor to rest upon'. Stewart's thoughts turned to returning home, although even in his current frame of mind he could not completely forget the war, and noted, 'Castlereagh's view of the State of our Warfare is Statesman like & most able, It is the exact notion taken by Lord Wellington, and I am still willing to hope the Game play'd on the present Plan may ultimately succeed.' However, a tone of pessimism is apparent in Stewart's outlook:

> But the Idea of War in the North seems to have died away again, Prussia has lower'd her Tone & Bonaparte seems returning to Paris only to plan his new Dispositions in Spain, With respect to this Country, One can not be blind, The Cortes & Govt. are absorb'd in Idle Disquisitions party Squabbles, & seem occupied in every thing but the Real means of Resistance for their Country.[14]

News from Spain was certainly far from optimistic, especially as the French continued to harry the resistance. The most dreadful news concerned the defeat of a Spanish force under General Joaquín Blake by a numerically inferior French army near Valencia on 25 October. This also meant that the great city of Valencia was likely to fall, a colossal blow to the Spanish cause.

The bulk of Lord Wellington's army may have been resting on the Côa, but the British general had left a small force behind to watch Ciudad Rodrigo; Wellington was soon cheered to hear that a leading Spanish guerrilla, Don Julián Sánchez, had watched the fortress so closely that he had managed to take the French governor prisoner. The French were far from having everything their own way, and on 28 October, General Hill gained a stunning victory over General Drouet at Arroyomolinos de Montánchez in Extremadura. While all this was happening, Lord Wellington kept his thoughts firmly on Ciudad Rodrigo and remained determined to take the city over the course of the coming winter. Stewart was one of those waiting that winter. Using the enforced spare time, Stewart found his brother three-pointers, 'I hope & believe of the real Spanish Breed.'[15] The pause in the war also put Stewart in a reflective mood, and with the coming of another new year, he wrote to Castlereagh on 1 January 1812:

> I have been making a Calculation of our Wear & Tear & Casualties I will send it you in my next. In the 2 Years & 9 Months we have been in the Peninsula, About 24000 Men have join[e]d the original Army, & I think our losses have been 18000 or near it including Battles, Deaths, & invalided – This is a large number, the last <u>half Year</u> has been particularly calamitous, 3500 men, have died, which is by far than on any other similar period.[16]

Unknown to Charles Stewart, events in Paris would soon shape the future direction of the war in Spain. As expected, after a prolonged siege, Valencia was taken by the French on 8 January. This was indeed a huge setback for the Spanish, and one which marked 'the high tide of French conquest'. However, it would prove a hollow victory for the French Empire. Napoleon had never rated Wellington's abilities and forgot that military commanders should not underestimate their enemy. He now made the serious miscalculation of detaching troops from the Army of Portugal.[17] Wellington soon discovered that Napoleon had ordered soldiers to the north and east of Spain, weakening French forces sent to oppose him. This also made an attack on French positions more attractive to the British commander.

On 8 January, Wellington seized the initiative, and in the middle of a Spanish winter laid siege to Ciudad Rodrigo.

Wellington soon heard of Valencia's fall and realized that the French would throw their forces against him to save Ciudad Rodrigo. This meant that there was a degree of urgency in Wellington's calculations. Ironically, the success of Spanish guerrillas prevented news of the siege from reaching Marshal Marmont until it was too late. Wellington was not to know this. Once the French were driven from the outworks, and having refused to surrender, Lord Wellington ordered the assault on 19 January. This was sooner than Wellington would have wished, but he knew that the city had to be taken before relief arrived. Stewart wrote to his brother on the mood of the army on the eve of the assault:

> On our side, again, the trenches, crowded with armed men, among whom not so much a whisper might be heard, presented no unapt resemblance to a dark thunder-cloud, or to a volcano in that state of tremendous quiet which usually precedes its most violent eruptions. But the delay was not of long continuance; at a few minutes past seven o'clock the word was quietly passed that all things were ready, and the troops poured forward with the coolness and impetuosity of which British soldiers alone are capable, and which nothing could successfully oppose.[18]

The assault was bloody and the French put up stiff resistance. The allies stormed the walls but at great cost; among the casualties were Major General Henry MacKinnon, killed by a French explosion, and Lieutenant General Robert Craufurd, mortally wounded by a musket shot. The fighting continued in the streets and houses of Ciudad Rodrigo, and by Stewart's account, around fifteen hundred prisoners were taken. There then followed 'scenes of plunder and confusion', as the victorious army rampaged through the streets, where the sounds of occasional gunshots were combined with 'shouts and screams' which 'mingled fearfully with the groans of the wounded and the outcries of intoxicated men'.[19] Fortunately the plundering, although appalling, was swiftly brought under control. This had been a short and decisive offensive action. The Spanish government certainly grasped the importance of this victory and was quick to reward Wellington's achievements, creating him Duque de Ciudad Rodrigo.

Homeward bound

This great victory would soon be tempered by bitter news for Charles Stewart. Only a few months previously his thoughts had turned to his family back at home. Now he received the terrible news that his wife Catherine had died on 11 February. In London, a government official, Edward Cooke, had been concerned that Stewart might find out through the papers. He wrote to Lord Wellington on 12 February to warn him of what had happened, sending the letter via a senior officer about to sail for Portugal. Catherine had suffered from 'a small knob or Protuberance in the middle of the Head' which had been 'imperfectly cut last year'. She then had another operation to remove it, and although it 'was trifling & the Wound was healing' an open carriage ride and cold bathing 'brought on a sudden & most violent Attack'.

Cooke wrote that Lady Catherine had died 'with tranquillity and Ease', but knowing 'how this most unexpected & afflicting Event will affect Charles' hoped that Wellington could 'find means to prepare him for it, & weaken if possible the Result of Suddenness and Surprize'. Wellington certainly did his best to help Stewart, lending the adjutant general his carriage as he was simply 'so prostrated with grief that he could not ride', and accompanied him for an entire day trying to offer comfort.[20]

Alison's 1861 biography insists that Stewart received this news when he was on his way home on sick leave. Cooke's letter and letters between Stewart and Wellington make it clear that he was still on active service. This was about to change, as Castlereagh felt that his brother should now leave the Peninsula:

> But, it is now for you, my Dearest Charles, when you have indulged the full measure of your Grief, to reflect on what is due to those who remain. Your Dearest Boy, consigned to my Care . . . will be cherished by Ly C. and myself with a tenderness that can leave you no anxiety . . . but there are a thousand indescribable and indispensable motives which after such a Calamity require that we should See you here, I do trust therefore, that without delay you will return to England. I am sure Lord W. will facilitate and leave the option open to going if you wish to resume, but whilst I press your coming, I feel that I ask nothing that as a Soldier you should not grant, It is impossible for human nature after such a Shock, to pursue any duty with Equanimity, I think you owe it to yourself as well as to your Family, not to attempt it, and professionally I consider you are not pledg'd to return to a Situation you never liked.[21]

Castlereagh's advice was straightforward and left open the possibility of Stewart's return to Wellington's staff. It was a momentous decision for Stewart to make: stay with the army following the success of Ciudad Rodrigo, or leave the role he had carved for himself as a senior member of headquarters staff. After a frustrating campaigning season in 1811, the allies were now on the offensive, and following the capture of Ciudad Rodrigo, Lord Wellington's thoughts naturally returned to Badajoz. Throughout Wellington's campaigns, Stewart had almost always been at the British commander's side. Charles Stewart had endured the dangers, retreats and glories of the Peninsular War since 1808. He had risen to the rank of major general and had earned himself a reputation for bravery. Castlereagh was obviously concerned that his brother would be unable to continue while labouring under feelings of guilt and grief. At home he could be comforted by his wider family. Castlereagh, who had been so keen for Stewart to join Wellington's staff, had offered his brother the chance to resign from a position that had never been congenial to the dashing hussar.[22] Stewart took his brother's advice. Having returned home, General Stewart seemingly kept a low profile. Coming to terms with his wife's death and getting to know his son Frederick would have taken up much of his time. Memories would have been all around, perhaps prompted by Thomas Lawrence's striking painting of Catherine as Saint Cecilia.[23]

This low profile was not to last thanks to events at home and abroad. The first stage was the revival of Castlereagh's political career. In February 1812, domestic political changes saw Castlereagh return to office as foreign secretary in the place of Lord Wellesley. A few months later, on 11 May, the prime minister, Spencer Perceval, was assassinated. The new prime minister, the Earl of Liverpool, wanted both Castlereagh and Canning in his cabinet. Negotiations to bring Canning back into office came to nothing, a situation that allowed Castlereagh to strengthen his political position. As Liverpool would lead the government from the House of Lords, Castlereagh added the leadership of the House of Commons to his responsibilities. Castlereagh now enjoyed a new and powerful political prominence as both foreign secretary and as the government's spokesman in the Commons.

Internationally, while Britain found itself having to fight the United States, with hostilities declared in June 1812, the British would also forge new alliances with Russia and Prussia. At the centre of these European alliances was Tsar Alexander I, a formidable man whom Stewart would soon come to know well. Alexander was an intelligent and capable ruler of the vast Russian Empire, although his succession in 1801 had been far from straightforward. Alexander had become emperor while still in his 20s, after the court elites had grown tired of his father, Tsar Paul I, who was overthrown and murdered.[24] Russia had been allied with France since the Treaty of Tilsit in 1807, but Alexander and his advisers believed that eventually the French Emperor would turn on them. As part of the agreement at Tilsit, Napoleon had demanded that Russia adhere to his Continental System, which meant a ban on both British ships and goods, harming the Russian economy and straining relations between the two powers.[25] By 1812 matters were at breaking point. War between the two powers began when French troops crossed the Russian border in June 1812. The French reached Moscow by mid-September, remaining there until Napoleon ordered the belated evacuation of Russia's ancient capital over a month later. The retreat from Moscow would turn into a military disaster for France, with Napoleon leaving most of his Grande Armée to perish in Russia.[26] French arms had suffered a catastrophic but not fatal setback. Napoleon had managed to return to Paris on 18 December, and far from being crestfallen was soon implementing plans to put together a new army.

Alexander wanted to assume the offensive against Napoleon, despite misgivings from many around him. Watching events closely was one of Napoleon's reluctant allies, Prussia. This proud kingdom had been militarily defeated and humiliated by France, and in the process had lost its status as a great power. Napoleon's disastrous Russian campaign seemed an ideal opportunity for the Prussians to turn the tables on France. They took their chance in late December 1812, without bothering to seek permission from their king. The Convention of Tauroggen, agreed by the Russian and Prussian armies, allowed Alexander's troops to occupy East Prussia. Frederick William III of Prussia was in an unenviable position. The King was right to be afraid of Napoleon, who might seek revenge on Prussia and destroy the much weakened country once and for all. Prussia's position was also dependent on the attitude of the Austrians. The upshot was a series of diplomatic manoeuvrings between Austria, Russia and Prussia, which resulted in Frederick William being reassured that Austria would not be bought off by Napoleon with promises of future territorial gain. The delicacy of these negotiations was increased by the fact that the Emperor of Austria, Francis I, was also Napoleon's father-in-law. Napoleon had married the Archduchess Marie Louise in 1810, and she had seemingly secured the future of the Bonaparte dynasty by bearing a son, the King of Rome, in 1811.

As these momentous events unfolded, Castlereagh's thoughts turned to his half-brother. Alison argued that Stewart was in line for a diplomatic role as early as January 1813, but a delay was caused by his reluctance to leave behind a military career. Castlereagh 'seeing his contest of feelings . . . applied for, and got for him, the military decoration of a red ribbon' of the Order of the Bath, thanks to a direct application to the Earl of Liverpool. Castlereagh laid his brother's merits at the feet of the prime minister on 23 January 1813:

> My brother has been at the head of the Staff of the (Peninsular) army since the commencement of Lord Wellington's command. He has always courted active service whenever it could be found, having relinquished the situation of Under-Secretary of State for that purpose. Exclusive of two campaigns with the Austrians, under the Archduke Charles, he has served under Lord Moira, Abercrombie, Moore, and Lord Wellington. He has been repeatedly wounded, suffered severely in his health, and has hardly ever been employed in the active command of troops without having his conduct particularly approved in the published orders.[27]

Stewart was nominated a Knight of the Bath on 1 February 1813 (becoming a Knight Grand Cross of the Bath on the enlargement of the Order in January 1815).[28] It was a crowning moment to his military efforts, which were also recognized by the Portuguese government's award of the Order of the Tower and Sword.[29] Although Sir Charles Stewart had returned home covered in military glory, he was still unemployed. Lord Wellington had made it clear that he would not give Stewart an independent command, effectively ending his active military career. Stuck at home, Stewart had missed the fighting and hard-won British triumphs in the Peninsula, which had seen a grateful government bestow new honours on its commander Lord Wellington, including an earldom and then a marquessate.[30]

Meanwhile, Russian troops advanced through Prussia and reached Berlin on 4 March. The French garrison was abandoned and the Russian troops were welcomed as liberators. Even before Berlin was taken, Frederick William III had decided to enter into an alliance with Russia. It was the start of a partnership between Alexander and Frederick William which would continue to be in evidence for the rest of the war. Both powers were also keen to see Austria join them, but for now this was a start. On 17 March 1813, the Prussians declared war on France. Already an alliance had been forged with Russia, and Britain had sent Viscount

Cathcart, a veteran general officer, as its representative to Alexander.[31] With the accession of Prussia into the new coalition against France, the foreign secretary, Lord Castlereagh, needed another trusted diplomatic agent. That trusted agent would be his half-brother, Sir Charles Stewart. It was a role which would prove an *entrée* to an entirely different theatre of operations, negotiating with emperors, kings, princes and ministers. It also determined the future direction of Stewart's career over the course of the next ten years, a decade which would prove to be a tumultuous period in European history.

Chapter 4

ROVING AMBASSADOR

Sir Charles Stewart's appointment as minister to Prussia has generated some censure, viewed by some as a foreign secretary indulgently appointing his brother to this lofty position. In an age when patronage was everything, this is too simplistic and lacks credibility, and does not explain why Stewart would be a key figure in the final campaigns against Napoleon.[1] Sir Charles Stewart was the ideal choice for this pivotal role, which was not going to be the usual ambassadorial posting with a fine embassy, but one regarded by contemporaries as 'a military mission'. Stewart was being accredited to a king who had declared war on Napoleon, and Britain's new representative would be expected to attend the Prussians on the battlefield. Stewart, used to the rigours of military campaigning and the sights of war, would easily fit into such a diplomatic posting.

George Jackson, an experienced junior diplomat, would serve as Stewart's assistant throughout the campaign of 1813–14. Jackson has left behind a memorable diary of this time, and from the start this incisive official recognized that Stewart 'must content himself with his double character of General and negotiator'.[2] This was no place for a civilian diplomat. Indeed, when the Earl of Aberdeen, a refined and cultured man with no military experience, was sent out to mainland Europe later in the year, he told Castlereagh, 'The Privations and sufferings of following Head Quarters are nearly as great as in a military life, but without any credit to be obtained.'[3] This is not to belittle Aberdeen but illustrates that Britain's representatives would have to undertake their diplomatic missions in the middle of a war zone. Both Lord Cathcart, the ambassador to Russia, and Sir Charles Stewart had lived with war for much of their professional lives and would not be put off by the need to conduct diplomacy across the battle-scarred fields of Europe.

Jackson's mother took a rather less charitable view of Stewart's new post. The idea of military ambassadors and ministers did not sit well with a woman who had two sons in the diplomatic line. She wrote to George Jackson, 'At Sir Charles Stewart's mission I am not well pleased. I am quite tired of Generals being sent out as negotiators; and there never came any good of it yet.' Perhaps saving her anger for last, she castigated Castlereagh, who in her opinion had 'more love for his brother than regard for the interests of his country, and with amiable weakness has given him the first and best thing that came into his hands'.[4] This attitude is perhaps understandable and has probably coloured subsequent accounts of Stewart's appointment. Poor Mrs Jackson must have been annoyed that as her two sons lacked Stewart's brilliant connections, they would have to make their own way in the world.

Stewart's original instructions were rather vague, and 'as unsatisfactory as it could be'. Stewart and Jackson went through their orders, which directed them to place themselves 'under the control and guidance' of Lord Cathcart, who was senior both in terms of position and military rank. Stewart was having none of this. He swiftly complained to his brother that he was going out with 'his hands tied' and 'his mouth closed', not the usual diplomatic language, and nearly unthinkable for anyone else to use. This obviously did the trick and Jackson could report that 'the change Sir Charles desired was instantly made, and he is now to act in concert with the noble viscount [Cathcart] – cojointly with whom he is to sign the treaty.'[5] Stewart certainly had a point, as any subordination to Cathcart would limit his independence to act as he saw fit.

Stewart was accredited to Frederick William III of Prussia. Born in 1770, Frederick William, who succeeded to the throne in 1797, had 'a sharp, if reticent, intelligence', and was a peaceful man 'who eschewed the quest for glory and reputation'. The King was also inclined to 'ask for advice and to vacillate'.[6] Frederick William was certainly decisive in one respect, and that was to restore Prussia as a great power. Alongside the declaration of war, the Russians had secretly committed themselves to Prussia gaining greater German territory. Lying behind this was the reality that Russian troops now occupied the former Prussian lands in Poland, and Tsar Alexander I had no intention of giving these up. Prussia would need to be compensated elsewhere. Frederick William had previously accepted Napoleon's gift of the Electorate of Hanover, the German homeland of the British Hanoverian monarchy (which Napoleon later incorporated into the Kingdom of Westphalia, ruled by Jérôme Bonaparte). After the war was over, Britain would naturally insist that Hanover should be in the hands of its own royal dynasty. At this stage, both Russia and Prussia looked to the territory of Napoleon's ally, Frederick Augustus, King of Saxony, as likely Prussian compensation.

Stewart was not just being sent to deal with Prussia. He was also charged with liaising with Charles-Jean, Prince Royal of Sweden, to whom the new ambassador 'had especial letters of authorization as to all matters of a military nature'.[7] These Swedish royal titles had been recently acquired by their holder, better known as Jean-Baptiste Bernadotte, the son of a minor functionary from Gascony. Bernadotte's meteoric rise in the army had been a classic example of the post-French Revolutionary career open to talent, culminating in Napoleon's making him a marshal of France. Connected by marriage to the Bonaparte family itself, his spectacular rise would reach even greater heights, when he was elected by the Swedes as heir to Charles XIII in 1810. Bernadotte was to be no slavish follower of Napoleon and having resigned his French commission, the new Swedish Crown Prince realized that his adopted country's future was best served by reaching an accommodation with Russia rather than with France.[8] Accordingly, the two countries signed an agreement. As part of this new understanding, Russia agreed to Bernadotte's demands that Sweden should annex Norway, at that time ruled by the King of Denmark, who also happened to be an ally of Napoleon. Realpolitik undoubtedly swayed Bernadotte, but the personal rivalry and hatred which had grown up between the Prince Royal of Sweden and the French Emperor may also have played their part.

Such was the diplomatic web that Sir Charles Stewart, given the local rank of lieutenant general, would have to negotiate.[9] Sailing from Yarmouth aboard the frigate HMS *Nymphe* on 13 April 1813, Stewart arrived a few days later in Hamburg, then occupied by Russian troops.[10] During his short stay in Hamburg, Stewart found himself immersed in military matters, notably with the formation of the Hanoverian levies. Soon afterwards Stewart set off for Berlin, arriving on 22 April. On his arrival, he found that Frederick William had already left, and was expected to meet Alexander in Dresden, the capital of Saxony. Stewart decided to follow. Arriving in Dresden on 26 April, he was unable to immediately present his credentials to Frederick William III but was able to meet the Prussian chancellor, Karl August von Hardenberg. The chancellor was from 'a Hanoverian family of progressive reputation', and by sheer hard work and intelligence would earn a reputation as one of the greatest civil administrators in Prussian history.[11] Stewart's first meeting with the formidable Hardenberg went well, and the new ambassador reported back to London on his 'very satisfactory general Conversation with His Excellency'.[12]

Sir Charles Stewart was able to present his credentials to Frederick William on 27 April. Stewart told his brother that 'It was not possible to have been received in a more gracious, or satisfactory, manner.' The King had been at pains to stress the importance of the new alliance with Britain and the constraints Prussia had been forced to accept by France. He expressed his regard for Stewart as 'an Officer of Character . . . who had seen much Service, being placed near His Person'. Stewart advised the foreign secretary, 'I did not fail to avail myself of this Opportunity of assuring His Majesty that it would be my constant Ambition to be worthy of Marks of His Confidence and Favor.'[13] In contrast, George Jackson recorded in his diary that the King 'still had the fear of Boney before his eyes', but noted he was exceedingly gracious to Stewart by complimenting him on his military exploits.[14]

Stewart the diplomat was obliged to remain 'reluctantly' in Dresden conducting 'preliminary negotiations', including the details of the British subsidies. In reality, Stewart the general was desperate to see military action. Stewart was annoyed with Cathcart, who was able to indulge his military passions by leaving with Alexander to join the allied armies. Stewart fulminated that although he was 'anxious in no way to impede the negotiation' he was 'urged by the natural impulses of a soldier, to be a witness of the grand conflict about to take place'. Clearly Stewart's impulses had to play second fiddle to his diplomatic mission, but Jackson could not help wryly recording that this was 'a pretty fair exemplification of the wisdom of sending out a brace of military negotiators'.[15]

Stuck in Dresden, Stewart wasted no time in venting his frustrations back to Castlereagh on 5 May: 'Lord Cathcart informed me it was his Desire, as he was under the necessity of following His Imperial Majesty that I should remain at Dresden for the purpose of commencing with Baron de Hardenberg, and the Russian Plenipotentiaries, the previous Discussions of the important Objects of the subsidiary Convention.' Stewart had 'felt a good deal of difficulty in having to enter alone into these important Concerns, and stated my reasons to Lord Cathcart'. These reasons were now elaborated to Castlereagh:

> His Lordship observed there would be only preliminary Conferences and nothing binding in any shape, and, as he seemed decided on this subject, I had no Choice. He informed me that he had opened verbally to His Imperial Majesty, and his Minister, Monsieur de Nesselrode, the general Objects of the Convention . . .
>
> Immediately on Lord Cathcart's Departure, His Excellency pressed me very much to commence my Communications with him, and to give him the Heads, in writing, of the Treaty about to be negotiated. Feeling it was my essential Duty (being separated from the Army by Lord Cathcart's Directions, and finding the Russian Ministers, as well as the Prussian, remaining here to commence Negotiations with me) to facilitate, to the utmost of my Power, the Progress of Affairs.[16]

Stewart dined with the Russian and Prussian ministers, and was able to discuss matters freely with them 'privately and unofficially . . . in an adjoining Room'. Stewart at first hand observed the closeness of Russia and Prussia during these discussions: 'a long conference ensued, in which I found M. de Nesselrode and Stein supporting Monsieur de Hardenberg in all the language he held.' Discussion had also turned to the future of Hanover:

> to the Aggrandizement of the Electoral Dominions, that there would be no Difficulty nor would there be to the Cession of Hildesheim, but that there would exist an insuperable one to the Annexation of Minden and Ravensberg [sic], which Baron Hardenberg declared no Consideration would ever induce His Prussian Majesty to accede to.[17]

Stewart had made important contacts in Dresden, including two of the Tsar's main advisers, Count Nesselrode and Baron vom Stein. Stewart also met Count Lebzeltern, one of the Austrian foreign minister's protégé diplomats. At one dinner on 1 May, Hardenberg seemed very pleased with the burgeoning alliance, and as Jackson wrote, had made reference to the motto of the Order of the Bath, *Tria Juncta in Uno*, to describe the new allies. This, however, Lebzeltern 'in a manner disdained'.[18] This was a timely reminder that the Austrian Empire had still not committed itself.

Austria's foreign policy was directed by its very capable minister, Clemens von Metternich, a man who would loom large in the next decade of Stewart's career. Born in 1773, Metternich, in common with many Habsburg servants, was not Austrian. Metternich's family came from the Rhineland. 'Cosmopolitan and rationalist', Metternich has also been termed 'the greatest diplomat of his age'. He learned the art of diplomacy as ambassador to Saxony, Prussia and France, and while serving in Paris, Metternich had come to know Napoleon well. In 1809, Metternich was appointed Austrian foreign minister.[19] 'Thin and handsome with piercing blue eyes', Metternich was a supremely egotistical man, capable of incredible hard work, and 'often impressed others with his perfect manners and aristocratic bearing'.[20] Metternich certainly strained every sinew to ensure the Habsburg monarchy's survival. To this end, he had helped to broker the marriage alliance of Napoleon and Marie Louise, which had resulted in a lot of mistrust between Britain and Austria. Britain was right to be wary, as Vienna by this stage was certainly 'tilting strongly' towards the anti-Napoleonic alliance yet was still prepared to make peace terms with France.[21]

The initial diplomacy in Dresden being completed, Sir Charles was anxious to march off to the sound of the guns. George Jackson incredulously noted: 'The King had given him no invitation to accompany him, but as a military man he is mortified, he says, to be in the rear of the army; the more so, as accounts have arrived that a battle is on the eve of taking place.'[22] It is hard not to criticize Stewart for simply deciding to leave Dresden and follow his own desires to see action, but hindsight would prove that being in the field was the right place to be. Unfortunately for Stewart, his stay in Dresden meant that he missed the Battle of Lützen fought on 2 May 1813. The battle had been an attempt by the allied armies to surprise the French, who were advancing into Saxony towards Leipzig. The result was optimistically described as a bloody draw. One important diplomatic result of the battle was to convince King Frederick Augustus of Saxony to reaffirm his alliance with Napoleon. This decision would have dire consequences for both the King and for Saxony. The Austrians meanwhile continued their own diplomatic game, and sought terms from Napoleon which included the restitution of all of the Habsburg monarchy's lost territories.

The allies had evacuated Dresden shortly after the Battle of Lützen, with the French not far behind them. The allies headed for Bautzen, to the east of the Saxon capital, while Napoleon established himself in Dresden. Stewart, not surprisingly, found himself back in the thick of political negotiations, but George Jackson could see that his mind was on martial glory: 'Sir C's thoughts are so taken up with the military arrangements of the allied army, that he has neither patience nor inclination for diplomatic discussion.' More worryingly, according to Jackson, Stewart felt out of his depth, and the manoeuvrings around the subsidy treaty were so complicated that he intended to write to Lord Castlereagh 'suggesting that no time be lost in sending out a proper person, completely qualified to master such details, or in proposing that some person should go from hence to discuss the Treaty in England'. Stewart was having to learn fast, but his self-doubt does not necessarily provide convincing evidence that he could not cope.

This episode has all the look of that crippling uncertainty in his own abilities that would dog Stewart in his diplomatic career, which was such a long way from that effortless success he enjoyed as a military officer. That said, he was still behaving as only a general and not as a diplomat in the field, to the irritation of others, notably Baron Hardenberg. The Prussian chancellor even buttonholed

Jackson to express his frustrations with Britain, and especially with its minister, over the lack of progress on the proposed treaty. Hardenberg remarked 'that Sir Charles Stewart's military duties no doubt prevented him from entering into the discussion of it so fully and promptly as was desirable'. From this Jackson deduced that Hardenberg 'would have been better pleased had our Government sent him a colleague more at leisure to confer with him'.[23]

Stewart explained the delays to his brother on 17 May from Wurzen, advising him, 'The constant Movements of the Army have prevented until Yesterday any further Measures being adopted, but being invited with Lord Cathcart to a Preliminary Conference on that day with the Plenipotentiaries of His Imperial Majesty & the King of Prussia, we proceeded generally to discuss the objects of the convention'.[24] On 18 May, Stewart went further, giving Castlereagh a summary of progress to date, an honest account of Britain's allies, and news of the arrival of a senior Austrian diplomat, Count Stadion. Stewart also advised, 'Our subsidiary Convention proceeds slowly' and pointed at a distinct lack of cooperation from his fellow British ambassador: 'I have the points with Prussia chiefly to fight myself, as Lord Cathcart thinks them less momentous; indeed the whole of this has been very dilatory, and I see no end to it; but this is not my fault'.[25]

At least Sir Charles Stewart would not have to wait long for a battle. While Vienna danced its waltz with Napoleon, the Russian and Prussian armies would again bleed in the field. On 20 May, the allies and the French fought at Bautzen. Stewart was completely in his element as a soldier and was joined in his warlike exploits by another Peninsular War veteran, Sir Robert Wilson, who was acting as a military liaison officer with the Russian army. Wilson was a flamboyant and brave soldier, who would finish his career highly decorated by a number of sovereigns (but not by his own). Writing a few days later, Wilson recollected what had happened at Bautzen. Having heard cannon fire, Stewart and Wilson both rode forth to the scene, and to their alarm witnessed an allied withdrawal from a crucial part of the battlefield:

> The point was the key of the position of the advanced-guard, and the most prejudicial results must have been the consequence of its premature occupation . . .
>
> Sir Charles agreed with my opinion. I brought back the guns and the retiring battalion. We then advanced at the head, caps in hand, and accompanied with loud cheers. The enemy fell back, but again we were obliged to retire by fresh succours sustaining the fugitives. Again and again we rallied and charged; and finding about forty Prussian lancers we dashed in among the enemy's infantry, while our own pressed forward to help our inferiority. The enemy threw their fire upon us before they gave way, and in flying singed us; but we were revenged.[26]

On the second day both men were again in the field, but their efforts were to no avail, as the result was another allied mauling at the hands of the French. Stewart perhaps rather downplayed his role in the official correspondence to his brother, remarking on 20 May, 'I witnessed two very gallant Charges of Russian Light

Cavalry, as well as extreme good conduct throughout the Troops engaged.'[27] Colonel Hudson Lowe, who was acting as British liaison officer with the Russian German Legion, was more fulsome in his account of Stewart's heroics: 'Lord Cathcart and Sir Charles Stewart were in every part of the Field during the Two days, the former generally near the person of the Emperor, the latter was on the last day almost personally engaged, in Company with Sir Robert Wilson whose active exertions were very conspicuous.'[28] Clearly, Stewart's account of the battle was well received in London, as Colonel Lowe wrote the following month, 'Lord Cathcart is not much pleased with his Dispatch of the Battle of Bautzen not having been published, while that of Sir Charles Stewart has appeared in the Gazette.'[29]

A Continental Peace

More alarming for Castlereagh was Stewart's reporting of secret peace negotiations with France. Stewart had discovered the details of these communications, and having talked to Count Stadion, could advise the foreign secretary privately, 'It is broadly admitted that a Continental Peace, separated from a Maritime Peace, may be negotiated.' Stewart would remain vigilant, as 'it is well to keep a good look out on every thing that is going forward.'[30] At least on the military front, Napoleon's forces did not have things all their own way, and over the next few days they suffered reverses while engaging the allied rearguard.

Just as importantly for his mission, Stewart seemed to be getting on with everyone, except perhaps Hardenberg. Wilson was certainly very happy to have Stewart with the armies, which is perhaps not surprising as the two men were so alike.[31] Wilson lost no time in telling the Prince Regent's cousin, the Duke of Gloucester, that the new minister to Prussia had certainly 'greatly improved' his own position. Superlatives poured forth from Sir Robert, who could not praise Stewart enough as a 'truly excellent gallant Gentleman' who was 'very much liked by the Prussian & Russian Courts and Camps'.[32] This report is not to be taken lightly. The charming and urbane Stewart, brother of the British foreign secretary, and a famed general staff officer, was clearly establishing a rapport with both allied royalty and military officers. This charm was soon to be tested to the limits.

For Stewart, Bautzen had rekindled his passion for war, but he would have to put these military pleasures aside and work hard to secure Britain's interests, as diplomacy took a far more complicated turn. Napoleon had decided to stop his advance on the allies, who had established their headquarters at Reichenbach in Prussia. The French Emperor had sent out peace feelers, overtures which led to an armistice on 4 June. Not only was the armistice agreed by Austria, Russia and Prussia; more seriously, nobody had bothered to include the two British plenipotentiaries in these discussions, or inform them of the result. Cathcart seemed to be completely in the dark, while Stewart only discovered what was afoot through an article in the *Moniteur* of 25 May, which stated, 'Buonaparte intended to assemble a congress at Prague, and that Austria had assented to this arrangement.'[33] Four points had been put to Napoleon. Perhaps the most significant was the abolition of the Duchy of Warsaw, a state created from Napoleon's political reorderings and ruled by the King of Saxony. Its territories would be shared among the allies. The other terms were territorial acquisitions for Prussia, the return to the Austrian Empire of its lost Illyrian provinces, and the removal of French fortresses in North Germany and Poland. These were very lenient conditions, and no mention was made of the Low Countries, the restoration of Ferdinand VII to the throne of Spain, or the future of the Confederation of the Rhine, made up of those German states which accepted French hegemony. On 6 June, Stewart, writing from Reichenbach, could hardly contain his fury to Castlereagh:

> The news we send home is not the best, and, from what I see, I fear political treachery and the machinations that are in the wind more than any evils from Bonaparte's myrmidons. We must keep a sharp look-out, especially since our refusal of Austrian mediation. We are not considered (from all I see going on) in the Cabinet . . . I fear the Swedes will go, and Bonaparte gets 20,000 Danes in the North.[34]

Stewart believed that Bernadotte had 'not been managed as he should have been by Russia' while the 'disorder' in Alexander's army was 'great'. At least the Prussian military, who were 'infinitely better', had done well, 'and will do much more in a little time. You cannot send them too much ammunition and arms.' Stewart, feeling out of humour with the Austrians, added his strong distrust of them in his letter, and especially towards Count Metternich. Stewart suspected Metternich of using Habsburg family ties to Napoleon to secure a good deal for Vienna, while warning Castlereagh that the other powers might call a congress. In that case, Stewart advised his brother, 'If you acquiesce in sending a negotiator, pray select a very able man. Depend upon it, he will be required. I fear military diplomatists will not be quite satisfactory to you.'[35]

Despite Stewart's doubt in his own abilities, the convention between the United Kingdom and Prussia was agreed at Reichenbach on 14 June 1813. The treaty was very precise in its terms of the financial subsidy for Prussia.[36] Two days later, Stewart wrote to Castlereagh convinced that Austria could be brought into the alliance 'by shewing we look to War even without her, to convince her that England and Sweden are firmly united to Russia and Prussia, and finally to make her adhere to Propositions which Buonaparte (it is declared) will not accept, is the surest mode of gaining her as a Belligerent'. Stewart also communicated his displeasure at the ignoring of British interests:

> I expressed to the Chancellor Hardenberg my Incompetence to answer him as to the Sanction of England to the late Proceedings . . . The most important points appeared to me to have been neglected in the Propositions alluded to, and those most interesting to England; Without Reference or Instructions I had no reason to believe Great Britain would take any part in what had occurred, but upon the

complete fulfillment of the late Treaty I relied. His Assurances in answer, were cordial and satisfactory.[37]

The British had been ignored, and despite Stewart's bluster, on 27 June Austria, Russia and Prussia agreed terms for an armistice, which additionally stated that if France did not agree to these terms by 20 July, Vienna would declare war.

Britain was understandably annoyed at these events, while the Russians and Prussians were not overly enthusiastic about these terms. Metternich himself likely believed that Napoleon would not accept them.[38] Although sidelined, Sir Charles Stewart still had the advantage of having money. Stewart told his brother, 'The very great distress in which the Prussian Finances are, and the important consequences that may result if Great Britain can make no Advance of a part of the Subsidy to this Power, has been so strenuously urged upon me, that I have consented after much deliberation to draw Bills for £100,000'. This money was later the cause of some disagreement between Stewart and Cathcart as to the intended recipients, while such financial aid for the allied war effort made the neglect of British interests even more surprising.[39]

Stewart kept himself very busy, travelling from Reichenbach back to Berlin, where he was able to enjoy life as a soldier in the Prussian capital by inspecting the militia; he may also have indulged other passions around this time. Stewart recollected that military headquarters played host to a number of high-ranking women, including Princess Pauline of Württemberg among others. Stewart clearly enjoyed their company and wrote later that his 'anecdotes' of this time 'might prove more interesting to many than my military narrative'. Whether Stewart's flirtations went further is impossible to say, as his account, written long after his second marriage, merely noted 'that female society of the most perfect description was within our reach; and its allurements and dissipations often divided the mind of soldier and politician from their more severe duties'.[40]

From Berlin, Stewart travelled to Greifswald, where on 5 July he had his first meeting with Bernadotte.[41] From the start Stewart was impressed with his fellow soldier who 'was no ordinary man'. Stewart could not be 'dazzled by his brilliancy' but was specifically tasked by his government to ascertain Bernadotte's 'real views, and how far the warmth of his expressions and splendour of his designs would be borne out by the reality of his services to the general cause'.[42] More importantly for British interests, Bernadotte had confirmed that a secret meeting had taken place between the Tsar and the Emperor of Austria, which seemed to indicate a growing understanding between the two empires.[43]

Back in Reichenbach, George Jackson reflected in his diary on the progress of Britain's diplomatic efforts, after he had dined with Lord Cathcart. Cathcart seemed very pleased with himself and perhaps a little jealous of Stewart. The dinner led Jackson to compare the two military negotiators, who despite having 'very different qualities' were 'about on a par in diplomatic ability'. Jackson also noted that Baron Hardenberg's 'ill-humour and backwardness to enter into discussion is owing to the little confidence he has in his colleagues, and his annoyance at their unusual mode of transacting business'. Despite this, Jackson could not help but be very tolerant of Stewart's foibles:

> In the latter respect Sir Charles, I fancy, is the greater sinner. But he is a very active and dashing officer, and socially, a most pleasant and excellent fellow, while for the rest, he is the brother of the foreign secretary of state, and that fortunate circumstance for him must be accepted, I suppose, as making up for all his deficiencies as a diplomatist.[44]

This diary entry reflects Mrs Jackson's comments on the connections of Sir Charles Stewart, but the other points on his social skills should not be underestimated when judging his capabilities in dealing with sovereigns, ministers and generals. In contrast, Jackson did not hold that high an opinion of Lord Cathcart, and he was almost contemptuous of 'the old man's deep faith in his great talents as a negotiator and the expertness with which he wields alike the pen and the sword'.[45]

Stewart may have fumed at not being in the smoke of battle, but he was not idle. As well as dealing with the 'very great Embarrassment' faced by the Russian German Legion's lack of funds, he was also in a position to pass on details about the peace talks to his brother. Thanks to Bernadotte, Stewart soon discovered that the deadline for French agreement to the Austrian terms had been extended to 10 August. However, as Stewart told his brother on 15 July, he had heard nothing from Edward Thornton, Britain's representative to Sweden, or from Lord Cathcart about the negotiations. It was only due to the Swedes that Stewart could advise Castlereagh that 'no great Results have arisen' from the talks with France, and that 'the main points seem to have been settled before the meeting'. Stewart was most unhappy about the way in which the British diplomats were being frozen out, and candidly vented his frustrations to Castlereagh:

> I do not conceive that the British Ministers present or the Prince of Sweden took prominent parts upon . . . the prolongation of the Armistice which was arrang'd between Austria & France & this demonstrates, what I ventur[e]d to state some long time since, that when these 2 latter powers have settled their Edict it will blazon forth & there is not Energy enough to resist it.[46]

Stewart was at least in his element after his arrival in Stralsund to again meet Bernadotte. As he advised his brother on 16 July, he had gone 'in conformity with that part of my instructions which gives me military Superintendance [sic] as far as Gt Btn is concern[e]d of the Prussian & Swedish Armies & the Auxiliary Corps under the Orders of the Prince Royal of Sweden'. This military force, the Army of the North, was now to become the centre of Stewart's attention. He now took this official opportunity to act as a general officer. In several of his letters to Castlereagh, Stewart could report on the strengths of the various armies. As a professional observer, the reports he provided would be very useful for the ministers in London. He could also get rather carried away and sometimes informed his brother, almost rapturously, that he was playing the role of military strategist.[47] These observations from a military man again show the advantage of having a soldier in this post. Such work would be unthinkable for a civilian diplomat and was a reminder that diplomacy was one thing, but only military might would liberate Europe from Napoleon's empire.

Most pressing from Stewart's point of view was to ensure that the Russian German Legion and the Hanoverian levies 'in which Gt Bn. are particularly interested' were brought together as an army corps. Stewart told his brother that he would inspect the troops in the absence of Bernadotte and the Prussian general, Count Walmoden. The Hanoverian levies were especially worrying as they 'exercise in every way English Prussian French after the fancy of their Councils' and had 'not been brought together or work'd even in Brigade'. Stewart, drawing on his experiences in Portugal and Spain, was the perfect officer to get these men into fighting form:

> This I hope to get remedied placing them all on the System laid down in HM's Regulations, which shall be adhered to – The Officers are all very inexperienced & Gen[eral]l Lyon represents to me how desirable it would be to get some Officers from England for the levies – perhaps Yr Lordship in considering the manner in which the Encrease to the Corps are to be Officer[e]d would be able to have some British Officers appointed as in the Portuguese Services, I throw this for Consideration.[48]

Stewart reassured his brother that he would 'studiously Endeavor to follow the opinions' of Bernadotte and 'the wishes' of Walmoden in any of his decisions. He also sought Castlereagh's agreement to this course of action, hoping that the foreign secretary and the Prince Regent would appreciate that as the man on the spot he should be allowed to make decisions on his own initiative, 'As accruing out of the critical period in which we are now call'd on to act with Vigor & which may not allow of References home.'[49] Stewart was very impressed with the troops, as Colonel Lowe reported, 'At Stralsund I had the advantage of meeting Lt General Sir Charles Stewart, who I found had already made an inspection of the Legion and transmitted a Report of it to His Majesty's Government. His Opinion of it is so favorable that He has recommended to be immediately taken into His Majesty's Service as part of His Electoral Troops.'[50]

Stewart did not forget that he was meant to be a diplomat. A few days later he told Castlereagh that he had had a detailed conversation with the Prince Royal of Sweden, advising the foreign secretary of the three main questions which would need an 'immediate decision' from the British government. The first was that if the armistice with France was 'by any unforeseen occurrence . . . prolonged' what would be 'expected' of Bernadotte? Second, if Bernadotte decided to remain in Germany over the winter, which Stewart believed he did not 'positively object' to, would Britain give an increased subsidy for the coming year? Stewart reported, 'This point seems strongly urg'd.' The third was the worry that if Napoleon accepted the proposed peace terms, 'it should be practically known that the Corps of the Russian German legion to be consider[e]d <u>as</u> a Corps at the Disposal of Gt Britain'. In this case, would it then accept orders directed from London?[51] Interestingly, for whatever reason, not long after he wrote this, Stewart's initial enthusiasm for Bernadotte seemed to evaporate, the minister reportedly telling Sir Robert Wilson that the Prince Royal was 'unworthy of trust'.[52] Perhaps Stewart had not been happy with some of these conversations with the wily Bernadotte, but, however that may be, his concerns and wariness would soon be overtaken by events on the ground.

In Spain, Lord Wellington had earned further laurels through his great victory against the French at the Battle of Vitoria on 21 June 1813. This battle sounded the retreat on Joseph Bonaparte's rule as King of Spain, and much of the King's personal treasure was taken. News of this victory had reached George Jackson in Reichenbach by 19 July. Jackson wrote to Stewart to advise of possible secret diplomacy and allied reactions to Wellington's triumph:

> I spoke to him [Cathcart] likewise of the reported Interview between the Emperors of Austria & Russia – H[is]. L[ordshi]p. denies any knowledge of it, & I have not been able to discover that it has actually taken place, but it is certain that the Emp. Alexr. has been absent for two or three Days fr: Peterswalde under Circumstances of the greatest Secrecy, travelling in a small open Carriage in the most private Way possible, & with a Guide, to conduct Him thro' the bye ways & Passes in the Mountains. –
>
> I am happy to tell you that the Effect produced by the late Victory of Ld. Wellington, as reported fr' the French Hd. Quarters, seems to have had the happiest results in inspiriting the Councils of Austria, & in giving fresh Vigor to the publick Feeling in this Quarter.[53]

Although Stewart had earned the Prince Regent's regard for his work, this must have been a frustrating time. Both Stewart and Bernadotte were being deliberately kept away from the peace talks. George Jackson, who was still in Reichenbach, at least kept Stewart informed of the negotiations. On 27 July, Jackson reported that the French representative, Armand de Caulaincourt, had not arrived in Prague on the expected date of 24 July, and had 'since learnt that War between Austria & France is now considered as certain'.[54] Another letter, dated 2 August, told Stewart, 'The Intelligence from Prague continues to be of the most satisfactory Nature.' Finally, on 12 August, Jackson informed Stewart, 'I stated to H. My's Ambassador at the Ct. of Russia with my Belief that a Convention had been signed between the Allies and Austria.'[55] Jackson was quite right. Despite British frustrations, the negotiations which took place in Prague proved to be a diplomatic disaster for Napoleon. The collapse of this diplomatic initiative meant that the armistice deadline of 10 August passed without a successful outcome, and Austria declared war on France.

Sir Charles Stewart was caught up in the mood of excitement which followed the Austrian declaration of war. Having returned to Reichenbach himself, he wrote a very emotional letter to Castlereagh:

It is difficult to convey to Your Lordship the Enthusiasm this News has created here; the Spirit of the Austrian Army is also at the highest pitch and when the three Allied Sovereigns meet at Prague it will be a proud Sensation for such British Subjects as witness the Event that the continued vigorous and energetick Conduct of our own Country, the wise Administration of the Prince Regent's Government, and the glorious Exploits of our Arms, have ultimately and exclusively brought into Action such a powerful Alliance against the Tyranny and Ambition of France, as leaves no doubt of a glorious Termination to the Contest. That doubts were entertained at Prague until the last Moment is not unnatural if one considers the past Conduct of Austria.[56]

Austrian attempts at mediation were at an end. Although Vienna had now acted 'nobly and magnanimously', Stewart, who was about to depart for Prague with Lord Cathcart, retained a certain lingering bitterness at recent events, especially as he had learned the full details of the treaty of 27 June, which was 'kept concealed from Great Britain in consequence of Austria's requiring this as a Stipulation'. To Stewart, this was inexcusable since the signing of the agreement between Britain and Prussia at Reichenbach. Stewart objected most strongly on this Subject to Hardenberg, who 'promised me in confidence a Copy of the Treaty, and defended his not communicating it by throwing it on Russia'.[57]

Napoleon now faced a huge allied coalition ranged against him. Already before this deadline had passed, Lord Castlereagh had decided to send out a new British diplomat tasked with negotiating with Austria. The new ambassador was George Gordon, fourth Earl of Aberdeen, a classical scholar, still in his late 20s. A friend of the foreign secretary, Aberdeen was cut from a very different cloth. Armed with a letter from the Prince Regent to the Emperor of Austria, Aberdeen set out to join Stewart and Cathcart. Castlereagh's instructions to the Earl revealed a new sense of optimism in London: 'The antient Jealousy, which divided the Courts of Vienna and Berlin, is now apparently, for the first time, buried in a Sense of common danger.'[58]

With the Austrians now part of the military coalition, and with Wellington making progress in the Peninsula, there was now a real possibility that Napoleon's imperial domination could be brought to an end. On 12 August, Stewart could report that 'the Prince of Würtemberg [*sic*], of whose Flight from his own Country your Lordship is already apprized' was 'most anxious to serve in any manner in the Hanoverian or other Levies, and offers His Services to the Prince Regent. – Your Lordship will be able to send me the Pleasure of His Royal Highness with instructions on this Subject.'[59] The Kingdom of Württemberg, a member of the Napoleonic Confederation of the Rhine, had to this point happily acquiesced in the French domination of Germany. Any such royal defection should have alarmed the French government.

These were worrying times as well for the British. Their allies still seemed content to offer peace terms to Napoleon without reference to London or to its negotiators, and they would continue to do so. Sir Charles Stewart would be well placed to check these attempts. Stewart was not only at the centre of Britain's efforts against Napoleon, he would prove time and again that Castlereagh had been right in sending him into the heart of the action. The scene was now set for a showdown between Napoleon and the allies, which would determine the fate of French power in Germany. In the process, Sir Charles Stewart would again take the fight to the French through diplomatic channels and through the judicious use of his cavalry sabre.

Chapter 5

THE BRANDENBURG HUSSARS

The Austrian Empire had joined the allied coalition. Napoleon's ambition for his dynasty and for France now faced its most serious challenge. Sir Charles Stewart, along with Lord Cathcart, represented the British government's interests as the allies sought to throw the French out of Germany. This would not be an easy task. Napoleon's armies were weakened, but nobody would write off the French Emperor's chances of defeating the allies through his military prowess. At least there was a seemingly united front against the French, after the labyrinthine peace negotiations had broken down. Stewart, the blunt soldier, rather than the smooth diplomat, had wasted no time in showing British anger at the secret negotiations. As George Jackson noted in his diary, Stewart caught up with the Prussian chancellor, Hardenberg, on 14 August, 'and peremptorily demanded' a copy of the treaty signed by the three governments. Hardenberg was not a man used to demands, and 'his temper, naturally so calm, could not quite unmoved withstand the shock of Sir Charles's impetuosity.' Even Jackson, normally rather taken aback by such behaviour, could not hide his pleasure, and in the confidence of his diary wrote 'yet Hardenberg I must confess deserved it.'[1]

Jackson could see that this was not the time for the usual civilities. The allies, happy to take British money, had deliberately kept London's representatives out of the negotiations. Stewart had every right to be annoyed, although at least this rough brand of diplomacy was blunted by the presentation of 'the Snuff Box with His Majesty's Picture set in Diamonds, for which His Excellency desired me convey the humble Expression of his Acknowledgements.'[2]

The day after he had hectored Hardenberg, Stewart journeyed to Landeck, where the Prussians had established their military headquarters. On arrival, Stewart was informed that the French were on the move, and he resolved to follow the Prussians once more as they set out for Prague. Before leaving Landeck, Stewart found time to write to Castlereagh to provide a frank assessment of Prussian strengths and weaknesses:

The King of Prussia, as well as the Emperor, deserves the highest Credit for his firmness throughout; and from accurate Observation I am persuaded His Majesty only requires to be in good Hands to take the high Line on every subject. If His Majesty had more confidence in himself His interests would be better attended to; – sensible and amiable to a degree, He is timid and reserved, and is too easy with those who surround Him. The Chancellor Hardenberg although a most excellent Man, is arrived at an Age, when neither his Power nor Faculties enable him to go through the weight of Business that falls to his Lot. – Foreign Affairs, Finance, and War, are all united in his Person; Any change in the Minister or dividing his Labours would perhaps give an impression now of a change of Politicks, so things are suffered to go on, But an Observer cannot help lamenting that the Administration & Resources of this Country are not better regulated.[3]

Prussian arms were at least impressive: 'The Assistance afforded by Great Britain and the Delay occasioned by the Armistice has enabled Prussia to bring into the Field 183,000 Men, she is thus far superior in numbers to either of the other Powers.'[4]

On the military side, the allies now had three armies in the field. The main force, under the command of the Austrian diplomat and soldier Karl Philipp zu Schwarzenberg, numbered 220,000 men. Throughout the campaign, Prince Schwarzenberg would show he had the necessary qualities to keep the allied forces together. The Army of Silesia, under the command of the veteran Prussian general Gebhard Blücher, stood at 105,000 men. Finally there was the Army of the North, commanded by Bernadotte, a force of 140,000 men.[5] Against this allied army of nearly half a million, Napoleon had probably some 100,000 fewer, but, more importantly, he had less cavalry. Napoleon's prospects were also not helped by the drain on resources and men imposed by Wellington's campaigns. However, with Napoleon in personal command of the French forces in Germany, the allies could not be complacent.

Stewart arrived in Prague on 18 August. Writing to Castlereagh, Stewart advised that one of his first actions was to apply for a passport for the Prince Regent's brother, Ernest, Duke of Cumberland, who was to join Prussian military headquarters. However, 'Being this moment arrived and not having been presented Either to the Emperor Francis, or Count Metternich, I fear I may write imperfectly.'[6] Stewart had an opportunity in Prague of enjoying a long and detailed conversation with Metternich. The Austrian foreign minister helpfully gave Sir Charles Stewart a potted history of his policies towards France, the state of the Habsburg monarchy, and the mistrust that the British had towards him.[7] Perhaps as importantly, Stewart, thanks to Hardenberg, now had the copy of the secret Treaty of Reichenbach. This was now forwarded to Castlereagh with a most secret and confidential letter of 20 August. Stewart stressed the delicacy of this communication from Prussia:

I have now the Satisfaction of inclosing to Your Lordship in Strict Confidence a Copy of this Treaty. – I say Strict Confidence because the Chancellor Hardenberg assured me that the Communication of it to me was a mark of personal favour and partiality, which he would have shewn to no other Person; and Your Lordship will Easily imagine that, if Russia has not made this Communication through Lord Cathcart, or if Count Lieven [Russian Ambassador to London] has not mentioned it, the Confidence from Prussia, in the first instance, might lead to unpleasant Feelings between those two Courts.[8]

On 19 August, Stewart was present as the Emperor of Austria, the Tsar of Russia and the King of Prussia reviewed the troops, a few miles outside of the Bohemian capital. Stewart was almost overwhelmed by the sight of the allied forces, a 'most military Spectacle' of seventy thousand infantry and seven thousand cavalry. To Stewart, the 'Composition of this army was magnificent', although with his trained soldier's eye he still observed 'a great many young Soldiers in it'. But, recollecting these events for Castlereagh, Stewart could write that 'the System . . . that reigns throughout, and the Military Air that marks the Soldier, especially the Hungarian, must ever distinguish it as the finest Army of the Continent.' The Russians, he observed, had 'a more powerful Soldier' while the Austrian general officers 'are of a superior class to those of the Russians' and its army had a 'finer' style, 'with the exception' of the Tsar's artillery. Once more transported in delight, Stewart witnessed the moment when the allied sovereigns 'nailed in unison their Standards to the Pole in front of the Army as a token of their firm Alliance; this was a most exhilarating Moment.'[9]

This firm alliance was soon in action against the French. Napoleon, now joined by the cavalry under the command of Joachim Murat, King of Naples, marched out of Dresden on 16 August. The French Emperor's intention was simple: to systematically destroy the enemy's forces. The allies struck first, and under the command of Prince Schwarzenberg attempted to retake Dresden. The assault, watched by Alexander and Frederick William, was thrown back by the French, who had returned in strength. Napoleon was determined that the allies would not take possession of the Saxon capital. On 27 August, the allies had to admit defeat.

Stewart, along with his ADC, had been involved in the assault. As Stewart later recalled, when the Austrians attacked the advanced works, daylight was already fading. This led to 'some disorder' and together with 'Prince John of Lichtenstein and my aide-de-camp . . . we were in the rear of their batteries before we were aware of our danger'. Luckily for Stewart and his companions, the fog of war meant that they were not discovered by the French. Stewart wrote, 'In this extremity, our only chance was to dash through, trusting to our being undiscovered in the mêlée, which, in the obscurity of the evening, occurred.'[10] The allies had suffered heavy casualties and retreated into Bohemia, but luckily the French pursuit was not that brilliant. If Napoleon had been in command, things might have been different.

Napoleon had won at Dresden, but French arms had suffered defeats at Grossbeeren on 23 August and at the Katzbach on 26 August. However, the most decisive setback for France was at the Battle of Kulm on 29–30 August. Sir Charles Stewart was no diplomatic bystander at the battle, which took its name from a village in northern Bohemia. The French army of thirty thousand men, commanded by General Vandamme, faced a numerically superior allied force. If the French broke through they would be able to menace the allies. At all costs the allied commanders had to make a stand and stop the enemy's advance. Vandamme, 'an arrogant man' who was 'in a hurry' to achieve military glory, made a number of mistakes, the greatest of which was to underrate his opponents.[11] This was a dangerous flaw and Vandamme threw away any advantages Napoleon had gained at Dresden.

On the first day of the battle, Vandamme attacked the Russian contingent under the command of General Count Ostermann-Tolstoy, numbering 14,700 men. The Russians fought this attack off but only at the cost of heavy casualties.[12] Stewart wrote in admiration that 'the Russian guards covered themselves with glory.' Among the wounded on the first day was Sir Charles Stewart, who received a 'severe wound' in the thigh, caused by a splinter from a cannon shell.[13] Stewart's sangfroid was readily apparent by the fact that he 'continued in the field, however, till the victory was secured in the evening, when he was conveyed to his tent, fainting from loss of blood'.[14]

In any other circumstances, a battlefield was no place for a diplomat. But Stewart's exploits were already causing a sensation among Britain's allies, as revealed by the other British general officer present, Sir Robert Wilson. Writing from Töplitz on 31 August, Wilson reported to Lord Cathcart that Stewart was still in some pain but hoped there would be 'no dangerous consequence'. Wilson added, 'This accident to an Officer so eminently useful on every occasion and who has gained the highest Consideration in all the Allied Armies excited universal regret.'[15] Amid the pervading martial spirit at allied headquarters, Stewart's bravado was becoming legendary, and although rather unorthodox behaviour in a diplomat, was earning him respect at least as a military man.

In Stewart's absence, on 30 August, the French were comprehensively defeated at Kulm. The Prussians launched an assault to the rear of the French army, and the Austrians and Russians attacked the French front. Vandamme could not answer all these challenges and was forced to retreat. Vandamme, who had overseen the 'disaster at Kulm', was taken prisoner and presented to the Tsar and the King of Prussia.[16] Fighting aside, there were also new military responsibilities for Sir Charles Stewart. Castlereagh's instructions, issued on 31 August 1813, directed his brother to 'immediately' take on the superintendence '(as far as may be necessary to provide for British Interests) of ye. Russian German Legion, & the other Levies, and you will report to me, for the Information of H.R.H. the P. Regt. the progress which you should have made'.[17]

The Prince Regent had nominated the Tsar a Knight of the Garter on 27 July 1813.[18] This mark of friendship between Britain and Russia was not without its difficulties. The Prussians felt that the Garter should also be given to Frederick William. Jackson was obliged to pass these concerns on to Stewart, who in turn 'privately mentioned' Prussian desires to Castlereagh.[19] Stewart, recovering at Töplitz, wrote of Prussia's grumbles to the foreign secretary on 4 September:

> In giving Your Lordship the Sentiments and Feelings of the Court at which
> I am accredited, and in putting you in possession at the earliest Moment of the
> Insinuations that are made to me, I am actuated solely by a desire that the Prince

Regent's Government should not be under the necessity of taking any decision without having ample time for mature Deliberation. –

It has often been urged by the Chancellor Hardenberg what a striking difference exists and how great a disparity there is between the Assistance afforded by Great Britain to Russia and that which is given to Prussia, when the numbers of Forces belonging to the latter actually in the Field exceed those of the former Power.

To all this and similar reasoning I have the most simple and satisfactory answers to produce; but it is evident the late determination to invest the Emperor of Russia with the Order of the Garter has caused a considerable Anxiety upon the part of the Prussian Government that a similar Honour should be extended to their Sovereign.

I understand the King himself has a very strong feeling upon the Subject – The nearness of his Connection with our Royal Family, has been urged as an additional, Reason for his being equally distinguished with His Imperial Majesty.

I have not as yet had any direct Communication with the Chancellor Hardenberg upon the Subject, but my Opinions have been sounded at his desire, and I am given to understand that he means shortly to have some Communication with me upon this Subject.[20]

Stewart further advised that he had 'discouraged and shall continue to do so, all idea of this measure' until he knew Castlereagh's thoughts on the matter. However, as 'it may be pressed upon me at a distant period, I am anxious that you should have it this early under Consideration. I shall in no shape give the Idea the least Encouragement as things at present stand, and I shall I hope, prevent the Chancellor Hardenberg's coming to the point.'[21] Things were at least moving forward diplomatically. On 5 September, Britain's new ambassador to Austria, the Earl of Aberdeen, arrived at headquarters. The following day, Aberdeen wrote to assure Castlereagh that Stewart 'was up to day, without the least degree of fever, and with a little time and quiet will probably be perfectly well – I saw the Emperor's Surgeon, who attends him, this morning, and he confirmed this statement.'[22]

In a most secret letter of 6 September, Stewart was able to pass on more Prussian news to his brother. Hardenberg had seen him that morning 'by order of the King, to express His Majesty's anxious Solicitude for my Situation & Recovery'. Hardenberg took the opportunity to engage the British minister in a detailed and confidential conversation on allied diplomacy. At the heart of this diplomatic activity was a new treaty of alliance to be agreed between Austria, Russia and Prussia: 'In which they are to bind themselves not to lay down their Arms until a Peace can be obtained from France, on terms approaching as near as possible to those of the 16th. of May.' Hardenberg hoped, 'As each Nation will make the same Efforts . . . he trusted the Support England was to furnish for another Campaign would be equal.' He confirmed that as soon as the treaty was 'in shape' it would be 'communicated to England & Sweden'. The treaty had lofty ambitions, and the Prussian chancellor revealed, 'Hopes are entertained that Denmark in the End, sooner than see herself the Victim of her own bad Policy, will also join the Alliance', although Stewart added, 'This however, is probably remote.' Allied expectations were optimistic, as Stewart added, 'It is with considerable Satisfaction I also inform Your Lordship that great Expectations are entertained by the Emperors of Austria & Russia that Bavaria is about to declare and take part with the Allies. Communications of the most confidential Nature have passed, and the Emperors have themselves carried on the Correspondence.' Stewart had caught some of Hardenberg's infectious optimism, but remained level-headed:

If this fortunate Event should take place, the King of Wurtemberg [*sic*] would unquestionably follow:–
Other States of the Confederation would flock in: The liberation of the centre of Germany would be the first Fruits that would be reaped; and their Forces acting in the Rear of Bonaparte would tend more than any thing to precipitate his Ruin. –
The Chancellor is easily elated, & easily depressed therefore I receive his opinions cautiously; But he added He firmly believed the War would yet be put an End to before the Winter.[23]

After Stewart had moved on to Prague, he was able to send the Foreign Office a copy of the proposed treaty on 17 September. Stewart saw 'nothing objectionable in this treaty, nor any thing that militates against existing Engagements with us'. However, Spain and the Netherlands were not mentioned and had as yet 'never been alluded to in any of the Treaties that have yet been framed and, although this is to be lamented, from the Conversation I had with the Chancellor there seem strong objections in all the three Powers'.[24] Stewart was also aware that he had neglected one key part of his role: the superintendence of Bernadotte's army. Moving to reassure Castlereagh on 23 September, Stewart wrote, 'I shall with as little Delay as my present Circumstances will admit, immediately proceed to the Head Quarters of the Prince of Sweden and Count Walmoden, for the purpose of commencing the Work.'[25]

Having been occupied by Prussian concerns over the Garter, Stewart himself was to be honoured by the sovereigns. On 27 September, he received a letter from the Tsar awarding him the fourth class of the Order of St George, for his gallantry in the field. This was to be the first of a number of new honours awarded. From the King of Prussia, Stewart received the Order of the Black Eagle, the highest of the Prussian Orders of Chivalry.[26] This bestowal of Orders was highly significant, and these great honours helped cement the alliance further. As Stewart noted, these were 'testimonies of the allied courts towards the British nation in my person'. As for George Jackson, one can sympathize with his comment, 'We *civilians* are the only undistinguished persons.'[27]

War gave way briefly to ceremonial when the Tsar was invested with the Garter. On 27 September, the British representatives were on hand at Töplitz to witness the investiture, with Stewart having arrived back that same day from Prague, 'sufficiently recovered' to return to headquarters. This Garter mission was led by

Lord Cathcart, along with Sir Thomas Tyrwhitt, Gentleman Usher of the Black Rod, 'who had suffered not a little difficulty and embarrassment in his heavy equipages, traversing the bad roads, and mixing in the columns of march in the mountains'. However, the small inconvenience of a war was not going to stop the British representatives or their mission, and the Tsar was duly invested 'in a little nutshell of a room'.[28]

Once he had fully recovered from his wound, Stewart left to join Bernadotte, 'to endeavour to bring him into cordial co-operation with the other Allied armies'.[29] Bernadotte had not been the most forward of the allied commanders as he had his own serious problems to worry about. Bernadotte wanted Norway, which Russia had earmarked as a quid pro quo for the Swedish Crown Prince's acquiescence in Alexander's annexation of Finland, formerly part of Sweden. Troops would be needed to fight the current ruler of Norway, Frederick VI, King of Denmark, who still maintained his alliance with Napoleon. Bernadotte's reticence also stemmed from the quality of the Swedish army.[30] It was in this atmosphere that the allies were pushing Bernadotte to use his troops against the French, and this was the lion's den in which Sir Charles Stewart now found himself. At least he was not on his own, as he would be working alongside the Tsar's representative, Charles-André Pozzo di Borgo, a Corsican whose dislike of his countryman Napoleon Bonaparte stretched back some twenty years.

Leipzig and more peace terms

In Germany, momentous events were underway. On 6 September, a French attempt to threaten Berlin, led by Marshal Ney, was defeated at the Battle of Dennewitz, while that month saw the Russians fighting behind the French lines and reaching Kassel, capital of the Kingdom of Westphalia, ruled by Napoleon's brother Jérôme Bonaparte. It was not surprising that Napoleon's allies in the Confederation of the Rhine looked to depart the sinking French ship, as Stewart had noted. The first major defector was Bavaria, which had gained much from the French alliance, having been raised into a kingdom by Napoleon. It now joined the allied cause by signing an agreement with Austria on 8 October. This desertion was certainly to prove timely.

Napoleon abandoned Dresden, and taking the King of Saxony with his army, had headed for Leipzig, which now saw a concentration of French forces. The allied armies were heading for Saxony's second city as well, and the scene was set for the battle which would determine the fate of Germany. Pressured by Stewart and Pozzo di Borgo, even Bernadotte was now marching in the direction of Leipzig, although 'in very hesitant fashion' which meant he missed the first day of the battle.[31] The Battle of Leipzig, which would involve half a million men, opened on Saturday 16 October, with fierce fighting across the sectors of the battlefield. On this first day of the battle, the allies were superior in numbers, but were of course missing Bernadotte. British unhappiness with Bernadotte was recorded by Colonel Hudson Lowe, who recorded what took place as Blücher was planning the disposition of the allied army:

It happened opportunely that Lt General Sir Charles Stewart arrived on the Ground . . . He wrote a letter immediately to the Prince Royal of Sweden, expressive of General Blücher's desire . . .

Not content with this, Sir Charles Stewart, at the request of General Blücher, forewent the Gratification of being personally present at the Outset of the Attack, and repaired himself to the Prince Royal to urge his instant movement & Cooperation.[32]

Stewart was unimpressed by Bernadotte's progress up to this point, and he found himself riding between the Prince Royal's headquarters and that of the Prussians, in order to ensure the Army of the North played a decisive role in the campaign. In a secret and confidential letter to Lord Castlereagh written on 17 October, Stewart did not bother to conceal his frustrations with Bernadotte:

I feel it an incumbent Duty to His Royal Highness the Prince Regents Government to put Your Lordship in possession of my candid Sentiments on the Prince Royal of Sweden's late Operations and the part I have deemed it my duty to take. It will be for your Lordship to judge if I have outstepped the bounds of Propriety; But an anxious Observer and well wisher to the Success of the Common Cause could not reconcile it to himself placed as I have been, and honoured by the Confidence of my Government, of the King of Prussia and of the Emperor of Russia, to be silent.

I have no hesitation in declaring to Your Lordship that indisputable proof can be adduced by Military Authorities that if the Crown Prince had done his Duty the whole of the French Army engaged against General Blucher on the 16th would have been destroyed.[33]

Stewart at least had the chance to indulge himself in the military struggle again, which must have come as a relief after dealing with Bernadotte's evasiveness. On 16 October, as well as playing the role of go-between, Stewart had been assigned by Blücher to the head of the Prussian cavalry corps under the command of General Yorck, a remarkable appointment for a British officer and diplomat.[34] Yorck was involved in some of the bloodiest fighting on that first day of the battle, losing about a third of his corps in the process. At one point, the Prussian cavalry was involved in a particularly fierce engagement. As Sir Charles Stewart told his brother, 'There were several brilliant charges of Cavalry – The Brandenburg Regiment of Hussars distinguished itself in a particular manner, & supported by infantry charged a Battery of 8 pieces which they carried.' However, the dispatches sent back by Stewart had the 'good taste' not to mention that he had led this gallant charge himself. The French gunners would have had no idea that at the forefront of this furious cavalry action was His Britannic Majesty's minister to Prussia.[35] A clue in Stewart's dispatches was his note, 'My Aide du Camp Capt During an Officer of Merit has unfortunately (I fear) fallen into the Enemys hands.' This proved to be an unfounded rumour, but Castlereagh might have wondered how and why his brother's ADC, a man whose subsequent career would be entwined with Stewart's, was so close to the thick of the fighting.[36]

The allies had not managed to defeat the French on this first day and the next day saw a lull in the level of fighting. This suited the allies perfectly, as Bernadotte's army had still not arrived in force, and further reinforcements from Dresden, commanded by a Hanoverian in Russian service, General Count Bennigsen, were also expected. Hostilities recommenced in full on the last two days of the Battle of Leipzig, on 18–19 October. On 18 October, the French were forced to fall back as the allies' greater numbers were brought to bear, their numbers slightly increased by the desertion of Saxon troops. Bernadotte's army was also in action, with the small numbers of British troops in his army involved as well. If the deployment of Sir Charles Stewart's sabre had not been extraordinary enough, the British now surprised the enemy with its use of Congreve Rockets. With some pride Stewart could report how the British detachment in Bernadotte's army used the rockets to disrupt a French attack on General Bülow's Prussian corps. As a foretaste of warfare to come, Stewart commented that the rockets 'produced an impression upon the enemy of something supernatural'.[37]

For Stewart, the start of the Battle of Leipzig's final day was marked by a furious row with Bernadotte, who approached the British minister 'with a look bordering upon suppressed anger'. Bernadotte had been unhappy at Stewart's behaviour and his role in pushing the Army of the North into a more offensive position. Stewart was not the kind of man to be intimidated by another general, even if he happened to be the heir to the Swedish throne. Stewart reminded the Prince Royal that he was 'charged generally with the military interest of Great Britain in the north of Europe'. Further, as Britain 'paid the Swedish army' through its subsidies, Stewart was responsible for telling his government 'whether that army did what I considered its duty to the common cause actively or passively', and these reports 'must operate seriously upon the alliance'. Stewart's account only barely glosses over his war of words with the Swedish Crown Prince, and, as he recalled, 'Certain expressions of his own were most explicit, and this was not a moment for diplomatic concealment. I spoke my opinion openly and firmly, but respectfully.' Stewart then tried some flattery, assuring Bernadotte that he 'felt honoured' by his friendship but again returned to the charge. It took courage to tell Bernadotte to his face that 'my anxious efforts were to assist the Swedish nation; but I could never see their chief depart from what I knew were the true interests of his situation, without remonstrating boldly.'[38]

Stewart's campaign did the trick; the British minister 'felt restored to favour' and as a mark of special attention was invited to dinner. Stewart was also greatly assisted by the Tsar's representative to Bernadotte, Pozzo di Borgo, who had also made himself 'very unpalatable' to the Prince Royal. The two ambassadors clearly supported one another, to the extent that Stewart was able to prevent Pozzo di Borgo's removal from Bernadotte's headquarters. Bernadotte was apparently impressed with Stewart's resolve, and his determination to stand up for his point of view.

On the final day of the battle, the French were on the back foot, and a retreat was ordered by Napoleon. The French rearguard was tasked with keeping the allies at bay while the French Emperor and most of his forces could escape from Leipzig. Frederick Augustus of Saxony was offered the chance to join the retreating armies, but the King could not desert his own country. Both sides had suffered huge losses, but for Napoleon, his desire to project French hegemony had been destroyed. There were more losses as Napoleon's army sought to get away, among them Prince Poniatowski, a marshal of France, and one of the heroic figures of Polish history.[39] The allied armies fought their way into Leipzig, entering at different points. After the city was taken, the Tsar, the King of Prussia and the Prince Royal of Sweden met in the city's main square. Poor Frederick Augustus of Saxony was pointedly snubbed by Alexander and then informed that he was under arrest. The King was then taken under Prussian escort as a prisoner to Berlin.

The choice of Stewart to lead a Prussian cavalry action was a real compliment to his fighting abilities, and undoubtedly increased his standing and prestige with the allied leaders, even if it was a distraction from diplomacy. As events unfolded, being on the battlefield again proved exactly the right place to be, as there was an attempt at some underhand diplomacy during the fighting. One Austrian general, Count Meerveldt, had been captured by the French on the first day of hostilities. Napoleon had used the Austrian general as 'an ingenious device to excite delay and discussion amongst the allies'. Released on parole, Meerveldt was sent to Francis I of Austria with peace terms.

This attempt at negotiation did not escape British attention. In this case, Sir Robert Wilson was the agent of discovery, on 19 October. He immediately wrote a dispatch and sent his ADC, Captain James Charles, to find Lord Aberdeen. The civilian diplomat was not to be found, but luckily, Captain Charles found Sir Charles Stewart on the battlefield, 'on the right of Genl Benningsen's [*sic*] corps', and showed him Wilson's note. This was fortunate, as Stewart was about to send off his own nephew, Captain John James, with his account of the battle. Captain James, who was serving with Stewart as a volunteer, had already seen his share of fighting, but he now found himself undertaking a rather different role. Stewart's own report to Castlereagh was to the point: 'I have heard Genl. Meerveldt who was taken on the 16th. was sent back on his parole by Bonaparte with propositions of peace to the Emperor . . . as to terms of peace that if England would give up Hannover, Lubeck & Hamburg, the independence of Holland might be arranged & Italy be made an independent Monarchy.'[40]

Stewart realized there was no time to find Aberdeen, and sent Wilson's note to London immediately, as this was 'intelligence of importance'. Stewart took full responsibility for his actions, and he explained the circumstances to Wilson and Aberdeen later.[41] Aberdeen was certainly not happy at Stewart's resolve and complained to Castlereagh that his brother 'who is always active, almost smuggled it from me – I hope we shall meet soon again, it is always the greatest satisfaction to me, and I hope he is not sorry either'. Lord Cathcart was also apparently 'greatly offended' by Stewart's speed in sending off the news. Outraged pride notwithstanding, Stewart had been quite right to put his country's interests ahead of the bruised feelings of his fellow plenipotentiaries. Needless to say, this rather improvised method of reaching a negotiated settlement did not succeed; unfortunately for Stewart's peace of mind it would not be the last attempt.[42]

As a final postscript to Leipzig, Bernadotte and Stewart struck up a friendship, cemented by the Crown Prince making Stewart a Knight Grand Cross of the Sword after the battle. Stewart had done his country a great service by ensuring Bernadotte's continued and active participation in the alliance.[43] Writing to Colonel Lowe on 26 October, Stewart was clearly taken aback by Bernadotte's gesture:

> Pray tell General Gneisenau that after all my Battles with the Prince Royal He has sent me today to my great Astonishment with one of the most flattering letters you Ever read His Order of the Grand Cross of the Sword –
>   It was only 48 hours before I had a fight with him –
>   This will amuse Blucher and Gneisenau not a little, beg Gneisenau to let the King know this if he has Communication with him[.][44]

Colonel Lowe was in no doubt that Sir Charles Stewart had done much to maintain the alliance with Bernadotte. Writing privately to Colonel Henry Bunbury at the War Office in late November, Lowe had nothing but praise for Stewart's role: 'What he [Bernadotte] has already done I am inclined to Attribute in a principal degree to the Awe in which He stood of the Superior virtue and Remonstrances of Sir Charles Stewart, and perhaps to some little return of his passion for military Fame on the day, when all Europe was a Spectator.'[45]

Stewart was now tasked with accompanying Bernadotte into Hanover, as the allies prepared to liberate the dynastic homeland of Britain's royal family. Stewart was placed in an awkward position, as it seemed possible that the Duke of Cumberland would accompany some of the troops into the electorate. Bernadotte was none too pleased at this prospect. Stewart explained to the Duke on 31 October that 'the Regency will be immediately established for all Civil Functions' and the 'Whole of the Military Arrangements are placed under the Prince Royals directions'. As Stewart had been ordered to organize the Hanoverian army, there would be nothing for Cumberland to do, leaving the Prince Regent's brother as 'neither . . . the Initiative or Organ of any arrangement'.[46] Problems with Cumberland aside, the liberation of Hanover was achieved quickly.

On 2 November 1813, Stewart was in Göttingen, seat of Hanover's famous university, and from where he proudly reported to London 'The Liberation of His Majesty's Electoral Dominions'. Allied troops had entered Hanover the day before to a very warm welcome: 'The Enthusiasm, Loyalty and unbounded Joy of the People is not to be described, and although ten Years have separated this Country from their legitimate Sovereign, it is obvious He lives in their Hearts with the same deeprooted Affection as ever.'[47] Stewart's role in Hanover was about to be cut short, as he was soon needed elsewhere thanks to more diplomatic intrigue.

Napoleon had been forced to retreat towards the Rhine, and travelling at great speed, many stragglers were left behind. He was pursued by the armies of Prince Schwarzenberg and that of Blücher, newly promoted to field marshal. However, a new peace initiative was about to stall the allied efforts. A French diplomat, the baron de St Aignan, had been caught up in the allied advance and sent on to the allied headquarters at Frankfurt. He was presented with yet another set of allied terms, which were in the circumstances very generous. In London, the British government was again forced to watch helplessly. To add to the problem, Lord Castlereagh could see the cracks appearing among the three British diplomats, assisted by the allies playing divide and rule. Aberdeen was one of the worst offenders. He astonishingly wrote to Castlereagh, in a letter marked 'For Yourself Only' on 29 October, not only to advise the foreign secretary of the continuing peace talks but pointedly to pass on Russian comments about Lord Cathcart. Stewart had his own issues with Cathcart, but Aberdeen was acting with incredible indiscretion.

The Tsar's representative, Count Nesselrode, had flattered Aberdeen that he should be 'the only person informed of what is now proposed to be done in the way of overture'. Aberdeen then proceeded to parade Nesselrode's denigrating comments on Cathcart. According to Aberdeen, Nesselrode, 'although not very wise himself has the most perfect contempt for Cathcart, and frequently expresses it. He says it is impossible to communicate with such an idiot – and that he is the Emperor's footman &c &c.' Wisely Aberdeen did not try and run down Stewart to his brother, even though relations between the hussar and the civilian scholar were evidently strained since the incident at Leipzig. Despite this, Lord Aberdeen still needed Stewart, writing on 5 November, on the eve of the allied entry into Frankfurt, 'I hope to God we shall soon see you, yet I do not know how your motions will agree with this wish.' Aberdeen was even forced to fall back on compliments, congratulating Stewart for standing up to Bernadotte, and advising that the Prince Royal, 'Finding that he cannot bully you, he is now on another tack; a better one I allow, but one which I have no doubt will equally fail in preventing your vigilance.' Aberdeen was also keen to patch up their friendship, and added as a postscript, 'I hope you repent of your silence to me at Leipsic [sic]; it was not fair or friendly, and I am sure could not have been deserved by me.'[48]

As for Napoleon, he now had to think about the new allied terms. In order to gain peace, Napoleon was to evacuate Germany, Spain and Italy. France was to be returned to its 'natural' borders and would be allowed to keep conquests in the Low Countries. These proposals were in direct contravention of British aims. Britain was desperate for the French to be removed from the Low Countries and was equally determined to see the restoration of an independent Netherlands, under the House of Orange. More dangerously, there was even a reference to Britain's Maritime Rights, the basis of British sea power. No government in London would ever agree to a discussion of these rights.

In Frankfurt, Britain's man on the spot was Lord Aberdeen, who had no objections to the proffered peace terms. How seriously the various allies took them is debatable, but it showed once again the willingness of Austria, Russia and Prussia to make terms, while ignoring British war aims. As Aberdeen wrote to Lord Abercorn on 15 November, 'You will however learn that an overture has been made by us. I have highly approved of it, but I fear it will come to nothing.'[49]

Why Aberdeen agreed to these terms is hard to explain, but his reasoning was buttressed by a surprising confidence in his own genius as a diplomat.

Aberdeen's sense of superiority had even extended to lecturing Castlereagh, informing him on 12 November that he had about him 'so much of the Englishman as not quite to be aware of the real values of Foreign modes of acting'.[50] Aberdeen also believed that he was the better diplomat than the Austrian foreign minister, Metternich, whose egotism was likely increased by his recent promotion to the rank of prince. This confidence was based on Aberdeen's having got to know Metternich 'pretty well' as he had advised the foreign secretary on 10 November. The upshot of this was that he dismissed Metternich to Castlereagh as 'not a clever man, but . . . tolerably well informed'. It is to be hoped that Metternich did not see this comment, but he would undoubtedly have found it amusing.[51] It needed Stewart to ride to the rescue and save Aberdeen from his own foolishness. Stewart was expected to arrive at Frankfurt, but had fallen ill en route. When he did turn up he again proved to be a far more active man than Aberdeen and the Earl's superiority came crashing to the ground.

Stewart soon learned of what had been going on, and lost no time in telling Aberdeen exactly what he thought of the peace terms. Stewart's annoyance is apparent in his account to Castlereagh of 28 November, pointedly blaming the Austrians, as Hardenberg had 'declared to me that his Mouth had been sealed wth regard to Communication with me . . . by a Promise exacted from His Excellency Prince Metternich'. Stewart then proceeded to rubbish the proposed peace terms, so recently agreed to by Aberdeen:

> Had I had the good fortune to have been taken into the Consultations which have preceded the Documents I now transmit, I should not have presumed on an infallible Judgement, nor should I have considered that on the Rhine the Prince Regent and his Government would depart from those great Principles in opening Negotiations to which the attention of His Majesty's Ministers at the allied Courts were called, when we were upon the Oder, and the Armies of France still unbroken & unbeaten.
>
> Your Lordship has distinctly pointed out 'the Points on which His Royal Highness's Government in Negotiation can under no Circumstances relax, the Faith of His Government being formally pledged to their inviolable Maintenance Spain–Portugal–Sicily–The fulfillment of our existing Engagements with Sweden.'[52]

Aberdeen's plans were scuppered. As the Earl succinctly told Castlereagh on 28 November, Stewart 'having strongly represented the whole proposal as unsatisfactory', he had gone to Prince Metternich to tell him 'that he must undo everything which he had fixed with the Emperor Alexr'.[53]

Unfortunately for Britain, its diplomatic arrangements were proving clumsy, and, in this instance, Aberdeen had fallen straight into the trap of allowing himself to belittle Cathcart. Stewart had shown his coolness in these most difficult of circumstances, but things could not go on as they were. It was becoming essential for the British to be represented by one man who could make decisions on the spot, without constantly referring back to his political masters. This was all the more necessary as the French Empire was beginning to crumble. After the Battle of Leipzig, Württemberg had rushed to join the allied cause, notwithstanding its elevation into a kingdom thanks to France. Hanover had been liberated, while Napoleon's Kingdom of Italy was also looking decidedly rocky. Napoleon's militaristic and absolutist monarchy was still a force to be reckoned with, but at this stage, all options seemed to be open as to the kind of France that might emerge from the war.

Chapter 6

THE FALL OF FRANCE

The Dutch Republic was one of the first conquests of the French Revolutionary Wars. The country's Stadtholder, Willem V, Prince of Orange, was forced into exile, while the Dutch state was transformed into a French client republic. Later, as part of the Napoleonic mania for family monarchs, it became the Kingdom of Holland, ruled by Napoleon's brother, Louis. By July 1810, Napoleon had grown tired of his brother's rule and annexed the country to the French Empire. In November 1813, the Dutch, with a long history of independence, began an uprising in The Hague, amidst calls for liberation and the return of the House of Orange. The British saw this as another opportunity to deal a blow to the French and sent Willem VI, Prince of Orange, the son of the last Stadtholder, back to his native country. The Prince was accompanied by a new British diplomatic representative, the Earl of Clancarty. Arms and troops followed, and although military operations did not go smoothly, the French hold on the Netherlands was systematically challenged. It was another sign that Napoleon's domination of Europe was becoming increasingly precarious.

In Britain, Lord Castlereagh's policy revolved around the signing of a Grand Alliance, which would bind the different governments to a common war aim. Aberdeen could confidently report to Lord Abercorn on 4 December that Austrian acquiescence was guaranteed, that Russia, thanks to his efforts, 'may yield', while Stewart 'has had no difficulty with Prussia'. Much to Castlereagh's chagrin, both Austria and Russia in fact refused to sign any such agreement.[1] Meanwhile, the Frankfurt negotiations had continued to cause trouble, despite Stewart's efforts. Napoleon had accepted the proposed terms as a basis for peace talks, and it was agreed by the allies to send Pozzo di Borgo to London to discuss matters directly with Lord Castlereagh. Nobody bothered to run this idea past Stewart, Cathcart or Aberdeen. All of this was too much for Sir Charles Stewart. George Jackson noted in his diary that Stewart was already 'out of spirits', feeling he had 'overstepped the mark in his remonstrances with Lord Aberdeen', and was 'not yet quite in charity with the [Prussian] Chancellor'. Jackson, however, took control, and on the 'pretext of indisposition' went to Hardenberg 'to settle for Sir Charles the business of the "Black Eagle," which he is authorized to accept'. Jackson, seemingly performing Stewart's role, probably used this meeting with Hardenberg to discuss matters of diplomatic importance between Britain and Prussia.[2]

Stewart and Jackson had disagreed with the choice of Pozzo di Borgo as the allied representative to London. This mission was dangerous for the British negotiators, who would be sidelined by the Tsar's agent. By sending Pozzo di Borgo, the allied courts might 'get rid of the difficulties that are said to be felt of having three British ministers here'. Hardenberg was particularly unhappy with Stewart, as Jackson recorded after a dinner with the British minister and the Prussian chancellor on 6 December. Hardenberg had delayed sending Stewart the French response to the peace terms, which was 'not surprising, considering the very lively scenes that have occurred between them on the subject of Saint Aignan's minute'.[3] Bernadotte and Aberdeen were clearly not the only ones to be on the receiving end of Stewart's rough wooing.

It is also possible that Stewart had plunged into a bout of depression. Sir Robert Wilson believed that Stewart would resign as he had grown 'tired of his position, and will daily become more so as his sphere of action is reduced'.[4] It is unlikely that Stewart would have simply walked away from his post, but he quickly snapped out of his mood, resuming the role of an efficient man of business. As Aberdeen tartly remarked, having 'contrived to get a copy' of the French response, Stewart sent Jackson off to London with this intelligence, ensuring that Pozzo di Borgo was not the only diplomatic source for the British government. Jackson promptly left for Britain, travelling via The Hague.[5]

British diplomacy was in danger of becoming ridiculous, with foreign policy run by memoranda. For example, Lord Castlereagh had written a lengthy treatise to his brother on 4 December, on the shape of the post-war settlement in Germany. Rather unhelpfully Castlereagh told Stewart that the 'difficulty of yet seeing daylight through the affairs of Germany makes me unwilling to attempt to send you any thing like official Instructions'. The foreign secretary was at least able to offer practical guidance on the Saxon issue. As the Austrians were unlikely to let Prussia swallow Saxony whole, Stewart was asked to use his offices to 'moderate the Prussian Temper'. Castlereagh was far from being misty-eyed about Frederick Augustus as 'no Sovereign can have less Claim to Favour or even Mercy than the King of Saxony'. The British simply did not want to see differences break out between Vienna and Berlin, 'upon whose future Concert every thing hinges'. Perhaps sensing further areas of trouble between the allies, Castlereagh also advised his brother 'to the necessity of keeping back Controversy, and combining every Effort against the Common Enemy'. A copy was sent to Aberdeen as well, with both being asked to gather information 'without agitating Matters that had better sleep for the present'.[6]

Castlereagh had tried hard to run Britain's diplomatic efforts at a distance. These were extraordinary circumstances, which required extraordinary measures. The other allies had their sovereigns and senior ministers on hand to negotiate, and Britain could not rely on its policies being represented by three diplomats who were sometimes more at odds with each other than with the other powers. On 20 December, the British cabinet considered the allied request for a single representative. Rather than rely on Pozzo di Borgo, they agreed to send the foreign secretary out to mainland Europe. Castlereagh set out on 26 December.

At least Castlereagh's arrival would put an end to the allied confusion of dealing with three British negotiators. This does not mean that Stewart's work should be underestimated or dismissed. Stewart had acted with energy and decisiveness throughout 1813, especially in discovering details of the various peace feelers and in keeping Bernadotte onside.

Bernadotte though was another source of irritation for the British in December 1813. Stewart had rejoined Bernadotte's army in Hanover 'to look after the Crown Prince'.[7] Stewart was increasingly concerned by Bernadotte's reluctance to assist the uprising in the Netherlands and by his preoccupation with Denmark. Stewart felt annoyed enough to send off a letter of complaint to his brother on 23 December.[8] Amidst all this gloom, a few days previously on 19 December, Stewart had witnessed happier scenes with the entry into Hanover of George III's youngest son, Adolphus, Duke of Cambridge. The population was delighted to have a member of its royal family back as Stewart recorded: 'Here was a Language that spoke from the Hearts which I am quite unequal to describe, and there was a Loyalty & Devotion displayed which would have done honour to Britons and which British Dominion so universally inspires.'[9]

Napoleon had been given a precious breathing space, since there had been no major invasion of France in November 1813. However, to the south, Wellington's forces had crossed into French territory.[10] Napoleon's chances of a negotiated settlement were certainly becoming slimmer, but that door had not been completely closed, as the allies had issued a declaration in early December offering France a vague promise of more territory, rather than just its 'natural limits'. True to form, Stewart had initially condemned this declaration as 'much too tame, and in other respects highly objectionable'.[11] By the end of 1813, the allies were poised to move west in force. Despite Russian objections, Austrian troops advanced through Switzerland and crossed the Rhine at Basel on 20–21 December. The Tsar delayed his crossing of the Rhine until 13 January 1814, the Russian New Year.[12] Sir Charles Stewart witnessed this momentous event and was quite overwhelmed by the sight of the armies, especially the Tsar's forces: 'Some of whom had emerged from the steeps of Tartary bordering the Chinese empire, traversed their own regions, and marched, in a few short months, from Moscow across the Rhine, one was lost in wonder, and inspired with a political awe of that colossal power.'[13]

Meanwhile, Castlereagh had arrived at The Hague on 7 January 1814. For the first time, the British foreign secretary could see for himself that the French were in retreat. Leaving his wife Emily in the Netherlands with Clancarty, Castlereagh travelled onwards, arriving at Frankfurt on 15 January. Three days later his carriage rattled into Basel. By the time Castlereagh arrived, the allied armies had crossed the frontier and established a new headquarters in France, at Langres. As the allied sovereigns had left Basel, Prince Metternich was given an opportunity to make a play for the ear of the British, without fear of interruption from the Tsar. Metternich was soon delighted by his British counterpart.[14] Perhaps more importantly for Britain's interests, Castlereagh was able to confirm his country's determination to see a strong and independent Netherlands, and reiterated his government's refusal to discuss the issue of Maritime Rights. At this stage, Castlereagh had no time to be won over by Metternich's diplomatic charms, as he needed to move on to Langres, arriving in the town on 29 January.

Castlereagh had momentous diplomatic negotiations on his mind. The results of the recent peace talks had come to fruition, and a new congress was to meet at Châtillon in Burgundy. From Langres, Castlereagh wrote to Stewart to send him instructions, while gently chiding both his brother's and Lord Cathcart's mania for seeking any opportunity to get involved in the fighting.[15] Castlereagh should also have been concerned with the Earl of Aberdeen. Writing to Lord Abercorn on 30 January, Aberdeen was keen to slight his two fellow plenipotentiaries, although the young Earl never spoke of Stewart in the way he did of Cathcart. Aberdeen was overconfident that he was their superior in the diplomatic line. Cathcart was 'a man of very moderate talents, but stiff, pedantic, and difficult'. His relationship to Castlereagh's brother was more complex:

> I rate Stewarts' [*sic*] talents higher, but he is shatter-brained, obstinate, and wrong-headed. Although he has certainly good qualities, and we remain on the best terms, I have been deceived in him two or three times, and in cases which have contributed to affect my opinion of him materially.[16]

This letter should not be taken at face value but rather as a reflection of the ongoing friction between Stewart and Aberdeen, apparent since Leipzig.

Napoleon, faced with the allied threat to the heart of his empire, had been far from idle. The French Emperor had left Paris, where he had been collecting reinforcements, to arrive with his army at Châlons-sur-Marne on 26 January. The French, always determined to gain military superiority, soon engaged with the allied armies, and the first major clash of arms culminated in the Battle of La Rothière on 1 February 1814. The French army was commanded by Napoleon, the allies by Blücher. The French managed to hold their position but were forced to withdraw as night came on, leaving a substantial part of their artillery behind. For Napoleon, it was his first defeat on French soil. The allies were elated. Lady Burghersh recorded Stewart's reaction to the news: 'The loss was severe; I don't know what. C. Stewart says he left the dead yesterday piled up in heaps.'[17]

Lady Burghersh was accompanying her husband with the army. Still only in her early 20s, Priscilla Fane, Lady Burghersh, was the daughter of William Wellesley-Pole, and Lord Wellington's favourite niece. Her husband, John Fane, Lord Burghersh, had been appointed as military liaison with the Austrian army in September 1813, despite attempts to give this role to Sir Robert Wilson.[18] Burghersh, born in 1784, was very well connected himself, as the heir to the senior politician John Fane, tenth Earl of Westmorland. A professional soldier and later a famed amateur musician, Burghersh would become a close friend and diplomatic colleague of Stewart's. The warmth of Sir Charles Stewart's attachment to both is obvious in their correspondence, and in Lady Burghersh's recollections. She was fortunate enough to remain with the army and was on hand to witness the momentous events which were to follow.

As the allied troops advanced through France, Stewart observed that the population 'appeared to . . . generally favour the allies; they seemed weary with the wars they were engaged in, and still more weary of their military ruler'. However, the allies soon learned that the population had been armed, so that the commander, Prince Schwarzenberg, 'was induced to issue a general order to treat all the natives as enemies who were found with arms in their possession'.[19]

For Stewart, warfare gave way to diplomacy at Châtillon when negotiations commenced on 5 February. The French were again represented by Armand de Caulaincourt. Lord Castlereagh 'supervised the allied plenipotentiaries informally', but the diplomatic trio of Sir Charles Stewart, Lord Cathcart and Lord Aberdeen took the lead for Britain.[20] Rather ruefully, Stewart noted 'during the whole of this period when the military operations were carried on I was prevented by my diplomatic duties from witnessing, and consequently detailing any personal observations on the military movements during the same interval'.[21] Castlereagh's position was clear from the start. France must withdraw to its pre-revolutionary borders, while the interests of certain key states remained central to Britain's war aims, especially so in the case of the Netherlands. Castlereagh also had other problems, having to contend with the Tsar's plan to place Bernadotte at the head of a future French government.[22]

Bernadotte was also at the root of other problems. Castlereagh was told that Blücher expected Napoleon to 'next fall upon him, when he wd. not be strong enough to stand his ground', forcing him to fall back. If he was reinforced, the Prussian commander assured his allies, 'he would "hold on"'. Castlereagh had no idea why Blücher could not receive reinforcements. However, he then found out that the extra troops were under Bernadotte's command 'whom they wd. not venture to disoblige'. Castlereagh was having none of this and sent Stewart to resolve the issue, as recalled by the Earl of Clanwilliam:

> W[ith]. all the drawbacks that hang ab[out]. Sir C. Stewart, he certainly was zealous, intelligent & plucky. And it so happened that there was a sort of camaraderie betwn. Him & B[ernadotte].
>
> So he told his friend roundly that he must give up the Corps to Blücher, as the successful carrying out of the plan of the Campaign depended on Blucher being enabled to advance on Paris; that he must not risk the suspicion of a doubtful allegiance to the cause he had espoused; that he must not forget the great claims Gt. Britain had on him, whom they had assisted & subsidized. Stewart reminded him, that at that very moment we were in material possession of the Baltick; that in fact Sweden lay at our mercy.
>
> Bernadotte gave-in at once. Blücher was reinforced and advanced on Paris, and the success of the Campaign was – & was <u>thus alone</u> – achieved.[23]

Stewart had materially assisted the allied cause once again. The military reinforcements would be needed, as Napoleon was more interested in turning the tides militarily on the allied armies to negotiate from a position of strength.

Poor Caulaincourt was playing an unenviable role, and his effort to buy time for Napoleon was not fooling anyone. The French negotiator was regarded with some sympathy, including by Stewart, who saw that Caulaincourt 'was sincerely desirous of obtaining a peace for his emperor, whose predicament he evidently saw became daily more perilous.'[24] At least the negotiations were conducted in a civilized way, as Lady Burghersh noted to her mother: 'I am to meet all the negotiators the day after to-morrow at a great dinner, given (as it is his turn) by C. Stewart.' Sir Charles was also able to oblige Lady Burghersh's literary tastes by lending her his copy of Lord Byron's latest work, *The Corsair*.[25]

A few weeks of this stalled diplomacy was enough to try any diplomat's patience, especially Stewart's.[26] In a rare outburst of temper to George Jackson on 26 February, Stewart gave full vent to his frustrations: 'You have made a very unfair attack upon me, my dear Jackson, for in the name of God, how could I send you any news, when we were four days here without communication, and Caulaincourt is still as dumb as ever.'[27] Stewart, as usual, hit the nail on the head. The French representative was in no position to negotiate seriously, and his hands had been tied from the start. Napoleon might have been less obstinate had he known that the tottering French Empire was being undermined by his former foreign minister, that great survivor, Charles-Maurice de Talleyrand-Périgord, prince de Bénévent. Talleyrand had sent a royalist agent, the baron de Vitrolles, to Châtillon; Vitrolles urged the allies to march on Paris, assuring them that they would be welcomed by key figures in the French capital.

Diplomacy was temporarily interrupted when the French overran the town of Châtillon, forcing the allies to move to Troyes and then on to Chaumont. Having had enough of French delaying tactics, on 9 March 1814 the allies signed the Treaty of Chaumont, a new general treaty of alliance, preventing any power from making a separate peace with Napoleon. The French were then given an ultimatum to accept the pre-revolutionary borders. Caulaincourt's reaction to all of this was relayed by Stewart to Lord Burghersh, along with some bottles of wine, on 11 March, after the allies had managed to return to Châtillon:

> Caulaincourt asked for an interview & Conference to-day, which sav[e]d us any direct proceeding – He has given us in our sitting a Tableau Historique de   .
> l'Europe, a Great deal of Crimination, Invective against Russia and England, particularly pointing out their Aggrandizement, &c &c – in short a most bitter paper – We ask'd for an Acceptance or Refusal of our Proposal – He then produced a Declaration which he begg[e]d to add to our proceeding verbally – viz that the Empr of the French w[oul]d renounce his Titles, acknowledge the Independence of Germany Holland under the P[rince] of Orange, Spain under Ferdinand, Switzerland under Antient Constitution.[28]

Stewart was far from impressed and told Burghersh that he believed 'this Proceeding is Evidently for Delay', also taking the opportunity to send 'some Good wine, and what I have in the larder to-day.'[29] Napoleon's chances of saving his throne were becoming less likely; only the day before Caulaincourt's 'Invective', the French Emperor had been categorically defeated by Blücher at Laon. The talks were finally broken off on 19 March, and with it 'Napoleon had lost his last chance to negotiate with the allies.'[30]

Interestingly, the Congress had reinvigorated Aberdeen's sense of superiority towards his diplomatic colleagues, Stewart and Cathcart. Left behind in Châtillon with Castlereagh, Aberdeen wrote to Lord Abercorn on 20 March. Rather haughtily, the noble Earl advised, 'Neither Cathcart nor Stewart are the men I should wish to act with, but by good temper and discretion they can both be managed.'[31] Stewart fortunately was not party to Aberdeen's rather misguided condescension, and he could enjoy these last acts of diplomacy with the Napoleonic regime:

> To the memory of these interesting days I must add, that the conviviality and harmony that reigned between the ministers made the society and intercourse at Chatillon most agreeable. The diplomatists dined alternately with each other; M. de Caulaincourt liberally passing for all the ministers, through the French advanced posts, convoys of all the good cheer, in epicurean wines, &c, that Paris could afford; nor was female society wanting to complete the charm.[32]

Time was fast running out for Napoleon, but even so he was not completely at bay, and the two sides were involved in fierce fighting at Reims, the ancient city where France's kings were crowned. The city was taken by the allies on 12 March, but Napoleon wrested it from their hands on the following day. Although it showed that Napoleon was not to be trifled with, in many ways Reims was a pyrrhic victory. Napoleon now authorized Caulaincourt to open full negotiations with the allies, but they were no longer interested. Meanwhile, in the south of the country Lord Wellington was threatening Toulouse, and on 12 March Bordeaux became the first French city to openly declare for the restoration of the Bourbon monarchy.

Onwards to Paris

Now that diplomacy had run its course, Stewart and Cathcart had both left for the wars, in attendance upon their respective courts. The allies still had to deal with a significant force under Marshal Marmont, and the inevitable clash came only 70 miles from Paris, at the Battle of La Fère-Champenoise, fought on 25 March.[33] Lord Cathcart found himself momentarily in charge of Russian artillery, while Stewart was in the thick of the action. As the battle raged, Stewart noticed that 'a lovely and most interesting Frenchwoman', the wife of a colonel, had been captured by a troop of Cossacks, and intervened to rescue her from 'these wild soldiers.' However, Stewart had no time to listen to her story and so entrusted her safety to his orderly from the King's German Legion, the gallant general consoling himself 'with the thought that when I returned at night to my quarters I should receive the gratitude of a beautiful creature, and pictured to myself romance connected with this occurrence'. However, as the fighting continued, she was taken by 'the same Cossacks . . . or others more savage and determined, and perceiving my faithful orderly hussar and prize, fell upon him, and nearly annihilating him, reseized their victim'. Stewart immediately went to the Tsar, but no trace of the colonel's wife could be discovered. Stewart could only write, 'I drop a veil over the horrible sequel which imagination might conjure up, and I took much blame for my neglect of a sufficient escort.'[34]

The Battle of La Fère-Champenoise had been a costly victory for the allies, and Marmont was able to withdraw his troops. On 29 March, the Austrians, Russians and Prussians were on the outskirts of Paris. The assault began the next day, and the Russians took Montmartre, a key part of the city's defences. Luckily for the population, there was to be no savage battle to take the city, and the French had no desire to risk the destruction of Paris. Marshal Marmont, in the vanguard of defending the city, had already been visited by Talleyrand. It is very likely that Talleyrand persuaded the marshal that Napoleon's cause was finished. Marmont agreed to surrender. The fight for Paris was over, although Napoleon still remained as Emperor of the French. Overcome with the news, Stewart wrote to his brother on 30 March, 'After a brilliant victory, God has placed the capital of the French empire in the hands of the Allied sovereigns – a just retribution for the miseries inflicted on Moscow, Vienna, Madrid, Berlin, and Lisbon, by the desolator of Europe.'[35]

The allied armies, led by the Tsar, the King of Prussia and Prince Schwarzenberg, entered Paris on 31 March 1814. Sir Charles Stewart was also among the first to enter Paris, behind Alexander and Frederick William. Cathcart and Stewart certainly stood out from the crowd: 'Lord Cathcart, in scarlet regimentals, his low, flat cocked-hat forming a striking contrast to all the others. Sir Charles Stewart was covered with orders, and conspicuous by his fantastic dress, evidently composed of what he deemed every army's best.'[36] George Jackson, who had shown great dedication to Stewart in his mission, accompanied him and described to his family back home the wonders of the scene, writing on 1 April: 'We are here at last; have entered in triumph and are in possession. Paris has been taken, or has surrendered, so bewildered are we that we hardly know which.' He saw Bourbon flags and white cockades and heard 'vivas for Louis XVIII' but added, rather ominously for the future, 'How they will like their most Christian king when they get him remains to be seen.' Jackson and Stewart seemed overwhelmed by the events in Paris. Jackson remarked that 'when I sat down with Sir Charles to concoct a report of the day's proceedings, I felt, and he no less so, though he is rarely at a loss for grandiloquent phrases', that it was harder to write of 'a pageant you have had a part in than one of which you have been merely a looker-on'.[37] Stewart's account to Castlereagh was more optimistic, both about the future, and for Louis XVIII: 'The restoration of their legitimate King, the downfal[l] of Bonaparte, and the desire of peace, have become the first and dearest wish of the Parisians.'[38]

Tsar Alexander, without discussion with his allies, took it upon himself to enter into talks with Talleyrand, to settle the fate of the French Empire and of its emperor. The Tsar was no friend to the exiled Bourbons, and there was still a possibility that Alexander might support a regency for Napoleon's son, the King of Rome, or even back Bernadotte, the heir to the Swedish crown. Talleyrand however was able to persuade the Tsar to support the restoration of Louis XVIII, in negotiations which have been described as 'entirely unconstitutional' and 'illegal'.[39] On 2 April 1814, what was left of the French Senate formally deposed Napoleon. On 4 April, George Jackson noted in his diary the British concerns that they were being excluded again.[40] Fortunately for the British, with Alexander now convinced that Louis XVIII was the best guarantee of stability, the Napoleonic loyalists had lost. With some relief, Stewart could advise his brother of the Tsar's resolve.[41] On 6 April, the Senate effectively ensured the restoration of the Bourbons to the throne of France. The French imperial dynasty was put aside, as Stewart told his brother: 'Napoleon Bonaparte has accepted the terms offered by the Allies for his future existence, and that of his family'.[42]

The resulting Treaty of Fontainebleau exiled Napoleon to the Island of Elba, and allowed him to keep his title of emperor. The choice of Elba was not applauded by Lord Castlereagh who arrived in Paris in company with Prince Metternich on 10 April. The Earl of Aberdeen summed up the blunt British attitude about these proceedings, writing home on 18 April to condemn 'the extraordinary and absurd convention', but noted that Alexander 'had gone too far for Castlereagh to interfere'. Elba was very close to Italy and for that matter to France, but there was nothing the British foreign secretary could do to prevent Alexander's fait accompli.[43]

Stewart was soon enjoying the charms of Paris, where 'every demonstration of joy, luxury, and gaiety was exhibited. The theatres and the public places, the balls, and the entertainments, kept the conquering armies in a fever.' This heady atmosphere soon got Stewart into a scrape. Coming home from the festivities rather the worse for wear, having been to the opera and then a ball, he had not returned to his apartments until two in the morning. After having supper, he took off his hussar's uniform, including the pelisse with his 'stars and foreign orders (some of which I had set in diamonds)'. Leaving his window open, he slept very soundly, but found the next morning that 'thieves (and no doubt assassins, if I had stirred from my heavy sleep)' had made off with everything: 'Official boxes, uniforms, and clothes taken from my very bed; my swords and pistols; all my stars and orders; and in short every thing I possessed.' As all his clothes had been stolen, Stewart was 'without the means of getting up', and although the French authorities tried to find the culprit, his possessions were never recovered. Stewart himself 'had reason to believe afterwards that a French valet de chamber I engaged on entering Paris was an accomplice, if not the chief actor'.[44]

It was perhaps just as well that Stewart left the capital on official business. After welcoming his brother to Paris, Stewart was sent south to Toulouse to offer Wellington the appointment of ambassador to France. He arrived in the city on 21 April in 'dirty overalls below but plastered with crosses and stars above', and was naturally invited to a ball, given by the inhabitants of the city for the British army. At this moment Stewart's valet 'absconded', which prompted Stewart's suspicions of the man as the thief of his clothes, orders and papers.[45] Wellington accepted the embassy and set off for Paris, riding between Castlereagh and Stewart when he arrived on 4 May. Wellington also had a new title. The Prince Regent had raised Wellington to a dukedom, in recognition of his remarkable string of victories.

Having returned to Paris, Stewart soon managed to find himself in more trouble. The Duke of Wellington was invited to a 'magnificent ball' given by Stewart, at which the Tsar of Russia and the King of Prussia were present. Wellington arrived with his two nieces. One of those nieces, Lady Burghersh, had already established herself as one of Stewart's most intimate friends. The comtesse de Boigne, the daughter of a French diplomat, noted in her memoirs what happened once Alexander left, and the Tsar's brother, Grand Duke Constantine, had asked for a waltz:

> He was just beginning to dance it when Sir Charles Stewart stopped the orchestra and asked for a quadrille, which Lady Burgers [*sic*] wanted. He was devoted to her. The conductor hesitated, looked at the Grand Duke, and continued the waltz. 'Who has dared to insist on having this waltz played?' asked Sir Charles. 'I', answered the Grand Duke. 'I alone give orders in my house, Monseigneur', said Sir Charles. 'Play the quadrille', he continued, turning to the conductor.[46]

Constantine, not surprisingly, 'went away very angry . . . accompanied by all the Russians'. Matters were apparently smoothed over, and a potential diplomatic incident as a result of the cancellation of the waltz was averted. The comtesse was clearly unimpressed by Stewart, whom she censured by adding, 'That, I fancy, was the first of the impertinences which Sir Charles scattered throughout a progress which he began as Lord Stewart and continued as the Marquis of Londonderry.'[47]

Louis XVIII arrived in Paris on 5 May, and although the Treaty of Fontainebleau had resolved some matters, more negotiations were still necessary to settle the affairs of the Kingdom of France. The resulting Treaty of Paris, signed on 30 May 1814, was generous towards a beaten enemy. France's frontiers were reduced to those of 1792, and Britain agreed to return a number of French colonies. Plundered artworks, taken as trophies of war and placed in the Louvre by Napoleon, were not ransacked by the victorious allies. Belgium (the former Austrian Netherlands), with its important Scheldt Estuary, was to be part of a new enlarged Netherlands, soon to become a kingdom under the House of Orange, while the independence of Switzerland was guaranteed. Prince Metternich could be pleased, as Austria received Venetia and Lombardy, while the Kingdom of Piedmont received the Republic of Genoa.

As one of the British diplomatic representatives, Stewart was busily involved in these negotiations. The comtesse de Boigne later recollected that when her father was one of the French delimitation commissioners, Stewart and Baron Humboldt were the two negotiators who 'disguised their demands under polite phrases'.[48] Clearly the comtesse's father felt the steel under Stewart's charming exterior. The peace would take longer to finalize, and with so much still to be decided, the allies agreed that they would meet in a great international congress at Vienna. This did not mean a stop to the victory celebrations, which moved across the Channel in June, as the Prince Regent had invited the allied sovereigns to London.

The London visit did not go quite to plan. The Prince Regent was repelled by the Tsar's sister, the Grand Duchess Catherine, who arrived ahead of her brother.

The Grand Duchess in her turn did not hide her dislike of the Regent. The Prince Regent was then insulted by the Tsar himself, who made a point of staying at a hotel rather than at St James's Palace, which had been offered for the visit. The Tsar then spent his time consorting with the government's political enemies and generally making life more complicated for the Russian ambassador to London, Count Lieven. Things went from bad to worse at the Guildhall, when the Grand Duchess Catherine, who disliked music, tried to stop the orchestra playing 'God Save the King'. Between them, the two Romanovs 'seemed to vie with each other to annoy the Prince and his government'.[49]

The Emperor Francis had decided not to make the visit, and in his place Prince Metternich proved himself the suave courtier, and in contrast to the Russian Emperor and his sister, proved a great success with the Regent. However, the proposed congress at Vienna was pushed back, and while the allied sovereigns and representatives were in London, they agreed that it should open in October. Much to Castlereagh's frustration, nothing else was achieved, and it became clear that nothing would be until the Congress of Vienna opened.

Sir Charles Stewart had been fully immersed in the London celebrations, and 'constantly accompanied my friend Marshal Blucher to all the feasts and dinners given to him'. Stewart was also able to translate Blücher's 'animated speeches, which were always given in German, to the public company'.[50] Animated is a more genteel word for the Prussian's 'uncouth speeches' which were 'translated with unusual tact' by Stewart.[51] All in all, Sir Charles Stewart could look back at the events of the past year with a great deal of pride. He had shown courage in his dealings with Bernadotte and had performed his duties as minister to Prussia to the entire satisfaction of his government and of the Prince Regent himself. His country now duly showed the high value it placed on Stewart's efforts: he was rewarded with a formal promotion to lieutenant general in June and on 1 July was honoured further with a United Kingdom peerage as Baron Stewart of Stewart's Court and Ballylawn. Further rewards had also come to the family. On 9 June, Castlereagh was himself honoured when the Prince Regent nominated him a Knight of the Garter, on the same day as the Emperor of Austria, the King of Prussia and the prime minister, Lord Liverpool.[52]

Lord Londonderry had written to Castlereagh from Mount Stewart on 12 June 1814 with a father's pride in the achievements of his family: 'For where can I find another Parent, whose latter Days, are equally brightened by the distinguished Atchievements [*sic*], and important Public Services, of both his Sons.'[53] However, the letter contained a concern over Stewart's prospects, telling Castlereagh: 'I long much to hear from D[ea]r Charles, & whether, he can give me any insight, or light, as to his future Motions, or Projects.' Stewart had achieved so much over the course of the past year. Time and again he had proved his worth as a diplomat, even if he over-indulged his passion for fighting at every opportunity. Even this had its place in that military air of 1813–14, which surrounded both the Prussian king and the Swedish crown prince. As a plenipotentiary in the middle of a war Stewart had performed well. The baron's coronet which he received had been well-earned. Castlereagh was also at the height of his fame, lauded as one of Europe's greatest statesmen. Having made use of his brother's services in the last struggle against Napoleon, Castlereagh would find a role for Stewart in the new post-Napoleonic world, as Europe's ministers and diplomats considered a continent at peace, after twenty years of almost continuous warfare. For now, all could indulge themselves in celebrating victory, but the hard work would soon have to begin.

Chapter 7

THE CONGRESS OF VIENNA

Napoleon, the colossus of Europe, had been exiled. The allies had certainly enjoyed themselves since Napoleon's abdication, with a riot of celebrations, first in Paris and then in London. The Congress of Vienna, due to open in October 1814, was to be their hangover. The foreign secretary, Lord Castlereagh, was focused on the negotiations to come, but his problems were compounded by the need to find a new ambassador in Vienna. The previous incumbent, the Earl of Aberdeen, had resigned from his post, making it clear that he had no intention of returning to diplomacy. The choice would have to be carefully made, as the role would guarantee the new ambassador a key place in Britain's negotiating team as a plenipotentiary at the Congress. Castlereagh needed someone who could be trusted implicitly, an ambassador who had the foreign secretary's complete confidence. The candidate for the post was in many ways obvious: Castlereagh's brother, the newly ennobled Lord Stewart. As the minister to Prussia, Stewart had already shown that he could be relied on to carry out sensitive missions successfully.

Stewart returned home to Ireland after the celebrations. Although he undoubtedly found the time to relax, he still had to deal with family affairs on Castlereagh's behalf, writing to the chief secretary for Ireland, Robert Peel, seeking government patronage for a client. However, there was little time to settle comfortably into the life of domestic politics and patronage, as Castlereagh was about to place his brother centre stage in international affairs.[1] Stewart was still at Mount Stewart when he was given his instructions for assuming the Vienna embassy. Responding to Castlereagh on 22 August 1814, Stewart also found time to grumble about his peerage fees:

> I have this day received your letter from Dover my Dearest B[rothe]r. It was the first Intimation that I had received of Aberdeens giving up his project of going. I shall endeavor to be with you at the time You point out altho' It is very difficult to get away from hence . . .
>
> With respect to the Peerage Fees, it occurs to me that it is a little hard to consider my Services or any reward I have obtain'd, solely politically. I am not so blind as not to know where I am of most use & I feel conscious, that at Culm [*sic*] & at the Battle of Leipsick [*sic*] I was of more use than in any diplomatick Concern, I admit I have the feeling that I should be sorry my Peerage was

consider'd merely as an Acknowledgement of one Species of Service, charg'd as I was with so much military Detail & Business, & I certainly should have declin'd it if it had been offer'd with this declaration.[2]

After returning from Ireland, Stewart was named as ambassador to Austria 'on the steps at the fete at Guildhall'. He kissed hands simultaneously as ambassador and as a Lord of the Bedchamber. To a man of Stewart's sense of honour these positions 'carried to my mind the grateful reflection that I had done my duty'.[3] Now the hard work would begin, and Stewart was to be thrown in at the deep end.

The British delegation to the Congress was led by Lord Castlereagh. The foreign secretary had set out for Vienna on 16 August, arriving in the city on 13 September.[4] Castlereagh had been given wide powers by the cabinet in London, and he would remain in constant touch with the prime minister, Lord Liverpool. Stewart was one of three plenipotentiaries under the foreign secretary. One was his colleague from the past year, Lord Cathcart, the ambassador to Russia, recently raised to an earldom. The other plenipotentiary was a 'civilian' diplomat, Richard Le Poer Trench, second Earl of Clancarty, and since 1813 ambassador to the Netherlands.[5] He was, like Stewart, a member of the Irish aristocracy, whose seat was at Garbally in County Galway. An intelligent and hard-working man, Clancarty proved to be one of the real workhorses of the British mission.[6] Castlereagh also brought with him Edward Cooke and Joseph Planta from the Foreign Office, as well as a number of assistants. Among their number was the young Irish peer Richard Meade, third Earl of Clanwilliam, who was one of the youngest diplomats at the Congress of Vienna, having just turned 19. Clanwilliam had close connections with Vienna through his mother, who was a daughter of Count Thun, a Bohemian aristocrat. Clanwilliam's contacts and linguistic skills were undoubtedly great recommendations.

Lord Stewart arrived in Vienna on 5 October 1814. There was a slight delay in Stewart's presenting his credentials to Francis I, Emperor of Austria, but on 9 October the new British ambassador was received. Born in 1768, Francis I had once been Francis II, Holy Roman Emperor, from 1792 to 1806. After Napoleon's reorganization of German territories and with 'future Habsburg possession of the imperial dignity insecure', Francis had declared himself Emperor of Austria in 1804.[7] Unlike his father, Emperor Francis 'was no scion of the Enlightenment'; endowed with 'particularly cautious personality traits', he was a reactionary, 'unsympathetic to even limited ideas of constitutional reform', a view undoubtedly reinforced by a 'very limited imagination'.[8]

Stewart assured the foreign secretary that he had been received by Francis I 'in a manner the most respectful towards the Government of His Royal Highness The Prince Regent and the most flattering to my own feelings'. Stewart responded with equal flattery. Perhaps as important was Metternich's warm reception, with Stewart reporting that the Prince 'was very cordial in promising me an entire confidence, hoping I should place the same in him. He seemed to consider that England and Austria were the only two Powers that really united cordially at the present juncture in political principles together'.[9] Metternich was wise to cultivate

Castlereagh's brother, and Stewart had more than got the measure of the Austrian foreign minister during the previous campaign.

Stewart now embarked on a new stage. Vienna, the capital of the Austrian Empire and seat of the Habsburg monarchy, was smaller than London or Paris, but it still ranked as one of the most glittering cities in Europe. Stewart certainly made an immediate impression on Vienna, as related by one French visitor, the comte de la Garde-Chambonas, 'a man of letters and a poet of some repute' whose recollections of the Congress are invaluable to historians. The comte recalled that during the Congress, the Prater had 'became more brilliant than it had ever been before'. Many persons of interest were those to be seen walking, riding or driving their carriages, but one particularly 'prominent figure among these was Lord Stewart, the English ambassador, himself driving a team of four horses which would have won the approval of the *habitués* of Hyde Park'. The comte was moved to remark on Stewart's equipage, writing that with all the dignitaries present 'a great number of carriages traversed the city in all directions, and that of Lord Stewart, the English ambassador, eclipsed all the others in virtue of its elegance and its appointments'.[10]

The comte took great delight in recording Stewart's movements in Vienna, and noted that at one ball, Stewart's vanity was on full display, explaining the origin of one of the Ambassador's Viennese epithets: 'Lord Stewart wanders listlessly from one room to another. He is simply anxious to be seen, and they have bestowed on him the sobriquet of "the golden peacock".[11] In addition to being seen everywhere, Stewart would introduce that most quintessentially British sport of fox hunting to Vienna. Baron Hager, who headed the Viennese intelligence mission during the Congress, even received a report from his agent 'oo' on the subject. On 29 April 1815, the agent reported that Stewart wanted to sell his 60 'magnifiques chiens de chasse'. No buyer could be found as the price was too high, and as the dogs were bred to purely chase foxes, no Viennese would purchase them, as this was a quite un-Austrian hobby.[12]

One aspect of Stewart's career at the Congress of Vienna cannot be ignored. He quickly became famous for his philandering, his drunken escapades and less than diplomatic behaviour. Stewart was a man in his 30s, and a widower. The Austrian capital contained many diverting attractions, which were multiplied during the Congress to cater to the expected influx of distinguished visitors. Stewart liked to take things to excess, and often did not know the concept of restraint. Historians have focused on this 'wild and extravagant' conduct, where Stewart 'drank and whored quite openly'.[13] This all makes Stewart one of the more colourful characters to talk about, but in many ways it also paints a sad picture. Without condoning Stewart's often crass behaviour, it is possible that he was plagued by bouts of depression. This might have led to his drinking too heavily and embarking, for want of a better word, on an orgy of pleasure seeking. It is a side of his character which would come to the fore in Vienna. Perhaps the best opinion on this behaviour was given by Countess Bernstorff, who saw Stewart in close proximity at the Congress:

> Lord Stewart amused them often, even if in an entirely different manner and always unconsciously and in a way rather unworthy of him. The reputation of

being a hero, which was well deserved, had preceded him. Even his appearance was taking, and made a stately appearance in his red uniform of hussars, and the one eye that was continually moist gave him a rather sentimental, but not disfiguring look.[14]

The Countess added that this good impression 'was soon obliterated by his aversion, which was disclosed more and more'. In what may also be a reference to that hard edge which Stewart possessed under the affable exterior, Countess Bernstorff spoke of Lord Stewart's 'unscrupulousness'.[15] The Congress would see Stewart enjoy himself to the full, but he would also be a great help to his brother Castlereagh, and he would show great resolve in the months to come, especially in the crisis of March to June 1815.

In anticipation of the Congress, the Austrian secret police had been busily preparing their networks of informants. This intelligence and spying operation was overseen by Baron Hager, who was 'relentless in the pursuit of his duties'. It was certainly true that the Austrian secret police would be kept busy by the antics of Lord Stewart. Indeed, they would come to gleefully report on the Ambassador. Their reports made for rather more exotic reading than those from informants who had to report on his brother, who was so clearly happy to be in the company of his wife Emily. As agent 'oo' informed Hager on 9 November 1814, Lord and Lady Castlereagh were observed 'everywhere', walking arm in arm around Vienna, enjoying themselves by looking at boutiques and shops.[16]

The secret police may have been busy, but there were enough issues facing the Congress to keep the assembled diplomats hard at work. The two thorniest and most serious problems were the fate of Poland and the future existence of Saxony. The Tsar wished to turn Poland into a kingdom under Romanov rule, while Prussia, in order to keep its status as a first-rate power, wanted compensation for land lost since the war. The Prussians looked to Saxony as the means of doing this. The King of Saxony had found himself on the wrong side at the wrong time and was in serious danger of losing his throne as the price for supporting Napoleon. Alexander seemingly held a strong hand, as both the lands of the former Napoleonic Duchy of Warsaw and the Kingdom of Saxony were currently occupied by Russian troops. The myriad of other problems included the abolition of the slave trade, the small matter of Sweden annexing Norway, the fate of Joachim Murat as King of Naples and future territorial arrangements for Napoleon's wife, Marie Louise. The Tsar, Alexander I, was also keen to do something for Napoleon's stepson, Prince Eugène de Beauharnais. It was in this atmosphere that sovereigns, princes, ministers, diplomats and petitioners arrived in the capital of the Austrian Empire.[17]

Stewart was soon busy organizing entertainments, as were so many other diplomats at the Congress. Stewart, however, was rather at a disadvantage by not having a grand palace. As Colonel Henry Hardinge reported, 'Lord Stewart has made his house very comfortable – it is too small for an ambassador's residence.' This did have one advantage, as Hardinge wrote, 'of restraining him from launching forth with such great expences as he otherwise would do if his house could hold huge assemblies'. Hardinge, related to the Pratt dynasty and so part of

Stewart's 'extended' family, obviously knew the Ambassador well enough to realize he would like nothing more than to spend large amounts of money. Acquiring a larger embassy would become one of Stewart's pet schemes.[18]

The Austrian intelligence system certainly got to work quickly. By 14 October, reports were sent to Baron Hager that Stewart's and Clancarty's letters had been intercepted, while on 17 October, agent Schmidt could inform the Baron that Stewart was counted as one of the regular visitors to the French plenipotentiaries, Talleyrand and Dalberg. A confidante of Talleyrand, Emerich von Dalberg, duc de Dalberg, had received his title from Napoleon. This did not stop him from favouring the Bourbon Restoration, and Dalberg had played a prominent part in the negotiations with the Tsar in Paris, which had led to the return of Louis XVIII. Talleyrand's presence at the Congress proved again that he was one of the great survivors of the age, and his metamorphosis as the king's minister had seemed effortless. It was fitting that during the Congress, Louis XVIII completed this transformation by creating him prince de Talleyrand 'in place of the already politically embarrassing' Napoleonic title of prince de Bénévent.[19] This was the man who would lead the embassy on behalf of a newly defeated France, but one now ruled by its restored Bourbon dynasty. In Stewart's letters, the proud Talleyrand was often referred to simply as 'Tally'.

Talleyrand had previously approached Stewart as an intermediary to Castlereagh. This had led to a meeting between Castlereagh and Talleyrand in Paris, when the foreign secretary was en route to Vienna.[20] Talleyrand was determined that France should not be excluded by the counsels of the four great allied powers and demonstrated his intentions on 30 September, just before the Congress was due to open. However, this was something that the representatives of Britain, Austria, Russia and Prussia were unwilling to concede. Events would change this position. It is significant that the Austrian authorities carefully noted all of those deemed regular visitors, and that Lord Stewart was the only member of the British delegation on the list.

Stewart would have to use all of his charms on Talleyrand, who was not impressed by either Britain or by Stewart's appointment. Writing to Louis XVIII, Talleyrand condemned what he saw as the selfishness of Britain's policies, which he believed was motivated by a desire to maintain its naval supremacy, and by a desire to humble France. To pursue these objectives, Britain wanted 'to bind Austria and Prussia close together . . . and to set them as rivals opposite France'. According to this grand plan, 'Stewart has been made English ambassador in Vienna. He is entirely favourable to Prussia, and was chosen exactly for that reason.' In order to placate Berlin, Britain would be happy to have Saxony 'sacrificed and delivered to Prussia'.[21] Talleyrand was correct in his assertion that Britain was prepared to give Prussia a free hand in Saxony, but his contention about a desire to denigrate France seems unlikely in the face of the moderate peace terms that Castlereagh had helped broker in Paris.

Stewart was soon involved in the intense diplomacy surrounding the impending Polish crisis. The British government was not prepared to let Alexander create a Romanov-ruled Kingdom of Poland, which would expand Russia's boundaries substantially to the west. At the diplomatic gathering in Paris, 'suspicions and indignation' had already followed the Tsar's plans for Poland, feelings which were extended to the Tsar's Polish adviser, Prince Czartoryski, the former Russian foreign minister. British suspicions were undoubtedly deepened by Czartoryski's inclusion in the Tsar's diplomatic entourage at Vienna.[22]

Castlereagh and Alexander met on 13 October to discuss the issue. The foreign secretary had handed the Tsar the British memorandum on Poland. It stated that the British government was opposed to the Tsar's plans, although not to the principle of a 'liberal and important aggrandizement of the Polish frontier'. Even more critical of Alexander was the memorandum's assertion that if the Tsar was 'seriously impressed with the necessity of ameliorating the condition of the Poles', this could be achieved already as 'the power is sufficiently in his hands at present with regard to his own Polish provinces and his fair proportion of the Duchy of Warsaw'. Further, if Alexander wanted to restore Poland as a kingdom it should be 'really independent as a nation'. Only this course 'would be applauded by all Europe and cheerfully acquiesced in both Austria and Prussia'.[23]

Stewart had been fully engaged in these diplomatic efforts and had been sent ahead in a gallant charge against Alexander soon after his arrival. Against the background of the worsening situation over Poland, Stewart summarized his efforts to date in a letter of 15 October to Castlereagh:

> Perhaps it may be worth while to put to paper the heads of a conversation I had with the Emperor of Russia, when I paid my duty to His Imperial Majesty the other day on my arrival at Vienna, as it tends to prove, either that H.I.M. is desirous of showing that all the Colossal Objections to his immediate projects on Poland are on the side of Great Britain, or that H.I.M. is an unfaithful reporter of Prince Metternich's opinions on this very grave and important question.
>
> His Imperial Majesty conversed at much length on the immense sacrifices of Russia, and putting these in the foreground of his Statement, he declared how doubly necessary it became him, on the present settlement of Europe to attend to their permanent Interests. That his moral feelings however, and every principle of justice and right called upon him to use all his power to restore such a Constitution to Poland, as would secure the Happiness of so fine and so great a people. The abandonment of Seven Millions of his subjects were he to relinquish his Polish Provinces, without a sufficient Guarantee to Russia of the great utility and advantage of the measure, would be more than His Imperial Crown was worth . . .
>
> His Imperial Majesty continued, that his character was well known and ought to give full confidence to Europe; – I remarked we could not at all times ensure to ourselves an Alexander on the Throne; to which H.I.M. replied, The Grand Duke Constantine imbibed entirely his sentiments, as well as his two Brothers; that he was happy also to believe the proposition he had stated, and the mode in which he viewed it, were seen by Prince Metternich in the same light.[24]

Metternich's agreement was all the more surprising, as Stewart could assure the Tsar that the Austrian foreign minister 'had held a very different language to me'.

Perhaps worried about Austrian policy, Stewart told his brother, 'I have not had an opportunity of seeing Prince Metternich since this conversation, but I shall not fail to apprize him of the extent to which he must have been misunderstood.' More alarmingly, set against British fears about Russian plans, Stewart added, 'His Imperial Majesty alluded rather in a menacing manner to His present Military Occupation of Poland, and seemed to be certain of the facility with which he could retain it.' As for the Tsar's brother, the Grand Duke Constantine reportedly 'talks a language most hostile to the English, and I understand has declared confidentially that Great Britain alone stands in the way of his being created Viceroy of Poland'.

Stewart returned to the subject of Metternich, who was 'not acting with that straight forward Policy which becomes him at so critical a juncture, holding off from a close connection with Prussia by a disinclination to guarantee Saxony'. Having been on the receiving end of Metternich's brand of diplomacy before, Stewart knew what he was talking about. Writing in very frank terms, Stewart warned 'that the same line of Politics which I thought I observed during the whole of the last Campaign, still regulates this Minister'. As a result, 'He is rather forced into any decision by circumstances and events or by the continued goading of those whom he fears and respects, than Disposed to take such manly measures as are becoming the first Minister of a Great State.' Just as worrying as Metternich's apparent slipperiness was the policy of France, which aimed at nothing less than the break-up of the alliance:

> It is also certainly evident that France at the present moment is on her side endeavouring to disunite the Confederacy; and perhaps no policy would be more dangerous than to incur the risk of breaking up the Alliance which had brought about the liberation of the world; nor would it be justifiable to deluge Europe again with a new War for a portion of Territory more or less, if it could be avoided.[25]

Stewart also advised on what might be done if Russia was determined on being 'impracticable upon the moral point' of creating a Kingdom of Poland.[26] It was becoming clear that Britain needed a line to France, in case of future necessity. This is the significance of Stewart's visits to the French delegation.

Stewart was not only chosen to meet with Alexander, he was being used as Castlereagh's personal representative to Talleyrand. Who better than the foreign secretary's charming but determined brother as the agent in these meetings, especially to a mistrustful Talleyrand, who would of course know that Stewart spoke with his brother's full authority. Stewart had been playing a clever game, and he had taken care not to antagonize Alexander and risk a rupture with Russia. Indeed, at a ball held by the Russian ambassador to Vienna, Count (later Prince) Razumovsky, Alexander had 'in shaking Lord Stewart by the hand, said, I am surprized you will speak to me as we differ so much'. This goodwill apparently did not extend to the Grand Duke Constantine, who was pointedly not invited to one of Stewart's entertainments 'because since the Paris Ball he has shewn Lord Stewart such a decided aversion, as to make it awkward'.[27]

Stewart's attentions were not just focused on negotiations. The subject of expenses and the need for a grand house also occupied his time. A suitably splendid embassy was not a whim, but in terms of European politics was a suitable reflection of Britain's prestige. Stewart had set his sights on one 'very eligible House next Year for the Embassy at this Court' which would likely become available 'on account of the derangement of Prince Stahrembergs [*sic*] Affairs for his either selling or letting it that a very advantageous Bargain might be made for it, If Your Lordship would give authority to any one to this Effect'. Stewart was anxious that Britain should not be outdone by the other great powers, telling the foreign secretary on 3 November:

> Although Your Lordship may not think it expedient to adopt the same plan here as at Paris, still perhaps the Government would be favorably inclined to assist the King's Ambassador at this Court in obtaining such a Residence as would put him on an equal footing with the Ministers of other Powers possessing fine Houses in this Capital. Prince Talleyrand has already agreed for his present Hotel for the Ambassador of France, and Your Lordship is acquainted with the Russian Ministers House – If His Majesty's Government are disposed to afford any Aid, it would materially assist me in endeavoring to have that reception which the other Ambassadors here are displaying, and I hope Your Lordship will favor me with Your Instructions on the Subject.[28]

During the German campaign, Stewart had earned a well-founded reputation for bravery and had forged close links with the Prussian military establishment. Castlereagh now used this to his advantage. The Prussian chancellor, promoted to the title of Prince Hardenberg, had been sympathetic towards Britain and France over Poland, but Prussia 'was scarcely in a position to oppose the unequivocal wishes of the Tsar'. On 5 November, Hardenberg was ordered to cease any opposition.[29] As a result of this, Stewart was sent to consult with the Prussian general Karl Friedrich von dem Knesebeck, an early advocate of Prussia's abandonment of the alliance with Napoleon.[30] Stewart was now privy to Prussian infighting, and the thinking behind its Polish memorandum, thanks to Knesebeck's 'little Memoir on the Subject'.[31]

Lord Pumpernickel

Lord Stewart was certainly playing the role of Britain's trusted emissary, but he found it impossible to stay out of trouble for long, and one of the more bizarre episodes in Vienna took place during these negotiations of high European politics. Stewart 'had made his name as a fighter on the battlefields of Germany' and thanks to a street brawl, now 'maintained it on the streets of Vienna'.[32] Baron Hager reported the details of Stewart's fight to his sovereign, the Emperor Francis, on 1 November, noting that it would have turned 'nasty' if not for 'the timely intervention of the police'. However, the full and grisly details soon became the talk of the Empress of Austria tavern, which 'at the dinner hour . . . was thronged with illustrious and important personages, anxious to escape from the magnificent but somewhat solemn banquets of the Austrian Court'. One of those present in the tavern was the comte de la Garde-Chambonas, who recalled the story of what had happened to Stewart 'due to his overweening conceit':

> 'For the last four days', said some one, 'his lordship has not been seen on foot or in his magnificent carriage. According to rumour, his face has been more or less damaged. He had a quarrel on the Danube bridge with a couple of hackney drivers, and immediately jumping off his seat, his excellency, waving his arms like the sails of a windmill, challenged his adversaries to an English boxing match. The Vienna coachman, however, knows nothing, either theoretically or practically of 'fisticuffs', and consequently bravely grasped their whips, and first with the thongs and afterwards with the handles, belaboured his lordship with blows, without the least respect for his 'pretty' face. They left him lying on the ground, bruised all over, and disappeared as quickly as their horses would take them.[33]

The Genevan delegate, Jean Gabriel Eynard, also heard the details of this unfortunate event. He went further than Garde-Chambonas and described what occurred after a policeman had arrived on the scene. The erstwhile representative of the Austrian state was about to arrest Lord Stewart, when the Ambassador revealed his identity: 'But this only incensed the abuse, he now being thought a swindler.' This failure of recognition was followed by 'a loud barrage of "Goddamns"' from Stewart, and because of this, it was thought he might be a 'stable boy'. However, his identity was confirmed at the British embassy and the rather horrified policeman 'repeatedly asked to be forgiven.[34]

Garde-Chambonas also detailed another story about the Ambassador, noting 'milord has bad luck, but his conceit seems incorrigible.' On a visit to the theatre, Stewart had been behind the daughter of an unnamed comtesse. In the crush, 'and taking advantage of it, his lordship was guilty of an act of impudent familiarity, which he might have found to his cost could only be washed out with blood'. The woman in question 'quietly turned round and gave him a sound box on the ears as a warning to leave innocence and beauty alone'. Garde-Chambonas added, 'Naturally, his lordship has been the laughing-stock of everybody, as he often is, for nothing waits so surely upon conceit and fatuous vanity as derision.' This incident may well be the same story recorded by Charles Greville on 24 January 1815 at a party held at Chatsworth. He recorded the following in his diary: 'Lord Stewart's conduct at Vienna has excited much dissatisfaction, and it is thought impossible he can remain there after the disgraceful things which have happened to him.' In the Chatsworth version, the story has two separate incidents. When the same woman was accosted by Stewart for a second time, her mother 'immediately declared that there was a present person who was unfit to be in society. This made a great breeze, and Ld. S. was forced to apologize.' In this retelling, Stewart himself blamed his drinking as the reason for his lack of self-control.[35]

That Lord Stewart's conduct was being discussed in high circles in Britain was not desirable, and especially at the seat of the great Whig family of Cavendish, among people who were no friends to Castlereagh or the government of which he was a member. Stewart's behaviour was bewildering and he must have known the shock it would cause in Viennese society. He simply could not control his drinking or himself. Other outbursts of erratic behaviour were being carefully recorded by the Austrian authorities, as illustrated by agent 'oo', who reported to Hager the details of a conversation between Stewart and Napoleon's stepson, Prince Eugène. Stewart insisted that he had fought Eugène in Spain, something that Napoleon's viceroy of Italy had never done. Even the agent was moved to remark that this was yet another example of the 'incredible history' of Stewart's time as ambassador.[36]

It was this kind of behaviour which led one Viennese diarist to remark of Stewart: 'He is not well liked, has the reputation of a sot.' It also helps explain the Ambassador's rather less flattering nickname, derived from a contemporary comic character, of 'Lord Pumpernickel', as recounted by Count Nostitz, a Prussian in the service of the Tsar. Nostitz had his own harsh words for Stewart, whom he described as 'an insolent Englishman who seems out to kick everybody in the teeth'. Such apparent detestation should perhaps be seen as not just a personal attack but could well stem from the deteriorating relations between Britain and Russia, and also be a reflection of that determined style of diplomacy which Stewart had already demonstrated in his previous role.[37]

Stewart was reported by Hardinge to be suffering from a 'bad cold' on 11 November, which perhaps meant he would enjoy Viennese entertainments with more restraint, at least for a while. One such entertainment, at Lady Castlereagh's, gave rise to one of the more famous quips of the Congress, as Hardinge wrote. Castlereagh, Stewart and Metternich 'were waltzing at the same time, and as it attracted notice, no one else would move, in order not to disturb the joke which in an instant went round the room, that the Congress at length is in motion & very active'.[38] Castlereagh undoubtedly found the lack of progress frustrating, and he certainly had more important considerations on his mind than his brother's antics. The Tsar had shown no intention to move on Poland or Saxony, a stance he had reiterated to Castlereagh, Metternich and to Talleyrand. In this he now had the full support of Prussia, which as a quid pro quo expected to receive Saxony with Alexander's blessing. However, British public opinion, as well as that in other countries, had turned in favour of the King of Saxony, and the idea of handing over the kingdom in its entirety to Prussia was becoming less palatable by the day. The plan had become even more distasteful on 10 November, when it was discovered that Russia had allowed Prussian troops to occupy Saxony, 'apparently with British approval'.[39]

The saving of Saxony had not been uppermost in British minds and in this respect Talleyrand's analysis of British intentions had been quite correct. Thus Castlereagh could write to Liverpool on 25 October 'that the fate of Saxony should be considered subordinate, after the glorious efforts of Prussia in the war, to the effectual re-construction of that Power'. Poland had always been to the fore in British diplomacy, as the memorandum to the Tsar indicated. Now,

Lord Liverpool rushed to tell his foreign secretary that the attitude towards Saxon independence had all changed, in a letter sent from London on 18 November.[40] Events now brought Britain, Austria and France together against Russia and Prussia, a rather surprising reversal of diplomacy. Metternich and Talleyrand had their own pressures. The Emperor Francis had no great desire to see the King of Saxony deposed and went as far as to tell this to Alexander, while Metternich had not appreciated the way in which the handover to Prussia had been conducted. Talleyrand was in an even more difficult position, as he had always been under specific instructions to save Saxony, not least because Louis XVIII had dynastic ties to the fallen Frederick Augustus. War was a distinct possibility. Events had moved on from the rapturous entry into Paris in the spring, a situation which thoroughly alarmed Lord Liverpool who wrote on 25 November to express his concerns.[41]

Lord Stewart himself was reported by Karl Heinrich vom Stein, a member of the Prussian delegation, as now accepting a break-up of the alliance, and he spoke of 'dividing Europe; on the one hand Russia and Prussia, on the other the remainder of Europe'.[42] Stewart was also kept busy by his brother in other official capacities, as Europe seemed to be sliding inexorably towards a new war. He was appointed to a number of committees, including the Swiss Committee, although the slowness in settling the affairs of Switzerland would become a source of annoyance.[43] Stewart was also appointed to the Statistical Committee, which was used to calculate the number of 'souls', as the value of territories was measured in population numbers and not in size. Prussia had been opposed to allowing France a place on the committee. Talleyrand was having none of this, and once again using Lord Stewart as the intermediary, stated quite plainly that France wanted representation. As a sign of that kingdom's growing prestige, Talleyrand's efforts were successful, and France had been allowed to have a delegate on the committee (although the four allied powers had two each).[44]

The Saxon question had also reached a crisis point, with Prussia refusing to back down over its demand for the whole of Frederick Augustus's territory. However, the Prussians would soon discover that they could not rely on Alexander's full support, once the Tsar had got his own way over Poland. As the Tsar's troops occupied Polish territory, the other allies had finally realized that there was nothing they could do to thwart Russia's ambitions. Alexander was going to have a Kingdom of Poland.[45] Indeed, by 27 November, Stewart had predicted 'that the Polish question would now calm down, but that more emphasis would be placed on the Saxon question'.[46] This is exactly what happened, and it led to a sharp deterioration in the relationship between Metternich and Hardenberg, and publication of diplomatic correspondence.[47] It was not immediately obvious that war would be avoided.

As Stewart predicted, Saxony was now the most dangerous issue, with Prussia, seemingly fully supported by Russia, in belligerent mood. Lord Stewart had been acting as a go-between for Castlereagh and Talleyrand, and this is where his role perhaps came to fruition. Already by 25 December, Castlereagh had told Liverpool that 'France is now a principal in the question.' On 1 January 1815, Castlereagh informed the prime minister, 'I have felt it an act of imperative duty to concert with the French and Austrian Plenipotentiaries a Treaty of Defensive Alliance, confined within the strict necessity of this most extraordinary case.[48] Castlereagh's resolve was strengthened by news he received on 1 January of the signing of the Treaty of Ghent, formally ending the 1812–14 war between Britain and the United States. France was now part of a formal alliance. This defensive treaty between Britain, Austria and France was only in case of war, and news of its existence was kept from the other powers. The Tsar though would find out a few months later, thanks to regime change in Paris.[49]

The new treaty would not be needed. Although the Statistical Committee would play its role in allocating suitable recompense to Prussia, the resolution of the outstanding Polish issues at the ministerial conference on 3 January was the real breakthrough. By 7 January, Castlereagh found Alexander in 'a remarkably conciliatory mood', and two days later Razumovsky 'announced that Prussia should be satisfied with only a part of Saxony'.[50] Prussia was not impressed, and so the Saxon question remained unresolved. It was perhaps not surprising that Lord Stewart's ball on 20 January, in honour of Queen Charlotte's birthday, was a slightly sombre affair. Nostitz recorded that it was 'a brilliant assembly of rich men and women and high personages'. Something though was missing: 'Everywhere was English comfort, but nowhere joy, which is ordinarily not absent where there is pomp and splendour.' At least Stewart could be relied upon to add to the gaiety of the Congress. On 2 January, Hager had been informed that the British ambassador had appeared at a dinner given by Count Bernstorff in honour of the King of Denmark and the diplomatic corps, in 'indescribable' breeches.[51] Stewart also continued to keep the intrusive Austrian authorities happy. An unknown agent reported to Hager on 8 January that the Ambassador had spent the previous night at the house of a woman in Kaerntnerstrasse, between the hours of 11 pm and 2 am.[52]

As for Stewart's brother, Lord Liverpool became desperate for Castlereagh to return. Not only was he foreign secretary but also leader of the House of Commons, who answered for the government in that chamber. The prime minister wrote on 16 January, 'Last year we could spare you . . . Now, very few persons give themselves any anxiety about what is passing at Vienna, except in as far as it is connected with expense.'[53] The government's solution was to replace Castlereagh with the Duke of Wellington. The Duke certainly had the necessary authority and international prestige to carry this function out, and he arrived in Vienna from Paris on 1 February 1815. Wellington's arrival was the subject of the famous painting *Le Congrès de Vienne* by the French artist Jean-Baptiste Isabey. Wellington is shown in profile at the very left of the painting and Castlereagh is seated almost at the centre of the composition. Lord Stewart can be seen at the back, resplendent in hussar uniform and covered in his orders, standing sixth from the right next to Razumovsky.[54]

Before Castlereagh left for London, the Saxon question had finally been settled without war. On 8 February, Prussia had accepted that Saxony was not going to be extinguished. It acquired about a third of the kingdom, leaving Frederick Augustus with a reduced but viable state. Without Alexander's full support, Prussia was in no position to start a war.[55] Other territorial settlements were ironed out, including those involving Hanover, which was raised to a kingdom during the Congress. Castlereagh's departure was set for 15 February and it was time for him to settle his affairs; this included Castlereagh's letter to his brother of 12 February, requesting that Clanwilliam be attached to the Vienna embassy, the Earl 'being desirous of entering into the diplomatic line'.[56] With the most pressing problems resolved, the foreign secretary issued a circular on 13 February to all his ambassadors and ministers that 'the negotiations at Vienna are in a favourable train of amicable settlement.' Although there were still outstanding issues to be settled, he advised Britain's diplomats, 'You may venture to dissipate all remaining uneasiness lest the peace of Europe should be disturbed.'[57]

Stewart summed up progress at the Congress succinctly to his friend Lord Burghersh, now minister at Florence. Writing on 17 February, he noted that since his brother had left, Wellington was determined to regulate affairs with the Austrian minister: 'Metternich takes his fling, The Duke wishing to fix him to at least a particular hour in every day to communicate as to progress urg'd him to this Effect. Metternich fix'd between 4 & 5 every day.' The Tsar was also showing renewed interest in Marie Louise, Napoleon's empress. Alexander had 'with his usual Chivalry' supported the Empress 'against her Papa', the Emperor Francis. Leaving these details aside, Stewart's letter is remarkable for its pessimism about the future of Europe, in contrast to Castlereagh's optimistic memorandum. Stewart feared Alexander's Russia, and thought that the Tsar might seek future territorial acquisitions: 'with 500,000 men at his Back, He is a bold man who will say where He will stop, It is vain for Europe to hope for a long peace while Russia is actually on the Oder.'[58] Stewart's analysis was wrong: the peace of Europe would not be disturbed by Alexander's Russia but by France, as the allied sovereigns and governments would soon discover. In perhaps one of the grandest understatements of the period, Lord Stewart wrote to his brother of French politics, 'But we shall see how it will Turn out.'[59]

Chapter 8

VIVE L'EMPEREUR!

In March 1815, Louis XVIII's monarchy collapsed like a house of cards. On 26 February, Napoleon made a daring escape from Elba with a small group of followers, setting foot on French soil on 1 March. The Bourbon regime dispatched the army to put down a seemingly minor problem. The soldiers instead defected, and what had started as a mad gamble rapidly took on the mantle of revolution. Napoleon reached Grenoble on 7 March and the following day he was in Lyon. On 20 March, Napoleon was at Fontainebleau, from where he had left for exile less than a year before. The allies declared Napoleon an outlaw, but this made no difference to events in France. The same night Napoleon reached Fontainebleau, Louis XVIII left the Tuileries Palace; instead of returning to Britain, the King crossed the border into Belgium and settled in Ghent. The King was far from foolish, but he had paid the price for a series of blunders since the Restoration. From the outset, he rejected the Revolution by dating his reign from the titular Louis XVII's death in 1795, not from 1814. Louis had further insisted that The Charter, the constitutional bulwark of the Restoration settlement, be seen as freely granted by him to the French people, rather than imposed on the monarchy. The drastic reduction in the size of the French military should also have been handled with more skill. Now Louis XVIII added to his troubles by leaving the country. France awoke to cries of *Vive l'Empereur!* – the acclamations of Long Live the Emperor had seemingly consigned the brief restoration of the Bourbons to oblivion.

Stewart learned of Napoleon's escape on 7 March. The intelligence was relayed by the British consul at Leghorn (Livorno) to the minister at Florence, Lord Burghersh, who communicated immediately to Stewart.[1] The news was quickly known by all the sovereigns and representatives present in Vienna. The allies, so recently on the brink of fighting each other, now came together to defeat the newly returned Napoleon. However, Stewart's analysis of the allied powers, in a letter he began on 4 March 1815 was hardly promising, one cause of concern being Prince Metternich's 'increasing unpopularity'. Moving quickly to reassure Castlereagh, Stewart advised that Metternich was not as insecure as others thought, and the more he was attacked 'the more certain does He appear of retaining his hold on the Emperor's mind, and from all I can observe I am quite persuaded his reign is very far from being near at an End as many predict'. As for the prince de Talleyrand, Stewart recorded the Frenchman's dissatisfaction with Louis XVIII's closest advisers, notably the King's favourite, the comte de Blacas, and in general at the reconstituted Maison du Roi. Stewart did not trust Talleyrand, informing London that he was 'not quite so <u>Loyal</u> to the King as He would lead <u>some</u> to believe'. Particularly grating to Stewart was Talleyrand's boasting of 'declaring <u>He</u> can manage the King, <u>He</u> knows the Kings Interests & similar Assertions', and although this was combined with anti-Napoleonic sentiments, it was 'not quite the course' of a 'Loyal & Stout' supporter of the Bourbons.

Talleyrand was implicitly attacking the Ultras, which in turn was a none too subtle criticism aimed at the leader of that faction, the King's brother, Charles, comte d'Artois, by courtesy styled Monsieur. Stewart also advised Castlereagh that in some quarters Louis XVIII was being written off and a second restoration not seen as inevitable, especially by the Russians. Alexander himself had another candidate in play, Louis-Philippe, duc d'Orléans, the closest in line to the French throne after the senior branch. Stewart wrote, 'If the Nation will choose the Duke of Orleans, prevent a Civil War, & abide by the Treaty of Paris &c &c that the Emperor [Alexander] agrees to <u>support them</u>.' The Tsar, never that warm to the eldest line of the Bourbons, had been highly offended by Louis XVIII's outward arrogance towards him at the Restoration. Matters had not improved since then, as Stewart reported: 'The Emperor of Russia's hatred to the Bourbons had been much augmented by the Deceptions relative to the Duke de Berris marriage as well as the Defensive Treaty.' The treaty of January 1815 between Britain, Austria and France had been unhelpfully sent to Alexander by Napoleon, as a means of sowing dissension among the allies. The abandonment of the proposed marriage of Louis XVIII's nephew, Charles-Ferdinand, duc de Berry, to the Tsar's sister, was an added affront to the Romanovs.

Stewart had discovered that Joseph Fouché, the infamous regicide who had been Napoleon's minister of police, was involved in indirect communications with Metternich. In turn, Metternich had let it be known that he did not support the idea of a regency for Napoleon's son, the King of Rome, who was currently a virtual hostage in Vienna. Metternich was apparently still hedging his bets, reportedly saying 'as to the King [Louis XVIII], It remain'd to see what party adhered to him in France.' The Austrian minister might have been warming to the idea of Orléans and if he 'was preferr'd Austria would cheerfully acquiesce in the feeling of the People'. Stewart pithily summarized the Russian and Austrian governments thus: 'The former wants to rush to the change at once, the latter desires to see the Movement Spontaneous and general.'[2] Such was the disunity among the allies at Vienna. Napoleon though had made a grave error and had timed his invasion badly. The powers of Europe, still together at the Congress of Vienna, were able to meet easily and organize new military efforts against him. Whether Napoleon had made his move out of fear of being sent to a new place of exile or whether in response to his unpaid pension was in many ways irrelevant.[3] What was important was that Napoleon's timing allowed his enemies to move against him quickly.

There were still other occasional diversions for Stewart's pen. On 11 March, the Ambassador was writing home on the subject of his finances, while the following day he reported on a robbery at the embassy.[4] However, the forthcoming campaign against Napoleon naturally took up most of Stewart's hours. On 22 March, Stewart gave his brother another depressing picture of the allies, this time criticizing Prussia, which was happy to let the Duke of Wellington have command of the Anglo-Dutch army but not of any Prussian soldiers. Stewart felt bound to remonstrate with Wellington over this plan, as he was concerned that this left him with 'an inefficient Army'. Acknowledging that the Prussians were not prepared to see their troops commanded by a 'Foreign Officer', he argued, 'It would be quite a new order of things, to see the Duke of Wellington with a less efficient or a less offensive Army, than other Chiefs.'

As if this were not enough for Castlereagh, Stewart reported that both Alexander and Frederick William wanted to lead their armies in person, and 'from all I hear, that the Emperor [Alexander] is not anxious that England should play a very prominent part in the active offensive military operations'. At heart was Alexander's 'jealousy' of Britain which was 'deeprooted, & apparent and I think influences more than an anxious desire for the Common Weal'. Stewart was no mere observer of events, and the Ambassador reported that he had warned Metternich 'that I was persuaded & I was sure the English Government would feel that unless a very large force was entrusted to him [Wellington] He should not be first forward'. Having also met with the prince de Talleyrand, Stewart informed Castlereagh that 'Tally wanted to pledge the powers not only to maintain the Peace of Paris & present limits of France' but had sought assurances on the future of the artworks in the Louvre, left in place in 1814. Stewart's response left Talleyrand in no doubt that allied attitudes had hardened towards France. Having returned from signing agreements on Switzerland, Stewart gave the French minister the benefit of his opinion on the Louvre, pointedly describing its acquisitions as 'the Robberies' and as 'the Trophies of the former humiliation of Europe'. In vain 'Tally' had riposted, 'It was the only measure that would carry the great Bulk of the Nation with us.' Stewart was having none of this, and he told his brother that Talleyrand 'did not succeed in persuading us'.[5]

Stewart could at least reassure London that the delegates in Vienna were determined not to treat with a Napoleonic regime. Writing on 25 March, detailing the imminent treaty to be signed by the allies, he noted, 'It is very desirable however, notwithstanding the Delicacy of our Opposition at home, to shew decidedly to the French Nation, that after all that has occur'd of late, we will not consent to Bonaparte's Reigning'. Stewart was also relieved that the Duke of Wellington was about to leave the diplomatic line to take up his command in the field. Confiding frankly to Castlereagh, Stewart believed that once Wellington left, the British representatives would 'go on more diplomatically & less military', and with Clancarty in charge, progress was likely to be more rapid.[6]

The Duke left Vienna on 29 March 1815. This was a busy day for Stewart, who had been involved in negotiations with the French embassy over their embarrassed financial situation. Unsurprisingly, Napoleon was not of a mind to fund Talleyrand's diplomatic mission and had accordingly ceased any payments to Louis XVIII's representatives. Wellington had already advised of this impending financial crisis, and Stewart had been detailed to ascertain immediate French needs. Talleyrand and Dalberg had seen Stewart that morning, 'and stated, that as the English Ambassador Resident at this Court, They thought it necessary to lay a more detailed Statement before me, of what they had now calculated their actual Expences to require'. Dalberg had accordingly drawn up a note 'by direction of Prince Talleyrand'. Stewart could further relay the news that 'Prince Talleyrand stated it was his intention to remain attached with the French Mission to the Head Quarters of the Allied Sovereigns; That on entering into the French Territory their presence would be of great importance.' Things were obviously urgent for Louis XVIII's diplomats, and Stewart added, 'It appeared to me that the French Mission were really in the most extreme distress, and it was impossible not to be penetrated by the picture they drew.'[7]

That same day, Stewart sent another letter advising London of his intention to dispatch a British military officer, Lieutenant Colonel Church, to liaise with General Count Nugent in Italy. An Austrian general of Irish birth, Nugent was currently engaged in dealing with trouble stirred up in Italy by the ever flamboyant Joachim Murat, King of Naples. The problem of what to do with Murat had been an issue for the Congress, with Talleyrand under particular pressure from Louis XVIII to see that the Neapolitan Bourbons were restored, a situation which Castlereagh also desired. Murat had helpfully solved the allied dilemma by declaring for Napoleon after his escape, and rashly calling on Italian patriots to take the fight to the Austrians. Stewart believed that Colonel Church's role 'may be of the most essential consequence'.[8]

With a degree of unfounded optimism, perhaps brought on by Wellington's departure, Stewart wrote to his friend Lord Burghersh the following day, to assert that 'the utmost vigor, preparation and unanimity reign among all the Sovereigns of Europe against Napoleon'.[9] The unanimity spoken of above did not encompass the plenipotentiaries of His Most Christian Majesty the King of France. Now that Louis XVIII had gone into exile, Talleyrand, Dalberg and the rest of the mission in Vienna were in an unenviable position. On 1 April, Stewart, with some sympathy for the Frenchmen, reported on their plight. He told Castlereagh, 'Talleyrand & Dalberg are as much suspected now as Traitors by the generality of this Town, as [Eugène de] Beauharnois [sic], & Metternich for not giving in to these opinions is doubted also.' Stewart condemned such goings-on, 'So horrible are the Effects of what we see passing in France.'[10]

Napoleon's stepson, Prince Eugène de Beauharnais, was certainly being watched. Brook Taylor, the British representative in Stuttgart, reported that a messenger sent by Napoleon had been intercepted trying to reach Eugène, who had as yet shown no sign of rushing off to Paris. Metternich had told the Earl of Clancarty of the messenger's arrest, but in relaying the details of this escapade to Castlereagh, Stewart could not hide his distrust of the former viceroy of Italy:

> As I have had a good deal of personal Communication with Prince Eugene and as He has talked rather freely to me, I will fairly own, that I should have no great Reliance in his adherence to his German ties; If such an opening occurred as would give him a fair chance of recovering his position: Every Frenchman so

soon reconciles to himself his Conduct by his Interest and Prince Eugene has been so evidently laying himself out for the latter here, that if He finds it passed by in the General Arrangements, I would not answer for the Consequences[.][11]

Prince Eugène would not join Napoleon, although it was perhaps natural that he was suspected of wishing to return to France. As Napoleon's stepson, he had always shown great loyalty and had enjoyed a position of honour under the French Empire.

Stewart was trying his best to advise London on allied troop numbers, and the military campaign. However, as he wrote on 8 April, 'so much must depend on the first Movements of Napoleon, & so much, (must the Spirit, (which we have reason to believe, still exists in the South of France), operate on any Decisions that I believe up to this period, nothing is positively arranged beyond the Assembly of the Levies.' Another problem lay in 'the Jealousy that exists as to giving any Accounts of Numbers and the fears entertained by these Governments, that every Detail given to a British Minister, appears immediately in the English Papers'. With a soldier's eye for detail, Stewart praised those regiments which had passed through Vienna, but there were still worries about their lack of experience. Stewart was not able to send a detailed account of the army in Italy, but could at least report on the Austrian and Prussian troops being formed up, and the imminent move of the allied military headquarters to Ulm in Württemberg.[12]

Stewart had genuine concerns about the army under Wellington's command, which he communicated privately to Lord Burghersh. Stewart joked that the 'melodies at Florence must yield to the sound of trumpets', before telling his friend that he was 'a little afraid Bonaparte may be too rapid for the Duke'. Stewart complained that the troops in Belgium were not up to the task, while the British soldiers 'never have seen a shot fired, and are very young'. The best solution was to 'get everything we can from England, and at least 100,000 cavalry, and then we shall do'. If this was not bad enough, a few days later on 15 April, Stewart wrote to Burghersh about the disharmony on France's future, with Alexander again the prime mover, using the same vehemence of language as before. Stewart noted, 'We are indivisible as to war against him [Napoleon] But as to the restoration of the King, great intrigue exists, The Emperor of R[ussia] hates all the Bourbons & is convincd they can not reign in France.' More unsettling for the senior Bourbon line was the news that 'a strong party exists for the D of Orleans; The Embassy here & Tally are not very divided in their opinions, in short I see much Devilment on this head.'[13]

Stewart's correspondence with his brother shows time and again a sense of alternating determination and utter disunity in Vienna. Stewart added to this disunity himself by managing to fall foul of Alexander. On 22 April, he informed his brother that he had been effectively frozen out of the military conferences, and the Earl of Clancarty, the civilian diplomat, had been attending as the sole British representative. Stewart vented his anger at this decision but assured his brother that he would not let this incident 'relax my zeal to be of use to You as far as lies in my power'. Stewart was careful not to attack Clancarty, stressing his 'warm feelings' for his fellow diplomat, before launching into an astonishingly vituperative attack on the Tsar: 'You know the Character of a certain Sovereign & his Influence, His Extraordinary Vanity and His Jealousy of other Glory, – I should almost say a Plan entirely projected by the D of W[ellingto]n. would be the very inducement for the above person in an Individual Manner to oppose it.'

This private and secret letter then turned to French manoeuvrings, consisting of a 'very confidential Communication from the French Boutique'. Monsieur's man at the Congress, the comte de Noailles, was being sent to Ghent to pass on to Louis XVIII 'the opinion & desire of all the Powers that His Majesty should make a proclamation'. This proclamation was to be circulated prior to Napoleon's planned meeting with the representatives of France on the Champ de Mars. This piece of pure Napoleonic propaganda was part of the French Emperor's campaign to show the world he was a changed man who could settle down to life as a peaceful monarch. The allies wanted Louis XVIII to 'state His Desire of rallying round him all parties in the Nation & assuring them without distinction of all the Advantage of a Regime Constitutionelle'. Stewart was able to report on the details of Talleyrand's dispatch, which 'adds that the Powers regard such an Act as a great Auxiliary in the present war. They desire also that the King in his Declaration should throw on his Ministers all the faults committed.' Talleyrand was further urging Louis XVIII to form a new ministry which 'should offer a Guarantee to all parties in the State'.[14]

If disunity was the watchword among the allies, another secret letter written by Stewart a few days later revealed fissures opening up in Britain's mission to Vienna. Complaining again about his apparent sidelining, Stewart was unimpressed with the military arrangements, as 'the Great Powers evidently desire to swallow all the Cash, & they are jealous of our affording better terms to the smaller states'. Negotiations with Prussia 'are very warm' and Stewart criticized the Earl of Clancarty's dealings with the Prussians, as their 'oppressions' against the King of the Netherlands had engendered 'a strong prepossession' in Clancarty against them. Stewart did not spare Earl Cathcart, specifically his handling of the break-up of the Saxon troops under Prussian command. Cathcart's error was deemed the most serious as it undermined Clancarty's position with the King of Prussia's representatives. Even the Austrians 'grievously lament our not making more Battle in the beginning on this head'. Stewart and the Tsar were still on bad terms, with the Ambassador 'so much in a great Personage's Black Books, that I have given you little information as to Russian Forces', although he conceded Cathcart would be able to supply details on Russia's military strength. Stewart desperately wanted to be the focus of intelligence-gathering for his brother. Cathcart's role as the only person capable of procuring news on the Russians did not improve Stewart's mood.

In the hothouse atmosphere of Vienna, the frayed edges of the British mission were becoming clearer for Castlereagh to see. The only positive note in Stewart's letter was his recommendation of the recently knighted Sir Henry Hardinge to a major role in the coming campaign. Hardinge, related to Stewart through the Camden connection, was described in the highest terms, and 'if sent direct by Lord Wellington [*sic*] to the great Head Quarters I think it would be the best

Plate 1 Robert Stewart, 2nd Marquess of Londonderry, by Sir Thomas Lawrence. Exhibited at the Royal Academy in 1821, Lawrence's portrait shows Britain's foreign secretary at the height of his influence and fame. Lauded throughout Europe by his courtesy title of Viscount Castlereagh, the foreign secretary was one of the architects of the Congress System and of Britain's pre-eminent position amongst the great European powers
Mount Stewart Londonderry Loan
Photo © Trustees of the Londonderry Estate/Bryan Rutledge

Plate 2 Charles William Stewart, 1st Lord Stewart (later 3rd Marquess of Londonderry), by Sir Thomas Lawrence. The artist began work on this painting in 1818. By this time Castlereagh's younger brother was a key figure in Britain's diplomatic networks. Sir Archibald Alison wrote of the relationship between the two brothers: 'Though their characters were thus different, the tenderest friendship existed between them, which continued with the most eminent advantage to both through the whole of life.'
Mount Stewart Londonderry Loan
Photo © Trustees of the Londonderry Estate/Bryan Rutledge

Lady Catherine Stewart and Frederick Stewart.

Plate 3 Lady Catherine Stewart as Saint Cecilia and her son, Frederick Stewart, later 4th
Marquess of Londonderry, by Sir Thomas Lawrence
Mount Stewart Londonderry Loan
Photo © Trustees of the Londonderry Estate/Bryan Rutledge

Plate 4 Amelia Anne Stewart, Marchioness of Londonderry, by Richard James Lane
At the Congress of Vienna, Lord and Lady Castlereagh were spied on as they looked at boutiques and shops
© National Portrait Gallery

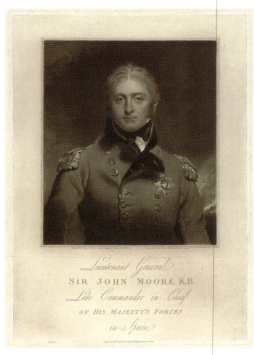

Plate 5 Sir John Moore by Charles Turner after Sir Thomas Lawrence (published 1809)
© Yale Center for British Art, Paul Mellon Collection

Plate 6 Arthur Wellesley, 1st Duke of Wellington, by William Say after Thomas Phillips; mezzotint published 8 November 1814

© National Portrait Gallery

Plate 7 King George IV after Sir Thomas Lawrence (based on an earlier painting of 1815). Prince Regent from 1811 due to George III's incapacity. After the limitations on the Regency ended in 1812, the political opposition under Earl Grey found themselves still excluded from office

© National Portrait Gallery

Plate 8 Napoleon I, Emperor of the French, from the studio of baron Gérard
© Rijksmuseum, Amsterdam

Plate 9 Charles-Jean, Prince Royal of Sweden, by baron Gérard. Elected as heir to King
Charles XIII of Sweden in 1810
Versailles, châteaux de Versailles et de Trianon
Photo © RMN-Grand Palais (Château de Versailles)/Gérard Blot

Plate 10 George Gordon, 4th Earl of Aberdeen, by Charles Turner after Sir Thomas Lawrence (published 1809) © National Portrait Gallery

Plate 11 John Fane, Lord Burghersh, after Sir Thomas Lawrence. A soldier and diplomat, Burghersh was also an amateur musician. Succeeded as 11th Earl of Westmorland in 1841 © National Portrait Gallery

Plate 12 Priscilla Anne Fane, Lady Burghersh (later Countess of Westmorland), with her son George Fane. By Porter, after Sir Thomas Lawrence (published 1831). A great favourite of her uncle, the Duke of Wellington, Lady Burghersh's quadrille caused a diplomatic incident in Paris © National Portrait Gallery

Plate 13 La famille royale et les alliées s'occupant du bonheur de l'Europe, published by Décrouant. This early-nineteenth-century depiction of the French royal family and their allies shows Louis XVIII and the duchesse d'Angoulême seated in the foreground. Standing behind, from left to right, are: the comte d'Artois, the prince de condé, the Prince of Orange, the duc d'Orléans, the Emperor of Austria, the Emperor of Russia, the King of Prussia, the duc d'Angoulême and the duc de Berry © National Portrait Gallery

Plate 14 Prince Metternich, after Sir Thomas Lawrence. Austria's foreign minister from 1809, Metternich was centre stage in the worlds of European diplomacy and politics throughout the Congress System period

Versailles, châteaux de Versailles et de Trianon

Photo © RMN-Grand Palais (Château de Versailles)/René-Gabriel Ojéda

Plate 15 Sir Henry Hardinge (later 1st Viscount Hardinge of Lahore), by and published by Charles Turner in 1833 © National Portrait Gallery

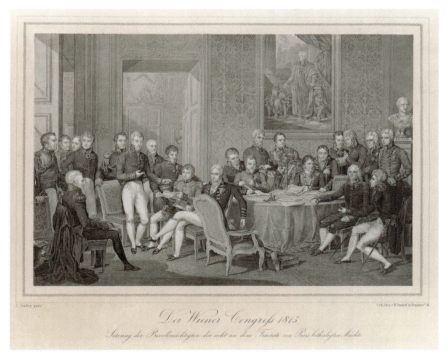

Plate 16 The Congress of Vienna by Bernhard J. Dondorf, after Jean-Baptiste Isabey © Rijksmuseum, Amsterdam

Plate 17 Key with the names of the participants at the Congress of Vienna
by Bernhard J. Dondorf, after Jean-Baptiste Isabey
© Rijksmuseum, Amsterdam

Plate 18 Catherine Fredrika Wilhelmine Benigne, Duchess of Sagan, attributed to Josef Grassi (nineteenth-century copy). While Napoleon threatened the peace of Europe, the Duchess's champagne-fuelled evenings kept the Austrian secret police very busy during May and June 1815
O. W. Klinckowström Art Collection Finnish National Gallery/Sinebrychoff Art Museum
Photo © Finnish National Gallery/Hannu Karjalainen

Plate 19 Caroline Amelia Elizabeth of Brunswick, Princess of Wales (later Queen Caroline), painted in 1804 by Sir Thomas Lawrence © National Portrait Gallery

Plate 20 Frances Anne Vane-Tempest, later Marchioness of Londonderry, by Sir Thomas Lawrence. Painted in 1818 at the time of her engagement. Her aunt, Frances Taylor, tried to prevent the marriage by accusing her niece's future husband of fortune hunting and his family of insanity

Mount Stewart Londonderry Loan

Photo © Trustees of the Londonderry Estate/Bryan Rutledge

J.F. HUTCHINSON. R.T.WILSON. M.BRUCE.

Plate 21 Sir Robert Thomas Wilson seen with his fellow conspirators in the Lavalette affair: John Hely-Hutchinson (later 3rd Earl of Donoughmore) and Michael Bruce. By an unknown artist. The affair caused fresh headaches for the British government in 1819 © National Portrait Gallery

Plate 22 Armand Emmanuel du Plessis, duc de Richelieu, by Etienne Frederic Lignon, after Sir Thomas Lawrence (line engraving 1824) © National Portrait Gallery

Nomination.'[15] Stewart's recommendation was taken up, and Hardinge, one of the most capable and resourceful of the younger British officers, would be appointed by Wellington to act as liaison with the Prussians. Stewart had also taken on the role of middleman between the allies in Vienna and Wellington, and was passing on useful information to the Duke, as shown in a letter of 28 April. This included news of General Gneisenau's plans from Sir Henry Hardinge, who was now in Liège. On top of this, Stewart had further responsibilities to add to his workload, as Castlereagh had charged him 'as last Year with the military Correspondence and duties of the Austrian Head Quarters to which the Emperor has very Kindly consented. I shall therefore be always with the Field Marshal.'[16]

'An infamous Army'

On 29 April, Stewart was appointed by Clancarty to the commission of subsistence for the military campaign, which brought on some gentle disagreements with his civilian colleague.[17] In case Lord Stewart was not busy enough, Wellington felt free to use the Ambassador as a conduit for his opinions on the allied forces. From the start there were problems with Wellington's Dutch troops and with his Prussian allies, led by Prince Blücher, while there were few experienced British soldiers to hand. It was to Stewart that Wellington sent his famous complaint of 8 May 1815 about the resources put at his disposal:

> I have got an infamous Army; very weak, & ill equipped, & a very inexperienced Staff. In my opinion they are doing nothing in England. They have not landed a man; they have not called out the Militia either in England or Ireland . . . and they have not sent a Message to Parl[iamen]t about the Money. The War spirit is therefore evaporating as I am informed.[18]

In a postscript on the other side of this letter is a personal touch. The Duke asked Stewart to send his best regards to the Duchess, along with Wellington's light-hearted but tacit acknowledgement of the strains the Ambassador was under: 'If you had not assured me so positively that you had no occupation at Vienna I should have been inclined to imagine that you had more than you could well manage!!'[19] Stewart soon found himself liaising between Metternich and Wellington as well. On 17 May, Prince Metternich thanked Stewart for a five-page letter from Wellington, 'Les idées de Mylord W'.[20]

Affairs in France and the Low Countries were not the only problems Stewart had to deal with during the Hundred Days. Joachim Murat's campaign had initially gone well, but the Austrians were relentlessly turning the tide. Thanks to Colonel Church, Stewart had a reliable informant on the ground.[21] However, it was Britain's official man on the spot who caused Stewart yet more headaches. Lord William Bentinck, a senior military officer and member of a Whig ducal dynasty, was Britain's representative to the Neapolitan Bourbons at Palermo. Bentinck's views were of another world to the Neapolitan King and Queen, and his support for the liberals and constitutionalism was causing worry in Vienna. Added to this was that Bentinck's vision of a liberal Italy did not have the sanction of Lord Castlereagh.

Bentinck was keeping Stewart updated on Murat's doings. Writing on 15 April, Bentinck could give an optimistic picture of events, 'Fortunately, he [Murat] has unmasked himself too soon & the Austrians may now fall upon & crush him.' The letter continued with a low view of Habsburg arms: 'I think the Austrians will be able to beat him . . . only because Murat has not the political courage & decision to conduct the great enterprise.' Bentinck was certainly to be proved right. Murat was declared an outlaw by the allies, and the Austrians had little difficulty in destroying his army. The Austrians could beat Murat, but they simply could not stomach Bentinck's transparently liberal attitudes. Clearly, from the tone of his letter, Bentinck thought little of the Austrians in return. As ambassador to Vienna, Stewart was made aware of Austria's unhappiness. On 22 April, he informed his brother, 'I have heard so much from the Austrian War Department about their Dissatisfaction with our Commander in Chief in Italy and those he employs in Confidential Situations.' Stewart was not overly interested in the niceties of the situation, and he looked at it in the cold necessity of realpolitik:

> Whatever is the real state of the Austrian Government in Italy at the Present moment, it must be prejudicial to our Interests to animadvert on it, & I fear from the Private letter of Ld. Wm. Bentinck to me, there is too much reason to believe, He is not sufficiently cautious in concealing his Sentiments.[22]

Prince Metternich's nose was very much put out of joint by Bentinck. As Stewart reported to Castlereagh on 13 May: 'Metternich now rides his stalking horse in Italy He thinks He's nothing to thank England for there, he wishes to see the Operations terminated by Austria alone.' Bentinck's ideas were eventually disowned by his own government. Murat suffered a harsher fate. After attempting to offer practical help to Napoleon without much success, his antics after the Emperor's defeat led to his being executed by a Neapolitan firing squad on 13 October.[23]

At least Stewart could look forward to a simpler military life. On 16 May, the Ambassador reported that he was now busy making preparations to leave Vienna. Stewart's most senior official, Robert Gordon, had presented his letters of credence, but there was the small matter of the Ambassador's suite to deal with, which meant disappointments for members of the Vienna embassy:

> Under these Circumstances, I do not feel authorized to propose to the Earl of Clanwilliam, the Earl of Ancram or Mr. Cartwright to go with me, and I shall leave them at Vienna, with Mr. Gordon, waiting Your Lordship's Decision on this Subject. Were I solely the Ambassador, and not a Soldier, there would be less difficulty, But as it is, the Outfit of all these Gentlemen for the field to which they are not called, would be attended with considerable Expence and Difficulty.[24]

Military life aside, worry over the future of France was still uppermost in Stewart's thoughts as revealed in a letter to his brother of 26 May. Perhaps against the background of his strained relations with Alexander, he warned Castlereagh against the influence of the duc de Richelieu and Pozzo di Borgo on French politics, laying bare again the air of distrust which swirled round the allies in Vienna. Richelieu, from a great French family, had served Russia in exile. The Corsican Pozzo di Borgo, once Stewart's colleague, was Russia's envoy to Louis XVIII. Stewart was afraid that undue Russian influence in any new French settlement would mean trouble: 'Though you destroy Bonaparte your Danger will be tenfold.' Stewart's paranoia was seemingly backed up by intelligence. In comparing 'what I hear is passing with Talleyrand' with fellow ambassador Sir Charles Stuart's correspondence to Castlereagh from Ghent, Stewart argued, 'You may rely upon it that the Emperor of Russia has every Engine at work to assume that Influence on a new State of things in France, which He thinks England so improperly and unjustifiably possessed during the late reign of Louis 18.'

To add to these concerns, Stewart still had a wary distrust of Prince Metternich, believing the Austrians retained their wild card to play in the shape of the Empress Marie Louise as a potential regent for her son, the King of Rome. Stewart told his brother, 'It strikes me from all I learn, that there is a quiet Coquetry with Maria Louise with a view to the . . . Regency, but this is only secondary with Metternich, yet he does not like to throw himself out of the Chance of Influence.' Stewart hypothesized how the succession of Napoleon II might be accomplished:

> If through the Russian sway, such an Event was on the Cards, and however Metternich may protest & aver the Empress's Disgust & Determination never to accept, still women change, & If Events or Arrangements are forc[e]d on such a Man, as the Austrian Minister, we know He bends to Circumstances . . . in such an Event as the Empr. of Russia's accomplishing the Regency, that He (Metternich) would govern France through His Superior Skill & Intrigue with a Daughter of His Imperial House.[25]

Stewart disingenuously added, 'I have no ground to suspect Metternich as Yet further than my not being able to account for his Conduct, on this Parma Question satisfactorily.' This point referred to the proposed compensation for Marie Louise in the shape of the duchy of Parma, another question that needed to be settled by the Congress.[26]

Stewart was certainly very well informed of Austrian diplomacy. One source for Stewart's intelligence was Friedrich von Gentz, secretary to the Congress of Vienna. It is probably no coincidence that on 2 June 1815 Stewart acknowledged a receipt from 'Chevalier Gentz' for a £400 payment. These payments were to be a regular feature of British diplomatic life in Vienna. Accounting for secret service funds at the end of 1820, Stewart noted that 'the payments to Genz [sic] speak for themselves. They were given with your Approbation previously obtained on each occasion. One payment was particularly for his Labors on Slave Trade, They [sic] others was for general good Services.'[27]

As for Talleyrand, Stewart trusted him about as much as he did Metternich, but at least cleared him of any Bonapartist sympathies as he told Castlereagh: 'You will hear of Talleyrands Notion as to recommending a provisional Government to the King – I am quite clear that He has irons in the fire in all Quarters and that He will play his Game to side with the powerful, altho' at present He is bought by all but Bonaparte'.[28] The French plenipotentiaries had more immediate, financial difficulties. Stewart reported that contrary to rumours, the money that Louis XVIII had secured for his exile was being used to meet his household expenses. Consequently 'the Embassy here found themselves in the greatest Distress, their Credits had been stopp'd & unless the liberality of the British Government would afford some momentary Aid, They were utterly incapable of existing.' That being proved, Stewart had been authorized to let the prince de Talleyrand have £1,000 of secret service monies, the same amount to be paid in regular instalments.[29]

Unfortunately Stewart's own expenses were causing the Ambassador as much concern. Writing to Castlereagh on 28 May, Stewart was 'again under the necessity' of asking for 'a further Sum of money in addition to those I have already been allowed'. The Congress was certainly an expensive business, and the negotiations had taken far longer than most observers had expected. Stewart then went into more detail. In response to former requests, Stewart had already been allocated £8,000. From this amount, £4,000 was swallowed up in transporting everything to Vienna while 'a large part nearly of all the remainder has been barely sufficient to provide myself with a suitable House & to furnish it in a manner not exceeding what was due to the rank of His Majesty's Representative.' Stewart was going through money like water, but he probably had a genuine grievance when he pointed out to his brother that 'Houses & means of habitation during the Congress in the Capital' were 'exceedingly exorbitant'. Stewart realized that the request would embarrass his brother, coming from his closest relation, but still hoped he might be allocated more monies 'without overstepping the bounds of propriety'.[30] Stewart's father, Lord Londonderry, had also got wind of the Ambassador's spending, and Stewart had felt compelled to write to Castlereagh on 13 May asking him to intervene.[31]

The prestige of the British ambassador, as representative of one of the great powers, could not be fashioned by mere economies. To celebrate George III's birthday on 4 June, Stewart held a truly magnificent ball. The comte de la Garde-Chambonas, who was present, left a memorable account of the occasion, noting that 'Nothing had been neglected to make the entertainment worthy of the memorable circumstances, and of the power represented by his lordship.' In the midst of this, 'Lord Stewart displayed a magnificence – or, to speak correctly, a profusion – of which few fêtes offered an example.' Clearly enjoying his subject, the comte wrote of Stewart, 'His excellency, however, who loved to be eccentric in everything, and whose eccentricities were not always successful, had hit upon the idea to add to his invitation a courteous injunction to come to his ball in the costume of the time of Elizabeth.' The British in Vienna certainly understood the dress code, but nobody else came in costume. Luckily for Stewart, 'those who had adopted the costume were sufficiently numerous to produce a very remarkable effect'. Stewart was certainly memorably attired:

As to his excellency himself, he wore his uniform of colonel of hussars, the scarlet of which was covered with embroideries, and a great number of orders, civil and military, to such a degree as to have led one easily to mistake him for a living book of heraldry.[32]

This certainly seems extravagant, but in the midst of the arguments and suspicions among the allies at Vienna, the ball was a rather grand way of bringing people together, and as the author recorded, such occasions, especially those lasting into the morning, were becoming a rarity at this stage of the Congress. Stewart was under constant pressure and perhaps needed to let off some steam. This was certainly one way to do so.

Europe might have been in turmoil, but during May and June 1815, the Austrian secret police found the time to continue their detailed surveillance of Lord Stewart's amorous activities. They had never stopped. For example, on 19 February, the authorities had noted that the British delegation had been 'captivated' by a Countess Zielinska, 'above all' Lord Stewart. However, it was the relationship between Stewart and Wilhelmine, Duchess of Sagan, which would greatly interest the Austrians. The Duchess, widowed some years before, had already been linked with Tsar Alexander and had conducted affairs with Prince Metternich and an Austrian officer, Prince von Windischgrätz. Her apartments at the Palm Palace would now play host to the dashing British ambassador. By 7 March their names had been linked together, but it was not until May that the reports really started coming in. On 12 May, agent 'oo' reported to Hager on Stewart's 'new eccentricity'. He had been spotted riding across the Graben and into the Kohlmarkt, his horse covered in lily of the valley, and he with an 'enormous bouquet' of the same flowers. The crowds in the streets had even stopped to look and laugh at the enamoured Stewart. The Austrians took pleasure in meticulously noting the evenings that Stewart spent at the Palm Palace, down to precise timings of when he arrived and left. The British ambassador was reported as being with the Duchess of Sagan most nights in those early days of June. Just as shocking was an intercepted letter of 7 June, which not only detailed one of Stewart's champagne-filled evenings with the Duchess but also noted that the British mission had been turned into 'en bordel et en trîpot' (a brothel and a gaming house), with hazard being played in Clancarty's own rooms.[33]

Stewart had certainly lived life to the full during the Congress. A draft Foreign Office letter of 9 June, which granted him an extra £5,000, had warned at the same time 'that from this period You will consider yourself as conscientiously bound strictly to limit the Expences of your household Establishment within the Amount of your Salary'.[34] Such pleasures aside, matters were now reaching their endgame. While Napoleon cast a menacing shadow over the participants in Vienna, the Final Act of the Congress was agreed by 8 June, and signed the following evening, 'the first and only time the congress had assembled in full'.[35] Stewart explained to his brother why he was still in Vienna on 10 June: 'I have been staying on these last ten Days here much against my will, expecting that the great work of the Treaty would be sooner accomplished and ready for Signature.' With faultless logic, Stewart asserted that 'it would be as well to put one's name to it.' Stewart did indeed sign for the British government, along with Clancarty and Cathcart. Needless to say, the charms of the Duchess of Sagan were not mentioned as a reason for remaining in the Austrian capital.[36] Others too were leaving, with Stewart reporting that Talleyrand was departing Vienna that day to join Louis XVIII, and, keeping true to the spirit of disunity, 'His Language of late has been much more Hostile against the Emperor of R. & it would appear that they have had a recent Difference.'[37]

The Austrian and Russian armies were moving westwards as part of the concerted military campaign against France. Clearly Castlereagh wanted a trusted eyes and ears at headquarters to report back to him on what was happening, and undoubtedly wanted his brother to leave Vienna as quickly as possible. Stewart had certainly intended to leave earlier, and Hager had been informed that the British ambassador had declared it his duty to join the allied headquarters on 1 June.[38] Once he had actually torn himself away from Vienna, his return to a martial way of life would rapidly be overtaken by events. Napoleon had no intention of waiting for the various allied forces to invade France, and with characteristic boldness struck at the armies closest to him, those of Wellington and Blücher.

Crossing the border on 15 June, the next day Napoleon engaged the Prussians at Ligny, while Marshal Ney fought against an allied force at Quatre Bras. Sir Henry Hardinge, who had been sent by Wellington 'to hang on' Napoleon's 'skirts', was particularly active in the campaign.[39] Hardinge was present at Ligny, and in the course of the battle his left hand was shattered, and had to be amputated. Marshal Ney failed to destroy the allied army at Quatre Bras, but just as significantly, Napoleon had not inflicted a crushing defeat on the Prussians at Ligny, who retired in good order. The Prussian army remained an effective and disciplined fighting force, and able to cooperate with Wellington. On 18 June 1815, Napoleon and Wellington finally met at Waterloo. Wellington's defeat would allow the French to advance on to Brussels, but the Duke was determined to ruin Napoleon's plans. The fighting was a bloody affair, but the planned arrival of Blücher's Prussians sealed Napoleon's fate. In desperation, Napoleon had sent in the Imperial Guard, but they were forced back by determined allied resistance. Their defeat was a symbolic passing of Napoleonic *gloire*.

News of Waterloo reached the Austrians and Russians, now at Heidelberg, at least by 21 June, when Stewart wrote to his mother, Lady Londonderry, 'I can not but feel deeply mortified that my Lot did not lead me to share a part, in the splendid Triumph that has added new Lustre to the British Name.'[40] Stewart still had a job to get on with, and on 29 June he wrote from Hagenau to his brother that he thought all were now agreed on the restoration of Louis XVIII, although there was 'a very considerable Interest as to the mode and Steps that are taken to place him again on his Throne, & the necessity of Security for the future, and Indemnity for the past'.

Stewart also passed on key information about Austrian attitudes to a second restoration of the Bourbon monarchy, set against the background of the prince de Talleyrand's disastrous meeting with Louis XVIII. Talleyrand had caught up with the King at Mons on 23 June, and had been, to all intents and purposes, dismissed from service. Now influenced more than ever by the Ultras, Louis XVIII was in no mood to forgive Talleyrand for his supposed impertinence in asking him to apologize for past mistakes. Stewart reported that Metternich had received this account the day before and had frankly asserted, 'That unless the King of France had his Eyes clearly opend & That he insisted upon what it was His own Interest to adopt, he should have the same Game to play over again some months hence.' Stewart further advised that even Alexander agreed that 'Louis 18 will now be best head for the Govt', although Stewart had heard the Tsar talk of 'consulting the Nation, & waiting until they should decide upon their King'. Stewart was not impressed: 'That To me it appear'd the French had no choice to make. The moment The Usurpation is at an end by the overthrow of Napoleon – The King of course resumes his rights.'[41] Stewart was reflecting the desires of the British government, who believed that Louis XVIII was the best choice to ensure stability in France. Now there remained the problem of how to bring about a second restoration. Before Louis XVIII could resume his reign, the allies would have to march on to Paris and install the King of France back in power.

Chapter 9

TO PARIS AGAIN

The allies had won the Battle of Waterloo. On 21 June 1815, Napoleon arrived back in Paris. He had risked all in his gamble for power, but still refused to accept that his imperial regime was dead. The French Empire was not quite finished, and on 22 June Napoleon abdicated in favour of his son.[1] The Bonapartists wanted to see the accession of Napoleon II, while the duc d'Orléans was mentioned by others as a compromise, a king ready to acknowledge the new France created since the Revolution. It was left to a regicide to ensure that Louis XVIII would again return as King of France. By so doing he would bury the French Empire once and for all. As Talleyrand had played a leading part in the first Restoration, Fouché, who had voted for Louis XVI's execution, would now make the second Restoration possible. Now in charge of a provisional government in Paris, Fouché was busy making clandestine plans which would ease a second return for the Bourbons. Meanwhile, Louis XVIII was heading for his capital, with Wellington and Blücher, but had seemingly learned nothing. The King found the time to issue the proclamation of Le Cateau-Cambrésis, which seemed to threaten dire retribution on those who had joined Napoleon's cause. Louis was not helping his chances of returning to power. Fortunately for the Bourbons, and with full allied backing, the prince de Talleyrand joined Louis XVIII at Cambrai. Talleyrand ensured that a second declaration was issued on 28 June, which effectively apologized for mistakes made, offered a general pardon with certain exceptions, and closed down the Ultra-Royalist agenda, at least in the short term.[2]

Lord Stewart remained with the sovereigns of Austria, Russia and Prussia, who were marching on Paris from the east. On 30 June, Stewart reported in a secret letter written from allied headquarters at Haguenau, north of Strasbourg, that commissioners had been sent out from 'the existing French Government at Paris'. These six commissioners had also seen Wellington and Blücher at Laon. The commissioners argued that Napoleon's abdication meant an ending of hostilities and asked that the former emperor be exiled to the United States. Stewart could assure his brother that the 'Determination of the Sovereigns was immediately taken' not to receive the commissioners, but 'by some mistake' they had arrived nearby. The British foreign secretary, who had been kept apprised of the allied squabbles in Vienna and on the march into France by his brother, would be concerned at the thought of any separate peace deal. In another secret communication to Lord Castlereagh sent that same day, Stewart passed on further details on the commissioners and his role in the affair:

> And They were so anxious to give the Allied Sovereigns a True Picture of what had passed in France, That the ministers of Austria, Russia, & Prussia present had consented to listen to such details as they might give, As it pledged them to nothing, & might take from them the possibility of doing mischief by their returning to Paris, with the Statement That They would not be heard, An Exasperation from such a proceeding might ensue, Napoleon being put aside, and ignorant of what the feelings of the most respectable part of the Representatives might be, It was deem'd wise to hear what they had to advance – Prince Metternich assur'd me this was the united opinion of the Sovereigns present, That They were decided equally not to enter into any Negotiation whatever. But to derive every advantage from listening to their Statements, and not irritating by a Total Rejection of them any of the most mischievous Spirits in France . . . His Highness was also extremely desirous that some person on the part of Great Britain should attend, It was now very late in the Evening, the Moments were precious as it was wish'd to despatch these Gentlemen immediately and although I felt the difficulty of taking a Step without Consultation, with my Colleague Lord Cathcart still as it appear'd to me rather a . . . proposition of placing me <u>au fait</u> at what might be decided on here, in order to communicate, if necessary in person with Lord Wellington [*sic*] I hesitated not in complying with Prince Metternichs wishes.[3]

Stewart was obviously anxious to put his brother in the picture, as he was rather exceeding his orders. Metternich had also learned his lesson from the previous tortuous peace negotiations and made sure that the British were represented. Stewart need not have worried. On 29 June, an allied army had reached Paris; the time for any kind of negotiated settlement was over before it had begun. This did not mean that the allies could simply walk into Paris, which remained very well protected by a significant military force. However, Paris bowed to the inevitable. The city capitulated on 3 July 1815 in a convention signed by Wellington, Blücher and the provisional government. By its terms, the French army agreed to evacuate the capital. The city was handed over to allied troops on 7 July, and the next day, Louis XVIII entered Paris. With this action, what soon became known as the Hundred Days campaign was concluded, and the second Restoration achieved. On 9 July, Louis XVIII announced a new ministry with the names of Talleyrand and Fouché prominently included.

Lord Stewart's journey with the Austrian and Russian headquarters had not been without 'many sharp actions' with the French. Perhaps with a sense of relief that it was all over, he wrote to his brother from Ligny, west of Nancy, on 8 July, detailing the reaction at headquarters to the capitulation. Prince Metternich was eager to get to Paris as quickly as possible, 'without Suite', but this brought its own complications, as the Tsar and the King of Prussia wanted to do likewise, leaving behind Francis I of Austria. This could be impolitic as 'an Interpretation might be put upon it as arising from His politicks towards the Empress Maria Luisa': in other words of favouring the accession of Napoleon II under the regency of his daughter. This meant there would be a delay before the three sovereigns could reach Paris. Stewart could report on the concerns at headquarters at 'the uncertainty of the fate of Napoleon' while Talleyrand's influence was 'much dreaded'. There was also talk of the three powers of Austria, Russia and Prussia agreeing a joint plan for the future, but Stewart was highly sceptical, telling his brother, 'I do not think however any Basis will be established.' More reassuringly for the foreign secretary, Metternich had confirmed to Stewart that 'the Interests of Austria' would be placed 'entirely' behind Castlereagh, 'such is his Confidence, & He will take no Decision without You.'[4]

Castlereagh had left for Paris, which was to be the scene of another great European diplomatic gathering. As Louis XVIII was announcing his new ministry, Lord Stewart was still with the Austrian and Russian armies, as he 'thought something interesting might happen on the upper Loire', but as he informed Robert Gordon on 9 July, 'in a day or so I shall probably proceed to Paris, Cast[lerea]gh is there.'[5] As the senior British official in Vienna, Gordon received much of Stewart's confidences over the coming months.[6] Despite the ending of hostilities, Stewart still reported on trouble from elements of the French population to Castlereagh as late as 12 July, but military concerns were about to give way to diplomacy, as Paris again beckoned.[7]

Paris was now a city under occupation. Stewart had arrived by 17 July, and his first priority, once installed in the Hôtel de Montesquiou on the Rue Monsieur, was to issue instructions to the British liaison officers to the allied armies who had been placed under his orders. This included gathering intelligence:

> The Sentiments of the Inhabitants and the opinions and feelings you learn are subjects of much interest and which you will not fail especially to report upon. If you deem it adviseable to take excursions to any quarters within the range of the Corps you are with for the purposes of information, you will consider yourself fully authorised so to do.
>
> The Cantonments of the Divisions and the movements from time to time are to be reported, and no Circumstance to be omitted of general Interest which a British Officer can much more fairly and without prejudice observe upon, than either the French Authorities to their Government who would be apt to picture Grievances in the most extravagant Colours, or the Officers of the Allied Armies who might be prone to commit excesses unwarrantably, which by good management and observation might be avoided.[8]

Stewart would receive regular reports from the British liaison officers throughout the summer of 1815 as a result of these instructions.

The allies had been generous to France when they had reached the capital in 1814, perhaps exemplified by the status of artworks 'acquired' by Napoleon. European statesmen had recognized that a great art collection had been built up in the Louvre, and accepting what had been achieved, made no attempt to effect a general restitution. Stewart had already revealed a harsher attitude when discussing the future of the Louvre with Talleyrand, and the French soon felt a distinct lack of clemency from the allied governments. The Prussians particularly wanted France to pay a high price for Napoleon's return, and the behaviour of its troops did nothing to help Louis XVIII. The debate about the terms to be imposed on France was not at all to Stewart's taste, who wrote in exasperated tones from Paris to Robert Gordon on 4 August:

> We go on here very slow, – the Allied Ministers are not yet agreed on the Securities they will require, France with 900,000 hostile Troops in her vitals, & not knowing what to expect is agitated convulsed, & may be desperate if decided measures are not soon taken . . . Make manifest the sacrifices she is to make, a certain positive surrender, that is known can be reconcil[e]d, an Undefined and expected spoliation, keeps alive every bitter feeling – The Govt. of France are timorous & might decline acting, Louis might be deserted, & then Our Troubles would be more embarrassing than they are now[.]
>
> I do not like our proceedings or our policy, God send a Change.[9]

It is hard to disagree with Stewart's analysis; better to let the French government know as quickly as possible what indemnities or punishments were to be meted out. Stewart's candid letter to Gordon shows the extreme anxiety that some of the diplomatic representatives felt about Louis XVIII. This letter is not a ringing endorsement of the second Restoration, and if Louis could be toppled with relative ease once, it could happen again. Then the allies would be faced with the question of who should rule France if the eldest Bourbon line failed. At least the Bonaparte dynasty was not in a position to challenge. Napoleon had never reached the United States; becoming a prisoner of the British, the Prince Regent's government had taken responsibility for him. It then exiled the former Emperor of the French to the South Atlantic island of St Helena, where he died in May 1821. Napoleon's son was also no threat. The would-be Napoleon II was kept as a prisoner in Vienna, although he enjoyed a more luxurious confinement as befitting a member of the Austrian royal family.

In late August, Stewart was sent to London 'by The Duke of Wellington & Lord Castlereagh to ascertain explicitly the sentiments of the Cabinet'.[10] Stewart arrived on 27 August, but left for Paris again soon afterwards, as Nicholas Vansittart, the chancellor of the exchequer, explained to the home secretary, Lord Sidmouth. Writing on 29 August, Vansittart acknowledged that Sidmouth's 'curiosity will naturally have been excited by the arrival of Lord Stewart & his speedy return to France'. Wellington and Castlereagh were concerned that the government 'was disposed to increase demands on France beyond what they thought could be obtained without a total breach even with the Loyal Party in France'. Although their concerns had been addressed by the prime minister 'in consequence of the last conversations with the Cabinet on the subject', Lord Liverpool's letter had only arrived after Stewart's departure. Wellington and Castlereagh were particularly anxious about French reactions to the proposed destruction of the fortresses at

Lille and Strasbourg, but Stewart had reported that at least 'there was reason to believe that the French Govt. was prepared to acquiesce in the other demands upon which we meant to insist.' These demands were spelt out by Vansittart:

1. The restitution of the territories annexed to France by the Treaty of Paris restoring the frontier of 1790.
2. The cession of the detached portions held beyond the general frontier of France in 1790 viz. Landau &, Philippeville besides some other small districts of no great importance on the side of Belgium.
3. The occupation for a certain number of years of the fortresses specified in the D of W's paper[.]
4. The continuance of an allied army (say 100000 men) in France during the same period at the expence of France.
5. The payment of a war contribution of say £24,000,000 . . . NB. it does not seem clear whether this is to include the maintenance of the allied Troops or to be distinct.[11]

Russian agreement had been secured for Britain's demands, although the Tsar wanted the allied occupation of any fortresses reduced from ten years to five. The Austrians were 'disposed to yield to our opinion', but Prussia remained 'obstinate & the Govt over awed by the army'. Perhaps more worryingly for British policy, Vansittart was hardly confident in the durability of the second Restoration, adding in his letter to Lord Sidmouth, 'I however have great apprehensions for France.'[12]

The allies soon showed their intentions with regard to the appropriated and stolen treasures which had made Napoleon's Paris the artistic capital of Europe. In August and September, allied representatives began removing their country's art from the Louvre. At the end of September, the four bronze horses stolen from St Mark's in Venice were taken down from the arch of the Carrousel.[13] Paris also saw upheavals politically, as time had run out for the prince de Talleyrand's government. A few days before the Venetian horses left Paris, Talleyrand had lost his hold on government. Stewart was an eyewitness to the goings-on in France and sent letters back to his uncle, Lord Camden, such as this report of 23 September:

The Govt, here are at an end – Talleyrand gave up Fouchet [*sic*], & would not entirely unite with the Dss D Angouleme & the Royalists, They were then too strong for him, & getting rid of the most wicked next . . . the most troublesome . . . What will come of all this God knows, I think the new Ministers will agree to our propositions.[14]

Stewart was correct in his predictions for the prince de Talleyrand. Louis XVIII wanted to be rid of him, and without royal backing Talleyrand's days in power were numbered. One of Talleyrand's last acts was to protest against the proposed allied peace terms. Prussia still wanted harsher penalties, but these terms were harsh enough. The allies were in no mood to listen to French protests. For Talleyrand, this was all academic; having threatened to resign, the Prince found that Louis XVIII took him up on the offer.[15]

In Talleyrand's place, the King appointed Armand Emmanuel du Plessis, duc de Richelieu, to head a new government. Stewart had previously warned about the influence of Richelieu, an émigré who had entered the Tsar's service. A liberal noble, Richelieu would become a very capable minister. However, writing to Gordon on 28 September, Stewart remained concerned by political developments in the French capital: 'I have not written to you lately, as the state of our negotiations have been so very uncertain & so undefined, I think the change of ministry is a court Intrigue & a R.[oyalist] plot, we must be upon our Guard in the North.' For some time, Stewart had been unhappy over the Tsar's influence in French politics. The appointment of Richelieu and the continued presence of Pozzo di Borgo, the Russian ambassador to France, were enough to give the British nightmares. Stewart warned Gordon, 'depend upon it the Empr [Alexander] outwits us all.'

France was witnessing a Royalist backlash against noted Napoleonic partisans, although the most prominent target, Marshal Ney, would not stand trial until November; found guilty of treason, he was condemned to death and shot in December. By this time, Stewart would be far away from Paris. The Emperor of Austria was about to leave on a tour of his Italian territories, and Lord Stewart was invited to accompany Francis I on his travels. This would mean a long absence from the embassy in Vienna, as he told Robert Gordon, 'I think the Emperor's stay in Italy will be till April or May next, this is a long period in these times, – however, I must go at present, & leave the future to take care of itself.' Turning to domestic French politics, Stewart was optimistic about the peace terms and believed that Richelieu would agree to the allied demands: 'I think the new Govt. will sign with us, they will yield the Enclaves, & we shall negotiate perhaps on the Cession of the particular Fortresses we demand en permanence.'[16]

Stewart's departure from Paris was scheduled for the beginning of October. However, before he could leave, the Ambassador had to deal with the mundane affairs of his finances. He wrote to Castlereagh on 3 October, having received news from his agents that 'it is not likely that the Salary of Ambassador up to the 4th of October will become in payment notwithstanding the new Regulations.' In that case, Stewart asked 'that in order to settle my Accounts previous to leaving Paris, I should wish to draw upon my Agents at the Foreign Office . . . the Sum of £2000 at Sixty Days Sight, and request in the event of the Salary to the above period not having been issued by the Treasury.'[17] Diplomatic life in Paris was clearly not cheap.

Stewart found himself travelling the roads of Europe once more, though now in peacetime. By 6 October, Stewart was at Dijon in Burgundy, where he again wrote letters on his financial affairs to Castlereagh. At least there were military diversions for Lord Stewart to enjoy in the form of an Austrian military display, and it never took much for the soldier to emerge in these letters to his brother.[18] Stewart's attendance on the Emperor was a great honour, but the Ambassador did not really appreciate it, as he confided to Robert Gordon:

> Metternich wrote to me in answer to my Enquiries as to attending the Empr. that none of the Diplomatick persons at the Court would be invited but as I had attended the Army, the Emperor would make particular & sole exception in

my favor my Brother wished me to avail myself of this, & altho' I had rather have gone to England until the Empr returns to Vienna, I have consented to Castlereagh's wishes, I mean to move about as much as I can, & if possible, see the whole of Italy.[19]

By 17 October, Stewart was writing to his brother from Geneva, to bring the merits of his private secretary, Major During, to Castlereagh's attention.[20] Stewart's absence from Paris meant that he was not party to the formal signing of the peace treaty agreed between the new Richelieu government and the allies. The second Treaty of Paris, signed on 20 November 1815, reduced France to its 1790 borders, created an army of occupation for between three and five years and imposed on the French government an indemnity of 700 million francs, on top of the charges levied for the upkeep of the occupying forces. The British, Austrian, Russian and Prussian governments also signed a new Quadruple Alliance on 20 November, further deepening their diplomatic ties, although the British were not enamoured of the Tsar's idea for a Holy Alliance between the nations. Alexander himself had already departed by this time, and on 12 November was 'enthusiastically and festively welcomed' in Warsaw when he entered the Polish capital on horseback.[21]

Stewart may have left Paris, but he was occupied by other affairs from the French capital, notably the financial circumstances of Admiral Sir Sidney Smith, who was resident in the city. Sir Sidney, a flamboyant and brilliant naval officer, who had earned the wrath of Napoleon himself, was another of the period's larger-than-life characters and in many ways cut from the same cloth as Stewart. It seemed as if Stewart was involved in so many different affairs, and with his customary attention to business he asked his brother 'if Govt. are likely to make him any and what advances'.[22]

Italian interlude and return to Vienna

By November, Lord Stewart had reached Venice. While in the city, Stewart wrote to Lord Burghersh to report his concerns about the French royal family: 'The Bourbons are behaving very foolishly – attempting to lower the Duke [of Wellington], I hear the Duc de Berri said Wellington could never be a great man, because Il est un Parvenu – The Duke of Wn told this story himself at a large dinner at Castlgh's, so it must be true.'[23] Stewart also wrote to Robert Gordon about the domestic arrangements of the embassy, while reassuring his colleague that he was being kept informed 'on all scandalous Topicks'. Stewart further reported that his ADCs 'long for the arrival of the Vienna Ladies You allude to, If they don't come soon, I think They will desert me.' Then came details of a bizarre romantic scrape: 'Mr. Griffiths tried to bamboozle me, & the Comtesse Zubeiski, to make love to me, Neither succeeded, & I gave Castlereagh the Information about him.' Gordon was obviously used to receiving such letters from his ambassador. Stewart stayed in Venice until December, before moving on to Milan. Always quick to pick up on political situations, the Ambassador passed on to Gordon his views of

Milanese attitudes towards the Habsburgs: 'The Austrians are held here <u>in horror</u>
It is a great pity but I fear they are too indolent slow & obstinate to change their
system, – the Empr is much more partial to the Venetians than the Milanese.'[24]

Stewart took the opportunity while in Milan to purchase a Titian for £1,200,
although 'Doubts were aft[erwar]ds thrown out' about the attribution. This
resulted in Clanwilliam's being sent to Rome with an introduction to Canova who
was under 'much obligation to Ld. C[astlerea]gh'. Canova convened a sitting of the
Accademia di San Luca, which then declared that the painting was not by Titian.[25]
Milan was also the scene for another of Stewart's personal episodes, as recalled by
Clanwilliam:

> Mrs F[itz]H[erber]t walking on the Milan Corso, on Ld. St[ewart]'s arm, her
> little son on the other side: – this boy tore x [across] the Corso, & kissed a young
> Hussar Officer. 'Why, my dear, how came you to know that gentleman?' on
> wh[ich]. the enfant terrible:- 'Oh, Ld. S., don't you know him? He always comes
> to Mama, when you go away.'[26]

The New Year brought two circulars from the foreign secretary to key British
ambassadors and ministers. Castlereagh's instructions, dated 1 January 1816,
showed how Britain was intimately involved in the affairs of mainland Europe and
wanted to be at the heart of international politics. The first was directed towards the
new treaty of alliance, formed 'for the preservation of the Peace, and independence
of Europe'. Britain's diplomats were to be proactive in 'cultivating the Confidence
of the ministers of those Powers . . . as having a common duty to perform' in
ensuring that Europe remained tranquil. The foreign secretary was also keen not
to isolate France. Castlereagh informed the duc de Richelieu that the treaty and
Wellington's appointment commanding the occupation forces arose from 'the
conciliatory, as well as liberal Views which animate the Allied Sovereigns to Louis
XVIII and his Kingdom, the first object of the Alliance in Truth being, to save
both, and through them the rest of Europe, from becoming a prey to revolutionary
Anarchy and Violence'.

Lord Castlereagh's instructions in his second circular were also very
clear: ambassadors and ministers were to write to the foreign secretary at least
once a week, the dispatch to be sent by the normal post or cipher, '& availing
yourself of any other opportunities as they may arise, to convey hence, whatever
further information you may judge likely to prove useful to His Royal Highness's
government'.[27] At the heart of all of this was still an unspoken fear about the future
of Louis XVIII's France. At the very least the allies were determined that events
in France would never again destabilize Europe. Stewart certainly saw diplomacy
in the same light, writing to William A'Court in Naples on 23 January: 'I own,
I consider all the efforts of us, Resident Ministers should strenuously be exerted
in urging in our respective situations the Decisions taken at Paris to be carried
forthwith into effect.'[28]

Castlereagh's successes would see the family further honoured in January
1816: Robert Stewart senior was promoted a step in the Irish peerage and created

first Marquess of Londonderry. However, for Lord Stewart the beginning of the New Year seemed rather lacklustre. After the excitements of the Congress of Vienna and the second downfall of Napoleon, a leisurely progress through Italy with the Emperor of Austria might have appeared somewhat dull. On 5 January, Stewart asked permission to host a ball to celebrate Queen Charlotte's birthday. Castlereagh was assured that the ball would cost a mere £400, which included supper at £160 and 'Wines and Refreshments' at £140.[29] There were also diplomatic conversations with Prince Metternich to be reported back to London, especially on alarms over Austrian relations with the Ottoman Empire and complaints about Bavaria.[30] However, this everyday diplomacy seems to have soon brought on one of Stewart's bouts of depression. Missing British company and society, which he had enjoyed to the full in Paris, Stewart was suddenly very vulnerable and alone.[31] Apologizing to his brother on 11 January for 'my blue Devils' which were 'somewhat constitutional', Stewart lamented that 'all the real good stuff of the family has been exhausted in Yourself.' The root of Stewart's depression might have been the realization that his role as a fighting ambassador was over. The idea of returning to peacetime Vienna was too much, and so an alternative scheme came into his head.

As the allied armies of occupation had been brought under the overall command of the Duke of Wellington, a new ambassador to France had been needed. In Wellington's place, Sir Charles Stuart had been appointed as Britain's representative. Stewart now wanted a transfer to take up this most glittering of diplomatic appointments.[32] Castlereagh was hardly likely to remove Stuart from Paris simply to accommodate his brother's whims, and the request was simply astonishing. Certainly Stewart was not thinking properly, and his depressive moods could obviously lead him seriously astray. Normally he was an astute diplomat, happy to carry out Castlereagh's instructions and help his brother in any way possible.

As if to make up for his behaviour, on 24 January Stewart wrote an overemotional letter to his brother, which was intended as a formal response to the instructions sent out by the Foreign Office in the New Year. Stewart assured Castlereagh, 'It would be difficult for me to convey to Your Lordship, the satisfaction & security that I shall in future feel, in fulfilling the Duties of the important Trust, committed to my Care, since my Course is marked out by so clear, so simple, & so satisfactory a Route.' Stewart was particularly impressed by the depth of Anglo-Austrian relations, while Metternich seemed to be a reformed character thanks to Castlereagh. Stewart reported: 'I should be most uncandid not to declare, that ever since Your Lordship has been in contact with Prince Metternich, his Character & Proceedings, in all points, bear a new aspect.' Stewart now looked forward to the birth of a new style of diplomacy, the 'Congress System', pioneered at Vienna and Paris:

> What has occurred of late, at Vienna, & Paris is a new diplomatic Era in History – May the advantage of it, be so appreciated, as to induce every 3 or 4 Years a reunion of the same Men, or those that fill their exalted positions, for the

purpose of keeping down petty Intrigue & Cabal; and consolidating from time
to time, more firmly, the great work of Peace they have Achieved.[33]

Showing his value to Castlereagh, Stewart advised that he was on 'the most
agreeable' terms with Metternich, while 'Count Stackelberg, the Russian Minister
here, is equally unreserved with me – General Krausemark, the Prussian Minister
(when he arrives) is a very old & intimate friend of mine, & we had the satisfaction
of observing the Prince of Sweden together.'[34]

Stewart was kept busy in Italy and following instructions received from
Castlereagh, the Ambassador had managed to conduct a long conversation with
Cardinal Litta, a senior Vatican official, to discuss 'the Religious Differences
existing between the Court of Rome & the King of the Netherlands', a discussion
which then touched on the Catholic population in Ireland.[35] Metternich had
also shown Stewart the latest dispatch from the Austrian ambassador to Spain,
Prince Kaunitz. Writing to Castlereagh on 3 February, Stewart reported that the
Austrian diplomat had presented 'a very unfavorable picture of the Conduct of
King Ferdinand and the Acts of the Government and the Intrigue and Spirit of
Party that reigns'. The Spanish army was reportedly 'wholly disorganized, and in
want of every Equipment but extremely disaffected especially towards the King'
while 'the Nation seems chiefly governed by the Monks, who yield in all Things
to the King's will'. As for Ferdinand VII himself, 'the main feature' of the King's
character 'seems to be a dread least he should be supposed to be influenced by the
Minister He employs'.

The Spanish were seeking a marriage alliance with Austria, as a counter to 'the
extreme discontent that still prevails at the Arrangement of Congress with regard
to the Duchies of Parma, Placentia and Guastalla . . . for the purpose of securing
the Reversion of the possessions of Italy to a younger Branch of the Spanish
Dynasty'. Ferdinand VII 'never could be satisfied with the Decisions at Congress'
and accordingly 'there was in preparation a Manifesto of His Majesty's Sentiments
more particularly on the Conduct held by Austria, which would be sent officially
to all the Courts of Europe.' Stewart further wrote of the 'great Intrigues in all
Quarters on the Subject' of Ferdinand's intended marriage into the Portuguese
royal house, and 'the extreme Jealousy of the Prince Regent of Sicily against His
Brother Prince Leopold, who it is said is to marry an Austrian Princess, and
separate Naples from Sicily, which is averred to be in contemplation'.[36]

Realizing that he was soon returning to Vienna, Stewart now wrote another
extraordinary letter from Milan to Robert Gordon, on the sexual conduct expected
from the embassy. Having dined with Major During and the Earl of Clanwilliam,
the Ambassador set out his thoughts:

> During & Clanwilliam arrivd this day & we have had a quiet dinner talking over
> Vienna Politicks Scandal Love Affairs &c. I have been very much amused – But
> indeed I should be unhappy by my Indiscretions to throw a State of Suspicion
> on your virtuous & moral Character, – The Wife of a friend ought to be sacred,
> I hope in my reflecting moments that I hold this Creed, But I am not quite sure

I can carry that Doctrine to His Mistress, You see how candid I am, & if I ventur'd to suppose You capable of an Offence, at least, I am sure, I could commit it without much Remorse Myself. If the Temptation was very great. You should not however, altho You are Diplomatick, be uncandid with a friend, on such a free Subject as Women, & I doubt whether You give me in your Broadbottom'd friend the real Reason for your Squeamishness. I should rather take Your Criterion of Report, & attribute Your horror, to some rounder bottom'd reason –

However it is my Business to be silent & not to say more – Us Englishmen abroad, have only one way of carrying on the War, And Don't fly out at my depravity when I lay it down We should defend each other, through thick & thin, – We should amuse ourselves, as much as possible, And knowing the Tenure of our Wild Oats to be short, We should spend them lavishly – But when we touch on Morality or lasting Attachment, I believe these Tenets can only exist in England when strengthened by Divine Law which aids Human Wisdom in the Contract, – I give you my Creed honestly, But if You shew me up in the Capital of the Austrian Dominions – I am ruin[e]d forever.[37]

Stewart's frustrations at this time were made worse by the perceived failures of the Austrian administration in Italy, and he had wasted no effort in denigrating Habsburg rule in Milan to Castlereagh, comparing it unfavourably to its previous position as a court city under the French.[38] On 4 February, Stewart set down a long and thoughtful letter on Austrian deficiencies. Stewart, with typical understatement, commented, 'All these proceedings are certainly impolitick and unwise, But I believe are really more to be attributed to the particular turn of the Emperor's Mind and Habits, and to the slow uniform, unchangeable and unchanged Mode in which the Austrians conduct their publick Affairs, than to any despotical or improper feelings towards this Country.' Although Metternich was 'disposed to see Things in a point of View infinitely more liberal and congenial to the Sentiments of this Nation . . . He has a party to manage whom He cannot always overcome.'[39] Domestic problems also arose while Stewart was in Milan, notably the residence of the British embassy in Vienna. Stewart had to conduct negotiations through Robert Gordon for purchasing the Starhemberg Palace, with the Ambassador prepared to pay £15,000 for the house 'with all the fixtures, Glass and Tapestry as it stands' and a further £4,000 to £5,000 for furniture.[40]

On 8 February, Stewart told the Foreign Office that the Emperor Francis was no longer travelling to Florence but would remain in Milan, make a tour of several towns and then return to Vienna. As there would be no accommodation for foreign diplomats, or for that matter the presence of Prince Metternich, who intended to travel to Rome and Naples, Stewart would not be in attendance. Instead, Stewart proposed 'either seeing the remainder of Italy or returning to Germany and Vienna'. This plan would at least ensure he was 'near some general Source of Information in order that I should not be supposed this Year to be desirous of leaving those duties which have been so graciously entrusted to me, and which I endeavor to fulfil, as well as I am able'.[41] However, while the court remained in Milan, Stewart continued to report on Austrian politics, including the continued concerns of war with the

Ottoman Empire, 'Russian intrigue in Italy' and the reactions to the publication of Alexander's Holy Alliance. To this last point, Stewart wrote rather dismissively, 'I think one can never sufficiently rejoice that the Prince Regent has Kept clear of committing His Name, to a Document, which, however harmless, it may be viewed in one Sense will ever be incontrovertibly stamped with Ridicule and Folly in the other.'[42] Russian diplomacy was very much on Austria's mind in early 1816, and on 2 March Stewart advised London of Austrian alarm over the closeness of Sardinia and Russia.[43]

Stewart left Milan on 24 March for what Clanwilliam described as 'a ridiculously rapid tour to Florence, Rome & Naples'. The Earl, who accompanied Stewart, noted that the reason for this rush was not political, but sprang from Stewart's 'having sentimentally promised to drive the D[uche]ss of Sagan in the Prater on May 1, a day of fête'.[44] On 5 April, Stewart reported from Florence that he had not met with Prince Metternich, who had decided to stay in Verona. The Austrian court had received news that Maria Ludovika, Empress of Austria, was dying, and so Stewart thought it likely that Metternich, in consequence, had changed his plans. While he was in Florence, Stewart had cause to gently reprove William A'Court, Britain's minister to Naples. A'Court had wanted Stewart to use his influence with Metternich to ensure the retention of Prince Jablonowski as Austrian ambassador to Naples. Stewart point blank refused, telling A'Court 'were I to use any little Influence which the Habit of close confidence with Prince Metternich might admit of I should think it was the very mode of losing the good opinion, that I naturally wish He should entertain of me.' From Florence, Stewart travelled on to Rome, where he learned that the Empress had died, and that the Austrian court was to return to Vienna.[45]

After visiting Rome, Stewart headed south to Naples, before journeying again to Florence. Writing to Castlereagh from that city on 23 April, Stewart took the opportunity to attack the conduct of Sir Charles Stuart in Paris. When he was in Naples, Stewart had seen a letter from Stuart to William A'Court 'in which the former begs the British Minister at Naples, to urge Mons. De Blacas's immediate return to France, stating that no Man will be so happy to see Him as Himself, and that nothing could be more important for the Country'. Stewart advised, 'Of this I do not pretend to judge but if I am not mistaken, Your Lordship's Sentiments as well as the Allies go to upholding the Duke of Richelieu and the present Ministers, and I doubt whether Mons. De Blacas's return would add strength to a Government which seems already overpowered by the party of the Thuilleries [sic].' The comte de Blacas, a royal favourite, was 'evidently, by his Language at Naples, placing all Acts of the present Government in France in the weakest and most invidious point of View'. Stewart continued, 'I understand He told Mr. A'Court, in Answer to Sir Charles Stuart's Message, that He was desirous of having an Order for His return in the King's own hand, but I have reason to believe, from information I received at Naples, that He is intriguing in every Quarter, to manage it.' Stewart undoubtedly enjoyed writing this, but he was right in advising of any potential destabilizing influences on Restoration France. However, his Italian journey was now at an end, and it was time to return to Vienna.[46]

The past few months had been rather unreal, as Stewart wrote to his father from Vienna on 5 May, recalling the events of his Italian tour, complaining to Lord Londonderry that 'the Country itself, (except immediately round Naples, The Lakes, & about Florence) very far behind any that I have before travers[e]d . . . The Climate far less agreeable in Winter than our own.' The population did not escape censure, as 'the Men are throughout the Country detestable, and I hardly saw a real beautiful woman.' At least Florence, which seemed 'to be the Head Quarters of the English in Italy', had its charms:

> There is an entire Colony of our Countrymen here . . . The Grand Duke's Court is very insignificant, & my friend Burghersh has really a sinecure, but amuses himself with the delights of Musick, in which He excels & He has a conclave of Squallers, male & female, who vibrate by his nod . . . He keeps a very hospitable & agreeable House, & is very much lik'd, – The Gallery at Florence for its unrivall'd Titians & other famous Pictures, & for its Venus, & Statues demand the utmost admiration, The Cathedral is also here magnificent, & the Town particularly clean & well pav'd.[47]

Stewart also recalled a seemingly trivial incident at Rome, which revealed the high regard in which Britain was held in mainland Europe, much to the annoyance of the French ambassador to the Holy See, when 'Cardinal Consalvi (Matilda's old Congress Beau) recogniz'd me . . . He seiz'd me by the Arm, & forc'd me up in my Shabby Blue Coat & Boots on the head of the Seat of the Corps Diplomatique.' The French ambassador 'publicly declar'd the following morning That He never consider'd England so great a Nation until He saw the crouching & Adulation of a Minister of the Church of Rome, to a wand[e]ring English Ambassador'. From Rome, Stewart had proceeded to Naples, but as he told Lord Londonderry, before leaving, he had paid his duty 'both to His Holiness the Pope (who gave me an Audience in his Night Cap at 7 in the morning,) and also to the King of Naples'. At the end of his journey, Stewart had accomplished the journey back to Vienna in nine days, rather worried that he had 'neglected' his 'official Correspondence'.

Lord Stewart might have neglected his duties a little, but he was still held in high regard, and the Prince Regent showed his continuing favour by making the Ambassador a Knight Grand Cross of the Royal Guelphic Order. Stewart was delighted at this honour, telling his father, 'I have been made happy lately by the Princes continued favors and Rewards to me, He has sent me the Grand Cross of the Hanoverian Order for the treaty I made with Prussia obtaining the Principality of Hildesheim &c for the new Kingdom & for my military exertions with their Army in 1814.' Well might Stewart tell his father that he was 'deeply sensible of the constant Affection' that the Regent showed him.[48]

The Royal Guelphic Order had been founded the year before. Although a Hanoverian Order, it was bestowed on a number of British subjects and became a way for the Regent to reward those who had been at the forefront of the military and diplomatic efforts against France, or who had been closely involved in Hanoverian affairs.[49] Stewart was certainly a worthy recipient. The Prince Regent would often use the classes of the Royal Guelphic Order to reward those who undertook personal services, a significance which would become apparent to Stewart when he became the spymaster in the Caroline Affair.[50]

Stewart had returned to Vienna to begin life as a peacetime diplomat, although he unhappily reported to Burghersh on 5 May:

> I hear all our salaries are about to be reduced ... The F.O. write in horrible Spirits losing their Candle Ends & Cheese Parings, Castlereagh says – The Nation last Year would have given Millions to save the Continent – at the Moment, The Continent & those who sav'd it sink into insignificance compar'd with our Imaginary Saving by the reduction of some trifling Office of 1000 £ a year.[51]

He still yearned for a leave of absence, but Stewart was back at work, writing to Castlereagh on 11 May to bring Captain Browne to his attention, who 'in addition to Major During my private Secretary' was 'considered as one of the Attachés, to whom some small Allowance may be accorded, the other young Noblemen are not in want of such Assistance'. Stewart had the highest praise for Browne's 'Efficacy, Attention and Diligence' and hoped he would receive a favourable response for 'an Object I have so much at heart'.[52]

There was actually little to report, with Stewart confirming on 21 May that Metternich had still not arrived back in Vienna. It was not until 10 June, that the frank diplomatic conversations with the Austrian foreign minister were reported again back to London. The Emperor Francis was due to return to his capital that month, and Stewart was able to tell Castlereagh that Metternich had 'alluded to the necessity of looking out for another Wife . . . His [the Emperor's] Interior would never be comfortable without one, and so strong are His passions, that His Health in a state of Celibacy would be soon affected.' In particular, Metternich sought a match with the Prussians, as 'An Alliance with the Crown of Prussia would be the most desirable and salutary Event possible for Austria.'[53]

Stewart was close to Metternich. This would prove invaluable to Castlereagh, who championed the warm friendship that now existed between London and Vienna, a situation which had seemed impossible a few years earlier. Stewart was very much the trusted confidante of the British foreign secretary and could be used as a conduit to the Austrian foreign minister, as is attested by a remarkable letter Stewart sent to Castlereagh on 23 June. Stewart had been ordered to sound out Metternich's views on Russian diplomatic overtures towards Britain. This had been delayed thanks to the Ambassador's falling ill, and to the Emperor Francis's return to Vienna, but Stewart had finally managed to hold 'two very long and confidential Conversations'. The first conversation had been held before Metternich had conferred with Francis I, the second just afterwards. Stewart 'ascertained immediately in the first Interview, that as yet the Emperor of Russia nor His Ministers had not addressed themselves to this Court in any Overture of a similar nature to that which has been under Consideration of the British Government'.

Stewart had been given discretionary powers to show Castlereagh's views on Russia to Metternich, and his dispatch is a testimony to the importance placed on relations between London and Vienna. Stewart admitted that he felt out of his depth trying to lucidly explain British policy towards Russia without the benefit of showing Castlereagh's own opinions. The Ambassador elaborated further on the difference of approach between the two courts over Russia:

> The Course of policy adopted by the British Cabinet towards Russia, has been hitherto stamped with Wisdom by its Success. But I do not think Prince Metternich feels that an exactly similar policy would do for the Court of Austria. The Approximation of their Dominions, Their great Military Array, Their History from time immemorial, afford a thousand points of Jealousy and foment numberless Bickerings, which never can enter into the relative Situation of Great Britain and Russia.[54]

The Ambassador developed his analysis, writing, 'The Difference that seems to exist, in Prince Metternich's Views of Your Lordship's Management of the Emperor of Russia, and His own arises in Your Lordship's general Desire, of yielding to His Imperial Majesty in little points.' The letter continued with Metternich's less than flattering opinion of Russia, together with Stewart's role in smoothing these differences:

> He thinks the national Character (independent of the Emperor's particular turn) overbearing, presumptuous and persevering against moderation, and Compliance, He is strongly disposed to believe that in proportion as You are passive, the Emperor of Russia will be Active . . .
>
> I told Prince Metternich in Reply although there might be Shades in your separate Opinions as to the Management of the Emperor, You both had the same End in View, and I believed in fact were very little separated, further than Circumstances or occasional Experiences gave stronger or lighter Shades to Your rising feelings.[55]

Castlereagh was also asked to take the Austrian ambassador to the United Kingdom, Prince Esterházy, into his confidence, in the same way that Stewart had been taken into Metternich's.[56] Stewart was now in a position of the highest trust and importance in the new post-Napoleonic world. Castlereagh saw Metternich and the Austrians as vital to his policies, and who better to have in Vienna, at the heart of a new international diplomatic network, than his own brother, Lord Stewart? It was hardly surprising that Castlereagh did not want to move his brother to the seemingly more glamorous posting of Paris. This letter, written just over a year after the Battle of Waterloo, sums up the nature of the ties between Castlereagh and Metternich, with Stewart and Esterházy the trusted agents of British and Austrian diplomacy.

Stewart took to peacetime diplomacy quickly, regularly sending his brother clear and insightful accounts of Austrian and wider European politics. Stewart was also part of a wider group of leading British diplomats, who wrote to each other on the affairs of their respective courts. Britain's pre-eminent position among the great European powers was seemingly assured; a situation encouraged and applauded by Lord Castlereagh at the Foreign Office. Stewart's role though was undergoing a change, even as he settled back into life in Vienna. While in Milan, he had already assembled and passed on information about the lifestyle of Caroline, Princess of Wales, the hated wife of the Prince Regent. This marriage would have a direct bearing on Stewart's career, as he would spend the next few years using his privileged contacts to become a rather exalted spymaster. The Ambassador would work closely with Captain Browne, put forward by Stewart for special recognition from the Foreign Office. The Caroline Affair would ensure that Stewart was not only at the centre of the new Congress Europe era of diplomacy, but also at the centre of a dysfunctional royal marriage.[57]

Chapter 10

THE CAROLINE AFFAIR

The 1795 marriage of George, Prince of Wales, and his first cousin, Caroline of Brunswick, was an unmitigated disaster. Perhaps it is unfair to say that she stank and he got drunk, but it is not that far from reality. The Prince of Wales, unimpressed with his wife's appearance and hygiene, had called for drink on their first meeting; on her part, she thought he was fat. Things went downhill from there. On their wedding day, the Prince was clearly the worse for wear. That evening the heir to the throne was still inebriated. However, at some point the couple consummated the marriage, and in 1796 Caroline gave birth to a daughter, Princess Charlotte of Wales, now second in the line of succession to George III. As the two royals could not stand the sight of each other, there was little chance of Charlotte being joined by siblings. By 1797 the couple had separated. Caroline was far from blameless, but she had been treated with a lack of respect, especially by her husband's current mistress. However, at the bottom of the whole business was a simple truth – the couple could not stand one another.

The formal separation meant that Caroline did not feel constrained as to how she conducted her life and the Princess began her own career of scandal. In the process, she would outdo her husband's famed affairs. This was a time when the law decreed that a Princess of Wales found guilty of adultery was committing high treason, a crime punishable by death. As the years went by, rumours about Caroline's lifestyle at her house in Blackheath, specifically about an alleged string of lovers, including George Canning and Thomas Lawrence, grew so much that even George III felt obliged to launch an investigation. This so-called 'Delicate Investigation' of 1806 dismissed rumours that a boy called William Austin was her illegitimate child, but condemned her conduct towards the opposite sex, which was deemed as inappropriate.

After the Prince of Wales became Regent in 1811, Caroline lost her only real protector in the royal family, as the King had always been fond of the Princess. Excluded from official life, the Princess of Wales looked across the Channel for a means of escape. After the first fall of Napoleon in 1814, mainland Europe was free to visitors from Britain. The Prince Regent was more than happy at the thought of his wife's departure. To a certain extent, this view was shared by Lord Liverpool's government. Negotiations were conducted between the Princess and Lord Castlereagh. Caroline was offered £50,000 a year to simply go away. This was accepted, and leaving her daughter behind, Caroline left Britain in August. The Prince Regent was delighted to be rid of her, and undoubtedly hoped that he would never have to set eyes on his wife again.

Caroline at first headed for Brunswick, but decided that Italy would be more to her taste. This caused headaches for the British government. After a sojourn in Rome, she headed for Naples, still under the rule of Joachim Murat. This was especially irritating for Britain, which wanted to see Murat deprived of his kingdom. Luckily for Lord Liverpool's administration, at the outbreak of new hostilities with Napoleon, Caroline left Naples behind. Travelling to Genoa, Caroline moved on to Milan, and then purchased a house on Lake Como, which she named the Villa d'Este. All the while the Regent had not been idle and 'had ordered his spies to follow Caroline, less for political reasons than to furnish him with evidence that might secure a divorce'.[1] In late 1815, Caroline departed on further travels, which included journeys to Sicily, Tunis, Malta and the Ottoman Empire. From Constantinople, Caroline travelled to the Holy Land, before returning to Austrian-ruled Italy.

The Caroline Affair now had a profound effect on Lord Stewart's career. His Majesty's ambassador to Vienna had little option but to become embroiled in this disastrous marriage. Stewart was always more than simply the recipient of intelligence passed on by spies. An active participant from the outset, Stewart would grow in the role to effectively become the director of the surveillance operation on Caroline.[2] His earliest involvement can be seen in reports to his brother from Milan, when he was accompanying the Emperor of Austria on his Italian tour. In a most secret letter of 9 January 1816, Stewart reported on 'a Subject which equally interests an Englishman & an individual plac[e]d in the High Situation which I unworthily fill, in a private manner rather than in an official form'. Stewart was being very cautious at this early stage, but felt duty-bound to pass on what he had heard of the Princess, who had recently left the city:

> Not but what I conceive I have ample grounds for representing in the most responsible manner to the Prince Regents Government all the scandalous Stories in general circulation here with regard to the Princess of Wales, but until I know how far delicacy would operate in the minds of the Prince Regents Ministers in concealing such unpleasant circumstances as I may detail, I am unwilling to give any official record.[3]

Stewart was 'very much in the dark as to all that the Law requires' but ventured to add 'I can entertain no doubt that the Scandalous publicity of the Anecdotes about the Princess of Wales will justify the Govt. in sending a proper professional person to reside at this place.' Stewart was in effect asking for a government spy to ascertain the veracity of what he had heard second-hand from the Austrians. In setting the tone for later operations, Stewart advised that although Prince Metternich had helpfully supplied him with the details of Caroline's behaviour, he 'would be sorry that the Austrian Govt., appear'd prominent or active in what they are not immediately concernd'. As Stewart warmed to his theme, he told his brother that if Caroline's 'conduct was not so scandalously profligate and the Taste exhibited so depraved, I really should have had difficulty in writing all this'.[4]

One of the Regent's early spies was a former Hanoverian official, Baron Ompteda, described by a contemporary supporter of Caroline as a man 'who bore his mortal ennui, and his disgrace with him into Italy. Drawn on by his promises, he degraded himself by the infamous trade of a spy'.[5] Ompteda had been recommended to the Prince Regent by Count Münster, the Hanoverian minister in London. The Baron's background is a timely reminder that the Prince Regent was also heir to the throne of Hanover. The Hanoverian politicians were 'especially concerned' to secure a divorce. Princess Charlotte could not succeed in Hanover due to Salic Law, but any disputed son from Caroline, however far-fetched a notion, could store up future problems for the Hanoverian succession.[6] Ompteda attached himself to the Princess while she was in Naples, and followed her to Milan. Although the Baron at first managed to fool the Princess, it seemed that his true purpose had not escaped the ever watchful Austrian spy network, as Stewart informed Castlereagh in early February. Stewart also outlined a possible counter-espionage operation being conducted in London, perhaps paranoia, but certainly worthy of a Regency melodrama:

> First, it appears the Prince Regent's Conduct is watched by some Person or Persons employed about his Person
>   Secondly – The Correspondence of the Princess of Wales in London and the Object & Purport of the mission She has sent there, may possibly be detected.[7]

The letter is filled with other pieces of information, including details of an informant, dubbed 'The Painter', who 'has not yet made any further disclosures, He has been absent at Como, I shall not let him sleep'. Before signing off, Stewart asked his brother if the Prince Regent could be induced to write a personal letter of thanks to Metternich 'for the very Secret and private Information He gives me and will continue to do from time to time'. Stewart believed that such a letter 'would flatter him . . . as he likes a little Attention' and would ensure continued cooperation from the Austrians, vital 'as nothing can elude the Police, No Post Office, Escritoire, or desk are safe from them'.[8]

Stewart soon changed gear in terms of spying, and in the process brought a man who would prove to be one of his most trusted friends into the operation. Captain (Thomas) Henry Browne was a talented young officer, who had earned the high regard of the Duke of Wellington. He had served with Stewart in the Peninsular War as deputy assistant adjutant general, and in common with many officers had returned home on half pay at the end of hostilities.[9] It had been the Hundred Days campaign that had brought the two men together again, when Stewart offered Browne the role of an ADC. Browne served with Stewart throughout, and after it was all over, accompanied the Ambassador to Paris in the summer of 1815. Returning with Lord Stewart to Vienna, Browne was appointed as private secretary to the Vienna embassy.[10] Browne, soon to be promoted to major, now enjoyed a far different role as the Ambassador's chief intelligence gatherer, working alongside another of Stewart's ADCs and private secretaries, Major George During.

As Stewart told his brother in a private and most secret communication of 13 February 1816, Browne was dispatched, along with During, to gather more hard facts about the Princess of Wales's alleged adultery. Stewart assured Castlereagh that he was 'fully aware this Business is of the most delicate nature, & until your excellent Advice, I had only my own Judgement to direct me'. He further advised Castlereagh that he had 'studiously avoided appearing in any shape in the Enquiries and During & Browne in their Interviews with the Painters &c have made use of every precaution are still unknown & have given no Rewards whatever'. Castlereagh had asked for 'English witnesses', but the Ambassador foresaw difficulties with this as the Princess's household was now 'nearly compos[e]d of Italians . . . few English if any would remain when so much disgusting Scandal is going forward'. Stewart reiterated the need for the British government to send 'a professional person here' who could gather the evidence together and forward witnesses for any future hearing in Britain, and 'would in like manner be placed in an underhand way in complete communication with the Austrian Police'. Stewart again warned that all of this needed to be done with the utmost discretion, as Prince Metternich remained anxious to prevent the Austrian government from becoming entangled in this affair, before suggesting to his brother how things might be arranged:

> The case stands thus, – The Facts & Crime must be discovered, – But The Informants & the principal Instruments of bringing the whole to Light must be kept in the back ground because the Love of upholding Decent Morality would not, in this malicious World be so attributed to them, as the desire of favoring the Prince Regents wishes.[11]

Stewart wrote about the current spy in the Princess's circle, Baron Ompteda, who had adopted the guise of 'an Illustrious Hanoverian Traveller – My Countenance was not the least necessary to the Sphere He already moved in before my Arrival'. Although Ompteda had approached Stewart for an introduction to the Imperial court, and had been invited on one occasion to the British embassy, the Ambassador had then 'avoided communication with him'. Once more showing his proactive role in this spy network, Stewart argued that Ompteda was of 'too high a Line to ferret out that Information, which a more Subaltern Individual, without the fear of compromising himself might achieve'. Clearly a high-class spy was seen as too risky, especially if he had a reputation to preserve. Stewart hoped that the foreign secretary would see things his way, and, always eager for his brother's assurance, added, 'I shall be very happy if you think I have acted prudently – & with sufficient circumspection.' Stewart's letter then touched on the issue of 'Ocular Demonstration'. The nature of this was laid out with extraordinary frankness by Stewart:

> This is always a very nice & difficult point & I wish you well to consider whether the excessive Indelicacy that the greatest Liberties would denote, between a

Princess of Wales, & a Common Courier, & Valet de Chambre, – Such as "kissing" rolling of the grass, Slapping on the Posteriors &c, would not in any Judicial proceeding go nearly as far as ocular Demonstration, or would the difference in the Situation of the parties in Life, be argued the other way as making the act improbable notwithstanding the Liberties.[12]

Stressing once more his inadequacy to conduct a spying operation, Stewart wondered if 'the placing the sifting & arranging the matter for the mature consideration of the Prince Regents Government in this Affair' could be given to 'some excellent Professional Man on the Spot'.

Stewart's letter then changed tack and turned to a matter only indirectly associated with the Princess of Wales, the proposed bridegroom of Princess Charlotte, Prince Leopold of Saxe-Coburg-Saalfeld. Charlotte had originally been engaged to the Peninsular War veteran the Hereditary Prince of Orange. Breaking the engagement off, Charlotte had later fallen for the charms of Leopold, a handsome but penniless suitor, and an officer in the service of Alexander I. Stewart, who clearly had good first-hand knowledge of Leopold, was asked for his insider information on the potential consort of a future queen. Stewart wrote that Leopold would 'do as well' as any other possible husband, while in terms of politics the Prince was 'certainly when I first knew him attached pretty strongly to the Emp[ero]r. of R[ussia]. – He changed latterly at Vienna.' Having clearly discussed the potential bridegroom with Metternich, Stewart could tell his brother that Leopold was held in high regard by the Austrians. Stewart then passed on more personal facts, telling Castlereagh, 'The Women (who after all are the best Judges) – say He is a little Canting and Sly. – Whether he kept aloof from Vienna Charms, or whether His physical powers are not beyond par, I will not determine, If the former, I conclude He will be more acceptable, If the latter, I should doubt whether He would not be less.' It is best left to the imagination how Stewart came by this information. Perhaps they had shared some of the same lovers, or Metternich had helpfully shown him Leopold's secret police file, while delicately not mentioning the bundles of surveillance reports on the Ambassador himself. Rather as an afterthought, Stewart devoted the last part of the letter to official business, dealing with Austria and Russia, which demonstrates how much of his time was now being taken up by royal business.[13]

Bartolomeo Pergami

The 'Common Courier & Valet de Chambre' mentioned by Stewart was an Italian called Bartolomeo Pergami. Stewart, in common with many others, referred to him as 'Bergami'. This man was to be the focus of the investigations into the Princess's conduct, and many would come to believe that he was Caroline's lover. If only this could be proved, then the Prince Regent would have ample grounds to be divorced from his hated wife. Pergami had been the Princess's courier but was promoted to major-domo by Caroline, who 'soon moved with him and his entire family into the Villa d'Este'.[14] Rumours had followed the pair as they travelled from late 1815, and details of their sleeping arrangements, of Caroline's clothes, and other sundry potential scandals were all to be analysed by the British government.[15]

Only when Caroline returned to the Villa d'Este in the summer of 1816 did she discover that Ompteda's attachment to her was not what it had seemed. It appeared that Ompteda had clumsily tried to bribe one of the Princess's servants during Caroline's absence, which had led the servant to confess all.[16] Caroline had been rapidly disabused, and her reaction was perhaps too gleefully reported by Stewart to his brother on 18 November. Perhaps feeling vindicated about Ompteda, Stewart wrote, 'I understand in consequence of the Princess's Suspicions she prevailed on an Englishman to challenge O[mpteda] in the true Stile [*sic*] of female profligacy satisfied to make these two men blow each others brains out'.[17] This was the end of the Baron Ompteda's career as a spy. It would also have been the end of Ompteda's existence if the 'Englishman' in question, one of the British members of Caroline's household, Joseph Hownam, had succeeded in killing him.

Stewart in the meantime continued to channel Austrian intelligence on the Princess to his brother. On 27 November, he informed Castlereagh that he had received more news on Caroline via Metternich, which 'are amusing in detail, but there is little of moment'. He also reported that Caroline had visited the former French empress, Marie Louise, in Parma, and on Ompteda's continued troubles from Hownam.[18] However, Lord Stewart's contempt for Caroline and for the low-born Pergami was given full rein in a most secret and private communication to Castlereagh of 13 December. It was bad enough that Pergami was foreign, it was even worse that he had been a courier. That such a man should be in the intimate company of the Princess of Wales was a complete travesty to Stewart.

The issue concerned Pergami's right to wear three Orders of Chivalry within Austrian territories. The decorations in question were those of the Order of Malta, the Order of the Holy Sepulchre and the Order of Caroline of Jerusalem. This third Order was a recent invention of Caroline, while the other two had been obtained for Pergami at the behest of the Princess. The Emperor certainly raised objections to the Order of Caroline, the official Imperial response being that 'as it is only the privilege of Reigning and Acknowledged Sovereigns to institute Decorations' no permission could be given. In a noticeable slip of that urbane mask, Lord Stewart added, 'The whole of these Transactions are really so very ridiculous, that it is difficult to treat them in any Manner, but as the offspring of a weak or insane Mind'.[19] Perhaps Stewart was venting his frustration at having to spend so much time on this affair, or maybe he really did think Caroline was somewhat unhinged.

The gossip and surveillance continued. On 5 February 1817, Stewart forwarded a report from Milan which 'is very horrid as it is really disgusting but P Metternich assures me it is undoubted Truth!!' Unfortunately, the disgusting report has not survived, but judging by later accounts it is all too easy to imagine these were yet more accounts of Pergami's relationship with the Princess, or gossip on their respective bedroom arrangements. In some despair Stewart added, 'What a melancholy thing it is for the Nation to be so disgraced!!' However, he could report that one of Caroline's female servants had arrived in Vienna. Stewart would investigate further: 'I know not if she can give any good or important Information, but by the next opportunity I shall endeavour to discover.'[20] It was certainly a comedown for Stewart to be involved in marshalling the various reports on a middle-aged Princess and her alleged Italian lover.

Even when the Princess of Wales was on her travels, Stewart could not be rid of her. Caroline was seen in Bavaria in March 1817, prompting the British minister to Stuttgart, Brook Taylor, to frantically write that the King of Württemberg was terrified that she would cross into his kingdom.[21] A little while later, Stewart had to deal with more issues, as Caroline had complained about the lack of respect shown to her by the Austrian authorities. Metternich had helpfully shown Stewart her original letter. To this effort Stewart, whose urbane exterior seemed to be slipping regularly now, could only bring himself to comment to his brother, 'The letter exhibits throughout such strange want of orthography & strange Expressions that it must excite the greatest mirth & ridicule.'[22]

At least up to this point, Caroline had kept away from his embassy. Stewart's peace of mind was to be rudely shattered when his brother informed him that the Princess of Wales was likely to head for the Austrian capital.[23] On 6 April 1817, Caroline informed 'the English Ambassadeur Lord Stuart [*sic*]' that she would expect the use of the Embassy when she arrived into Vienna, along with rooms for her retinue.[24] If Stewart had shown distaste for Caroline at a distance, then this was nothing as to how he felt about her in close proximity. Stewart did not reply until 8 April, and, careful to show respect to her title, if not for her, he assured Caroline that 'in replying to Her R[oyal] H[ighness] with the utmost Sincerity He will not be considered as deficient in the profound Respect due to the High and Illustrious name HRH bears.' He was not able alas to acquiesce in Caroline's request. Firstly, perhaps a little imperiously, Stewart informed the Princess of Wales that he did not 'recognize the Authority from any Instructions He ever saw or heard of that would authorize Her Royal Highness to take possession of an Ambassadorial Residence at a moments Notice'. Further, he was not 'prepared to admit that in the Capital of Vienna Her Royal Highness is to assume Her Rights as Wife of the Prince Regent after the usual Etiquette'. As a final insult, he added that had this 'been in contemplation Lord Stewart apprehends He would have received the Commands of that Prince and that Government Whom alone He serves'. As a practical afterthought, Stewart advised the Princess that as the embassy had 'only one Floor furnished' this 'entirely precludes the Accom[m]odation Her Royal Highness orders, and Vienna does not afford the facilities of procuring furniture for such a Suite in a few hours'.[25]

Confronted with the royal ogre in Vienna, Stewart decided to take a diplomatic holiday, and to take the embassy with him. When Caroline turned up, Stewart was not in attendance. Joseph Hownam wrote to the Ambassador 'to express the astonishment of Her Royal Highness in finding His Lordship had just left for the country. Her Royal Highness requests His Lordship will wait upon her as soon as possible.'[26] Stewart must have known that he would be secure in the Prince Regent's and the foreign secretary's approbation for his decision to insult the Princess of Wales in the Austrian capital. The Emperor of Austria had also declared that it was impossible for Pergami to be received at court, and perhaps following Lord Stewart's lead, Francis had also ordered Prince Metternich to advise Caroline 'that on account of different preparations & affairs, in which the Emperor was engaged' she could not be received either. Stewart hoped that Castlereagh would approve of his actions: 'I shall deeply lament if Your Lordship is of opinion, that in maintaining what I consider as the Dignity of the King's Representative, at this Imperial Court, I have departed from the line of prescribed respect, which the Title of H.R.H. demands.' Stewart added that he did not see why he should be 'turned out of my House, not to make way alone for H.R.H., but for Italians . . . & God knows whom'.[27]

The snub to the Princess was absolute. One of the attachés, Thomas Cartwright, had been left in charge. As Stewart made clear to his brother, the next most senior figure, Robert Gordon, along with 'the rest of the Embassy had accompanied me out of Town'.[28] To have left a minor official in charge was a very calculated insult, and the Princess and her household were furious. Hownam wrote to Cartwright in high dudgeon, passing on Caroline's command that Lord Stewart explain himself in writing. Stewart, through Cartwright, was convinced that Caroline knew her request would be refused 'purposely to be able to complain of my Conduct beforehand, whatever Line I might deem proper to adopt'. He also again made it clear that he was answerable only to the Prince Regent and his government. Cartwright was left to issue the Princess with passports (she was travelling incognito as the Duchess of Cornwall), and it must have been with some relief for all of the British diplomatic staff that the attaché could report on Caroline's departure for Trieste on 17 April.[29]

The one event which changed the Caroline Affair for ever was the death of Princess Charlotte in November 1817. Charlotte had married Prince Leopold in May 1816, and the country was overjoyed when news was announced of the Princess's pregnancy. The joy turned to national mourning when Charlotte was delivered of a stillborn son, followed by her death from a haemorrhage. Many had looked to Charlotte and Leopold as the great hope and future of the monarchy, but now the Prince Regent had lost his daughter and grandson. The Hanoverian dynasty was now suddenly bereft of a next generation. None of George III's many other children had managed to have legitimate heirs, although there were certainly a number of illegitimate offspring around. Princess Charlotte's death now led to a rush from three of the Regent's brothers to get married.

Stewart perceptively saw that any restraint shown by the Prince Regent towards his wife would now completely vanish. Caroline had been the mother of a future queen, perhaps her last protection. Stewart, at this time on leave and staying with his parents at Mount Stewart, was just as stunned as many others in the country at 'the 'Catastrophe', which he knew Castlereagh would particularly feel 'from the peculiar Share you had in forming that Union'. Turning to his Faith as a way of dealing with his emotions, he told his brother sadly, 'Nothing ever occurr'd perhaps, in which we so little see through the Intentions of the Almighty, and the Stroke seems to be one which puts at defiance all human Calculation as to the wisdom & necessity of this sad Blow.' Stewart was also the man of business, and he found time to turn his thoughts to the practicalities of the new situation:

> I know full well how much the Event will rouse (after the acute Afflictions have subdued) all those secret burnings & hatred in the Regents Mind against the Pss of Wales, and I have no doubt He will urge the question of Divorce upon his Govt. in a manner they will find it difficult if not impossible to resist, I am apt to believe I could be of some use to You (after a short time) in London – As HRH talks to me in a manner sometimes that He wd be afraid to do to You – If therefore for any good purpose You can recall me, I rather wish you would.[30]

Stewart was proved right, and the renewed activity on behalf of the Prince Regent would lead to the formation of the Milan Commission in August 1818. This would be a more official operation, sanctioned by the British government. Stewart was to take a very prominent role and would well served by Henry Browne, who would come into his own as a loyal and stalwart ally. By so doing, Browne would cement their friendship further. Browne's work was recognized early on by the Prince Regent, who had already made him a Knight of the Royal Guelphic Order in March 1818.[31] The bestowal of the Guelphic Order on Browne was especially significant. As a technically foreign decoration, the Regent could use this Hanoverian Order of Chivalry to reward those who had undertaken personal services to him. Browne had more than earned these marks of favour, which were also undoubtedly meant as spurs to further efforts to help gather as much evidence as possible on Caroline. If this was the intention, Browne would not disappoint. The downside was that Stewart and Browne would become very public figures, and both the Ambassador and his secretary would be insulted as little more than purveyors of filth to the British government.

Chapter 11

VANES AND TEMPESTS

Diplomacy and the Caroline Affair were temporarily put on hold in early 1818. Instead of returning to the embassy, Stewart's time was taken up with his own personal problems. This latest episode sprang from a Chancery Case brought to examine his fitness to marry an heiress over twenty years his junior. In the process, the Stewart family would be dragged through the mud. The heiress in question, Frances Anne Vane-Tempest, was the daughter of Anne McDonnell, Countess of Antrim, and Sir Henry Vane-Tempest, of Wynyard in County Durham. After Sir Henry's death in 1813, Frances Anne found herself at the centre of a complicated tug of war between her mother, Lady Antrim, and her aunt, Frances Taylor. As a result, she was made a Ward of Chancery in 1814.[1] In 1817, the widowed Countess of Antrim married Edmund Phelps 'who had formerly been in a very different situation in society' as related by Mrs Taylor in her evidence to the Chancery Court. Giving full rein to her vitriol, Mrs Taylor went further, noting that she had been 'informed & believes' that Lady Antrim's new husband 'was engaged as a Public Singer at Vauxhall & who since such marriage & on a Petition of s[ai]d. Countess has obtained his Majesty's Letters Patent authorizing him to take the name & bear the Arms of Macdonnell'.[2] It was in this volatile family feud that Lord Stewart became entangled.

The whole affair might never had happened, but for Stewart's extended absence from his embassy. In May 1817, Stewart was writing to his brother from Vienna about his leave; the following month he was in Carlsbad (Karlovy Vary).[3] By August 1817, Stewart was back in London, where he took the opportunity to roundly complain to William Hamilton, the undersecretary at the Foreign Office, of the 'delay in the execution of his orders, with respect to the Payments of the Contingent Expences of my Embassy'.[4] Stewart's correspondence shows that he was at Mount Stewart in November 1817, but by early 1818 he had returned to London.[5] Stewart, who was 'well known' to both the Countess of Antrim and Edmund McDonnell, had been introduced to Frances Anne at her mother's house in February 1818. Stewart met her again at Lady Antrim's house and at public events: specifically the Queen's Drawing Room on 26 February and at Almack's on 4 March. However, trouble was brewing. Mrs Taylor had received a series of anonymous letters detailing a plot to marry Frances Anne to Stewart. On 13 March, in advance of a dinner given by Lady Antrim for the Prince Regent, this correspondence between 'a Lady of Rank' and Mrs Taylor came to Stewart's attention. It was apparent that the Ambassador, a widower since 1812, was swept away by the young heiress, as outlined in his testimony: 'Her peculiar character of mind her excellent understanding & the personal qualities with which she is gifted made a strong impression.'[6] Frances Anne's reaction was rather less of the swept-away kind, but it seems that after due reflection on Stewart's merits as a possible suitor, she became convinced that he would make a good husband. However, knowing her aunt's opposition, Frances Anne 'concealed her growing feelings' from Mrs Taylor.[7] In April 1818, Stewart's proposal of marriage was accepted, and he wrote to both Lady Antrim and Mrs Taylor as Frances Anne's guardians. The Countess of Antrim was delighted, Frances Taylor was far from thrilled.

Mrs Taylor regarded the Ambassador as too old. She also suspected Stewart of being a fortune hunter and charged him with being in 'embarrassed circumstances'. She added more spice to her charges and accused Stewart of having 'dissipated & irregular' habits and, to add more venom to the mix, she topped this off by claiming that Stewart's family suffered from hereditary insanity. Frances Anne's concealment of her attachment had also led to further complications, especially as Mrs Taylor was convinced that the marriage was a plot hatched by Lady Antrim, Edmund McDonnell and Lord Stewart. As Mrs Taylor's evidence charmingly put it: 'And notwithstanding the said Infants inexperience of the World the s[ai]d. Countess of Antrim Mr Mc Donnell and Lord Stewart obtained the said consent of the said Infant to marry his Lordship.'[8]

The accusation of insanity centred on Stewart's sister, Lady Caroline Wood. Her husband, Thomas Wood the Younger, swore an affidavit for the court on 17 April 1818 to attest to the circumstances of Caroline's ill health, together with his condescending opinions:

Saith that shortly after the birth of the s[ai]d. 4th Child Lady Caroline being on a visit to Aldboro' in Suffolk to her Sister Lady Charles Fitzroy [Frances Anne Stewart] without regarding the circumstance of her then late confinement and also that circumstance which in all Females requires particular care and attention Bathed in the open Sea which produced an immediate irregularity in her constitution and a temporary affection of the mind.

Saith that after sometime the constitution being restored to its regular habits her recovery became complete and has ever since remained so & that she is in no respect mentally affected or her judgment in any wide impaired – but on the contrary.[9]

Things got worse for the Stewarts when it was alleged that 'insanity prevails in some branch from which His Lordship is immediately descended.' It was further claimed that in May 1813, Lord Ellenborough had tried to stop his son Edward Law marrying another of Stewart's sisters, Catherine Octavia, and made inquiries as to Caroline's illness.[10]

Stewart's first affidavit, sworn on 17 April 1818, was, from necessity, a wide-ranging affair: both to refute the accusations of fortune hunting and to defend his reputation and that of his family. Reminding the court that he had been raised to the peerage for his services in the Napoleonic Wars, Stewart then proceeded to outline his financial means and personal attainments. Aside from stoking contemporary gossip, the Chancery Case is useful in giving a clear insight into Stewart's finances at the time. His positions as colonel of the 25th Light Dragoons, governor of Fort Charles in Jamaica and as a Lord of the Bedchamber brought in an income of around £3,700 a year. Stewart's salary as ambassador to Vienna was £12,000 a year. On top of these emoluments, Stewart received monies as a life tenant from family estates in Ireland. In total, he estimated his personal property 'to be of the value of £26000 or thereabouts exceed[in]g his debts which Debts are merely his current Expences . . . for Articles furnished for his use & now on their way to Vienna'. Stewart then launched into a measured counter-attack against Mrs Taylor's character assassination:

> Saith he considers himself to be free and that he is in fact free from Debt except as aforesaid and that he confidently refers to every Act of his Life to manifest that his habits are not dissipated or irregular but depo[nen]t. saith he submits to the Court whether he can be expected to answer general pers[ona]l detractions without a single fact stated from which the conclusion is drawn –
>
> Saith he does not believe that insanity prevails in any branch of the Family from which he is immed[iatel]y descended or that Insanity has shewn itself in a manner to have rendered Coersion [*sic*] necessary in more than one Member or in any member of the Family . . . but he saith that Lady Caroline Wood one of Depo[nen]ts. Sisters had in or about the year 1807 an indisposit[io]n. the circumstances of which are detailed . . . by the husband of the said Lady Caroline Wood . . .
>
> Saith that he hath been well known to the Countess of Antrim & to Edmund Mc. Donnell Esq. for many years & from such knowledge he had prior as well as subsequent to the said 26 day of Febry 1818 frequently visited them.[11]

Stewart's further affidavit, sworn on 20 April 1818, reassured the court that there had been no 'collusion or conceit' on his part to bring about the marriage. He further told the court that he was 'incapable' of proceeding in such a dishonest way as this would 'have been equally an insult to Lady Frances and an eternal dishonour to himself'.[12]

The Countess of Antrim's affidavit, sworn on 20 April 1818, was a strident defence of both her conduct and Stewart's character. Lady Antrim stressed her 'most familiar and intimate' connection with Stewart and the Ambassador's acquaintance with her husband. Since Stewart's return he had 'been very intimate with & frequently' in her house. Lady Antrim had introduced her daughter to Lord Stewart on account of the his 'great worth and high Honor & Integrity but without the least Idea that it would lead to any address on his part in the way of marriage'. When Mrs Taylor revealed the contents of the letters she had received about the affair, Lady Antrim stated her ignorance of any plan to arrange the marriage. Believing Stewart to be 'unimpeached in Character & Honor', she had treated 'all such anonymous communication with total disbelief'.[13]

The case lasted three months. The lord chancellor, Lord Eldon, consented to the match, although Mrs Taylor's 'threat of appealing to the Lords' delayed matters further. It was not until 3 April 1819 that Stewart and Frances Anne married at the Countess of Antrim's house. In recognition of Frances Anne's great wealth and property, Lord Stewart took the surname of Vane, while the marriage settlement included three trustees to look after the new Lady Stewart's interests. The settlement implicitly recognized Frances Anne's status as an heiress, as highlighted by Diane Urquhart, who noted that Stewart had 'a somewhat unusual and unstately legal position as he became, in essence, a life tenant on his wife's estate'.[14]

However, it was impossible for Stewart to stay in London and wait for the marriage to go ahead; he had to return to Vienna to prepare for the first European congress since 1815, called against the background of the continuing allied military occupation of France. Put in place after Napoleon's second abdication, the occupation had 'quickly became unpopular in France, even among the royalists'. Understandably, the French wanted to be rid of this force as soon as possible. In 1817, the Duke of Wellington, commander of the occupation army, agreed to reduce troop numbers. By the following year, the Duke had been 'finally won over to an early withdrawal when he realized that a prolonged occupation would only render the King unpopular'.[15]

Stewart had not entirely neglected business during his stay in London. He had taken on new personnel, as a number of friends and family were appointed to the embassy: George FitzRoy and John Bloomfield in February 1818, and Lord Camden's heir, the Earl of Brecknock, in April 1818.[16] However, the Earl of Clanwilliam had left the embassy in 1817 to become Castlereagh's private secretary. On 9 June 1817, Stewart had written sternly to Clanwilliam over his refusal to stay in Vienna until the end of that month. Stewart informed the Earl that he was 'always desirous' to meet the views of those attached to his embassy, 'but on the other hand I expect in return they will conform to my orders' or those of the senior official in his absence. If this was not possible, Stewart would request their removal.[17] It was fortunate that Clanwilliam returned to London.

The Congress of Aix-la-Chapelle

By the summer of 1818, Stewart was again at the heart of diplomatic affairs, his domestic concerns put aside as preparations were made for the Congress of Aix-la-Chapelle (Aachen). On 24 August, Stewart advised Castlereagh of his arrival the day before in the German 'watering Place' of Franzensbrunn, having stopped off en route in Hamburg to pay his respects to Prince Metternich. Despite his absence from his post, Stewart was soon in Metternich's confidences and could report on the Austrian minister's current pet project. This was to orchestrate a meeting with Lord Castlereagh in Paris, as the foreign secretary would be attending the

Congress of Aix-la-Chapelle in person. Stewart argued that this would only arouse suspicion in the minds of the other allies.

Metternich had also taken the opportunity to pour forth his 'dissatisfaction' with the Tsar for causing a delay to the new congress and voiced his suspicions about Russian intrigues over Spain. The Spanish certainly had their own axe to grind about their South American colonies, and the issue would come to the fore in European affairs. Prince Metternich was keeping himself busy, and despite Stewart's advice that he was unlikely to meet Castlereagh in the French capital, the Ambassador thought it probable that the Austrian minister would decide to go to Paris nonetheless:

> As he has an idea, from his personal influence, and some late Correspondence that he has had, that he might devise the means of reconciling Monsieur to the King's Government. In short, it appears to me, that the Prince secretly wishes, from one Cause or other, to be at Paris, for a week or Ten Days, and my Belief is, He will go, at all events.[18]

Stewart was keen for his brother to be in full possession of the facts, having clearly failed in his attempts to persuade Metternich to steer clear of Paris. With Metternich's proposed meddling in French politics, Castlereagh was advised to 'consider this, in your Decision, whether it would not be as well to have more Ministers there, than One'.[19]

By a separate letter sent that same day, Stewart was able to give his brother a more detailed account of his interview with Prince Metternich. Stewart was happy to report that 'in the little personal Communication' he had enjoyed with Metternich 'the whole of his views, so completely coincide with those which Your Lordship was pleased to communicate to me, as the general notions of the Prince Regent's Government, previous to my Departure.' Metternich wanted the new congress to be 'specifically' limited to the stipulations of the second Treaty of Paris signed on 20 November 1815, with the status of the allied occupation force the most pressing issue. Metternich was desperate to avoid opening up the Congress to 'all the Branches and progress of Discussion, which other unsettled points in Europe would entail'. To Metternich, this would simply 'give rise immediately' to dangers from 'the Jacobinical Impressions, that are rapidly encouraging on all sides' that the Congress was 'to new-model and re-model existing arrangements, & to open those Doors for Discontent, Speculations, & Diplomatic Intrigues, which it is so much the interest of the Quadruple Alliance for ever to keep closed'.

France was very much on Metternich's mind. Stewart reported that the Austrian minister was 'not satisfied or entirely tranquil, as to the State of France, although he does not fear any immediate results that may attend the withdrawal from the military hold of the Country'. Metternich was prepared to concede that French political life, especially under the duc de Richelieu, was 'regularly proceeding to a state of consolidation', but he still had misgivings, notably on the long-term future of the senior Bourbon line. As Stewart advised, 'He is by no means satisfied that that Ministry's views are exclusively directed to, or that the bulk of the People of France are disposed to look to the exact legitimate line of succession, as that most conducive to the real interests of the Country.' To Metternich, 'the dangerous Period for France' was not the withdrawal of the allied army 'but when the King dies, & the immediate succession of Monsieur shall be called into action'.

The interview then turned to the German Confederation and the issue of the Barrier Fortresses, before returning to the occupation army, and a remarkable testimony to the high regard in which Wellington was held by Metternich: 'His Grace's means of information & observation – the high trust that has been reposed in him, & his universal Fame, will lead his views to be looked upon, almost as natural Decisions.' In Stewart's opinion, 'The continuation of the Conferences at Paris, & the general System adopted towards France need suffer little alteration, & every advantage may be taken which the remainder of the Period allows of.' As to Metternich, his 'desire to do a great deal, and yet to put off actual Decisions, or doing any thing, until the last moment, is so well known to Your Lordship, that You will not be surprized, that the Report I am enabled to send You, is so little precise'. Castlereagh though could be reassured that Metternich was a firm ally and that 'all points will be carried, as England & Austria may deem most wise, and advantageous for the common Cause'.

A thornier issue for Metternich was the future of the Quadruple Alliance itself, and France's position vis-à-vis the alliance. The French government had already made overtures to join the formal alliance. Stewart told Castlereagh, 'The Delicate Question with regard to the Efforts on the part of France to become a Member of the Alliance will be met in this Quarter with a decided Rejection.' Metternich had already advised the duc de Richelieu, through the French ambassador to Vienna, that he thought it unwise for Louis XVIII 'to press such a subject'. Metternich believed that 'the true position for the King of France to stand in, is the Ally of the Alliance, which has saved His Throne, and the civilised World, and that any attempt to alter these understood relations could not but be pregnant with mischievous & prejudicial effects'.[20]

Having finished this detailed account, Stewart relayed yet more information in a third letter, again dated 24 August. This was obviously a busy day for Stewart's pen, the Ambassador making amends for his long absence. This further piece of news concerned the French prime minister, Richelieu, who was not only favourably disposed towards Vienna but also apparently behind the proposal to enlist Metternich's help in uniting the comte d'Artois with Louis XVIII. In relaying this information to Stewart, Metternich allowed himself the opportunity to unburden himself of his frustrations with Bourbon France, knowing full well that this would be forwarded to Castlereagh:

> He does not defend many Transactions of the King & His Government; but shews incontrovertibly how much his Power & his Government have been enfeebled by the Ultras, who have fed & kept alive the Hopes of Jacobinism and the seeds of universal Discontent. He calls the attention of Monsieur to the difference between a Royalist, and a legitimate Royalist. The friends of every new Dynasty to which there is a Head, are Royalists. The Swedes are Royalists.

The French might denominate themselves Royalists, under any Successor to Louis XVIII; but the true interest of the presumptive Heir to the Crown, was to make the People feel, that Royalism & Legitimacy were inseparable – that this has unfortunately not been the Course of the Advisers and Friends of Monsieur . . . and so long as he keeps aloof, from the King & His Government, under his present feelings, so long does he endanger his own Succession, & encourage all those evil Passions, which must grow out of the discordant State of Parties, which now exist.[21]

The Emperor of Austria, 'sensibly alive to the interests & future establishment of Monsieur', was giving his Imperial backing to Metternich's mission. With all this in mind, Stewart could only ask his brother whether it would be worthwhile to go to Paris, along with Wellington.[22] Secret service papers reveal that he was also busy getting information from Gentz as well as from Metternich. The Ambassador was able to enclose a present from Gentz in the form of 'a little Brochure . . . as it is a short & clear Expose of the Doctrines held here'. Perhaps anticipating further services from Gentz, he drew on £250 of funds on 4 September.[23]

By 29 August 1818, Stewart was in Carlsbad, where he had more news for the foreign secretary: this time on Napoleon's son, the former King of Rome. Stewart wrote that the titular Napoleon II would no longer be styled as Duke of Parma but as Duke of Reichstadt, and addressed as Serene Highness. As Stewart mischievously noted, 'In all probability, it will not fail to produce a salutary effect upon the imaginations of those who, without grounds for their Suspicions, have affected to mistrust the Sincerity & Loyalty of the Austrian Cabinet, with regard to the future Destiny of this young Prince.'[24] British politicians were certainly very interested in Reichstadt. On 3 September, Stewart advised Castlereagh of his return to Vienna, but he had almost immediately gone to Baden to meet with the Emperor and the new Empress of Austria, Caroline Augusta of Bavaria. It was no coincidence that Marie Louise and her son, Reichstadt, were there.

Aside from the usual platitudes, the Emperor Francis was keen to talk to the British ambassador about the Duke of Reichstadt: 'He thought the last Act of Change in His Title &c &c would shew Europe how completely determined His Imperial Majesty was to extinguish, as far as possible, every Remembrance of the Napoleon Dynasty.' The Emperor, for good measure, 'added, with great Emphasis, it was impossible, He ever could be too sensible of all he owed Great Britain'. Just as importantly, Stewart took the opportunity to meet Marie Louise and the Duke of Reichstadt, and then to relay his views about the Duke, together with his low opinions of the heir to the Habsburg throne, Ferdinand:

After an Audience of The Empress, I had one of The Archduchess Maria Louisa, and the young Duke of Reichstadt. She was very desirous of shewing off the Boy, and having Him taken notice of. He appears to me however, not so promising as He was – His Head looks large & heavy, and if You were not called upon to notice Him, as the Child of a particular Person, You would pass him, without Remark. The long, curling, white flaxen Hair which He had so peculiarly, is shorn quite close. His Tutors seem to pay great Attention to Him; and He stood up beside His Mother to receive me, with as much Ceremony and Etiquette, as The Imperial Prince.

The Latter, to whom I next paid my Duty, is not improving much, in any one of those Qualities or Attributes which are undoubtedly called for, in The presumptive Sovereign of a great Empire.

The Archduchess, and the young Duke, accompanied by General Neipperg, set out, in a Day or two, on their Return to Parma.[25]

Such were Stewart's preparations as he made ready for the Congress of Aix-la-Chapelle. However, as he had advised in his letters to the Foreign Office, the withdrawal of the occupying troops, the key matter for the new congress, was already being addressed.

In September 1818, the participants began to arrive in Aix-la-Chapelle, a recent territorial addition to Prussia. Perhaps unsurprisingly, there had been dissension among the allied powers over who should be invited, but it had been agreed that only members of the Quadruple Alliance should attend, together with France. Britain would be represented by Lord Castlereagh and Lord Stewart, while Wellington was invited as the commander of the occupying army.[26] The atmosphere at Aix-la-Chapelle has been described as capturing some 'of the festive atmosphere of Vienna' with its 'customary dinners, concerts and balls'.[27] To add to the feelings of festivity, Stewart's friend, the famed British portrait painter, Sir Thomas Lawrence was present, with commissions from the Prince Regent. Lawrence's friendship with Stewart dated back several years. In 1814, the Ambassador had probably helped smooth the painter's entry into the Prince Regent's circle. Stewart took every available chance to help the painter's career; for example, in March 1816, Stewart had written to Lawrence detailing 'a very short, very decided and very prompt' plan to paint not just the Austrian and Russian sovereigns, but other famed figures of the day including 'Schwarzenberg, Metternich, *Madame Murat*, and *Young* NAPOLEON'.[28]

The two emperors, Alexander and Francis, both sat to Lawrence during the Congress, as did many of the leading participants, including Prince Metternich, Count Nesselrode and the duc de Richelieu. Lawrence noted, in one of his letters, that Stewart had accompanied him for the sitting with Alexander, using the occasion to converse with the Tsar.[29] Meanwhile, Lord Stewart also caught some of the festive atmosphere, obviously getting carried away as related by the Earl of Clanwilliam:

Ld. Stewart was also at Aix. He and I had a 'jaw['] one night, at Lady C.'s supper-table, ladies present. In a sort of angry joke, he shied a large potatoe [*sic*] at me, wh[ich]. splashed agst. the wall. I lost my temper, & when he took up an[othe]r potatoe, in horse-play, I lifted a bottle by the neck, & threatened to break his head! He saw I was dangerous, & stopt. I may assume I was in the right, for His Exc[ellenc]y. recd. a wigging frm. his brother.[30]

Although the Congress rapidly approved the allied military evacuation from France on 1 October 1818, trouble lay in wait for the British with a new Russian proposal for a great pan-European alliance 'to maintain the general peace and the treaties of 1815'.[31] This idea was stillborn without British participation – and there was simply never any real chance that London would agree to such a general binding agreement. Equally, the British gave short shrift to the idea of allied intervention in Spain's South American colonies, although proposals put forward for mediation involving the Duke of Wellington ultimately came to nothing.

A number of other issues were raised at Aix-la-Chapelle, including Bavaria's territorial dispute with the Grand Duchy of Baden, the slave trade, piracy, the conditions of Germany's Jewish populations, Swedish obligations to Denmark, and Napoleon's imprisonment.[32] However, despite the signing of a declaration on 15 November 1818, possibly the main tangible results were the reaffirmation (in secret) of the Quadruple Alliance and a public protocol inviting France to participate in future reunions. No date or location was fixed for a future congress, but the French could be pleased that they had returned fully to the international fold. With its remaining indemnity written off, France saw the last allied troops leave its soil on 30 November.

Lord Stewart was back in Vienna at the end of November 1818, but the capital was quiet throughout early December. Although the Emperor Francis returned on 3 December, Prince Metternich did not do so until 12 December. Alexander I had also arrived in the Austrian capital, but news received on 13 December of the Grand Duke of Baden's death had muted any festivities or welcome. Castlereagh had sent instructions for Stewart to meet with the Tsar, and despite the intelligence from Baden, Alexander had agreed to see the British ambassador. On 21 December, Stewart reported on his interview with the Tsar to the foreign secretary. Despite the differences of approach at Aix-la-Chapelle, Alexander held Castlereagh and the Liverpool government in the very highest esteem. Superlatives poured forth from the Tsar, although there was undoubtedly some courtly flattery behind these words. Alexander told Stewart that he 'took the greatest Interest in the preservation of the existing Government and the System of Politicks of the two Courts'. Alexander had been pleased to meet Castlereagh again in person, and clearly disliked the idea of an alternative government as 'New Men would come with new Ideas, and there might be bad Men amongst them.' The Tsar's opinion of the current ministers, 'all those whom He knew . . . or heard of', was that they 'were good moral Men'. Indeed, for Alexander it was Britain's 'preponderance of Moral Conduct, over a contrary Action' which had led to the 'present repose'.

The interview moved on to Spain, and specifically Castlereagh's interview at Aix-la-Chapelle with the Tsar, which the foreign secretary 'fortunately had, at the Moment of His Imperial Majesty's Departure'. Alexander had promised to rein in his diplomats in Madrid, and stop them from raising unrealistic expectations of allied intervention in the Spanish colonies. Stewart took delight in mimicking Alexander's characteristics, telling Castlereagh that he had been treated to those habits the Tsar 'is singularly partial to, with those significant nods of the Head and important manner'. This was followed by a shrewd estimation of Alexander's character: 'that although He undoubtedly plumes Himself, on being the Pivot of the Whole European World, Each Subject, which He touches and Each Issue, which He draws, in the course of Conversation can only give food for Satisfaction'. Stewart further advised that the Tsar wanted to enjoy complete candour with Castlereagh:

> That He [Alexander] should in future, have no reserve with Your Lordship, from the frank manner You had addressed Him, a frankness of which You had given the most unequivocal, and incontestable proofs at a time when it was not even necessary, except from Your Honorable Feelings, and that as the only way for good Men to do Business, was to be entirely sincere.[33]

In return, the Tsar would 'not hesitate' to communicate with the foreign secretary directly 'on any interesting Subject' which he hoped would be proof of his good opinions of the current British government.

The Tsar's conversation had then turned to Bavaria's claims against Baden, left over from the Congress of Aix-la-Chapelle. Remarkably Alexander was quite open about the problems Baden was causing to the alliance, as Austria was keen to support Bavaria's position. The foreign secretary might well have been alarmed to read Stewart's dispatch. Alexander reported that the Empress of Austria, Caroline of Bavaria, was 'extremely cold' and had 'attacked Him on the [Baden] Affair which was certainly very awkward'. The Tsar cleared Metternich of subterfuge, but he suspected intrigues, telling Stewart that as Francis I supported his wife he was 'not so pleasant as He was at Aix la Chapelle upon the Bavarian Question'. With Britain, Russia and Prussia united on the issue, the Tsar was optimistic about the affair being settled, although he invited Stewart to wait on him again for a second interview.[34]

Stewart took every opportunity to discuss policy with the Russian delegation. Writing again on 21 December, he reported to Castlereagh on his meeting with Count Capodistrias, who remained joint foreign minister with Count Nesselrode. The conversation had again turned on Spain and Baden, but what is striking is the usefulness to the Russian mission of face-to-face meetings. Telling Capodistrias of 'the favorable manner in which (I Knew) Your Lordship had written Home, with regard to Your personal feelings towards him after Your last Conferences', the Russian foreign minister was equally candid to Stewart:

> He remarked that the Reunion at Aix had tended to make All parties better estimate each others worth, and to become personally attached, and that he trusted to preserve Your Lordship's good opinion. – I observed also He spoke much in praise of Metternich, and as the latter had done the same of Him, Harmony is becoming more universal.[35]

This universal harmony should of course not be taken at face value: diplomacy does not necessarily mean telling others your true feelings, but clearly the Russians felt that the Congress had been a worthwhile undertaking. However, harmony was soon dispelled, this time thanks to France, where political infighting between the prime minister and Louis XVIII's favourite, Élie, comte Decazes, whom the King was determined to keep in office as minister of police, was far from conducive to stability.

As Philip Mansel has argued, opposition to Louis XVIII's government came both from the right in the shape of the Ultras and from the more enthusiastic liberals on the left. This meant that by 1818 the French government was 'beginning to be torn apart by the magnetic attractions of the right, advocated by Richelieu and the left, pushed by Decazes'. The result was that there 'was no longer a firm political base for a Government of the centre'.[36] Alexander I for one was deeply unhappy about the state of French politics, as Stewart reported in a further dispatch of 21 December. Having spoken to the Tsar at a 'Magnificent Entertainment' the night before, Alexander had asked for the second interview to take place the next day, prior to his departure from Vienna on 22 December. The fall in French funds and 'the Schism that appeared in the Ministry' were of great concern to the Russian monarch. Warming to his theme, the Tsar wanted to remind Castlereagh, through Stewart, of 'His fixed Opinions upon the radical Disease that pervades this unhappy Country; the manner He had talked of its State to the Duke of Wellington and Your Lordship, and His full Conviction that we ought never to be lulled into Security'. As a consequence, the Tsar believed that the Quadruple Alliance should be bound 'still closer and closer' and that if France ever had the opportunity 'of creating Discord amongst us' the results could lead to renewed warfare. The Tsar was far from impressed with Louis XVIII, criticizing the King's speech to the Chambers, and his appearing 'no longer looking gratefully to those powers, who restored Him to His Country'. Britain could be reassured that if events ever turned to war, Alexander 'would be first in the Field of Battle'.

Discussion had then returned to Spanish affairs. Stewart voiced British concern that the Tsar's orders to his diplomats in Madrid would simply be ignored by the Russian ambassador, Count Tatishchev. The Tsar was crystal clear: 'If he does not fulfil my Instructions to the Letter which I now send, I shall recall him instantly.' It merely remained for Stewart to remind Alexander that the Duke of Wellington was proposed as sole mediator, and that this should be clarified in the Russian dispatch. On Baden, the Tsar could not see any likely agreement with Austria but would leave Capodistrias behind in Vienna for a few days to see if progress could be made. The talk of allied unity was fast disappearing in the winter days of Vienna. Stewart confirmed this himself after seeing the Tsar, when he waited on Francis I to present a letter from the Prince Regent. The Emperor Francis had clearly had enough of Alexander, and Stewart 'found at this Interview His Imperial Majesty very dry and caustick as to The Emperor of Russia, and evidently out of humor, and when I alluded to the Departure of the Latter, He said "Yes He is glad to go away because He finds we are not agreed with Him here."' As for Alexander, he was reported as spending the evening 'for the first time' at Metternich's, before setting off the following day for St Petersburg.[37] This hints at possible bad blood between Metternich and the Russians. Indeed, in Stewart's dispatch No. 18, also dated 21 December, Metternich's annoyance with Russian diplomats is obvious, with the Austrian minister talking of Pozzo di Borgo being 'as bad as Mons. de Tattischeff [*sic*] at Madrid'.[38]

At least Stewart had the satisfaction of helping Sir Thomas Lawrence, who was in Vienna, where the Emperor of Austria sat for him again; others sat for Lawrence as well, including the Ambassador himself. Lawrence wanted for nothing, as the painter wrote, 'Lord Stewart's friendship is equally zealous and active in securing facilities for my Professional mission, and in making my stay as agreeable as possible at moments when I am not employed upon it.'[39] Meanwhile in Paris, the result of the latest round of political intrigues led to the temporary eclipse of Decazes. Louis, in order to placate Richelieu, had agreed to remove Decazes from government on 23 December. However, Richelieu's attempts to form a more Ultra-leaning government ended in failure. The duc de Richelieu resigned on 26 December 1818. His government was replaced by a ministry led by General Dessolles, but in reality dominated by the more liberal Decazes. The new government was not only 'clearly more liberal and left-wing than its predecessor' but marked the end of the desire 'to live above parties'.[40]

Such was the state of Europe at the end of 1818. The new year of 1819 would bring more challenges. Stewart would be drawn fully back into the Caroline Affair as the Milan Commission prepared its evidence against the Princess of Wales. The new year would also bring a resolution to Stewart's personal life, as he would return to Britain in order to marry Frances Anne. Stewart had served British interests admirably with his work leading up to the Congress of Aix-la-Chapelle. The Ambassador had continued his good work in the immediate post-Congress period, ensuring Alexander's cooperation in British foreign policy, building relations with Capodistrias and in laying bare Austrian irritation with Russian foreign policy. Stewart though was preoccupied with his personal business and after marrying, would be absent from international affairs until the summer of 1819. It was a pattern which would manifest itself at other times during Stewart's remaining tenure of the Vienna embassy, a pattern which could only be detrimental to his brother Castlereagh.

Chapter 12

THE MILAN COMMISSION

On 24 August 1818, Stewart approached Prince Metternich on a subject 'deeply important' to the Prince Regent 'in soliciting Such Assistance as the Austrian Government can give' to the proposed Milan Commission – formed to gather the necessary incriminating evidence against the Princess of Wales. Discretion was needed, and Metternich was informed that 'the less their object is known the better.' Stewart further hoped that the Austrians would 'render the protection & assurance required as far as possible to these Gentlemen [the Commissioners] during their stay' in Milan. Metternich was careful in his answer to this request: 'It must be noted here that Lord S never received any further Official Communication to say the Emperor had formally agreed to the proposal.' Stewart only received a verbal agreement. Still this was enough, and Stewart could assure his brother that he believed the Austrian authorities would give the Commission 'every facility support & assistance'.[1]

The chairman of the Commission in London was a senior member of the legal profession, Sir John Leach. In Milan, the Commission had three members, William Cooke, John Powell and Henry Browne. The Commission started its work in September 1818. Stewart's secretary, Henry Browne, would be the linchpin of the mission. On 8 September, the Ambassador could advise his brother that he was dispatching a former official from Austria's Milanese government who was 'to proceed at the same time with Major Browne to that place'. The official was 'intimately acquainted' with the affairs of the Princess of Wales when she lived on Lake Como. Stewart, always eager to please, added, 'I trust the whole of the arrangement will be approved by the Prince Regent.'[2]

Stewart's activities had attracted comment in Britain. Even before the Milan Commission had been set up, the anonymous author of *Journal of an English Traveller* had written of the Ambassador's doings. Stewart's role was now disseminated further as passages from the *Journal* appeared in an 1818 biography of Princess Charlotte by Robert Huish. This publicized Stewart's snubbing of Caroline at Vienna and his 'friendship' with the spy Ompteda.[3] Stewart found himself again in the middle of the Prince Regent's desire to be rid of Caroline. It would prove a very hard place to be: dealing with the heir to the throne, the British government, the Hanoverian minister, Count Münster, the two legal teams and the Austrians.

The Princess of Wales's team were busy trying to rubbish Lord Stewart's name. Henry Browne, soon to be promoted to lieutenant colonel, sent a translation of a letter from Pergami to the 'Advocate Godazzo' dated 4 December 1818, which noted 'that it is necessary You should <u>procure</u> attestations that the persons sent away have been paid by an English Gentleman, and if possible, that this Gentleman was the <u>Minister at Vienna</u>'. Caroline was also involved in these attempts to blacken Stewart's character.[4] The gloves were well and truly off. Meanwhile the Milan Commissioners proceeded with their work quickly, and by the summer of 1819 presented their final report to Sir John Leach. Despite all precautions, the Milan Commission had not gone unnoticed by Caroline, who wrote:

> My traducers and enemies in England have again held secret inquisition at Milan, through the means of spies and many old servants who have been sent from the house for bad conduct. A Mr. C –, Mr. P –, a Colonel B –, and Lord S –, have been making all kinds of inquiry into my private conduct.[5]

However, instead of providing continued assistance with these efforts, Stewart would take a lengthy leave of absence from the spying operation in 1819. Personal affairs for once got in the way. On 3 April, he married Frances Anne in London. But Stewart did not entirely neglect official business. On 24 April, the Ambassador sought patronage on behalf of his ADC, George During, another actor in the Caroline Affair. During was appointed consul general at Trieste. Stewart then journeyed north to his wife's estate at Wynyard. From there he wrote to his brother on 1 May, requesting the appointment of William Bradford as chaplain to the embassy in Vienna.[6]

Stewart was then further distracted by another delicate affair, albeit an official one, in the summer of 1819. The French government was unhappy with Britain's ambassador to Paris, Sir Charles Stuart, which in turn was another problem for the foreign secretary. Castlereagh needed a trusted agent to unravel the causes of these complaints and report back to him. So, Lord and Lady Stewart's journey back to Vienna would be delayed by a stay in Paris.[7] The importance of Stewart's position is again apparent, able to undertake discreet operations on behalf of the Foreign Office. Stewart arrived in Paris, 'this extraordinary Capital', in August 1819. Having conducted talks with leading members of the royal family, including Louis XVIII, the comte d'Artois and the duc d'Orléans, Stewart sent back his views on the current state of French politics to his brother: 'The mass of the nation prefer monarchy, of this there is little doubt, But none like the present Gov[ernmen]t'.[8] Having got the routine politics out of the way, Stewart proceeded with his investigation into Sir Charles Stuart.

The French government had grown increasingly dissatisfied with Stuart's behaviour. Lord Stewart soon discovered that the main source of irritation was Sir Charles Stuart's supposed relationship with Sir Robert Wilson, who was in Paris at the time. Wilson had been Stewart's companion in arms during the German campaign, but since then, Stewart and Wilson had gone their separate ways, politically as well as professionally. Sir Robert Wilson was very much out of favour with the restored French monarchy. This went back to an extraordinary incident Sir Robert had masterminded in 1815–16, when he had been instrumental in securing comte Lavalette's escape from prison. Lavalette, a former Napoleonic official, had been sentenced to death for his role in the Hundred Days. The comte's escape, involving disguising himself as a woman, and government searches across Paris, was a tale of derring-do worthy of any novel. Wilson had been put on trial for his part in Lavalette's escape and had spent three months inside a French prison. The trial was hardly great propaganda for the French government, and he had not hesitated to express his antipathy towards the Bourbons.[9] Naturally, any contact between Stuart and Wilson would make the French government suspicious. Stewart quickly dismissed these concerns in a secret letter to Castlereagh, dated 14 August, confidently reporting that there was nothing to complain about in terms of Wilson, while Sir Charles Stuart's role as ambassador was judged 'infinitely more advantageous to his own Government than at any former period'.

Having dealt with the supposed political objections, Stewart turned to the rather more delicate nature of the Ambassador's sexual habits. Castlereagh could be reassured that Sir Charles Stuart's 'irregularities' were not done 'in the glare of Day', while his 'orgies are in secret & in the Dark . . . they are not unknown & his Enemies take advantage of them'. If anything, Sir Charles's behaviour had even improved, or at least was 'not so bad', but as Lord Stewart wrote, such conduct 'has been talk'd of & itself known so long and been unnoticed' by the Foreign Office, that Stuart could not really be dismissed on these grounds. Stewart again proved that he was the perceptive diplomat, advising London that the Ultra Royalists in particular had an axe to grind against Sir Charles Stuart. All in all, Stewart believed that 'the Prince Regents Govt could not have a better Servant here . . . at the present moment'. The Foreign Office was minded to agree and left Sir Charles Stuart in post.

The Princess of Wales could not completely escape Stewart's attentions, and he ended his letter with a postscript on the subject. The British government wanted the Princess to remain abroad, and Stewart agreed that 'the supposd Return of a certain person' was a 'Menace', but at the moment he had not heard any news of her having crossed into France, but 'only the Message from Calais that she was expected there'.[10] This turned out to be a false alarm. Having finished his work in Paris, Stewart hardly rushed back to his embassy. Advising Castlereagh of his return to Vienna on 1 October 1819, Stewart needed time to re-immerse himself in European political affairs: 'I can not immediately become acquainted, or accurately informed of the general State of the Political Concerns at this Court, and I must claim your usual indulgence until I shall have an opportunity of instructing myself on all that is most important.'[11]

Lady Stewart suffered a miscarriage after their return to Vienna in October. Desperate to have an heir, this affected her physically and mentally, and she became depressed by Viennese society and the round of diplomatic entertainments.[12] Stewart though had to get back into the thick of things. Regular conversations were resumed with Prince Metternich through October and November. These ranged from proposing London as the scene of regular and permanent diplomatic conferences, the current state of French politics, and the popularity of the new Queen of Spain.[13] But it was the state of the French monarchy which was rarely from Prince Metternich's thoughts, specifically fears as to what might happen after Louis XVIII's death. At heart, the Habsburg court still worried about the fragility of the Bourbon Restoration, as Stewart reported on 29 November:

> He [Metternich] talks of three formidable Parties being in existence. One, looking to the Young Napoleon here. Another, to Prince Eugene, But the most formidable of all, to the Prince of Orange. The conduct of His Royal Highness, Prince Metternich declared encouraged this latter Party, even so far, as to have taken into his employ, many French Officers on half Pay, and to have made promises to others, As all these Ideas are old, I only relate them to Your Lordship as having had new birth for the purpose of pressing His Highness's views as to the latter points of his last Memoire.[14]

The education of the duc de Chartres was also on Metternich's agenda. Chartres, heir to the duc d'Orléans, had been sent to the Lycée Henri-IV in Paris, and as Stewart reported: 'It appears the mode of educating the Duc de Chartres has given serious offence to the King as favoring a levelling System wholly objectionable for any member of the Royal Family.' Louis XVIII's complaints had fallen on deaf ears, and thereby 'placed the House of Orleans in great disfavour', leading to 'much party feeling and discussion on the subject'.[15] These were the concerns of Europe at the close of 1819, but the new year of 1820 would bring fresh alarms.

In Britain, the Caroline Affair had continued to be a thorn in the side of the Liverpool government. During June and July 1819, the cabinet had been involved in discussions with the Prince Regent over the best course to adopt: they were told in no uncertain terms that the Princess of Wales had to be divorced. The Liverpool government was unhappy about the prospect of a trial conducted by the Houses of Parliament, exposing to full daylight the varied unsavoury royal scandals.[16] For the meantime, Caroline remained in mainland Europe and the matter could at least be left where it was for now. Things would be even better if the Princess were persuaded to remain abroad permanently. Ministers were involved in negotiations with Caroline's main adviser, the highly ambitious Whig lawyer Henry Brougham, to try and bring such a situation about.[17] Then an event occurred which changed Caroline's status.

George III, for nearly ten years incapacitated and unable to rule, died at Windsor Castle on 29 January 1820. The Prince Regent now succeeded as King George IV. If George hated the thought of his wife as Princess of Wales, this was nothing in comparison to how he thought of her as his Queen. The King harangued Lord Liverpool on the subject, and in February it seemed as if the government was on the verge of resignation. On 14 February, Castlereagh saw the King and attempted to bring him to reason and accept the government's plan to persuade Caroline to stay abroad. Castlereagh managed to win his sovereign round.[18] Having heard of these events from his brother, Lord Stewart wrote candidly to Castlereagh about the likely problems ahead for both of them, including the possible resignation of

Liverpool's government. In a letter to his brother, dated 8 March 1820, Stewart wrote, 'If You can count on any thing Living You may count upon me, It is a poor return, I admit, for all I owe You.' Stewart went further and told Castlereagh that he would resign from his embassy if he left the Foreign Office. Although he disagreed with Castlereagh on the King's attitude to the divorce, Stewart was at pains to stress his loyalty and confirmed he would 'never . . . act upon a separate opinion'.[19]

Stewart was proved correct in his assumption that George IV would not rest easy until he was divorced, a point reinforced to him by a letter from Sir Benjamin Bloomfield, the Keeper of the Privy Purse, dated 12 February.[20] Disagreements with Castlereagh aside, Stewart's work was at least recognized by the King, who bestowed on him the colonelcy of the 10th Hussars. Stewart received the news in March 1820, and ever the military man as well as the diplomat, regarded this appointment as 'the greatest Mark' of the King's 'personal feeling & professional Approbation'.[21]

There was more to diplomatic life than just the Caroline Affair. In January 1820, Europe was shaken by revolution in Spain, with Ferdinand VII forced to accept the liberal 1812 Spanish Constitution. Produced in the midst of war against the French, the constitution contained some radical ideas, including 'the nation proclaimed to be sovereign', combined with the 'most severe restrictions' on the King's powers.[22] In the following month, Europe was rocked again by the assassination of Charles-Ferdinand, duc de Berry, third in line of succession to the French throne.[23] This brought down Decazes and returned a 'reluctant' duc de Richelieu to office as prime minister.[24] Stewart also worried about British political unrest, but the danger to his brother was more immediate than he could have guessed. Castlereagh, along with the rest of the cabinet, had been marked down for assassination by the members of the Cato Street Conspiracy. This bloodthirsty attempt to overthrow the government, which took its name from the would-be revolutionaries' meeting place off the Edgware Road, had been infiltrated by government spies. The conspirators were arrested on 23 February, and executions rapidly followed. On 10 March, a very relieved Stewart thanked God for his brother's 'providential Escape' and pleaded with Castlereagh to be vigilant, arguing, 'Your Life is Your Countrys & not Your own . . . your too careless regard of Your own person is indeed a Crime.'

Stewart was now becoming quite the master of underhand diplomacy and could report to his brother that thanks to Metternich, he was now privy to the private correspondence of Prince Esterházy, the Austrian ambassador to London. This in itself was a quite remarkable circumstance. Despite receiving a 'satisfactory' letter from Bloomfield, Stewart warned his brother that George IV was in the habit of being 'very open' to Esterházy about his annoyance with the Liverpool government, whatever he might have said to his ministers. Stewart added that Hanoverian interests could cause trouble as Count Münster 'is not quiet as the letting the affair [i.e. Caroline Affair] be managed in a tranquil Shape, He considers the Honor of <u>Hanover</u> implicated, more especially if <u>She</u> is to take a Foreign Title'. As if this were not enough, the King was unhappy with Sir Charles Stuart.[25] Thanks to Stewart, the government was aware of the monarch's double-dealing, but the letter reminded the cabinet that George IV was also King of Hanover and would expect his dynasty's German interests to be looked to.

On 29 March, Stewart reported more clandestine news, this time forwarding Metternich's reports on Bonaparte plots and connections to the Whig peer Lord Holland. Stewart remained sceptical, as he confided in a most secret and confidential letter to Castlereagh:

> This seems so incomprehensible that I made the Prince repeat it twice to be quite sure I heard right.
>
> It is needless for me to say more until Your Lordship has the full information, with all the papers, before you. At the same time I cannot help remarking that there is a degree of circumspection and doubt necessary to be held in view when one examines the numerous reports of a hired and paid Police.
>
> Your Lordship Knows we are a little fond in this Court of Secret information, and plots, I shall therefore add no more at present on this Subject.[26]

The paranoia of the Austrian government had been increased by the revolution in Spain, and Metternich's fears were given full rein in his discussions with Stewart. It also brought home to the Austrian minister the state of the Habsburg dynasty itself, as Stewart advised on 9 April:

> The weakness of the Crown Prince augments as he advances in years, and Metternich (I know) bitterly laments now, that he did not counsel (as he once projected) that he should be declared <u>Incapable</u> when he was yet in his infancy. Now, Alas! he is far too advanced in Age, and although there is a moral certainty that his incapacity will preclude his wisely administering the Government of the Empire, still he has been brought so much out that there would be much greater difficulty if not entirely, in putting him aside.[27]

Unfortunately, Stewart noted, 'The Younger Brother also affords little more promise, and the picture of what possibly may arise here is not bright.' The Ambassador continued that he was writing this letter 'at a moment when I see the mind of Metternich much depressed with gloomy forebodings at the black prospect that lowers around, and they may have a tinge of Contemplations'.[28]

Although the Milan Commission had completed its work, Henry Browne remained in place as Stewart's trusted agent in the city. Stewart himself was acting as go-between for the various parties in London, Vienna and Milan, which kept him very busy, as one letter to Castlereagh makes clear. Stewart had been commanded to see Metternich, to remind him that Colonel Browne 'cannot be acknowledged as authorized to announce any sentiments to the Milanese Government, and the Governor is not to take any cognizance of his being at Milan'. Stewart was also left to guide the Austrians on matters of etiquette, insisting that the Milanese should address Caroline correctly if she travelled as Queen, as well as offering advice to the authorities there on the right of Pergami to wear his Orders of Chivalry. It also seemed that news had reached the Foreign Office of Browne's too great enthusiasm as a member of the Milan Commission, and Stewart had to deal with this problem as well. Always loyal to a friend and colleague, the Ambassador rushed to defend his man on the spot, as he told Castlereagh, 'I am sorry there should be a little annoyance at this moment for my Friend Browne, but his over zeal makes him, "I fear" rather intimidate the Governor', Browne's letters and the governor's annoyance had led the authorities to complain to Metternich.

The real problem of course, as Stewart pointed out, stemmed from Browne's semi-official position and his not especially secret work, 'and Although Browne means admirably he does not enough consider his actions cannot be authorized, and his positive open interference only mars what he wishes to aid'. Stewart advised his brother that he had sent fresh instructions to the colonel and could 'entertain a confident belief that the conduct at Milan will be precisely what is wished'.[29] As was often the case with the nervous Stewart, he hoped that his actions would be approved at home, but he had been right to defend Browne, who was in a very difficult situation. As secretary to Lord Stewart, and a member of the Milan Commission, Henry Browne was to all intents and purposes Britain's representative to the Milanese government in the Caroline Affair.

The British government still hoped the Queen would remain abroad. Stewart, thanks to Metternich, was in receipt of intelligence and downright gossip picked up by the Austrians. Stewart warned his brother that Caroline was being 'urged' to return to Britain. As if to back up this news, he forwarded an account of events in Paris, and of eavesdropped conversations involving Sir Robert Wilson, who had become a partisan of the Queen. According to the report, 'Sir R: Wilson avowed that it was the decision of the opposers of Government in England to induce' Caroline to return. Perhaps with a wry smile, Stewart told his brother that even Wilson was aware of the Queen's behaviour, Sir Robert having remarked, 'it was impossible to be sure of the Princess's [*sic*] acting for any time decently'. Meanwhile in Milan, Henry Browne was keeping a careful eye on the Queen's movements. Military habits die hard, and remembering that he was addressing his superior officer, Browne always addressed Stewart as 'My Dear General'. Writing on 27 April, Browne reported that although Caroline remained in the city, 'every preparation' was being made for her 'speedy departure'. Browne added a detailed account of the Queen's current companions. One of them, a Professor Rasori, 'is one of the most violent Demagogues existing . . . He is moreover a cunning, designing, & remarkably clever fellow, a great meddler in politics'. Just in case Stewart had not got the message, by the next report Browne described Rasori as a 'very shrewd fellow & violent jacobin'.[30]

Stewart was also in the middle of other sensitive matters, including the forwarding of Austrian secret correspondence to his brother. One item concerned George IV, in which the King had declared that he and Metternich were the two people in Europe marked out for assassination, further adding a request for the Order of Maria Theresa. Stewart remarked that the letter 'was in German & I saw it by accident it not being intended, I am sure for my inspection'. Stewart's linguistic abilities, combined with his new passion for spying, meant that Castlereagh was kept apprised of everything, even the King's private musings.[31] Showing that nothing escaped the attentions of His Majesty's diplomats, Stewart further forwarded some scandal fresh from Rome, via Sir William A'Court in Naples.[32] A'Court could report, perhaps too vividly, that 'one of the Pope's Chaplains, a red-stockinged Gentleman, was caught by the Police a few nights since . . . in full canonicals, sodomizing a huge whisker faced Grenadier of the Holy Father's Swiss Guard.'[33] Stewart's reputation as a gatherer of intelligence was spreading, and it is noticeable that A'Court had sent the report on to Stewart, for onward transmission to London.

Browne was being ever vigilant in keeping Caroline's movements under surveillance. On 15 May, Stewart sent one of Browne's reports to his brother, which summed up the difficulties that the colonel was up against. It also revealed the personal enmity in which Stewart was held by the Queen:

> You may conceive, my Dear General, my private feelings, on the necessity which exists (& no one can doubt of it's impervious existence) of permitting this infamous Woman to continue her horrid Career, as 'Queen of England' – They might be less acute, had not the whole of the evidence passed under my own eye, & left a decided conviction, that nothing was wanting, in that respect, for the full accomplishment of the ends of justice, & the assertion of our national Character.
>
> You may be proud of her bitterest hatred, which she never omits an opportunity of expressing, & I am too proud of being honorably associated with those, who detest her name.[34]

Browne stood ready to depart 'in the conviction, that the truth sought for by the Commission, was found'. As a final flourish, the colonel added, 'Your approbation will form no small part of my reward, as my attachment & gratitude to you can never diminish.' Stewart, when passing this on to his brother, admitted he was 'quite in the dark' as to what the government intended to do with the Milan Commission's work, but concluded that Sir John Leach would 'send Browne his orders'.

Turning to Browne's future prospects, Stewart told his brother he was determined that the colonel should not be overlooked.[35] This sentiment was a little premature, as Browne's work in Milan was far from finished. The Liverpool government still hoped the Queen would stay abroad, but unfortunately for the British ministers, Caroline had different ideas. The Queen was listening to other counsel than Henry Brougham, most notably that of Alderman Matthew Wood, a radical politician from the City of London. To people like Wood, Queen Caroline had to return to Britain: the resulting political storm might just bring down the Earl of Liverpool's administration and lead to a new government committed to reform.

The Queen's trial

Queen Caroline was persuaded by the radical arguments and she set sail for Britain, arriving at Dover on 5 June. The government now had no choice but to act, and on the following day, Lord Liverpool in the Lords, and Lord Castlereagh in the Commons, each delivered a sealed green bag, which contained the evidence against the Queen. After debates in Parliament, the Lords moved to examine the evidence by a secret committee, finishing their work on 4 July. The committee found that Caroline had 'formed an intimacy of the most criminal nature with a foreigner' and that her conduct 'had in other instances been marked by circumstances of a licentious nature, unbecoming her rank and station'.[36] The upshot was the introduction into the House of Lords of a Bill of Pains and Penalties, which if passed would secure George IV his divorce and deprive the Queen of her title. The work of the Milan Commission was soon to be exposed to the glare of daylight, and not just in any forum, but in the House of Lords, where the peers would find out just how busy Stewart and Browne had been.

A courier was dispatched from London to Milan, with the details of the bill, which Henry Browne received on 15 July. The following day, Browne reported to Stewart, 'No sort of preparation had been made to receive the Witnesses & they were insulted by the Mob.' More seriously Browne reported, 'The Work & Intrigue going on here, in the radical class – there is no lie untold, no measure however infamous, to which resource is not had, for the purpose of intimidating the Witnesses & disgusting them – It is made as hot a party business here, as in London.' To reinforce the point, Browne added, 'The fate of Italy seems tied to the Queen's apron-string.' Browne had at least received 'advice & support' from Sir Thomas Maitland, governor of Malta and lord high commissioner of the Ionian Islands, who had shown 'zeal & energy in the affair'.

Browne's letter shows that he was having to move quickly to make provisions. The lack of preparations likely stemmed from the government's expectation that Caroline would stay away, but as they now had to proceed against her, nobody had thought to advise Stewart or Browne. Maitland's arrival and assistance must have come as a great relief. Perhaps of even greater alarm for Stewart was the government's concern that the Queen's supporters were determined to blacken his name. Browne wrote that the ministers now sought copies of Stewart's previous correspondence on issues relating to the Queen, especially one letter from 1819, 'on the subject of the Witnesses at Vienna'. Castlereagh's private secretary, Lord Clanwilliam, told Browne that the foreign secretary was 'exceedingly anxious to have some further information on this point' as the government was afraid that Stewart might stand accused of impropriety in securing evidence. Despite these worries, Browne, the capable and efficient man on the spot, was happy that events were now moving forward. Browne expected the bill to appear in that day's *Milan Gazette* which he believed would 'make a change, or at least a hesitation, in public opinion'.[37]

Browne's optimism had somewhat faded a week later, but the Austrians at least were being cooperative. Stewart had leaned on Prince Metternich, and the colonel duly showed his appreciation for the Ambassador's 'intercession'. Poor Browne had received yet more demands from Clanwilliam with regard to obtaining correspondence, documents 'relative to the refusal of the order of Malta', and other papers. However, as Browne wrote, 'These are only to be had, (in the form to be of use) from the Police & the Tribunals.' Browne's problems again stemmed from his non-official status in Milan, and he argued, 'If I had full powers & had only to ask ... You know full well, how different is my situation, & that I have asked repeatedly & in vain for these Documents, which are so essential.' Even more annoying to Browne was that fact 'that they exist within a hundred yards of me & that I am unable to procure them'. The colonel was resigned to 'wait with patience, in the hopes of relief from you, as without You, the whole affair would long since have fallen to the ground'. This was certainly an acknowledgement of Stewart's role. Stupidly, the government had made Browne's job harder when it had allowed a group of Italian witnesses to be insulted and attacked at Dover on their arrival. Not surprisingly Browne advised that the incident had 'produced the most serious effects here, & Pergami, who has been here this week past, is most active, with all his Crew, in circulating lies'.[38] Castlereagh, with his own Caroline issues to deal with, probably did not unduly worry about Browne's problems in Milan. The government wanted results, without pausing to think about their man on the spot.

Things were getting very ugly in Milan in the summer of 1820, and in Italy generally. Browne had received news from Sir William A'Court in Naples and Lord Burghersh in Florence, on the state of unrest in their 'respective Neighbourhoods'. Armed with this, Browne had gone to the Austrian governor of Milan, at the express order of the Foreign Office, in what seems like a coordinated plan to frighten the Austrians into even more cooperation. The colonel informed Stewart on 28 July that Caroline's case was taking on the tone of political radicalism in Milan. In his reports, Browne disseminated news of the Milanese 'Coffee-rooms' awash with talk of 'insurrections & Constitutions' and the liberals proclaiming 'the approaching fall of Tyrants'. Browne was not overly worried by all of this, and although the liberals were 'ripe for any & every thing' they were 'cowards at heart, and will not venture a step, so long as a single Austrian Battalion shall remain here'.

Still it was prudent to keep an eye on events, and Browne hoped that Austria would have the foresight to send more troops in case they were needed. Using a phrase calculated to alarm Metternich, the colonel could tell Stewart, 'A Political Leader of the Democrats here, said in Society a few evenings since "The Queen of England <u>shall</u> triumph, & we want only two or three Questions of this nature, to establish the reign of common sense, & to rid us of all our Tyrants at once." ' Browne, with his soldier's hat on, still remained optimistic and believed, 'Troops will keep all this boasting perfectly quiet, and the larger the Mustachios the better.'[39] If Browne's reports were seen by Prince Metternich – and Stewart may well have passed these on – they would certainly have terrified him. With the governor of Milan being informed of threats from liberals, and with reports coming in of Caroline being used as a stalking horse to attack Habsburg rule in Italy, it looks suspiciously like Browne and Stewart were putting pressure on the Austrians, by deliberately using the spectre of revolution to secure what was needed.

Stewart was also pushing his relationship with Prince Metternich, believing that the Austrians would be as zealous in 'the cause of real justice and morality'. The Ambassador felt no compunction in presenting a shopping list of demands.

Firstly, Stewart wanted to know if Pergami had ever been 'confined under any criminal charge' and if so, where. If this could be shown, could the witnesses be sent to London? The British government also wanted information on Pergami's Orders of Chivalry, and on anything which confirmed the Italian's 'low origin' as well as that of his family, including Count and Countess Oldi, and whether they had kept a brothel. If they had, the politicians in London wanted to know 'how this is authenticated'. Stewart then turned to the Queen's stay in Vienna, and, showing that he was well aware of every piece of prurient gossip and rumours, asked for more:

> The British Government request that the Landlords, waiters &c may be examined at the Inn her Majesty resided at, at Vienna, to ascertain how the apartments were distributed, what the conduct of the Suite was at Vienna and . . . touching the extravagance of Her Majesty's appearance and her conduct while resident at Vienna.[40]

This request was basically a carte blanche for anything that the Austrian government had picked up in Vienna and Milan, 'That can throw light upon or adduce proof, corroborating testimony of the charges preferred against her Majesty the Queen, under the bill now brought in by the Lords Spiritual and Temporal assembled in Parliament'.[41]

Stewart might have transformed himself into a spymaster, but he could still get himself into trouble. The summer of 1820 witnessed one such incident involving Austrian royalty. The witness to the scene was Martha Wilmot, wife of William Bradford, recently appointed as chaplain to the Vienna embassy. In July and August, Stewart was regularly travelling between Vienna and Baden. Needing to follow the Imperial court to Baden, he had taken his wife with him, presumably at the end of July.[42] The Stewarts gave a ball for Henrietta of Nassau, the wife of the Emperor's brother, Archduke Charles. The Archduchess was 'particularly fond of dancing' and must have looked forward to British ambassadorial hospitality. She was certainly 'enjoying herself in that amusement' when Lady Stewart retired to her bedroom, attended by her husband. Stewart then sent a message ordering the music to cease, but the musicians 'continued playing, while her Imperial Highness continued dancing, on which Ld S. came forth from his Lady's bower and with his own lips order'd them to cease!' The Archduchess promptly left in anger but somehow the incident had been hushed up, although Martha Wilmot reported that 'from that period none of the Imperial family has entered their doors!'[43]

This was certainly stupid behaviour, and smacked of that attitude which had seen Stewart fall out with the Grand Duke Constantine in Paris. In mitigation, Stewart was clearly still anxious about his wife's health; added to this was the strain of the spying operation and the different demands of the British government and the Austrian authorities. This strain might just have been too much. The news of course reached London. The Duke of Wellington repeated the story to his confidante, Harriet Arbuthnot, in February 1821. The Duke was clearly unimpressed with the Stewarts and, more worryingly, he had heard further reports of a Habsburg snub to the Ambassador in direct retaliation.[44]

The incident did not merit a recall, despite Martha Wilmot's assertion that Stewart would not be permitted to return as ambassador, especially 'as 'Ld S: has appeared before the Emperor in dirty boots and otherwise with so little respect of demeanour that he will no longer endure him. Whether this report be true or false it may give you an idea *how* they are liked in Vienna! and no wonder. Their pride renders their very kindness an insult.' This comment smacks of pure malicious gossip.[45] It is possible that another diplomat would have been censured for such conduct, but no such censure seems to have occurred. Whatever happened, Stewart's relations with Prince Metternich were apparently unaffected. But, it is hard to escape the impression that the Stewarts were flouting the rules of society. The Stewarts obviously enjoyed flaunting their wealth, inspiring comment and resentment, as Martha Wilmot's description of one entertainment illustrates. Lady Stewart was 'decked out like the Queen of Golcondo [*sic*], seated on a sofa' while Stewart was his wife's 'most humble slave'.[46] At least the Stewarts were happily married, but they could not afford to alienate Austrian society too much. Meanwhile, back in London the political establishment assembled to hear the sordid details of a broken royal marriage.

The trial of the Queen in the House of Lords began on 17 August. The peers 'in their legislative-judicial capacity' were to decide on Caroline's guilt or innocence.[47] One of the prosecution's star witnesses was Theodore Majocchi, who had given evidence to the Milan Commission. Questioned by the solicitor general, John Singleton Copley, Majocchi provided seemingly damning details of the Queen's and Pergami's intimacy on their travels, down to the arrangements made by the major-domo for Caroline's baths. Henry Brougham, appointed the Queen's attorney general, took the lead for the defence, and he soon destroyed Majocchi's credibility with his cross-examination. The evasions from the witness, including 'I don't remember' or 'I don't know' (evasions which became famous as 'Non mi ricordo'), did much to undermine the prosecution.[48] This was not enough and Brougham determined to attack Majocchi further, painting him as a paid government stooge. By so doing, Brougham brought in Lord Stewart and Colonel Browne. Brougham started with Stewart:

About what time did you quit the service of the Marquis Onischalti [Odescalchi] at Vienna? About two years ago.

Into whose family did you then go? The Ambassador's of Vienna.

The English Ambassador? The English Ambassador gave me something to live upon.

What was his name? Lord Stewart.

Did you go as a postillion, lacquey, or courier, into his service? Lord Steward [*sic*] gave me only my living.

Do you mean that you became attached to his embassy as a sort of private secretary, or what? I was always at the embassade [*sic*].

Were you in his house on the footing of a private friend? No, not as a friend.

When did you first see his Excellency, the English Ambassador? I do not remember; I saw his secretary.

What was the secretary's name? Mr. Durin[g].[49]

It is apparent that Majocchi was not officially employed, but Stewart had kept the prosecution's star witness to hand, possibly using clandestine funds to help him. This was not in itself a crime, but in the context of the trial allowed the defence to politely besmirch the Ambassador.

Brougham then turned his attention to Henry Browne. Majocchi claimed in the cross-examination that he did not know either During's or Browne's nationality at that point, as they had both conversed with him in French. He further told Brougham that he was not in any employ at the time, which allowed the Queen's attorney general to again hint at a government conspiracy to buy Majocchi's evidence. Under questioning, Majocchi informed the House of Lords that he had gone to Milan with his father to meet with Browne. Brougham found this rather hard to understand. He asked why Majocchi had left Vienna, after meeting the recently promoted Colonel During, to go all the way to Milan simply to see Colonel Browne. Brougham was unsubtly hinting at illicit payments, and wanted to know if Browne had given the witness money, allowing the Queen's lawyer to imply corruption. The questions became increasingly sarcastic in tone, amidst cries of 'order' preventing Majocchi from answering.[50]

When asked, 'Did you ever go before, by your father's desire to speak to Colonel Brown[e], or to any body else?' the witness confirmed that he had not. Then moving to the point, the Queen's attorney general wanted to know, 'How did you support yourself on the journey from Vienna to Milan, when you went to speak to Colonel Brown[e]?' To this, the witness confirmed that his father had paid for the journey. Brougham wanted more details:

Has he made a private fortune by the lucrative trade of a carter or carrier? He has not.

Has your father any money at all but what he makes from day to day by his trade? No.

Did you live pretty comfortably on the road from Vienna to Milan to speak with Colonel Brown[e]? We wanted nothing.[51]

Brougham wondered whether Majocchi had complained to Browne about having to give up a lucrative position at Vienna, to which the witness gave one of his evasive 'Non mi ricordo' answers.[52] Having implicated Colonel Browne with accusations of underhand payments, it was time to attack Lord Stewart again.

Majocchi confirmed that he had temporarily rejoined Odescalchi's service, as a cook for three months, after returning from Milan. This seemed rather too convenient for Brougham who asked if Odescalchi was a friend of Stewart's. Majocchi could only answer 'I do not know'. This answer was repeated when he was asked whether Lord Stewart had ever been seen at Odescalchi's house. Perhaps his guard was down, but Majocchi again directly implicated the Ambassador:

Having no wages, how did you support yourself from the time you left Vienna
to the time you came back and went to Hungary with Onischalti [*sic*]? The
Ambassador gave me something to live on.

Did the Ambassador give you any thing when you went to Milan? Non mi
ricordo.[53]

Majocchi made matters worse for Browne by admitting that the colonel had paid
for him to travel back from Milan to Vienna.[54] Brougham could be satisfied that
some peers would suspect both Stewart and Browne of having bribed witnesses to
testify to the Queen's adultery. This interpretation was unfair to both men, who
were often without direct instructions, and somehow had to keep the Majocchi
family in funds. They had certainly made payments to support Majocchi in Vienna
and in Milan, while Stewart had unofficially attached this prosecution witness to
the embassy. Odescalchi was probably in on this too.[55]

The Queen's supporters, who included authors of atrocious stories and doggerel
verse, had a field day with Majocchi and his 'Non mi ricordo'. Inevitably the Milan
Commission was swept up in this, much of it centred on Colonel Browne.[56]
Browne appeared in poetical efforts as well, but many pro-Caroline writers failed
to make the link between Browne and Lord Stewart, which had been spelt out
so clearly by Brougham. At least the author of '*The Royal Italian Jugglers' Count
Milani and Countess Colombier* made the connection. These jugglers, otherwise
the prosecution's Italian witnesses, had been 'preparing their Tricks for public
exhibition'. The act had been a great success abroad:

They were honoured on the Continent with the patronage of distinguished
members of the Corps Diplomatique at Naples, Vienna, &c; and, having had an
opportunity of going through their whole performances before a select company
of the *most respectable English* at Milan, were advised and encouraged to exhibit
to the English nation, for their instruction and amusement.[57]

The 'jugglers' had many tricks, being able to 'see through *painted canvas and deal
boards*' and able to 'hear and explain the *most secret whisper* even through *two
decks of a ship in full sail*: and their intelligence is so remarkable, that, although
kept absolutely *separate from each other*, they can freely communicate each
other's thoughts and intentions'. In this brief satire, the writer had brought in Lord
Stewart, the Milan Commission, and Sir William A'Court in Naples.[58] Stewart was
fortunate that he was rather out of the line of fire, perhaps because his brother was
closer to hand and made a far easier target. As such, Castlereagh was singled out
for very unpleasant, often anti-Irish, attacks.

On 25 August, Stewart's former brother-in-law, Lord Ellenborough, spoke up
for him in the House of Lords. Ellenborough informed his fellow peers that to his
recollection, Stewart had been present in Britain from July 1817 to March 1818.
Ellenborough went further and told the peers that he had met Stewart on the Dover
Road in August 1818. For this reason, 'It was impossible' for the Ambassador to
have seen Majocchi in Vienna or to have had 'any communication' with the witness

after he had left for Milan.[59] Of course, Stewart's absence or otherwise would not preclude his role as spymaster against Caroline, but Ellenborough's intervention was timely.

The government's agents were not happy at Stewart's name being brought into the frame. In Milan, a British official, F. Seymour Larpent, told Stewart to take a less high-profile role. Larpent advised that all documents sent from Milan 'should be entrusted at Vienna to some inferior officer' who could then transport them to London. Larpent went further, and asked, 'As a matter of delicacy and propriety with respect both to our own Government and the Austrians' every piece of evidence laid before the House of Lords should appear to have 'been obtained at the request and instigation of the Attorney General'. This would have the advantage 'so as to take away arguments which may be otherwise used of any great zeal or interference on the part of either Government and to appear as if done at the request of the law officers'.[60] The damage had already been done by Brougham; that horse had long since bolted and feverish attempts to close the stable door were a little late. Stewart was having none of it, and he bluntly told Larpent that such subterfuge would hardly get very far, especially as the Austrians were in possession of his official correspondence relating to the Queen. Further, the attorney general had not made any requests or written 'a single line' to Stewart. In this predicament how could a man of honour 'transfer all my official Conduct upon Him?' In his defence, the Ambassador could at least advise Larpent that he was involved in facilitating passports for the Queen's legal team, as well as for the prosecution. Stewart added, 'It is now too late to retreat from a Line which certainly was marked out from England.'[61]

Safe in this knowledge that he was carrying out his instructions, Stewart was immune to any cautionary words, and along with Browne, was still working flat out in the government's cause. Throughout August, Stewart was pressing Metternich constantly for assistance in obtaining the necessary incriminating documents from the Austrian authorities in Milan. The tone showed he was being harassed by the British government to make progress.[62] In September, he was writing to Metternich about the Queen's representatives. He tried to appear impartial and forwarded complaints from Caroline's defence team who had encountered obstacles 'in collecting and forwarding the various evidence which is to appear in Her Majesty's behalf'. The Ambassador may have had an eye on any future leaking of letters, and he could assure Metternich that he had 'not omitted any Application, according to his Instructions to the Austrian Govt. to invite them to afford every facility in their Power to the Legal Advisers of Her Majesty the Queen of England'. This is also the same man who had written to one of Caroline's lawyers in Milan, a Mr James, that he could not 'speculate as to what Her Majesty's Law Advisers may recommend as proceeding further with a Defence so crippled'. So much for trying to appear impartial. Stewart's dislike for the Queen readily shines through his correspondence, although letting slip his opinions to her own legal advisers was perhaps not wise.[63]

In Milan, Browne could tell the Ambassador that 'no one of respectability has yet demanded a Passport' to go and appear as a witness for the Queen. Browne remained cheerfully optimistic and, referring to news from London, believed 'things at home go on steadily & well, & think at all accounts, Government has made out it's [*sic*] Case'. However, like Stewart, the colonel was aware of the dangers of being accused of securing witnesses through wholesale bribery. Browne had asked the solicitor general to examine all the financial transactions made '& that the more it is sifted, the more honorable it will appear, both to the Employers & Employed'. Indeed, Browne now stood on his dignity as a British officer to refute any accusations of impropriety with regard to money: 'It is as clear & bright as polished Steel, & I feel prouder in the integrity of all the money transactions, than in any operation of my life because the temptations to which I have been exposed, in regard to money, needed all the inflexibility of the English Character to withstand.'

Lord Stewart and Colonel Browne had been subtly and cleverly insulted by Henry Brougham in the House of Lords. Browne had especially been pilloried in the popular prints, although surprisingly Stewart had escaped most of the insinuations, with most of the vitriol, much of it deeply unpleasant, being directed at his brother, Castlereagh. In London, the crowds grew more restive as the trial progressed, with Castlereagh and the home secretary, Lord Sidmouth, marked out for regular abuse. It was fortunate that Lord Stewart was in Vienna, and even more so that his role seemed to be lost on those outside the rarefied audience in the House of Lords. This is very hard to understand, as Brougham had grasped what Stewart and Browne had been up to and had spelt this out at the trial.[64] It is more surprising so few linked Browne, one of the lead bogeymen in the popular press, back to his direct superior in Vienna. Stewart's position could have been made very uncomfortable. Lord Ellenborough's defence of Stewart would not have helped much if the Queen's partisans had really decided to go after the foreign secretary's brother. The trial was not over, but in Vienna, Lord Stewart had many other things to distract him. Revolution in Spain had been followed by revolution in Naples as Ferdinand I, King of the Two Sicilies, was forced to accept the 1812 Spanish Constitution in July 1820. These revolutions were likely to keep Stewart busy, and he might have felt that at long last he could put Queen Caroline out of his mind.[65]

Chapter 13

A VANE HEIR

Queen Caroline's trial continued in London. Stewart, safe in Vienna, could be relieved that having been attacked in the House of Lords, the cheap and popular prints had largely failed to make the connection between himself and the Milan Commission. This had long been feared by the Liverpool administration. For example, in the midst of the clamour at the start of the trial, the government had been mortified at the thought of Stewart's involvement being used against them; he had even been forced to defend himself to his brother about 'the charges of the Queen against my conduct' which were part of 'the Yellow bag'.[1] With his role in the spying operation now over, it was time to return to full-time diplomacy. Unfortunately, with Europe convulsed by revolution, a resumption of diplomatic certainties was not on the cards, and problems with the Congress System would come to the fore. Stewart also had to deal with a more serious Metternich, described in a most private and confidential letter sent to his brother on 3 February 1820: 'His Labor is incessant now. He has laid aside all trivial pursuits neither Play, Women, or Conviviality engross Him; the two former He has quite abandoned, and He seldom goes into Society'. Instead, Metternich's 'whole Mind and time' was spent in 'His <u>Cabinet du Travail</u>, which He scarce ever leaves'.[2]

Stewart's time in the latter half of 1820 was taken up with preparations for a new European congress called against the eruption of revolutionary fervour in Spain and Naples. From London, Castlereagh relayed to his brother George IV's 'regret' over events in Spain, together with the King's 'Surprise and Grief' at the Neapolitan revolution, especially as the army in Naples, according to the royal opinion, 'had no Grievance whatever'. Castlereagh, who had little time for reactionary monarchs, acknowledged the danger posed by events in Naples to international affairs. As he told his brother, 'However anxious the British Govt. may be to witness the progressive advancement of rational Liberty throughout Europe', revolution in Naples would cause special problems for foreign policy, 'from the tendency it must have to excite uneasiness in the Austrian Cabinet for the Security of Their Italian possessions'. Castlereagh charged his brother to advise Austria that Britain was prepared to give them almost free rein in Italy, and 'assure P. Metternich that we shall as far as possible endeavour not to embarrass them in acting upon it'.[3] Metternich had already drawn up a note for 'all the Austrian Ministers in Italy' comparing 'the difference, and leading features of the three

Revolutions of Europe—France, Spain, and Naples'. Stewart himself saw the French and Spanish revolutions as 'equally deplorable' but those 'at least bear the Character of their being effected by the whole Nation, the Governments being most imprudent and Tyrannical'. Naples was different, as the revolution there was 'the work merely of a deluded and factious Sect'.[4]

Alexander I was thoroughly alarmed by these revolutions. Unsurprisingly, the Tsar was one of the prime movers behind calls for a new congress to be held at Troppau (Opava) in Austrian Silesia. In advance of the Congress, Stewart relayed to the Foreign Office his insights into Alexander's frame of mind, evident in recent Russian correspondence with the Emperor Francis:

> The Emperor of Russia invariable in his Sentiments and unchangeable in the Principles of the Quadruple Alliance, trusts it is not yet too late by the Application of the Sage and Energetick means of the Four Powers which have already been exerted so Efficaciously at Aix la Chapelle to arrest the Evil of Revolution which is making such rapid progress and His Imp: Majesty felicitates Himself that His Allies <u>now</u> see the Danger with which Europe is threatened. (This evidently alludes in pique to His Imp: Majesty having taken a separate line towards Spain.)

The timing of the Congress of Troppau was dictated by Alexander's attendance at the Diet of Warsaw. The Tsar judged his presence in Warsaw as 'indispensably necessary', which meant he could not attend until early October 1820. Stewart also detected an underlying hostility towards Britain from Count Capodistrias in Russian correspondence, caused by 'ill Temper or a seeming indifference towards England and which I did not fail to comment on to Prince Metternich when he read me this Letter'. To Stewart, the most offensive passage declared, 'If the King of England is unable or does not attend this Reunion in Person, at least there would be the <u>Three Founders</u> of the <u>European System</u> Assembled to continue their Grave and important deliberations for its security and welfare.' As if this were not enough, Stewart reported that the Austrians would take full advantage of the situation:

> It appears to me that Prince Metternich will try to bend the positive proposition for a Reunion of Sovereigns into a Ministerial Conference of the accredited Ministers here, and afterwards when the course is shaped, it will be submitted to the Sovereigns at their Meeting as measures that have been proposed by Austria, discussed and decided upon.[5]

The Congress was potentially troublesome for Anglo-French relations.[6] A revival in French diplomatic ambitions was apparent and was already causing unease in Vienna, as Stewart informed London in early September: 'There is no doubt that the last French "<u>Mémoire</u>" in which the King of France's pretensions as Head of the House of Bourbon and consequently most deeply interested to take the lead in the Affairs of Naples, were put forward, has occasioned considerable Jealousy to this Government.'[7] Bourbon France, five years after Napoleon's final defeat, wanted to flex its muscles on the international stage. Stewart advised Castlereagh that Richelieu's ministry was growing in confidence to 'take prominent positions & regain amongst the Allied powers that Ascendancy which for a period has been dormant'. Anything affecting other Bourbon powers would excite the interest of the French monarchy. Richelieu was also particularly unhappy at the 'intimacy' of Britain and Austria over Italy, with French policy geared towards detaching Vienna from London and towards the embrace of Paris. Just as troubling for Castlereagh, the French prime minister seemed willing to conduct a personal vendetta against Sir Charles Stuart.[8]

Showing his usual political perception, Stewart summarized the problems of the great European alliance. In so doing, he was inadvertently spelling out the reasons why his brother's Congress System might ultimately be doomed to failure:

> The present Difficulties have undoubtedly brought forcibly into consideration, the Advantages & Disadvantages of the present Great Alliance, out of the five Powers who compose it, 3 have Monarchical Institutions the other 2 England & France have Constitutional Governments. The Measures of the former in all points connected with their publick Administration & safety should be rigorous prompt and immediate, In the Constitutional Govts they can be committed to nothing without previous Deliberation & Discussion, & though they can act upon a great Crisis or Contingency, they can not be pledg'd upon any probable Evil nor take part in any measures, to forestall Patiently.[9]

Stewart saw that Metternich was at a crossroads himself, as the Austrian minister had to decide whether he would 'stand singly with England' over this new European crisis.[10] Castlereagh's instructions and opinions of the Congress of Troppau were sent to Stewart in a most private, secret and confidential dispatch of 16 September. The foreign secretary advised, 'With all the Respect and Attachment which I feel for the System of the Alliance as regulated by the Transactions of Aix-la-Chapelle, I should much question the Prudence, or in truth the Efficacy, of any formal Exercise of its forms and Provisions on the present occasion.' Castlereagh had made clear the limits of Britain's involvement at Troppau:

> We desire to leave Austria unembarrassed in Her course, but we must claim for Ourselves the same Freedom of Action. It is for the interest of Austria that such should be our Position. It enables us in Our Parliament to consider and consequently to respect Her Measures as the Acts of an Independent State, a Doctrine which we could not maintain, if we had rendered Ourselves, by a previous Concert, Parties to those Acts; and it places us in a Situation to do Justice in Argument to the Considerations which may influence Her Councils, without, in doing so, being thrown upon the Defence of our Own Conduct.[11]

Before the Congress opened, discussions had touched on the subject of British naval protection for the Neapolitan royal family, but diplomatically it was made clear that Britain would not actively participate at Troppau.[12]

Stewart attended only as an observer, arriving in Troppau on 20 October 1820. At least Britain was not isolated. France 'did not want to appear too reactionary' and followed Britain's lead, sending just an observer, so that the two constitutional powers marched in step.[13] Stewart's uncomfortable status meant he soon felt his position as a second-class representative. Reporting back to Castlereagh on 23 October, Stewart wrote, 'Prince Metternich requested me to call upon him at one o'clock to-day, and I found there assembled the Ministers of the Sovereigns now present there, and those belonging to, or in the Suite of the Monarchs.' This was followed by the dubious pleasure of listening to Metternich's lofty outline of the Congress's aims. British sensibilities though would at least be respected. The day before, Stewart had told Metternich that he 'positively' declined to sign any Protocol, or to do any Act without positive Instructions' and 'would not go beyond the exact letter' of his orders. Metternich proposed instead that 'a Journal of deliberation' be made, to be signed only by Friedrich von Gentz.[14]

Stewart made himself useful, conducting a private interview with Alexander I on 23 October. The Tsar was in a bad humour following the second session of the Polish Diet. Alexander had been confronted by the 'emergence of a vociferous, liberal opposition', and the Tsar had left the country leaving instructions to his brother Constantine 'to have no scruples in overriding the Constitution' of the Polish kingdom if needs be.[15] Stewart soon discovered that Alexander was convinced of a grand revolutionary conspiracy, nothing less than 'a secret mischief that is undermining all our Governments', held 'together by a complete Intelligence and formed System of Action, and which is marching by rapid strides to revolutionize every state in Europe'. The danger to Europe would increase if the current British government were to fall. The Tsar had nothing but praise for Castlereagh, Liverpool and Wellington. But Stewart's report revealed the Tsar's obsession with revolution:

> It was not however, the immediate object of restoring the order of things at Naples and placing the King at liberty that should engross us; this was the Easier task that we had to perform – In His view our Great work was one of a much heavier nature, and all our faculties should be directed to counteract and oppose that fatal Spirit which was making such rapid progress in Europe, and to settle upon some principle of common action and conduct with regard to it, so that Military Revolution and the Machinations of occult Sects and Incendiaries, should be arrested and paralized.[16]

Stewart, a diplomat to his fingertips, advised the Tsar that this 'was a very Herculean, if not an impossible Task'. Treading carefully, Stewart told Alexander that these revolutionary outbursts 'broke out in different shapes and shewed itself in such various Colours in different Nations, that the same measures of precaution would not answer to each even if Nations were all in a position to adopt them'. The Ambassador then came to the nub of the matter, namely that the British government was 'from our construction more disposed to grapple with a danger when it arrived than seek to fight it at a great distance by an unintelligible and circuitous course'. As for the Congress of Troppau, Stewart's instructions had made it clear: 'Whatever was deliberated upon should be managed so as to avoid any general declarations, or universal pledges, and that the dissertation upon Abstract principles was considered by My Government as highly prejudicial.'[17]

Stewart kept Castlereagh informed of progress through secret and confidential communications, assuring his brother on 4 November that the French were not part of the '3 Monarchical Powers'. He kept close to Metternich and discovered that the Tsar had heard 'disagreeable intelligence' from St Petersburg of 'a movement in his Guards' duly reported to London on 15 November.[18] The mutiny in the Tsar's 'beloved' Semenovsky Regiment hardly endeared the idea of military revolts to Alexander.[19] The British though were walking a diplomatic tightrope. On the one hand, they had no desire to be seen as a reactionary power openly intervening in the internal affairs of other countries. On the other, they had already told the Austrians that they had a free hand to deal with Naples.

As Stewart told fellow diplomat Sir George Rose in November, Britain refused 'to become a party in any active interference which may be directed against Naples, and avoiding all responsibility under the engagement of a strict neutrality'. Stewart added that his 'watchful endeavours to maintain this Attitude' had received 'the support and concurrent sentiments of the Allied Cabinets, thereby securing to themselves a freedom of action, which it is hoped will be shortly developed, founded upon principles that may secure their future safety'.[20] With attention now focused on Naples, the British minister, Sir William A'Court, was suddenly placed in an exposed position. It was delegated to Lord Stewart to point this out: 'I am anxious to state explicitly that you are left at present to be guided by your own discretion and under your own responsibility'. A'Court would have to tread delicately in Naples. Stewart reinforced his message by reminding A'Court that 'although Emanating from the five powers, it has been planned, and adopted by three'.[21]

Troppau ended with an open rift in the Congress System and with Metternich's distancing himself from his formerly close relationship with Britain. The British and French anxiety to be disassociated from the monarchical states at Troppau was real. Siding with absolutist regimes would court grave unpopularity in London and Paris. However, with the British powerless to stop it, the final Troppau conference session on 7 December resolved that, if necessary, revolutions could be put down by allied armed force. That same day, Stewart sent London a copy of 'the Circular which has been finally agreed' which he understood was 'ultimately, the greater part from the Pen of Count Capodistria[s]' but which had 'undergone the pruning Knife of the Chevalier Gentz'.[22] After the Troppau Circular was 'conveyed' to Britain and France, Castlereagh 'accepted none of its propositions', and when news of the circular reached the press, the foreign secretary 'was forced to repudiate it publicly'.[23] The assembled diplomats agreed to meet again at a new congress planned for January 1821 and extended an invitation to the Neapolitan monarch, Ferdinand I, to attend.

Stewart remained in Troppau until late December 1820. Trying to repair diplomatic fissures, he had another personal interview with the Tsar, reporting on

Alexander's mood on 21 December. Alexander was 'personally, very flattering, and He said, "He however entertained little doubt that when the British Government, and Lord Castlereagh, had fully digested all the communications that would arise from Troppau, there would be a far different impression from that I seemed to entertain"'. Despite this unrealistic Imperial assumption, Stewart retained a sense of optimism. He advised Castlereagh, 'Something General will be done: But the strong sentiments of Great Britain, as expressed, will harmonize any Treaty or Formal Act into a General Statement of Principles upon Military Revolts and revolutions operated by illegal Means.' Stewart argued that any 'Formal Promulgation of what is intended for Europe' would be put on hold until the Neapolitan problem was resolved. As for the future, Stewart believed that as long as 'Great Britain and France are firm in non-accession to it, and set their face against the notions of carrying Neapolitan Remedies into the Spanish and Portuguese Quarters, we may look with confidence to a break up of Allied Conferences when the present object is disposed of.'[24]

Stewart also had to mend fences with Metternich, telling Castlereagh that 'When I went over Your Lordship's Paper with Prince Metternich, I certainly found Him much annoyed, He remarked that if all the other Powers had adopted a Line of Neutrality like England, Austria was lost, as She never could have taken upon Herself the Odium attending a separate Struggle with Naples.' The Ambassador further reported, 'It was therefore vital to Him, as Austrian Minister, to secure Russia and Prussia, This He had accomplished.' However, if Britain and France would not join the three other powers, Austria would secure its Italian interests through a possible 'Guarantee or Arrangement . . . and there would be some Understanding or general Declaration by such Powers as would come into it against Revolutions operated by illegal means.' Stewart was left unimpressed by the whole business, telling Castlereagh, 'I think it to be lamented that these great Transactions are clouded by a little rival Manoeuvring between the two operating Ministers which had infinitely better be avoided.' Britain's government could rejoice in one small crumb of comfort – they were less unpopular than France: 'The Proceedings of this French Government being reprobated as very inconsistent, and as it is now believed She will unite with us in our Jealousy on all Measures not consistent with Constitutional Ideas, there is not much Eagerness shewn for Her future opinions.'[25] Diplomacy was then suddenly and prematurely concluded. Stewart received news of a fire in his wife's bedroom and boudoir in Vienna, which meant he was forced to hurriedly leave Troppau, arriving back in the Austrian capital on 24 December. Fortunately, Lady Stewart 'most providentially escaped unhurt.'[26]

While Stewart had been busy in Troppau, the Queen's trial had not resulted in violent revolution in Britain as many had feared. By the end of October 1820, the defence and prosecution had summed up their cases. The peers voted to leave the divorce clause in the Bill of Pains and Penalties, and the whole was put to the House of Lords on 6 November. The result was 123 in favour and 95 against the bill. The government realized this was not an overwhelming majority and was unlikely to secure the divorce if it was pressed. The trial had shown that the Queen was likely guilty as charged, but the government saw no point in continuing, much to George IV's fury. As with so many great spectator sports, once the euphoria died down, the country rapidly returned to normal. Stewart still had secret service monies to account for, and in late December, in sending his account for the last five years, he noted that a number were connected to the spying operation on Caroline, including monies for Browne to travel to and from Milan, and other various expenses, including sums for £400 and £250. There were also the usual payments to Gentz.[27]

The new year of 1821 brought Queen Caroline unexpectedly back into Stewart's life. Letters once more were sent back and forth on the subject. Stewart dealt first with the government's concern over a parliamentary investigation into the conduct of the Milan Commission. This in turn had thoroughly alarmed the Austrians who would be shown as having 'aided and abetted the Enquiry'. Then came news of the attempted assassination of Colonel Henry Browne on 8 January. Browne's name had been to the fore during the Queen's trial, to the extent that Lord Camden had been obliged to come to the colonel's defence. Interestingly as Camden was Stewart's uncle, he perhaps saw defending Browne as a way of protecting his nephew. The opposition peer Lord Holland had been unimpressed, stating, 'He [Browne] might be a very deserving officer' but if Camden wanted to defend him via 'a long panegyric on his services in that house, it might be permitted to another to state what he thought of the conduct of Colonel Brown[e] in certain transactions as they stood on their lordship's Journals'.[28]

The 'atrocious and execrable Attempt' upon 'the Life of an Individual who has devoted himself to the Service of His Kings Country, with no ordinary Zeal' came as a shock to Stewart.[29] Insults had continued to be thrown at Browne after the trial had ended. Bad poetry was one thing, but Browne had put up with 'the attacks of knives and pens'.[30] Lord Byron, in a lapse of taste, was rather pleased that one of the king's agents had been attacked.[31] Browne was not badly wounded, and he was soon rewarded by appointment as a Knight Commander of the Royal Guelphic Order, George IV again using his Hanoverian honour to recognize services performed by those in the Caroline Affair.[32]

A new congress

Stewart's attention soon focused back on diplomacy and on his own family. In the diplomatic sphere, the next European congress opened on 12 January 1821 at Laibach (Llubljana), in the Austrian Duchy of Carniola. Adopting the same policy as before, the British government resolved to send Lord Stewart only as an observer. However, Stewart was absent from the opening of the Congress. With his wife's twenty-first birthday in January, there were various legal affairs to resolve along with the small matter of presenting Frances Anne with a 'diamond Bouquet'. Stewart was also distracted by news from Ireland, as his father, Robert Stewart, first Marquess of Londonderry, was dying. Frances Anne felt that her husband should distract himself by setting off for Laibach as soon as possible, and so off he went.[33] This new congress was determined to put an end to the revolution in Naples but would conclude with Britain further isolated from its European allies.

After his late arrival at Laibach, Stewart resumed his regular reporting on the diplomatic wrangling, and felt compelled to announce, perhaps a little prematurely, the death of the Congress System. This pronouncement arose from the attitude of Britain's constitutional ally, France. French politics was still dominated by the duc de Richelieu. However, Stewart noticed the increasing power of the 'close confidant' of Louis XVIII, the comte de Blacas, the former minister of the Maison du Roi, and currently French ambassador to the Holy See.[34] Blacas was very much identified with Ultra Royalist France and had been Talleyrand's bête noire in 1815. The comte was chosen to represent France at the new Congress, and he received new instructions from Paris on 18 January 'furnishing him with full powers to accede to all the resolutions of the allies'.[35] Prince Metternich had been working hard since Troppau to 'secure the aid of France not only in all the measures <u>to be</u> adopted in Italy, but likewise if possible to unite Her with the 3 other Powers in Their <u>immediate</u> Measures with regards to Naples'. Blacas was not slow to see the advantages. Having 'been of late a prominent figure in Italian politics', and now enjoying 'the chief direction of French Affairs at the Conferences', he was now presented, in Stewart's opinion, with 'an opportunity which was not to be lost'.

The Kingdom of the Two Sicilies was formally represented by Prince Ruffo, the Neapolitan ambassador to Austria. Ferdinand I, King of the Two Sicilies, had also been invited to the Congress of Laibach, and once safely out of Naples he repudiated the constitution he had agreed to. Ferdinand then made a pre-planned request to the other powers for help in putting down the revolution. Stewart saw the hand of Blacas behind this, together with one of Metternich's protégés, the Austrian diplomat Count Lebzeltern, although he could not definitely discover the extent of their involvement. If true, it would mean a closer rapprochement between Austria and France.

Blacas had his own game to play, namely to pursue the 'desire of France to raise Herself up in the Alliance' which 'has long been evident and in proportion as She gains consolidation in Her institutions by the encreasing [*sic*] strength of Her Government'. In addition to this, in Stewart's opinion, was 'the vanity belonging to all Frenchmen' which 'has been largely played upon in the person of Mr de Blacas'. The end result would be trouble for Britain. British policy was to avoid influencing France 'to any other line of Conduct' than one which 'their own views and Policy may lead them spontaneously to adopt'. Stewart believed that such a diplomatic line was a failure, and he relayed the dismal effects of this course of action back to London. During a conversation with Blacas, Stewart discovered that the French representative found the Austrians, Russians and Prussians 'so fixed in their purpose, and so determined to hear no Opposition to the exact course they chose to steer', that he would not even bother to stand in their way and would go along with whatever they decided:

We must therefore no longer conceal from ourselves that we stand alone in our position, and that Austria has embarked the other 3 Powers under Her Banners in Her present purpose.

She has facilitated immensely Her position by having succeeded through the means of Her various efforts and Negotiations to produce the present posture of Affairs, but as to what may grow out of it hereafter, it is difficult to determine.[36]

A letter had been prepared for the King of the Two Sicilies to send to his son and heir, the Duke of Calabria, acting as Prince Regent, which 'justified Ferdinand's violation of his oath' to the new constitution. A second letter was also prepared in which the new Regent 'was to keep secret or to publicize at his own discretion'. This outlined 'the pacific and amicable' allied aim of sending in Austrian troops.[37] Stewart's unhappiness with the allies was spelt out to Sir William A'Court on 28 January:

The point on which I feel the least satisfied is, that notwithstanding my earnest and urgent efforts, the King's Letter to His Son (which I conclude will be the first Instrument made public at Naples) carries upon it the expression 'Les Souverains Alliés' the second Letter also in one Paragraph has the same denomination for decisions in which our August master takes no part.

However the incalculable desire of unanimity and <u>Solidarité</u> amongst the Powers, and the Policy, in my humble opinion, once that our line is made clear, of not being too capricious, or traversing theirs, has led me to be satisfied with the clear manner in which the first part of the two Letters specify those Sovereigns of the Alliance, whose Sentiments the King's Letter can alone declare, and we can hardly insist upon directing His Sicilian Majesty's exact expressions to His Son.[38]

However, British diplomacy was not as innocent as Stewart implied to the Congress, as he told A'Court with some frankness: 'The nicety of the Question is, that on the first promulgation of this Manifesto, that Great Britain should not appear to be included and yet not to withdraw from an oral and intimate understanding with the other Powers.'[39] On 31 January, Stewart had to advise the Foreign Office that, thanks to Blacas, he discovered that a third letter had been sent to the Duke of Calabria. In this letter, Ferdinand advised his son to 'summon the Council, and demand of them to appoint a Council of Regency, and that His Highness himself should lay down this Character, it would then be for the Regency to take their determination'. Calabria was then to place himself at the head of his guards and 'to wait for further Events' at the fortress of Gaeta. Perhaps as much of a problem as all this underhand diplomacy was the weakness of Ferdinand himself. Stewart was under no illusions: 'He has not in his own inclination the least disposition for this Step, and would much rather go and hunt Wild Boars near Vienna.'[40] Stewart's next secret and separate letter to Castlereagh of 2 February touched on Browne's attack at Milan, before fully returning to business in his most secret and confidential dispatch of the same day. Aside from his criticisms of Metternich, Stewart reported that both Britain and France had been left out of meetings involving Italian representatives and again highlighted the divisions in the Congress System. Ferdinand was to have 'a constitution given to him cut and dry by Metternich and Capodistrias' while France was again in disfavour. Stewart noted, 'They will endeavour to get rid of France in the consideration of this discussion. They find Blacas already embarrasses them on the question of military contributions in case of resistance.'[41] Blacas though had been in a very uncomfortable position, having received yet further instructions 'to avoid committing France to taking any part in new hostilities in Italy'. On 2 February, he registered in the Congress Journal that in case of 'coercive measures, France would not participate in them'.[42]

The consequences of division at the Congress of Laibach soon became apparent. Faced with increased hostility from British public opinion, the foreign secretary issued a State Paper on 5 May 1821 which 'argued that the alliance could not be extended to become an instrument of oppression'.[43] More immediately the result of the Congress was felt by the Neapolitan revolutionaries. The Austrians marched an army into Naples, put the revolution down and put paid to any notions of a constitution for the Kingdom of the Two Sicilies. This was not the end of Italian revolutionary activity. Another revolution broke out in the Kingdom of Piedmont in March 1821, but by this time Stewart had handed over his responsibilities at Laibach to Robert Gordon. In Stewart's absence, it was left to Gordon to report back on Italian affairs to the Foreign Office.[44] Stewart though was not completely removed from diplomacy. Back in Vienna, he reported on the Laibach Congress in several lengthy letters to the foreign secretary during May and June 1821. Most significantly, on 30 May Stewart advised on Metternich's unhappiness with Britain:

> From the Commencement (the Prince added) I have never been mistaken in the magnitude of what I had to contend with. On this Ground Your Govt. has never done me Justice, they take their Views form the actual Appearances of the Moment, They never look . . . for the Mischief that is brooding, Their insular Situation removes them from all the Channels and Sources of correct information, whereas the central position of Austria gives her the most ample & enlarged Knowledge upon every point connected with the State of Europe; from a firm conviction therefore that the Evil was not partial but general, not only general but nurtured & disseminated from Paris, I framed all my Measures . . . all these Troubles have arisen from France alone and they have been aided & abetted by the mistaken policy & grievous faults of that Govt. and the support that I . . . supposed would be derived from the Liberalism of the Emperor of Russia.[45]

Metternich at least congratulated himself, 'The Emperor of Russia became happily . . . alive to all His former mistaken liberal views. He candidly avowed his Error. The Reign of those Ministers who led Him in his former path is at an end, & I pledged myself . . . to answer for the Emperor of Russia's Conduct until our next Meeting as for my own.'[46]

As at Troppau, Britain remained less unpopular than France. Stewart advised the Foreign Office in June, 'On the question of the Game France has played Prce. Metternich entirely concurs also in Sentiments with Sir Wm. A'Court, and in His Highness's expressions to me, reprobates the whole System of that power in the strongest manner.' Metternich reportedly had a 'total Impossibility in these facts, of Knowing how to trust France and such an evident contrast between the Acts of the King and His Governt: That it must create an entire want of Confidence and Respect in the whole French System.' Louis XVIII's representative was at least rewarded for his discomfort at Laibach, being made duc de Blacas.[47]

With the Congress ending unsatisfactorily for Britain, and with Prince Metternich increasingly prepared to ignore British sensibilities, Stewart could rest assured that he still stood high in George IV's estimation, undoubtedly reinforced by his zeal in the King's cause over the Caroline Affair. The continued royal favour was confirmed by George IV's command that he attend both his proposed visit to Ireland and the forthcoming coronation. The coronation, postponed thanks to Queen Caroline's return, was due to take place at Westminster Abbey on 19 July 1821. The command to Lord Stewart informed him that the King was 'desirous to call you near his Person; subject nevertheless, to the State of Foreign Politics, and to the Health of Lady Stewart . . . no one is more anxious for Her well-being than the King or more ardently hopes for an Heir Apparent'.[48]

The King's letter referred to Lady Stewart's pregnancy, which had added to Stewart's reluctance to participate at the Congress of Laibach. At some point, Stewart had obviously vented his frustrations on Robert Gordon. That such behaviour was out of character is apparent as the Ambassador felt compelled to apologize for his 'bad humour' which had given him 'unfeigned pain to see that a momentary Expression of my spleen should have hurt You'. One of Stewart's most attractive qualities had always been his willingness to lavish praise on his subordinates, and he assured Gordon, 'In a very long & indefinite friendship & under various points of Business, no one upon Earth can be more sensible of your merits than myself.' Just as importantly, in a world of patronage, Stewart would always be 'ready at all times to acknowledge them & to avow the great Assistance I have always derived from yr Ability Talents & Experience'.[49]

The spring of 1821 would bring great personal changes. The first was the expected death of his father Lord Londonderry in April, at the age of 81. Although his father had found every opportunity to complain about his second son's extravagances, Stewart had always seemed to take this in good part and had often used his brother to act as mediator. The second personal change was the birth of the long-awaited Vane heir. Lord Stewart's marriage to Frances Anne had seen him change his surname to Vane, but as yet there was no heir to the huge inheritance and coal mine riches in Durham. The Stewart dynasty was secure with Frederick, but he would have no rights to the Vane estates. Lady Stewart, who had already suffered a miscarriage, had worried that she would not be able to have children. Frances Anne's pregnancy was not completely trouble-free, with the fire in the embassy and her husband's absence at Laibach.[50] All this aside, she successfully gave birth to a healthy son, George Henry Robert Charles William Vane, on 26 April 1821.

There was now a male heir to the Vane estates, and no expense was to be spared to celebrate this glorious event, as Lady Stewart wrote in her journal.[51] A semi-royal christening was planned, and for the full details of this extravaganza, historians are indebted to Martha Wilmot.[52] The christening was planned for 4 June 1821, for the son pointedly described as 'the *heiress heir*'. The boy was 'the most exquisite infant' that Martha Wilmot had 'ever beheld', which she thought was rather unfair as the couple already had everything and '*seem* to possess Fortunatus's wishing cap . . . and as they do not *squander* the power of pleasing others, I suppose they must at last sink under the load which they accumulate on their dear selves'.[53] This is the rub of the matter and helps explain the harsh tone apparent in the journal. At some point the Stewarts must have disappointed the Bradfords' expectations, perhaps in the shape of ecclesiastical preferment, or from a perceived meanness.

To a correspondent, Lady Bloomfield, Martha Wilmot unleashed all of her feelings. The recipient was the wife of the King's Keeper of the Privy Purse, a man who was on very good terms with Lord Stewart. It is to be hoped that Sir Benjamin Bloomfield did not catch sight of this outpouring, written over the course of several days in early June. The recipient should have been slightly embarrassed, as the Bloomfields' son, John, was an attaché at the embassy. She opened with abuse of the Stewarts, before continuing with a deliciously vindictive hatchet job, especially so when describing the christening itself. The invite given by the 'mock Royals' specified that attendees should appear in full court dress. On arrival at the embassy, they were greeted by Frances Anne 'dress'd exquisitely in brussels lace, profusion of diamonds on her head, EIGHT THOUS[AN]D *p*[oun]ds *worth* of pearls on her broad expanse of neck and shoulders, and a bouquet of flowers in precious stones'. Not to be outdone, Lord Stewart was 'in full uniform, yellow boots and all, which *God forgive the wicked* always makes me think of a tame Jackdaw, to say nothing of a gold chain *clasped* with a ruby, an emerald and a diamond serpent!'

Prince Metternich stood proxy for George IV, one of the child's godfathers, Lady Stewart was proxy for her mother, the Countess of Antrim, and Lord Stewart was proxy for his brother. In the midst of this the 'unconscious little innocent was dress'd in blue satin, brussels lace and surrounded with every vanity and pomp which money could purchase'. Even Martha Wilmot had to admit the scene was something to behold, 'The entire scene was *theatrical*, but of the very first order.' The mother and heir were then 'displayed to public view and inspection'.[54]

Stewart also had other concerns. Joseph Planta had acknowledged the various sums spent over the course of the Caroline spying operation, as well as the £300 paid to Gentz, Metternich's secretary, for services rendered. Gentz certainly continued to do well from British secret service funds. Perhaps more tellingly, Planta used the opportunity to advise of the enormous strains his brother, now second Marquess of Londonderry, was under, while reassuring Stewart that the foreign secretary's 'Health continued good notwithstanding all his fatigues; indeed, he has borne them better than we could have expected.'[55] Castlereagh (as he will still be referred to) remained leader of the house as well as foreign secretary, and the ministry's leading spokesman in the Commons.

Added to this workload was the continuing abuse from the popular press, such as this effort from *A Slap at Slop*, over the results of the Congress of Laibach: 'LOST, THE BALANCE OF EUROPE as *privately adjusted*, according to a pair of *pocket* scales, by the Marquis of Londonderry; it was last seen *on a piece of paper* at Laybach [*sic*]. Please to bring it to the Foreign Office.' This edition contained other insults at 'BOB STEWART, an Irishman, who jobbed at the Castle, in Dublin, and *worked in the Yard*.'[56] Stewart could at least look forward to seeing his brother, as he was preparing to return home, in order to take his place among the assembled peers for George IV's coronation. However, the best-laid plans soon went awry. George Henry Vane caught a cold following a vaccination, necessitating a delay in the Stewarts' departure until late June. The Stewarts did not arrive at Dover until 8 August, long after the coronation.[57]

Lord Stewart was not in London when the final act of the Caroline Affair took place. The Queen had expressed her intention to play a role in the coronation ceremonial, but of course her husband was having none of this. She was determined anyway, and had to be physically barred from entering Westminster Abbey. The crowds, once so supportive, were unimpressed with this spoiling of the great spectacle, and Caroline had been forced to admit defeat with boos ringing in her ears. She died a little while later, on 7 August, the day before the Stewarts arrived back in the country. The death of the Queen allowed a pro-Caroline author, John Wilks, to rush out a biography in 1822. This revived memories of Lord Stewart's role in the affair, as evidenced by this passage, on the insults received from the Austrian court:

> The enmity of Lord Stewart, who was at that time ambassador from the English government to that of Austria, in some measure, however, accounted for such conduct, as he was one of the principal actors in the celebrated Milan Commission, to whose proceedings it will be hereafter necessary distinctly to refer.[58]

This was all too late, and the Queen's partisans had failed to hit their target when they needed. The tumult had died down, and if Stewart felt any discomfort at being mentioned in print like this, he gave no indication.

The Ambassador was about to embark on a rather extended leave of absence, as Stewart would not return to Vienna until the following summer, leaving the capable Robert Gordon in charge. Soon after their arrival in Britain, the Stewarts went down to stay at Castlereagh's house in Cray. Castlereagh though was absent, as he was in attendance on the King in Ireland, but Stewart's eldest son, Frederick was there to meet them, as was Emily, his sister-in-law. There had been diplomatic concern that George IV intended to travel to Vienna as part of his planned visit to Hanover, which would have necessitated Lord and Lady Stewart returning to Austria. Stewart was reassured from Carlton House that 'Vienna will <u>not</u> be in our route. This will ease both your mind & Lady Stewart's.'[59] Castlereagh would of course have to accompany his royal master to Hanover, but perhaps it was unfortunate that the two brothers would not in fact meet in the Austrian capital. Castlereagh and Metternich at least had an opportunity to meet in Hanover, where they 'tried to restore a common understanding following their disputes over the Troppau Protocol'.[60]

Now that there was no need to return to Vienna, the Stewarts could enjoy themselves to the full. There was a trip to Brighton, recorded in Lady Stewart's Journal, where her husband reviewed the regiment of which he was colonel, the 10th Hussars. She wrote, 'Charles, in his full General's uniform' had been very well received and that evening had provided a dinner at the riding school accompanied with 'an immense quantity of ale'. This had proved too much for Frances Anne, who was taken ill, but her immense pride in and love for her husband were apparent.[61] There were also other pleasures. Sir Henry Hardinge, a member of Stewart's extended family, and recently elected as MP for the Vane interest in Durham, became part of his close family in late 1821, when he married Lady Emily James, Stewart's sister.

Lady Stewart was enjoying society, but the couple's immense wealth soon began to attract unfavourable comment. Dorothea, Countess Lieven, wife of the Russian ambassador, caught sight of Frances Anne in London. Countess Lieven wrote to her lover, Prince Metternich, on 16 March 1822 that Lady Stewart 'looked to me like one of those effigies you see in Greek churches, with no colour or shading but loaded with jewels. She was wearing enough to buy a small German principality.' Four days later, she was able to amuse Metternich further, after actually meeting Frances Anne, commenting unfavourably on her appearance and size, as Lady Stewart was again pregnant. Much more importantly, the Countess advised Metternich that Lady Stewart 'is bored in Vienna. I told her there was nothing simpler than not to go back; I said that in the interests of a good many people.' Who the 'good many people' actually were is not spelt out, but the fact that this was written to Metternich indicates a willingness of the Austrians and possibly the Russians to be rid of Stewart from Vienna. Perhaps, after eight years, the Ambassador had been in place too long, but the real reason likely lies in the increasing distance between Britain and Austria. Having the foreign secretary's brother in Vienna, as the trusted eyes and ears of his government, could prove embarrassing in the long term.

Countess Lieven also gave her lover a glimpse into the opulence that Lord and Lady Stewart enjoyed, and one which likely raised eyebrows in some quarters. The Stewarts were content to spend lavishly, their desire for ostentation apparent. The Stewarts had rented a house in London and the Countess was one of those invited. Calling on Lady Stewart in April 1822 she was shown the bedroom:

Above the bed is a baron's coronet, the size of the crown of the King of Würtemburg [*sic*] on the palace at Stuttgart – red, velvet, ermine, everything that goes with it. From it hang heavy draperies, held up at the four corners of the bed by four large gilt figures of Hercules, nude and fashioned exactly like real men. The bed is as big as a room and almost on the level of the ground . . .

What an extraordinary family! I should lose my taste for luxury in that house: it
is displayed in such a vulgar way.[62]

The Stewarts did not care what others thought, and with an income of £80,000
a year were wealthy enough to enjoy thick skins. Openly flaunting wealth was
always capable of putting noses out of joint in London society, and in this case the
Russian ambassadress probably voiced the reaction of others.

Stewart was not yet ready to return, and aside from the purchasing of huge
beds, there was serious political work to be done at home. Stewart was now the
father of two sons, who were heirs to two dynasties: that of Stewart represented
by Frederick, and that of Vane, represented by his new son, George Henry. Lord
Stewart could be forgiven if he did think of a career change, perhaps to a position
at home. He had acquitted himself well at the two recent congresses, he had put
Queen Caroline behind him, and remained high in his sovereign's favour. Lord
Liverpool had intimated that he might one day stand aside in favour of his foreign
secretary, which would bring new opportunities for his brother. However, this
remained just a possibility, as the prime minister, on other occasions, indicated
that he was not about to retire.[63] It seemed that all was set fair for Stewart's
continued ascent in honours and responsibilities. Castlereagh might have ignored
his brother's requests for the Paris embassy in the past, but perhaps some other
post could be found which would be more congenial to Stewart and his new family.

Chapter 14

THE DEPLORABLE EVENT

In the spring of 1822, Stewart was enjoying life on leave and seemed to be in no rush to resume his diplomatic duties, although preparations were being made in Vienna for his eventual return. From the Austrian capital, one of the Ambassador's employees, Arthur Aston, wrote to Stewart to confirm that the 'various orders transmitted to me by Browne' were being carried out, including the completion of a 'Music Machine' which would be 'more powerful and complete than P. Metternich's, and to contain four different Airs'.[1] Vienna must have seemed very distant to the Stewarts. The couple also had much to celebrate with the birth of a daughter, Frances Anne Emily, on 15 April 1822. Countess Lieven was one of those invited to the christening which took place on 20 May. She noted that the event witnessed 'a great deal of vulgar ostentation' which 'took nearly the whole day'. The Countess was given another chance to comment on the overly decorated bed, and although she thought the whole thing was tasteless, it was obviously the fashionable place to be that day as 'the whole town came to see the farce'.[2]

Life in London was not just the usual round of pleasantries. Stewart soon found himself in the middle of another royal drama, as Castlereagh was now in difficulties at court. The King's current mistress, Elizabeth, Marchioness Conyngham, was not overly popular with many in society, who saw her as particularly grasping. Unfortunately for the foreign secretary, one of those who took a strong dislike to Lady Conyngham was his wife, Emily. The mutual dislike reached the stage where the royal mistress demanded that Castlereagh's wife be forbidden from all official functions, including the King's plan to attend a proposed congress at Florence. Such a request was patently absurd.

Dorothea Lieven found herself an active participant in the affair, trying to broker a peace settlement, while also witnessing the added strain this put on Castlereagh's health. On 2 June, she helpfully supplied Prince Metternich with all of the latest news. She painted a picture of a foreign secretary who was in 'a positive rage' and on the verge of resigning for the insult done to his wife. Meanwhile, Stewart seemed helpless as he witnessed the strain this all put on his brother's health. In some distress, he informed Dorothea that Castlereagh was 'disgusted with everything. One more reason for disgust – this women's quarrel – and the cup has overflowed.' Stewart was a witness to his brother's declining health, made worse as it was accompanied by political paranoia. Castlereagh complained of 'the new rival put up against him in the House of Commons, and the mistrust that he feels of all his colleagues'. Countess Lieven, acting as one of Metternich's spies, managed to extract more information from Stewart, who admitted that his brother distrusted his cabinet colleagues, especially the Duke of Wellington. The Countess was quite taken aback at this news, at which 'Lord Stewart burst into tears. He told me that Lord Londonderry was broken-hearted, and that he had never seen a man in such a state.' As a sign of desperation, he even asked if Dorothea could secure 'an open declaration of hostility from Lady Conyngham'.[3]

Stewart was again sent by his brother to Countess Lieven, and tumbled out more on his brother's paranoia about his colleagues, centred again on Wellington. By 10 June, the Countess could tell Metternich that the foreign secretary 'looks ghastly', had aged five years in a matter of a week and seemed to be 'a broken man'. Dorothea also believed that Castlereagh's paranoia was being magnified through his brother's own suspicions:

> I am afraid that Lord Stewart may be doing him a bad turn, and that his suspicions may have taken root in his brother's mind. Now that I know what those suspicions are, a number of circumstances come to mind that confirm me in my belief that he mistrusts the Duke of Wellington.[4]

Certainly Stewart had voiced his suspicions of the Wellesley family before, notably after his brother's duel with George Canning in 1809. The two brothers were used to speaking to each other frankly, and it is likely that Dorothea Lieven mistook this as Stewart's encouragement of Castlereagh's hostility towards Wellington. Whatever the case, Stewart would only have wanted to help his brother.

Castlereagh and Stewart still had official business to deal with, primarily connected to an impending diplomatic gathering in Vienna, called to discuss another European crisis. The Greeks had started a full-scale uprising against Ottoman rule: the cause was popular with many in Britain, but European diplomats were concerned about the wider implications. The diplomats and ministers were then due to attend the next congress, now scheduled to take place at Verona.[5] In reality, the Congress of Verona would also have to deal with the ongoing and deteriorating political situation in Spain. Metternich had always seen Castlereagh as a man he could work with and was clearly concerned by news that the foreign secretary might resign. Countess Lieven now took on an extraordinary new role, as an unofficial Austrian diplomat and raised the issue of the forthcoming meetings with Castlereagh. Dorothea could assure Metternich that the foreign secretary intended to come. She also got to work on George IV. Lord Stewart, somewhat amazed, told her, 'I congratulate you; you must be proud of yourself; you have made the King obey you on every point. My brother found him as prepared as if he was under orders; everything you wish is done, and we must all run at your bidding.' As the Vienna meeting and the Congress of Verona required the attendance of the British ambassador to Austria, Stewart's long absence was now brought to an end. However, he set out for Vienna with an air of trepidation, confiding to Dorothea Lieven, who recalled his 'despair', that 'it will end in disaster', although, as she said later, 'I never supposed that the phrase referred to anything but a political event.'[6]

On 12 August 1822, 'the Marquis of Londonderry, after several days of mental and bodily illness, died in a fit of derangement.'[7] Under the strain of his workload, with perhaps the row between his wife and the King's mistress as a tipping point, Castlereagh's health had deteriorated sharply. The paranoid persecution complex had reached fever pitch, and the Duke of Wellington had been so shaken by the state of the foreign secretary's health that he had advised that the greatest precautions be taken. As Dorothea Lieven reported, during the last interview held between the King and his foreign secretary, Castlereagh had 'accused himself of every crime; he threatened the King, and then kissed his hands, and wept; for half an hour he alternated between madness and repentance'. Castlereagh had then returned to his house at Cray where steps were taken to ensure the foreign secretary could not harm himself. However, these precautions were not enough, and on the morning of 12 August, Castlereagh's doctor went to attend him in his dressing room:

> The doctor went in after him, and found him standing up, his eyes fixed. He cried, '*Let me fall in your arms, it is all over.*' The doctor ran to him; at that moment, streams of blood gushed from an artery in the neck . . . In his right hand, he was holding a little pen-knife which he used to cut his nails; he fell stone dead.[8]

Historians have long debated the causes of Castlereagh's breakdown and death, examining at some length the conspiracies that the foreign secretary accused himself of, his delusions and paranoia. Numerous theories have been put forward over the years.[9] What is certainly clear is that Castlereagh was a prodigiously hard worker; by combining the roles of foreign secretary and leader of the House of Commons, he bore a huge strain on his shoulders as the government's lead spokesman in the lower house. When most of his cabinet colleagues sat in the House of Lords, this must have made for a lonely position. It is also no coincidence that Lord Stewart showed a tendency to depression at key moments in his career. Castlereagh might well have been suffering from similar symptoms of depression to those that gripped Stewart. However, Stewart had always managed to pull himself back from his depressive bouts, but in Castlereagh's case, the sheer strain of ten years of unremitting work seemed to cause a complete breakdown. Castlereagh was still at the peak of his political powers, and his health declined at a frightening speed. The foreign secretary's suicide was a terrible loss to the country, and a grievous blow to Stewart, who would now be without his brother's support and wise counsel.

The Duke of Wellington wrote to Stewart on 21 August, to tell him of his 'heartfelt grief at the deplorable event'. The Duke also gave an account of Castlereagh's funeral at Westminster Abbey, which 'was attended by every person in London, of any mark or distinction of all parties, and the crowds in the street behaved respectfully and creditably'. There had been one notable exception by a group of radicals at the door of the Abbey who 'were evidently employed for the purpose, and were ashamed of showing themselves'.[10] The Ambassador was now third Marquess of Londonderry, while his eldest son, Frederick Stewart, the chief mourner at his uncle's funeral, now became, by courtesy, Viscount Castlereagh. The Londonderry title had been enjoyed by his brother for only a short while, and it was as Viscount Castlereagh that he had become famous throughout Europe. It was this fact which led Lord Liverpool, at the foreign secretary's funeral, to offer the new Lord Castlereagh a post in government should Frederick ever desire office.[11]

Resignation from Vienna

There were practical arrangements to be made, not least of which was the appointment of a new representative to the Congress of Verona. The choice was clear. Only the Duke of Wellington had the necessary international prestige to take the foreign secretary's place. The choice of a new foreign secretary and leader of the House of Commons was also obvious. George Canning was the only real man of talent that the government could call upon in the House of Commons. This also meant that the new Lord Londonderry would be answerable to a man he detested. The death of his brother, coupled with the promotion of a family enemy, was too much. In a breach of etiquette, probably intended as a not too subtle insult to Canning, Londonderry wrote to both George IV and Lord Liverpool on 25 September 1822 to announce his resignation, rather than to the new foreign secretary.

Frederick had travelled to be with his father in Vienna.[12] Now, he was sent back to London with his tutor, carrying the two resignation letters. Trying to cope with the loss of his brother, the third Marquess of Londonderry wrote to the prime minister to make practical arrangements for Frederick, while also finding time to make the first of his preferment requests, seeking ecclesiastical patronage for his son's tutor, 'The only moral Obligation That my beloved Brother conceived He had to accomplish.'[13] This was to be the first of many references to his brother in such letters, which soon caused irritation to the recipients. The letter to the prime minister conveyed a mixture of emotions: the wrench caused by his brother's death, the desire to do his duty, distaste for George Canning and his own epitaph for his eight years' work in Vienna. Astonishingly, the resignation letter also contained some criticism of Liverpool's lack of communication, never a wise idea for anyone who might want future preferment himself, before turning to the subject of rewards for services rendered at Vienna.[14]

To George IV, the Marquess spoke of his 'deep and heartrending' state of mind, although he did not mention Canning by name, as this would have been rather tactless.[15] Lord Liverpool received the resignation letter at Walmer Castle in October from Sir Henry Hardinge. The castle was Liverpool's residence as Lord Warden of the Cinque Ports, and having retired there for health reasons, the prime minister sat down in November to reply to Londonderry 'not only as a Public Servant of the Crown, but as I hope a very old & sincere Friend'. The prime minister explained that he had no intelligence as to when Londonderry intended to return home, and had been unwilling to write until a new foreign secretary was appointed. More interestingly, Lord Liverpool also advised that the delay was 'fortified by the Information which I had received some Weeks before, from your Poor Brother, that the mission at Vienna would be relinquished by you at an early Period'. In consequence, 'He was desirous of making an eventual Arrangement, respecting the Succession to it.' According to Liverpool, things were so well advanced that when Canning received the seals of the Foreign Office, he had been advised by the King that the matter was 'as a Point settled'.

The prime minister admitted he might have made a mistake in not writing sooner 'but if I have, it proceeds from a good Feeling, & certainly no Want of Personal Kindness or Friendship towards you'. Liverpool added 'that upon the present as upon every occasion' he would be 'most anxious to manifest to you the Sincerest regard' as well as his 'desire to meet all your Feeling as far as my Public Duty will admit'.[16] The belief that Lord Londonderry intended to resign anyway hints at advanced discussions with his brother about a change in career. Londonderry had seen Britain further isolated in European politics; with a growing family, and coupled with Frances Anne's reported boredom, these factors may have convinced him it was time to leave Vienna. If so, he would have expected a new position, but with his brother's death all of these calculations were thrown out of the window.

One voice of reason at this time was an old friend and colleague, the Earl of Clancarty, the ambassador to the Netherlands. Currently on leave in Ireland, Clancarty was relieved to hear that the Marquess was 'bearing up, against the dreadful calamity which has befallen us all'. He too had heard of Canning's succession to 'our Great & Noble-minded Friend' and had 'remonstrated to the utmost of my power' against the new arrangements, but to 'little effect'. The Earl, as ever a clear-headed man in times of crisis, felt that Londonderry could continue at Vienna 'even under Mr. C.' but, if this should prove impossible, was anxious that everything should be done with the utmost circumspection. Any decision to 'retire from public life' should be made on personal grounds 'for the present at least'. This would avoid any chance of 'casting doubt upon the sincerity of your brothers forgiveness of his former opponent'. More importantly this might save Londonderry from destroying his career for good. For these reasons, a 'wish for retirement upon this change of situation, and on the business incident to it requiring your presence at home', would not 'hazard the revival of a bye gone controversy, by shewing enmity of distrust where your brother had long ceased to shew any'.[17]

In his irrational and angry mood, Lord Londonderry was in no mood to listen; his response to Clancarty, complete with contempt for George Canning, began with an attack on Lord Liverpool. By moving quickly to appoint a new foreign secretary, the prime minister had acted in a way which was 'so disgusting, in as far as common Gratitude to the memory of Him, who has alone upheld Liverpool's Administration'. The resignation would stand, and, Clancarty was told, 'nothing which I have heard' from the Duke of Wellington, who had recently arrived in Vienna, had 'Shaken my opinion'. It was perhaps natural that 'His Grace should wish me to sail in the same Ship in which <u>He</u> has been the Helmsman, at the point of Embarkation.' The Marquess was not overly friendly towards the Duke, adding, 'Whether it <u>arises entirely from Friendship to me</u>, or from other Causes, I will not at present time Examine; But State, as you perceive by my letters, The Duke of Wellington could have no influence <u>upon me</u>.'

Tragically, Londonderry knew that his brother was the better man for having been prepared to work with Canning, telling Clancarty, 'Altho' a Great Mind willingly forgives the injury done to himself' it was not 'so easy for One who idolized that Great Mind, and stood in the Affinity I did to Him, entirely to bury the past in Oblivion'. As for Canning, Londonderry was uncompromising: 'I cannot <u>respect the Man</u>.' Returning to Wellington, Lord Londonderry openly admitted that he was 'annoyed' at the Duke 'with his Great Name and celebrity, coming out under Mr Canning, to a Congress, where from circumstances, there is nothing now to do, where no credit or Character can be obtained'.[18] As so often in his life, Londonderry was acting without any kind of restraint, his behaviour probably heightened by the terrible loss he had suffered, which also now led him into an exaggerated sense of his new position as head of the family.

The Marquess of Londonderry further annoyed the government over the next few months. Writing to Robert Peel, now home secretary, Londonderry announced that he wanted to succeed his brother as lord lieutenant of County Down. Further, he wanted his cousin, Alexander Stewart, MP for County Londonderry, to succeed to Castlereagh's colonelcy of the militia. The regimental appointment would be a theme that Londonderry would return to often, reiterated in letters to both the prime minister and to the lord lieutenant of Ireland, Lord Wellesley.[19] It is obvious that the Marquess of Londonderry needed a restraining influence. Discretion was a better way of proceeding than constant harassment of His Majesty's government.

It was in this frame of mind that Londonderry attended the Congress of Verona with the Duke of Wellington. For some time, the Ambassador had been warning the Foreign Office of the problems with the Congress System, highlighted at Laibach where the French had sided against an isolated Britain. This was a process that would only continue. The duc de Richelieu had fallen from office in December 1821. France was now under the control of the Ultra Royalists, men who looked to the future, and the succession of Louis XVIII's brother as king. The Ultras had their own agenda and longed to intervene in Spain and aid a fellow Bourbon monarch, Ferdinand VII. As Londonderry had pointed out to Clancarty, there would be little for the British representatives to do or achieve.[20]

The Congress of Verona would see the start of a close and remarkable friendship between Alexander I and Frances Anne, now Marchioness of Londonderry.[21] It would also mark the decline of the Congress System, perhaps inevitable after Castlereagh's death. The process was further accelerated by Canning's less than enthusiastic commitment to it.[22] Sidelined at the Congress, it was not a glorious end to the third Marquess of Londonderry's time as ambassador to Vienna; he saw that, with France now having 'surrendered herself entirely to the direction of the Holy Alliance', the Ultra Royalists would get their chance to intervene in Spain. Londonderry further commented in a memorandum, 'It is too evident from the moment the four Powers have been agreed, that they have become more indifferent about England.' He still hoped that the system might survive, and 'that differing on many points, we are still enabled to preserve the spirit of our union'. This was perhaps rather unrealistic. Less than ten years after the Peninsular War, French troops would march into Spain to uphold Ferdinand VII's authority.[23]

While he was still abroad, Londonderry had broached the subject of honours.[24] Now came a new request for himself, in the shape of an earldom, with remainder to the eldest son of his second marriage. This was controversial in a society aware of the different gradations of rank. This would allow Frances Anne's eldest son to sit in the House of Lords as an earl, while Frederick would only sit in the upper chamber thanks to his father's United Kingdom barony. Undaunted by the troublesome nature of the request, the Marquess of Londonderry decided to press the point. Lying behind this was the Marquess's very great ambition for his family: to found two dynasties, one in Ireland and one in Britain.[25]

Lord Camden was roped in to soliciting for the honour, while Sir Henry Hardinge was acting as a go-between behind the scenes. Much ink was spent in lengthy letters between Camden and Hardinge on the subject during November and December 1822, with various options discussed, including a peerage for Frances Anne in her own right. Ironically, although Camden was seen as a key figure in obtaining the desired peerage, he might not have been that useful. In a private letter to the prime minister, Camden seemed embarrassed and apologetic about the whole episode.[26] It was left to the Duke of Wellington to resolve this matter. Acting with his usual efficiency, Wellington was working to end this potentially troubling affair. In that straightforward approach that the Duke preferred, he told Hardinge that he had secured the desired rank and further passed on his advice as to Londonderry's conduct:

> I write to You one Line to tell you that with Lord Liverpools Consent I have settled for Lord Londonderry His advancement in the Peerage He is to be made an Earl with remainder to his male Issue by Lady Londonderry
>
> If He will be only quiet, I shall be able to settle for him likewise the Londonderry militia
>
> Pray entreat him to be so.[27]

The Londonderrys were in Rome when they received the offer of the earldom in March 1823. The Marquess decided to take the titles of Earl Vane and Viscount Seaham. Lord Londonderry had taken a major step in his desire to found a new noble dynasty. The titles reflected Lady Londonderry's family background as well as a recently acquired estate at Seaham. Frances Anne was undoubtedly thrilled that her son had the courtesy title of Viscount Seaham and one day would inherit an earl's coronet.[28]

The Marquess and Marchioness of Londonderry made their way home leisurely, not just to go sightseeing, but out of concern for Frances Anne, who was again pregnant. In May 1823, the couple reached Paris. Not content with the earldom, Lord Londonderry annoyed Liverpool's government further by demanding a pension. Certainly there were precedents on his side, as the former ambassador was quick to point out, but the prime minister thought otherwise. The Foreign Office official Joseph Planta replied that he had only 'reluctantly' pressed the issue with Liverpool, and the prime minister's response to Planta was very clear. The letter was passed on to the would-be pensioner:

> I am persuaded that this Letter was written by our friend, without sufficient consideration; for independent of publick objections, I can conceive no step that would be more injurious to his reputation than his receiving the Pension which the King is authorized to grant to Ambassadors.
>
> The power of granting these pensions was rested in the Crown, as a remuneration to those Individuals who had served the Country abroad, and who had not the means of supporting themselves and their Families, upon their return home.[29]

Liverpool went further and suggested that 'the greatest injury would arise from his pressing it: I have no doubt that the consequence would be, that the power of granting such Pensions would be by Parliament further limited, if not altogether taken away.'[30] Liverpool was plainly concerned about public reaction to a pension being granted to a man married to one of the country's wealthiest heiresses. Londonderry could only see precedent, and if others had been awarded pensions, he chafed at any thought that he might be overlooked. He made his feelings plain in his response to Planta on 10 June, while still in Paris.[31]

The pension was a step too far for the prime minister, a fact which became public a few years later. In 1827, *The Times*, in the third Marquess of Londonderry's words, issued 'a Libel upon my Character in which it is stated, That upon an Application of mine for a Pension out 'of the prescribed form' Lord Liverpool had himself enclosed these words "This is too bad"'. In response to Londonderry's anger at this 'leak', the foreign secretary of the day, Lord Dudley, rather sheepishly admitted that although the phrase did not appear on the copies sent on request, it appeared 'endorsed on your second letter to Mr. Planta, in the hand writing, (as I am informed by persons acquainted with it) of the Earl of Liverpool'. The prime minister was a man of the utmost probity and expected the same of public servants. In this case, Lord Liverpool felt that Londonderry's conduct had fallen below his expected standards. This was not a brilliant state of affairs for the Londonderrys as they returned to Britain.[32]

The former ambassador was at least still the courtier, enjoying continued favour from George IV, not least over his agreement to resign the governorship of Fort Charles in Jamaica to accommodate Sir Benjamin Bloomfield.[33] This royal favour was enough to earn him an invite to join the King at Windsor on 21 June, with Wellington advising him to 'be prepared to stay at dinner and even to sleep at the Cottage. But I don't doubt that Lady L's situation will be admitted . . . if you wish to return to town.'[34] Frances Anne's 'situation' was of course a reference to her current advanced state of pregnancy. On 29 July, the couple celebrated the birth of a second daughter, Lady Alexandrina Vane.

The subject of the Londonderry militia still rankled, the more so as the colonelcy of the regiment was in the hands of Sir George Hill. The Hills were political rivals but were also loyal to the Liverpool administration, and the government did not want to alienate them. Wellington was in the thick of it again, and to make matters more complicated, Londonderry made distinct noises about separating from the government, which the Duke regarded as 'a subject which is so painful'. To a man of Wellington's temperament, to go into opposition for a private object was folly. Perhaps this advice was heeded as the Marquess did not go into opposition; he may also have realized that politically he was not as important as his late brother.[35] At least Londonderry kept himself busy with business connected to his wife's interests in County Durham. The Marquess and Marchioness of Londonderry had also acquired a sumptuous town house in 1822, worthy of their rank and wealth. Holdernesse House on Park Lane would become known for its lavishness as one of the greatest of the Tory political houses. As another string to his bow, the Marquess started to collect paintings on a large scale, writing to his friend Lord Burghersh in July 1823, 'My Correggios are the Wonder of the world.'[36]

This of course was part of the problem. The third Marquess of Londonderry had come a long way in a short time. Married to one of the richest heiresses of the day, he was determined to do right by Frances Anne's family, hence the desire for an earldom for the eldest son of his second marriage. The chance to found a new dynasty in the north-east of England, alongside the Stewart line in Ireland, was too great an opportunity to pass up. However, there were better ways to do it. There was also no longer the restraining influence of his brother to help, and the third Marquess had nobody to act as a brake on his always exuberant character. Snobbery and prejudice undoubtedly added to the mix, but Londonderry's behaviour after his brother's death had effectively destroyed his chances of an immediate return to public life. From enjoying a meteoric career on the battlefield and in the chancelleries of Europe, the third Marquess of Londonderry, once indispensable to his brother Castlereagh, would be left trying to rebuild his reputation. This was a terrible waste, but even if he had known this, or even suspected this, he seemed incapable of stopping himself. Well might his biographer, Sir Archibald Alison, note that after the Congress of Verona 'Lord Londonderry's official and public career came to an end.'[37]

The tragedy is that this public career did not have to come to an end. Instead of fresh laurels after ten years at the highest levels of British diplomacy, it was a far from splendid conclusion to a distinguished diplomatic career – an act committed in a fit of pique at George Canning's appointment to the Foreign Office. Without his eldest brother's guidance, he seemed intent on alienating as many influential people as possible. A man in very good health, and still only in his 40s, the third Marquess of Londonderry had so much still to offer his country. Instead, his story after his return from the Vienna embassy was one of frustration and missed opportunities. Only when it was too late did he realize the injury he had done to his own reputation. As he told a former political opponent in 1839, 'It is certainly possible that my mind has not march'd with the Events of the Times, as my Brothers would have done I know full well all its inferiority, but I mention these points at this moment of our Restoration to friendly intercourse and Correspondence as a Justification for myself, if my zeal & Devotion to his memory have led me too far.'[38] It was perhaps a very fitting epitaph to his devotion to Castlereagh's memory, but one which was to cause lasting damage to his reputation.

Chapter 15

GENTLEMANLY CONDUCT

Sir Archibald Alison tactfully wrote that like 'many other persons of warm feelings and a high chivalrous sense of honour, Lord Londonderry was apt, when he felt strongly, to indulge in perhaps too unmeasured expressions'.[1] This was a grand understatement. In February 1824, he refused the chance of a diplomatic career for his son, and threw a proffered olive branch back in the faces of Lord Liverpool, and his least favourite Tory politician, Mr Canning. In May 1824, Londonderry fought a duel with Cornet Battier, an extremely junior officer of his own regiment, earning a furious censure from the Duke of York in the process.[2] Such events were symptomatic of the third Marquess of Londonderry's post-diplomatic life: excluded from office, he was bitter towards former friends and always easy to offend, with no appreciation of how his own actions offended others. By providing a brief overview of key moments in Londonderry's life after his resignation, this concluding chapter explains why his great career was forgotten by the public by the time of his death in 1854.

Links with Londonderry's past life were soon broken. On 16 September 1824, Louis XVIII's death brought his Ultra Royalist brother, the comte d'Artois, to the throne as King Charles X. The peaceful succession indicated that the Bourbons had cemented their position within the French body politic. Just over a year later, on 1 December 1825, Alexander I of Russia died. Wellington wrote to Londonderry that Alexander's qualities as a man 'rendered him highly estimable & much to be lamented'.[3] The loss of these connections to the Marquess's former public career highlighted the different life he now lived: such issues of high European diplomacy were no longer part of his world. At the forefront of his concerns in 1825 was the need to introduce Castlereagh to his responsibilities in Ireland.[4]

On 17 February 1827, Lord Liverpool suffered a huge stroke. He made a partial recovery, but could not continue in office, and quickly retired. On 12 April, Wellington advised Londonderry that Canning had been appointed prime minister. The next day, Londonderry went to the King to denounce Canning and resign his place at court as a Lord of the Bedchamber.[5] Wellington, appointed commander-in-chief of the army following the death of the Duke of York, was not without his own petulance; he too resigned in protest. However, having waited for so long to reach the top of the political ladder, Canning had little time to enjoy it. Already ill when he accepted the premiership, Canning died suddenly on 8 August 1827.[6] Londonderry refused to revise his opinion of Canning. He wrote to Lord Burghersh on 20 October to complain about plans to erect a monument to the late prime minister 'for his great publick Services', which he felt was incomprehensible as nobody knew 'what They are or [could] state any one Act'. George IV appointed Canning's cabinet colleague Frederick Robinson, recently ennobled as Viscount Goderich, as prime minister. Like many others, Londonderry dismissively referred to Goderich as 'the Blubberer' from his predilection to burst into tears.[7] The new premier, a Tory in the same mould as George Canning, was happy to share office with moderate Whigs; there was no room for firebrand Tories of the likes of Lord Londonderry.

There was much at stake for the Londonderry 'party' in the uncertain political world of the late 1820s: if things went well there was the prospect of a return to office for Hardinge, a position for Castlereagh, and maybe even something for Londonderry at the head of this Anglo-Irish political squadron. Hardinge was alive to the possibilities and was keen to broker an understanding with John George Lambton, known as 'Radical Jack', the head of the leading Whig family in County Durham. An informal alliance between the Wynyard and Lambton interests would secure Lord Londonderry's future political influence in the City and County of Durham. This was all sound advice, and as with the accommodation between the Stewart and Hill interests in County Down, an arrangement was made with Lambton, ennobled as Lord Durham. By May 1828, Durham could write to Lord Londonderry, 'It is my anxious wish that, on all occasions connected with our mutual interests the most unreserved Confidence should Exist between us.'[8] In the autumn of 1827, Wellington undertook a tour of the north-east to boost support. Naturally, part of his itinerary included staying at Wynyard, and Lord Londonderry was much involved in the Duke's triumphant political progress.[9] This proved unnecessary as Goderich, never overly confident in himself, did not last long in office, resigning in tears on 8 January 1828.

Lord Londonderry's enforced absence from politics was at least a gain for the republic of letters, with the appearance of *Narrative of the Peninsular War from 1808 to 1813*. As adjutant general, Londonderry had witnessed key events and decisions as a senior member of Wellington's staff. The *New Monthly Magazine and Literary Journal* of January 1828 mostly praised the book, while remaining decidedly cool about Londonderry's politics. The review commented, 'Our author is better qualified to judge of particulars than of generals; or, to speak technically, we should have a higher opinion of him as a general of division, or of hussars, than commander in chief.'[10]

Following Goderich's resignation, George IV turned to Wellington to form a new administration. Hardinge was reappointed as Clerk of the Ordnance, while Lord Aberdeen returned to front-line politics. There was nothing for Londonderry or Castlereagh. The third Marquess harboured great ambitions, and wanted to be either lord lieutenant of Ireland or ambassador to France.[11] However, the Marquess of Anglesey remained as lord lieutenant, and that seasoned diplomat Charles Stuart returned to his old post at Paris, recently ennobled as Lord Stuart de Rothesay. If Lord Londonderry could not go to Paris as ambassador, he could at least go for pleasure. In the spring of 1828, Londonderry enjoyed life in the French capital, and relayed back to Wellington his detailed opinions on French politics under King Charles X. When it soon became apparent that he was attracting press attention he advised the Duke that he was quitting Paris early.[12] On his return, Londonderry wrote further on French political life for Wellington, notably on the future succession of the Orléans dynasty as the best guarantee of the French monarchy.[13]

Wellington's premiership would witness a further deterioration in his relationship with Lord Londonderry. Hardinge's career went from strength to strength: he was appointed secretary at war in May 1828, but without a seat in the cabinet.[14] Londonderry and Castlereagh remained excluded from office, even though both supported Wellington over Catholic Emancipation.[15] Harriet Arbuthnot recorded Londonderry's fury at this time, although she had little time for his complaints, writing in June 1829:

> The real truth is, Ld L[ondonderry] is so strange, so flighty, so intensely selfish & so governed by his most absurd wife that he is not fit to be trusted in any high office, besides which, when it is a question between him, the possessor of 80,000£ a year, & men like Lds Hill, Beresford or Stuart, who have very little beyond their profession for the means of existence, it wd be most unfair to prefer him.[16]

At least Londonderry was restored to the King's good books, seemingly through the offices of George IV's brother, Ernest, Duke of Cumberland. As things stood, Cumberland would one day inherit the throne of Hanover.

Castlereagh's exclusion from office was particularly unfair. Clever and potentially a capable man of business, he had not been given a chance to show his abilities. When a vacancy occurred at the Admiralty, Castlereagh was fortunate in having Mrs Arbuthnot as a decided partisan to argue his case with the Duke, whatever her low opinions of Lord and Lady Londonderry.[17] The plea worked and in June 1829 Castlereagh accepted office as a Lord of the Admiralty; an important first rung on the ministerial ladder.[18] On accepting office, Castlereagh sought re-election for County Down. The alliance with the Hills ensured he was returned without difficulty. The Wellington ministry, now strengthened with more 'Tory' members, was embedding itself into power, but by early 1830 George IV's health was declining.[19] The King's death would trigger a general election, and the increasing political uncertainty encouraged intrigues. At the centre of one was an unemployed Lord Londonderry. In May 1830, Mrs Arbuthnot was reporting on Londonderry's plotting with the recently recalled lord lieutenant of Ireland, Lord Anglesey, and the heir presumptive to the throne, the Duke of Clarence.[20]

Opponent of reform

In the early hours of 26 June 1830, George IV died peacefully.[21] In his place was his brother, William, Duke of Clarence, a straight-talking former naval officer, who became King William IV. In France, Charles X's reign was brought to a close, not by death, but by revolution on the streets of Paris. The Bourbon King's hardline policies led to the 'three glorious days' of 27, 28 and 29 July 1830. The King lost control of Paris and seeing that his reign was over, abdicated in favour of his grandson, Henri, duc de Bordeaux. There was to be no coronation for the young titular Henri V of France. The eldest branch was finished, and to forestall radical alternatives, the duc d'Orléans was called to the throne. The post-Napoleonic settlement had been overturned, and a new monarchy established with Orléans becoming Louis-Philippe, King of the French.[22] Shortly afterwards, another pillar of the Congress of Vienna settlement was overthrown, with the break-up of the United Kingdom of the Netherlands. The Catholic population in Belgium had never warmed to being ruled by the Protestant Dutch. Taking events in Paris as their model, an opera in Brussels inspired nationalists to start a revolution to overthrow Dutch rule.

In October, with Europe again ablaze from revolution, Londonderry's old friend, Lord Bloomfield, minister to Sweden, was writing not only about the overthrow of regimes, but about Lord Londonderry's latest memoir, and its reception. This book, *Narrative of the War in Germany and France*, was examined with interest in Sweden, with its account of the former Marshal Bernadotte, since 1818, King Charles XIV John. Bloomfield mischievously told the author that his 'Friend Charles Jean' had been unimpressed with another recent publication, and intended to use Londonderry's book as a rebuttal, noting that one of the Swedish courtiers 'has retained my Copy of your book <u>above</u> 3 months'. Bloomfield could also report that another courtier had 'expressed himself in general praise, & added that he thought your delineation of His Master was "bien caractéristique"'.[23]

While there were revolutions abroad, politics in Britain was far from stable. In the general election following the death of George IV, Wellington's government was left without a working majority. Hardinge was promoted to chief secretary for Ireland, but was no longer MP for Durham, having decided to take the Treasury seat of St Germans. Castlereagh had faced a contest in County Down, but he had won the day, and remained in office. The Duke tried to encourage moderates to join his government, but it proved to be a vain undertaking. The stumbling block was parliamentary reform. Londonderry also proved as obstructive as ever: he wanted recognition of some kind, and had now set his sights on becoming colonel of the Blues and one of the Gold Sticks. Previously held by Wellington and currently by the Duke of Cumberland, this prestigious Household office was a military and ceremonial position of great honour. Using the first Duke of Buckingham as a go-between, his ambitions were rebuffed. Wellington expected loyalty from Londonderry without conditions. More ominously, Buckingham hinted at strong opposition to any accommodation, especially from one quarter. This opposition was rather delicate for Castlereagh, and the Buckingham correspondence shows that Londonderry's heir did not agree with his father's tactics.[24]

In November, the Wellington administration lost a key vote, and the Duke resigned. In Wellington's place, William IV appointed the Whig leader, the second Earl Grey, as prime minister. Interestingly, Londonderry was being kept informed of political events by someone very much in the know. Lord Durham, who also happened to be Grey's son-in-law, was putting out feelers to his neighbour as a potential supporter of the new government. The political understanding between the two peers had deepened into friendship, and on 22 November, Durham appealed to Londonderry to support a measure of political reform.[25] Londonderry would have none of it. The revolutions in France and Belgium had seen two major parts of the 1815 Vienna treaty discarded; against this unravelling of his brother's legacy, any idea of reform at home was a step too far. Although he saw the dangers posed to France by the Ultra Royalists, when it came to Britain, Londonderry acted contrary to his own political good sense through blind opposition.

If Lord Londonderry felt paranoid about the dangers of revolution following the momentous events in Paris and Brussels, another shock occurred to further stoke his fears. The accession of Tsar Nicholas I in December 1825 came amidst confusion over the rights of his elder brother, Constantine. It was also marked by calls, at least from the moderate members of Russia's elites, for reform of the Romanov monarchy. These calls from the Decembrists led only to exile and executions. Nicholas, who had none of his eldest brother's charm, now witnessed a second attack on the Russian monarchy. In November 1830, a military uprising occurred in Warsaw, and in January 1831 the Tsar was formally deposed as King of Poland. Nicholas's response was to send in the army to restore Russian power. A new wave of political exiles was born. One of the exiles was Prince Czartoryski, well known to Londonderry from diplomatic encounters after Napoleon's first fall.[26] It was against this background of mainland European revolution that political reform was attempted in Britain.

Although Wellington set his face against reform, it was the right wing of the Tory party that was most vociferous in its opposition. Running with these Ultra-Tory foxhounds was the Marquess of Londonderry, who would behave throughout 1831 and 1832 as an unthinking political reactionary. His behaviour against reform caused him to be vilified, and he became one of the most unpopular figures in the country. He made himself all the more unpopular by being very much on Nicholas I's side.[27] The Polish cause commanded a great deal of sympathy from liberal opinion in the constitutional monarchies of Britain and France. With the passing into law of electoral reform in 1832, Londonderry's political capital was at an all-time low – seen as the friend of autocrats abroad and the enemy of reform at home. It cost him the chance of a new diplomatic career.

Lord Grey resigned from office in July 1834; he was succeeded as prime minister by Lord Melbourne. However, the Whig government lost office in November to the Tories, now led by Sir Robert Peel. Londonderry enjoyed a cordial relationship with the new prime minister, and in December 1834 Peel offered him a return to public life, as either ambassador to Russia or Master of the Buckhounds. Although Londonderry had wanted Paris, he was delighted to accept the embassy and by Peel's 'placing two Offices at my Sons Disposal'.[28] The opposition was outraged. As Londonderry wrote to Peel in February 1835, 'The Whigs mean to attack my Appointment, & that Lord Palmerstone [*sic*] is busy in pressing this Effort.'[29] By March, Londonderry realized that his proposed embassy would likely inflict terminal damage on Peel's administration. On 14 March, a political enemy, Charles Greville, wrote of the Commons debate on the appointment: 'The result is that Londonderry cannot go, and must either resign or his nomination be cancelled.

This is miserable weakness on the part of Government, and an awkward position to be placed in.' The following evening, Greville met Wellington. The Duke talked candidly about the affair and his low opinion of Lord Londonderry, coupled with rare praise for his abilities as a diplomat, remarking,

> He was not particularly partial to the man, nor ever had been; but that he was very fit for that post, was an excellent Ambassador, procured more information and obtained more insight into the affairs of a foreign Court than anybody, and that he was the best relater of what passed at a conference, and wrote the best account of a conversation, of any man he knew.[30]

On 16 March 1835, Londonderry tendered his resignation as ambassador.[31] However, this noble gesture did not save Peel who also resigned in April 1835. With Peel's departure, Castlereagh, who had been appointed vice chamberlain of the Household, also lost office.

Faced with another disappointment, Londonderry took himself off to Russia and on his return produced a new book, *Recollections of a Tour in the North of Europe 1836–1837*. Published in two volumes, it provides an intimate account of life in the Russian Empire under Nicholas I. Lord Londonderry's account, which benefited from revisions undertaken by his old friend Sir Henry Browne, was published in 1838.[32] Londonderry's book, dedicated to Sir Robert Peel, was very keen to stress that Nicholas I was not the tyrant of popular myth.[33] It also gave him a chance to air his views on Poland, which he visited after leaving St Petersburg, via Riga, on 9 February 1837:

> It is morally impossible that Poland can ever again be severed from Russia, and established as an independent kingdom, unless with the previous subjugation of Russia . . .
>
> Let the politicians of Europe weigh well these few observations, and ask themselves if promoting sedition, discontent, and democracy in Poland, can by any probability tend to the happiness and welfare of that nation.[34]

Returning via Prussia, the Londonderrys had been the toast of Berlin society, meeting with the Prussian royal family, ambassadors and spending much time with the Duke and Duchess of Cumberland. Londonderry had been much cheered by all the attention he received. As ever though, he saw himself as the pale reflection of his late brother, and described the attention 'as proud and flattering testimonials that, far more by the acts of another than by my own humble efforts, the name I bear will be remembered on the scene of Europe'.[35]

The Victorian age

On 20 June 1837, William IV died. The King was succeeded by his young niece, Princess Victoria of Kent, while the Hanoverian throne passed to the Duke of

Cumberland. Immediately, Lord Londonderry was seen as a figure of influence with the new King of Hanover.[36] This influence in Hanover was not matched by influence at home. With the Tories out of power, Londonderry was no nearer to office. This did not stop him cutting a dash in society. Amidst the splendour of Queen Victoria's coronation on 20 March 1838, the Londonderrys were on their best form, with Frances Anne, Marchioness of Londonderry, almost stealing the show. A member of the Londonderry circle, the young Tory politician Benjamin Disraeli, was moved to remark that she 'blazed among the peeresses' and 'looked like an Empress'.[37] Castlereagh had introduced Disraeli to Frances Anne at a ball in June 1835. The ambitious Disraeli told his sister that Lady Londonderry reminded him of a rhinoceros, but he was soon on very good terms with the family.[38] Disraeli also enjoyed the splendours of Holdernesse House, and thanks to him we have a glimpse of a glittering entertainment held by the Londonderrys as part of the coronation celebrations.[39]

The decision to dispense with the coronation banquet led to unfavourable comment in certain society circles. One upshot of this decision was the riot of medieval pageantry that was the Eglinton Tournament. Held at the Earl of Eglinton's castle in August 1839, the Londonderrys were again centre stage, as key participants in this revival of chivalry.[40] The Marquess of Londonderry agreed to serve as king of the tournament, although according to his own recollection, only reluctantly: 'It was only at the eleventh hour, I was applied to act as King of the Lists, – I felt my own inadequacy, but others failing, I was too happy to shew this proof of regard in acquiescing to the desire of Lord Eglinton.' Unfortunately, Londonderry afterwards became embroiled in an argument over the subscriptions to the Eglinton Trophy, an affair which rumbled on until June 1840.[41] Londonderry had lost none of his capacity for finding himself in trouble. At least the row over the Eglinton Trophy was conducted in ink. Before the tournament, Londonderry had become embroiled in a different kind of argument with the Irish Whig MP Henry Grattan. This political affair ended with an exchange of pistol shots in June 1839.[42]

With the Whig government of Lord Melbourne entrenched in office, there was little chance of Peel returning to power. With no immediate prospect of employment, the Londonderrys resumed their indulgence in travel, undertaking journeys to Portugal and Spain, and then to Constantinople. With the Marquess now something of a travel author, these journeys were published in 1842 in a two-volume set, *A Steam Voyage to Constantinople, by the Rhine and the Danube in 1840–41, and to Portugal, Spain &c in 1839.* In Vienna, Londonderry noted, perhaps rather unflatteringly, that the ambassador Lord Beauvale 'seldom gives any grand or general reception, his indifferent health being the reason for living privately'. Londonderry also had the chance to talk politics with Prince Metternich.[43] Travelling on to Constantinople, the capital of the Ottoman Empire, Londonderry soon made a new enemy. As a man who took offence easily, Londonderry came to dislike Lord Ponsonby, the British ambassador. Londonderry's complaints about Ponsonby were reproduced in print for all to see, as detailed in volume one of his travel journal.[44]

While the era of Victorian politics and diplomacy took shape, it was a world from which the Marquess of Londonderry was still excluded. Ernest, King of Hanover, also felt snubbed by the new order of things, and regularly corresponded with Londonderry (addressing him as 'Dear Charles') on a range of topics including his position in the British royal family and politics. Prince Albert, the Queen's consort since 1840, was often in Ernest's sights.[45] However, at long last for the Tories, Sir Robert Peel returned as prime minister in August 1841. This Tory government presented new opportunities, as was shown in the case of Londonderry's old friend, the diplomat and composer, Lord Burghersh. Appointed ambassador to Prussia, Lord Burghersh, soon to succeed as eleventh Earl of Westmorland, would remain Britain's representative in Berlin for the next ten years.

In May, several months before Peel's return to power, Londonderry had approached Hardinge with a list of the prized appointments he sought. These included the embassy in Paris or the lord lieutenancy of Ireland, judged 'Most Acceptable', although the Ordnance, without cabinet rank, was not so attractive. Hardinge was advised to 'make use of this letter if You deem it necessary.' Hardinge sent a detailed response to this request, noting that Castlereagh did not desire office.[46] Instead of Paris, the Earl of Aberdeen, reappointed as foreign secretary, offered the Vienna embassy, which was then declined. This brought a 'strong disapprobation' from Lord Burghersh. Londonderry responded to his old friend:

> To renew my old work in my Grammar School in Metternichs Ante Chamber at Vienna To travel those haunts no longer a Lothario but 60 & a family of Young Ladies To have the Contrast of the past with the present thrown in my Teeth . . . what object but one of Degradation & Disgust could Vienna but be to me – Paris far far different afforded every thing new.[47]

The Vienna embassy was given to Aberdeen's brother, Sir Robert Gordon. After his service in the Austrian capital as secretary of embassy, Gordon had enjoyed a successful diplomatic career, and the promotion was a fitting reward. Londonderry, however, was irritated by the appointment.[48] With the Marquess regarding the Vienna offer and Gordon's subsequent appointment as insults, Lord Aberdeen was forced on to the defensive. Londonderry's written comments across Aberdeen's letter leave no doubt as to the bitterness he felt, combined with bewilderment as to why he was not even offered the opportunity to go to Constantinople as ambassador to the Porte.[49] Despite the spat over the Vienna posting, Londonderry's ambitions were far from dormant. In June 1842, he revived his pretensions to the embassy in Paris.[50] Aberdeen advised that there was no vacancy, but moved quickly to cut this avenue off for the future, telling Londonderry on 1 July, 'You are quite aware that the nomination to this Post must be considered in a political, as well as in a diplomatic view; and that it is not exclusively the Act of the Secy of State.'[51]

The government though was still willing to oblige Londonderry, and if Paris was not to be, at least other responsibilities could be bestowed. Peel had already made Londonderry lord lieutenant of Durham in February 1842, in succession to the Whig peer William Vane, first Duke of Cleveland. Having been on far from cordial terms with the first Duke, Londonderry took pains to mend fences with the second Duke.[52] In 1843, Londonderry, who had been promoted to general in 1837, became colonel of the 2nd Life Guards in succession to Earl Cathcart, and consequently one of the three Gold Sticks.[53] In 1845, the family was further honoured when Castlereagh was appointed lord lieutenant of County Down. As Sir Henry Browne wrote to the Marquess, 'There never was any thing better done, than your securing the Ld. Lieutenancy to Castlereagh.'[54]

Even if he was out of high office, Londonderry was still seen as a man to approach. In July 1845, a former colleague from the Napoleonic era, Sir George Jackson, called at Holdernesse House seeking assistance in securing an interview with the Foreign Secretary. Since the heady days of the 1813–14 campaign, Jackson had served in diplomatic posts across the globe. From 1828, Jackson had been appointed to various senior roles associated with the abolition of the slave trade. As Londonderry wrote to Aberdeen on 28 July 1845, 'And with all my repugnance to ask favors I know not how I can well refuse Sir George who served under me from forwarding his Letter.'[55]

Londonderry's career was stalled, but Hardinge had returned to the office of secretary at war in August 1841. In 1844, he was persuaded to become governor general of India, in succession to the Earl of Ellenborough. Taking Londonderry's son, Lord Adolphus Vane (born in 1825), with him, Hardinge's tenure saw a number of reforms carried through. But his time in India was chiefly given over to events in the Punjab and a major military campaign against the formidable Sikh armies. The First Sikh War was a hard-fought affair, but military success and the subsequent treaty of 1846 allowed the East India Company to make further territorial acquisitions. The governor general was rewarded with a peerage, created Viscount Hardinge of Lahore. However, in a letter to Londonderry, Hardinge rightly saw the treaty as potentially no more than a temporary truce.[56] In late 1847, with Lord Hardinge's term of office drawing to a close, Adolphus took the opportunity to explore the country.[57] Hardinge returned home himself in 1848.

While Hardinge earned new military and civilian laurels, Lord Londonderry's name was attacked for his actions during the Irish Potato Famine.[58] As Trevor Parkhill notes, 'The public controversy into which the third marquess was drawn concerned the privations of his tenants in County Down, who were experiencing initially severe difficulties following the second successive potato-crop failure in the autumn of 1846.'[59] The very public nature of the criticisms did enormous damage. Sir Henry Browne was one of those who felt honour-bound to seek redress, although his letter to the Marquess of 14 September 1850 clearly hints that all was not happy on the Londonderry estates:

I had already, about a fortnight since, sent a strong article to the Sun which has an extensive Circulation . . . in which I expressed a firm conviction, that the attacks made on you were utterly groundless & false, originating in Presbyterian Ministers, & levelled at confessedly the best Landlord in the Kingdom, who had ever, in all his dealings with his Tenantry, wished them to feel & value as they ought, their Connection with him – that many, who have visited your Irish

Property, even though politically opposed to You, had not been able to deny You this justice of your unrivalled success in making your Tenants comfortable & happy, which they would prove to You in a thousand warm & affectionate ways, were they not misled by selfish designers – that You stood too high, to bend yourself with correspondence with them.[60]

Lord Londonderry's actions led to a strong attack on the family's political influence from the tenant-right candidate, William Sharman Crawford, who put up a strong showing at the contest for County Down during the 1852 general election.

Trevor Parkhill further argues that 'Given the extent and nature of the attacks on the third marquess's response to his tenants' difficulties during the potato blight and the direct electoral challenge to his standing', the election marked 'a beginning of the end of the old order he had so stalwartly represented.'[61] In contrast, Lord Castlereagh's reaction had been more straightforward. In 1847, he published an account of his travels in *A Journey to Damascus through Egypt, Nubia, Arabia, Petraea, Palestine and Syria*, produced in two volumes. Castlereagh wrote in the preface that he would not have 'ventured upon their publication' had he not 'entertained the hope of thus being enabled to add some slight contribution' to the relief efforts for Ireland.[62]

In these later years, as he was being criticized for his actions in Ireland, Londonderry undertook his greatest literary labour, editing his brother's letters for the twelve-volume *Memoirs and Correspondence of Viscount Castlereagh, Second Marquess of Londonderry*. Published between 1848 and 1853, the spark for this undertaking was a war of words with his old adversary Lord Brougham. In 1845 Brougham, excluded from public life since losing the Great Seal in 1834, brought out a new edition of his *Historical Sketches of Statesmen Who Flourished in the Time of George III*. Apart from raking up old history, Brougham was particularly harsh on the late second Marquess of Londonderry, describing him as a man of 'limited capacity'. Perhaps as hurtful was Brougham's complete rejection of Castlereagh's achievements in the Foreign Office, particularly after the end of the Napoleonic Wars. This was combined with a vicious piece of character assassination.[63] Although the third Marquess's work was meant as a tribute to his brother, some contemporaries were less than impressed. Lord Clanwilliam was a noted critic, not just on the grounds of what was excluded but also of the loss at sea of so many of the letters in the process.[64] Clanwilliam went further and described, what was for him, the whole sorry episode of Londonderry's taking possession of his brother's papers from the trustees, as it was 'well known his object was to sell them to [John] Murray for £.1000'. Clanwilliam's judgement was blunt: 'And this shows why the 4 vols. of Ld. C's papers, publ[ishe]d. by his Half-Brother, are rubbish.'[65]

The first volume of Londonderry's work appeared as revolutions again erupted across mainland Europe, including in France, Prussia and the Habsburg monarchy. The revolutions of 1848 affected many of the European powers: an early casualty was the July Monarchy of Louis-Philippe which fell in February 1848, to be replaced by a new republic. In the Habsburg empire, 1848–9 saw revolutions throughout the dynasty's territories, notably across the Kingdom of Hungary, but also in Galicia, Venice, Prague and the Imperial capital itself, Vienna. In March 1848, Metternich's government collapsed and the minister was forced to leave the capital. In December 1848, Ferdinand I, who had succeeded in 1835, abdicated in favour of his young nephew, Francis-Joseph.[66] Londonderry could only observe these events. Since Peel's resignation as prime minister in 1846, a call to arms was now a very remote possibility. Peel had remained close to the Londonderrys and had offered them patronage and office. When Peel died in July 1850, Lord Londonderry lost a valuable ally, although he remained active in political life: for example, strenuously opposing proposals to abolish the lord lieutenancy of Ireland in a speech in the Lords on 27 June 1850.[67]

Suspicion towards French ambitions was rarely absent from British opinion, especially among the generation which fought Napoleonic France. In a letter dated 24 March 1851 to Lord Londonderry, who was currently abroad, Browne showed this to the full, writing that if the Marquess chose to travel south from Paris, he could 'explore the Pass of Roncesvalles' with its history of past military glories:

> through which our Black Prince trod . . . with his English Archers, so many centuries before Wellington revisited it, with his conquering Army – the second humiliation of France – never forgotten – never forgiven, & which that France hopes to avenge, one day, with the 100,000 men garrisoning Paris, which, in so popular a cause, might solely entrust herself to her National Guard.[68]

This was, however, a France with another Bonaparte as head of state. Louis-Napoleon, the son of Louis, King of Holland and Queen Hortense, had been elected as president in 1848. The Londonderrys and the President were on close terms, something which would be used by Lord Londonderry to good effect in securing the freedom of Abd-el-Kader (as contemporaries wrote his name), a leading Algerian military and religious figure at the forefront of the struggle against French rule. In 1847, Abd-el-Kader had surrendered to General Lamoricière and then to Louis-Philippe's son, the duc d'Aumale, on condition that he would be allowed to go into honourable retirement. The French government subsequently refused this condition and imprisoned him. It was this affair which would do much to restore Londonderry's good name in the last years of his life, following the widespread criticisms he had received during the Irish Potato Famine.

Abd-el-Kader's imprisonment was a cause célèbre in France, and in Britain Lord Londonderry led the way in calling for his release, first of all writing to Louis-Philippe and to leading French ministers. The fall of the monarchy in France meant that nothing came of these appeals. The election of Louis-Napoleon Bonaparte presented a new opportunity. Prince Louis-Napoleon, the heir to the Bonaparte dynasty since the death of the Duke of Reichstadt in 1832, was an established member of the Londonderry social circle. Louis-Napoleon was a 'frequent guest, and almost a habitué, of Wynyard Park between his two captivities'. Alison recalled that on his later visits, Louis-Napoleon 'repeatedly conversed with Lord and Lady Londonderry on the breach of faith' over Abd-el-Kader. The President was soon in a position to make amends. Louis-Napoleon achieved 'supreme power' in 1851, and he secured the release of Abd-el-Kader the following year.[69] That same year of 1852 saw the French Republic transformed into the Second Empire and the President's transformation into Napoleon III, Emperor of the French.

In February 1852, the Tories returned to office as a minority government under the premiership of the Earl of Derby, winning a general election in June. Disraeli became leader of the Commons and chancellor of the exchequer, while Hardinge was appointed Master General of the Ordnance in March. This last appointment caused a rupture with Lord Londonderry, who wanted office for himself and had expected Hardinge's help. Londonderry was out of love with the political world; this was despite the fact that Lord Eglinton had called on the Londonderrys at Holdernesse House to advise, via Frances Anne, that Lord Seaham, was to be offered a number of places in government.[70] On 16 March, Hardinge put up a spirited defence of his actions.[71] The argument escalated, and later that same day, Hardinge, clearly responding to another barb, wrote, 'I quite agree with you that no farther advantage can arise from any further correspondence – but I peremptorily deny, that I have done or written any thing which requires yr. forgiveness.' All of this put Londonderry's sister, Lady Hardinge, in an awful position. One of her undated letters, but clearly post-dating this quarrel, has the line, 'As you never call on me or request me to call on you, I conclude we are to continue in a State of estrangement, which is certainly very sad at our age.'[72]

Although Londonderry was not to receive any office, the government was to secure him one last honour. In August 1852, the death of the tenth Duke of Hamilton caused a vacancy in the Order of the Garter. Londonderry's name was one of those put forward in consideration. Queen Victoria was no fan of the Marquess, and was not overly impressed with the idea, telling Derby that she was 'of opinion that it would not be advisable on the whole to give the Garter to Lord Londonderry; that the Duke of Northumberland had by far the strongest claim to this distinction'. On 14 September 1852, Londonderry's old chief, the Duke of Wellington, died, creating a second vacancy. Thanks to Prince Albert, Londonderry was now in line to receive this honour. On 17 September, Albert drew up a memorandum of his conversation with Lord Derby on the bestowal of honours and offices freed up by the Duke's death, noting among other things 'that Lord Hardinge was the only man fit to command the Army' and that the Garter should go to Lord Londonderry. Derby was now free to make the offer to Londonderry, which he did by letter also dated 17 September 1852.[73]

The letter was slightly delayed reaching the Marquess who was currently in Ireland. The letter had first been dispatched to Wynyard, then to Garron Tower and then to Mount Stewart. Replying from Mount Stewart on 23 September, an overwhelmed Lord Londonderry told the Prime Minister 'that by Her Majesty's gracious Act of favour She has recruited, and recalled again by the Brother, those proud names of Wellington and Londonderry to that Epoch when by their splendid and eminent services, they gave Peace to Europe.'[74] Despite the often strained relations between Wellington and Lord Londonderry, it was only natural that he was one of the pall-bearers at the Duke's state funeral on 18 November, along with a number of military veterans including Hardinge.

On 15 January 1853, Londonderry was summoned by Lord Aberdeen to travel to Windsor for the Garter investiture.[75] At Raby Castle, Londonderry's neighbour, the Duke of Cleveland, advised that he had also just received his own summons from the Bishop of Oxford. The Duke acknowledged this being 'so sudden a notice' but was clearly more in touch with railway timetables and sent his advice on travel arrangements.[76] A few days later, Londonderry was preoccupied with mundane political matters. On 20 January, he wrote to the foreign secretary on rumours that Castlereagh was to be called up to the House of Lords in his father's lifetime, through a writ of acceleration. Castlereagh had enjoyed a rakish reputation in his younger years; known as 'Cas' and 'Young Rapid', his attentions to the renowned opera singer Giulia Grisi had led to his fighting a duel with her husband in 1838. Castlereagh though had put this life behind him. He married the widowed Elizabeth Jocelyn in 1846 and settled down to life in her house at Powerscourt. Having served as MP for County Down for thirty years, Castlereagh retired from the Commons in 1852.[77] Londonderry was furious at the idea of his eldest son's elevation to the Lords, telling Aberdeen as much, revealing at the same time his disagreements with his son's current political conduct.[78]

Although he remained very active and still rode regularly, Londonderry was now in his mid-70s, and age was beginning to creep up on him.[79] An accident at the end of 1853 was followed by reports of his being ill. A concerned Disraeli wrote on 30 January 1854, 'I never heard of your illness for a long time . . . but I learned, at the same time, on the authority of one of your most intimate acquaintance, that there was no truth in it, & that you were happily quite well.'[80] Alison's account has Lord Londonderry in good health until February 1854, when he 'was seized with an attack of bronchitis . . . which from the first was attended by alarming symptoms'.[81] However, it was reported at the time that Londonderry had 'a 'sudden attack of influenza which proved too severe for a constitution already weakened by the natural decay of age'. On 6 March 1854, the third Marquess of Londonderry died at Holdernesse House surrounded by 'nearly all the members of his family' including his sister, Lady Hardinge'.[82] On Monday 13 March, Lord Londonderry's body was taken from Holdernesse House to King's Cross, attended by 'his three sons and other relatives'. At the station, a guard of honour was formed by the 2nd Life Guards to the strains of the Dead March from Handel's *Saul*. On Wednesday 15 March, the third Marquess lay in state at Wynyard and his funeral took place the following day in Long Newton. Among the pall-bearers were the Duke of Cleveland and Sir Henry Browne.

Londonderry's obituary in the *Gentleman's Magazine* listed his immense military achievements but briefly passed over his public career as a diplomat, before concentrating on his life post-Vienna. It also hinted at the long years of frustration:

The responsibilities devolved upon Lord Londonderry by the management of the property of his bride, embracing a considerable portion of the most important coal-mines in the country, opened a new field for the exercise of energies which the cessation of war had thrown into temporary inaction. His Lordship applied himself with a vigorous activity which formed one of his characteristics to the development of the vast resources of his estates.[83]

This politely ignored the fact that Londonderry's energies had been focused on diplomacy since the ending of the war, until his resignation from the Vienna embassy – his inaction had nothing to do with the years of peace. By the time of his death, only a few of those who had known Londonderry during his years of greatest public service were still alive. The close partnership between Castlereagh and his younger brother, which had done so much to shape European history, would soon completely fade from public memory. The result was to underestimate the third Marquess's unique and important career, and thereby reduce the close and intimate relationship between Castlereagh and his beloved brother to sometimes little more than a footnote. For Castlereagh, his fame would lead to numerous biographies and publications; his younger brother would not be so fortunate at the hands of history.

NOTES

Introduction: The dragon's crest

1   Louis J. Jennings (ed.), *The Croker Papers* (3 vols, London, 1884), vol. 1, pp. 346–7.
2   Elizabeth Longford, *Wellington* (this edition, London, 1992), p. 147.
3   Durham County Record Office, D/Lo/C167/1, Lady Londonderry to Alison, 30 May 1854; see also DRO, D/Lo/C168, Browne to Lady Londonderry, 18 July 1854; DRO, D/Lo/C543/13, fourth Marquess of Londonderry to Lady Londonderry, 30 November 1854; DRO, D/Lo/C543/21, fourth Marquess of Londonderry to Lady Londonderry, 20 February 1855; in letter 30 (n.d.) Frederick advised his stepmother, 'You shall have the copies of Ld. Aberdeens letters, as soon as I get back to Powerscourt.'
4   Sir Archibald Alison, *Lives of Lord Castlereagh and Sir Charles Stewart* (3 vols, Edinburgh, 1861), vol. 1, p. ix.
5   A positive account of the close relationship between the two brothers can be found in Theresa, Marchioness of Londonderry, *Robert Stewart, Viscount Castlereagh* (London, 1904), preface, pp. 3, 50.
6   Sir Charles Webster, *Foreign Policy of Castlereagh 1815–1822* (London, 1925), p. 39; Webster noted that this usefulness decreased after his second marriage.
7   Edith, Marchioness of Londonderry, *Frances Anne, The Life and Times of Frances Anne Marchioness of Londonderry and Her Husband Charles Third Marquess of Londonderry* (London, 1958); Diane Urquhart, *The Ladies of Londonderry* (London, 2007), pp. 9–69; H. Montgomery Hyde, *The Londonderrys* (London, 1979), pp. 18–43.
8   Wendy Hinde, *Castlereagh* (London, 1981), p. 191. See also Ione Leigh, *Castlereagh* (London, 1951), p. 292.
9   John Bew, *Castlereagh: Enlightenment, War, and Tyranny* (London, 2011), p. 223.
10 For example, Rory Muir, *Britain and the Defeat of Napoleon 1807–1815* (New Haven, CT, 1996), pp. 243–61, 280–342. Two earlier works should also be noted: Henry Kissinger, *A World Restored: Metternich, Castlereagh and the Problems of Peace 1812–1822* (London, 1957); Paul W. Schroeder, *Metternich's Diplomacy at Its Zenith, 1820–1823* (Austin, TX, 1962).
11 Charles Vane, third Marquess of Londonderry (ed.), *Memoirs of Viscount Castlereagh* (12 vols, London, 1848–53), vol. 1, pp. 1–2; Alison, *Lives of Lord Castlereagh*, vol. 1, p. 1; John Debrett, *Debrett's Peerage of the United Kingdom of Great Britain and Ireland* (2 vols, London, 1828), vol. 2, p. 634; see Hyde, *The Londonderrys*, pp. 265–8.
12 Alison, *Lives of Lord Castlereagh*, vol. 1, p. 1; Londonderry, *Castlereagh*, vol. 1, p. 2.
13 Created first Marquess of Hertford in 1793.
14 See Edmund Lodge, *The Peerage of the British Empire* (London, 1832), pp. 255–6; in *Debrett's*, Stewart is shown as having two other brothers, Alexander John (d.1800) and Thomas Henry (d.1810), in addition to another sister, Elizabeth Mary (d.1798); see Debrett, *Debrett's Peerage of the United Kingdom*, vol. 2, p. 635. *Debrett's* spells Catherine Octavia's name as 'Catharine'. Lodge's list tallies with Alison's account of the

family (and Lodge calls Catherine Octavia simply 'Octavia'); see Alison, *Lives of Lord Castlereagh*, vol. 1, p. 2. The third Marquess's surname after his second marriage was sometimes referred to as 'Vane-Stewart' (see, for example, Lodge, *Peerage*, p. 255).

15 Alison, *Lives of Lord Castlereagh*, vol. 1, p. 3.

16 Kent History and Library Centre, Pratt Manuscripts, U840/5, 10 October 1790.

17 However, 'After 1782 . . . the Irish Parliament . . . achieved an unprecedented, though still limited, level of legislative independence' (Bew, *Castlereagh*, p. 38).

18 Alison, *Lives of Lord Castlereagh*, vol. 1, pp. 3–4 on an incident involving a schoolfriend at Eton, Lord Waldegrave; see also Lodge, *Peerage*, p. 403.

19 Alison, *Lives of Lord Castlereagh*, vol. 1, p. 4; See Roger Knight, *Britain against Napoleon: The Organization of Victory 1793–1815* (London, 2013), p. 123.

20 Kent History and Library Centre, Pratt Manuscripts, U840/C50/1 (n.d. marked in pencil, c. September 1795).

21 Commissioned an ensign on 11 October 1794, promoted captain on 30 October, and to major on 31 July 1795. See H. G. Hart, *The New Annual Army List, Corrected to 7 February 1840* (London, 1840), p. 136.

22 Richard Bassett, *For God and Kaiser: The Imperial Austrian Army* (New Haven, CT, 2015), p. 192.

23 *Royal Military Calendar, or Army Service and Commission Book* (3rd edition, 5 vols, London, 1820), vol. 2, p. 411.

24 See Londonderry, *Castlereagh*, vols 1 and 2. See also Bew, *Castlereagh*, pp. 109–24.

25 *Royal Military Calendar*, p. 412.

26 Londonderry, *Castlereagh*, vol. 2, Camden to Stewart, p. 89.

27 *Royal Military Calendar*, p. 414.

28 Alison, *Lives of Lord Castlereagh*, vol. 1, p. 319.

29 *Royal Military Calendar*, p. 414; see also Alison, *Lives of Lord Castlereagh*, vol. 1, p. 319.

30 Bew, *Castlereagh*, p. 150.

31 Ibid., pp. 125–57.

32 Ibid., p. 151, p. 169.

33 Charles Esdaile, *Napoleon's Wars: An International History 1803–15* (this edition, London, 2008), pp. 24–38.

34 Michael Broers, *Europe under Napoleon* (this edition, London, 2015), p. 15.

35 Ibid., p. 19.

36 Philip Mansel, *The Eagle in Splendour: Inside the Court of Napoleon* (this edition, London, 2015), p. 16.

37 Esdaile, *Napoleon's Wars*, pp. 71–109.

38 See Esdaile, *Napoleon's Wars*, pp. 110–53. One of the main areas of disagreement between Britain and France was the continued British occupation of Malta. Napoleon had seized Malta from the Knights of St John, but the British had besieged the island, forcing the French garrison to surrender in 1800.

39 Arthur Aiken (ed.), *The Annual Review and History of Literature for 1805* (London, 1806), p. 291; see pp. 291–2 for the entire review and for extracts from Stewart's work.

40 Esdaile, *Napoleon's Wars*, pp. 154–5.

41 BL, Moore Papers, Add. MS 57543, ff. 56–7, 9 May 1808.

42 Ibid., f. 72, 31 May 1808. Stewart's letters to Moore are dated 25 April to 31 May 1808.

43 Lodge translates the family motto as 'The collar of the dragon is to be feared' (see Lodge, *Peerage*, p. 256).

1 Portugal and Spain

1 Charles Esdaile, *The Peninsular War* (London, 2002), pp. 53, 58; for an account of the events leading up to the uprising, see pp. 37–61.
2 DRO, D/Lo/C17/2, 8 July 1808.
3 DRO, D/Lo/C17/3, 15 July 1808.
4 Ibid.
5 Sir Archibald Alison, *Lives of Lord Castlereagh and Sir Charles Stewart* (3 vols, Edinburgh, 1861), vol. 3, p. 209.
6 DRO, D/Lo/C17/4, 24 August 1808 (wrongly dated November, August pencilled on letter).
7 Charles Vane, third Marquess of Londonderry, *Story of the Peninsular War* (this edition, London, 1856), p. 80.
8 DRO, D/Lo/C17/5, 1 September 1808.
9 See Rory Muir, *Wellington: The Path to Victory 1769–1814* (New Haven, CT, 2013), pp. 259–82.
10 DRO, D/Lo/C17/6, 3 September 1808.
11 Ibid.; Napier records that Stewart found himself embroiled in political intrigues which included a Hanoverian officer and the Portuguese Regency: 'General Charles Stewart, brother of lord Castlereagh, was the bearer of Von Decken's first letter; he would not knowingly have lent himself to an intrigue, subversive of his brother's views.' Sir William Napier, *History of the War in the Peninsula* (Oxford, 1836), p. 63.
12 Sir John Fortescue, *A History of the British Army* (20 vols, London, 1899–1930), vol. VI, p. 319.
13 DRO, D/Lo/C17/13, 8 October 1808.
14 See Huw J. Davies, *Spying for Wellington: British Military Intelligence in the Peninsular War* (Norman, OK, 2018), p. 63.
15 Londonderry, *Peninsular War*, pp. 93–4.
16 Esdaile, *Peninsular War*, p. 284.
17 Londonderry, *Peninsular War*, p. 94.
18 See DRO, D/Lo/C17/15, 29 November 1808.
19 Londonderry, *Peninsular War*, p. 103.
20 DRO, D/Lo/C17/15, 3 December 1808 (continuation of letter dated 29 November 1808).
21 DRO, D/Lo/C17/16, 5 December 1808.
22 Londonderry, *Peninsular War*, p. 110.
23 See Davies, *Spying for Wellington*, pp. 94–5, for details of the later intelligence role performed by the then Lieutenant Colonel John Waters.
24 Londonderry, *Peninsular War*, p. 112.
25 Ibid., pp. 112–13.
26 DRO, D/Lo/C17/19, 19 December 1808.
27 DRO, D/Lo/C17/20, 22 December 1808.
28 Londonderry, *Peninsular War*, p. 122.
29 DRO, D/Lo/C17/22, 2 January 1809.
30 William Fordyce, *The History and Antiquities of the County Palatine of Durham* (2 vols, Newcastle upon Tyne, 1857), vol. II, p. 325.
31 Alison, *Lives of Lord Castlereagh*, vol. 1, p. 330; vol. 3, pp. 208–9.

2 To war with Wellesley

1 DRO, D/Lo/C113/12, 20 March 1809.
2 Sir Archibald Alison, *Lives of Lord Castlereagh and Sir Charles Stewart* (3 vols, Edinburgh, 1861), vol. 2, p. 204; letter p. 205.
3 Ibid., vol. 1, p. 332.
4 Rory Muir, *Wellington: The Path to Victory 1769–1814* (New Haven, CT, 2013), p. 508.
5 DRO, D/Lo/C17/26 and 27, 5 May and 7 May 1809.
6 British officers in the Portuguese service received additional ranks. Stewart voiced his opinions on this subject to his brother; see DRO, D/Lo/C17/33, 29 May 1809.
7 George FitzClarence, first Earl of Munster, *An Account of the British Campaign in 1809 under Sir A. Wellesley in Spain and Portugal* (London, 1831), p. 13.
8 James Tomkinson (ed.), *The Diary of a Cavalry Officer* (2nd edition, London, 1895), pp. 10–11.
9 Sir Charles Oman, *A History of the Peninsular War*, vol. II, January–September 1809 (first published London, 1903; this edition, London, 1995), p. 330.
10 [P. Hawker], *Journal of a Regimental Officer during the Recent Campaign in Portugal and Spain under Lord Viscount Wellington. With a Correct Plan of the Battle of Talavera* (London, 1810), p. 56. Stewart is referred to as a 'Staff Officer'; not surprisingly it might have damaged the officer's career prospects to have criticized Stewart openly.
11 Charles Vane, third Marquess of Londonderry, *Story of the Peninsular War* (London, 1856), p. 160; Oman, *Peninsular War*, vol. II, p. 341. Sir William Napier, *History of the War in the Peninsula* (Oxford, 1836), p. 193; Munster, *An Account of the British Campaign*, p. 17.
12 DRO, D/Lo/C17/31, 15 May 1809.
13 DRO, D/Lo/C17/35, 8 June 1809.
14 Ibid.
15 DRO, D/Lo/C17/37, 12 June 1809 and D/Lo/C17/39, 18 June 1809.
16 DRO, D/Lo/C17/42, 1 July 1809.
17 Londonderry, *Peninsular War*, p. 176.
18 Ibid., pp. 181–2.
19 Ibid., p. 185.
20 Ibid., p. 186.
21 Ibid., p. 187.
22 Muir, *Wellington: The Path to Victory*, p. 339.
23 Munster, *An Account of the British Campaign*, p. 31.
24 DRO, D/Lo/C17/46.
25 DRO, D/Lo/C50, 18 August 1809.
26 DRO, D/Lo/C51, 21 August 1809.
27 DRO, D/Lo/C52, 24 August 1809. The letter noted that the posts of adjutant general and quartermaster general 'are not understood in our Army nor is the Business conducted through them in such a manner as to render the Officers, as interesting or important as they are in most other Army's [*sic*]'.
28 DRO, D/Lo/C55 (i), 19 September 1809.
29 John Bew, *Castlereagh: Enlightenment, War and Terror* (London, 2011), pp. 257–67.
30 See Giles Hunt, *Castlereagh, Canning and Deadly Cabinet Rivalry* (London, 2008), p. 137.

31   Alison, *Lives of Lord Castlereagh*, vol. 1, p. 354.

32   DRO, D/Lo/C17/53, 20 October 1809.

33   Ibid.

34   DRO, D/Lo/C17/55 (ii), 20 October 1809.

35   Londonderry, *Peninsular War*, p. 200.

36   DRO, D/Lo/C18/57, 7 October 1809; it talks of Wellington's possible appointment to the Ordnance. 'We must consider this only as a Wellesley Govt – if the Marquis gets the Garter, I hope the D of R. will resent it as he ought.' Canning is also attacked in an earlier letter (D/Lo/C18/56, 2 October 1809).

37   Alison, *Lives of Lord Castlereagh*, vol. 1, p. 354.

38   Ibid., pp. 356–7.

39   DRO, D/Lo/C113/15 Wellington to Stewart, 28 February 1810.

40   Ibid.

41   As well as minister to Portugal, Stuart was later appointed to the Portuguese Regency Council. For an overview, see Robert Franklin, *Lord Stuart de Rothesay* (Upton-upon-Severn, 1993), pp. 88–103. The minister's role in intelligence gathering is discussed in Huw J. Davies, *Spying for Wellington: British Military Intelligence in the Peninsular War* (Norman, OK, 2018), pp. 71–90.

42   However, for an alternative view of Craufurd's actions, see Davies, *Spying for Wellington*, p. 144.

43   DRO, D/Lo/C113/6 (a), Wellington to Stewart, 28 August 1810.

44   Londonderry, *Peninsular War*, p. 225.

45   Alison, *Lives of Lord Castlereagh*, vol. 1, p. 375.

46   Jac Weller, *Wellington in the Peninsula* (this edition, Barnsley, 2012), p. 135.

47   Alison, *Lives of Lord Castlereagh*, vol. 1, p. 380; see also Londonderry, *Peninsular War*, pp. 224–9.

48   Ibid., p. 379.

49   Charles Esdaile, *The Peninsular War* (London, 2002), p. 327.

50   Alison, *Lives of Lord Castlereagh*, vol. 1, p. 383.

51   Muir, *Wellington: The Path to Victory*, p. 399.

52   Londonderry, *Peninsular War*, p. 233.

53   Ibid., p. 237.

54   Esdaile, *Peninsular War*, p. 330.

55   DRO, D/Lo/C113/ 4, 5 January 1811; Alison, *Lives of Lord Castlereagh*, vol. 1, pp. 410–11; Napier notes that during the retreat 'the letters of general Spencer and general Charles Stewart appeared so desponding to lord Liverpool that he transmitted them to Lord Wellington'. See Napier, *History of the War in the Peninsula*, p. 311.

56   DRO, D/Lo/C113/8, Wellington to Stewart, 11 January 1811.

3   Great gallantry

1   Sir Archibald Alison, *Lives of Lord Castlereagh and Sir Charles Stewart* (3 vols, Edinburgh, 1861), vol. 1, p. 427.

2   Charles Vane, third Marquess of Londonderry, *Story of the Peninsular War* (this edition, London, 1856), p. 252.

3   Alison, *Lives of Lord Castlereagh*, vol. 1, pp. 423, 427.

4   DRO, D/Lo/C18/61.

5 DRO, D/Lo/C18/62.

6 DRO, D/Lo/C18/63.

7 Quoted in Alison, *Lives of Lord Castlereagh*, vol. 1, p. 451; see also Londonderry, *Peninsular War*, p. 278.

8 Alison, *Lives of Lord Castlereagh*, vol. 1, pp. 451–2.

9 Ibid., p. 457; Londonderry, *Peninsular War*, p. 284.

10 Londonderry, *Peninsular War*, pp. 284–5.

11 Ibid., p. 286.

12 Ibid., p. 287.

13 Ibid., p. 291.

14 DRO, D/Lo/C18/67. The letter had begun by complimenting Castlereagh's 'Exposé as to County Derry, Peninsula, & my own Domestick Politics.'

15 DRO, D/Lo/C18/70, 20 December 1811.

16 DRO, D/Lo/C18/71, 1 January 1812.

17 Charles Esdaile, *The Peninsular War* (London, 2002), p. 378; see also pp. 372–9.

18 Alison, *Lives of Lord Castlereagh*, vol. 1, p. 476, Stewart to Castlereagh, 21 January 1812.

19 Londonderry, *Peninsular War*, p. 310; for Stewart's description of Ciudad Rodrigo, see pp. 297–312.

20 DRO, D/Lo/C118/4; Rory Muir, *Wellington: The Path to Victory 1769–1814* (New Haven, CT, 2013), p. 515.

21 DRO, D/Lo/C118/3, n.d. See also Wellington's letter dated 19 October 1812 (DRO, D/Lo/C113/3).

22 On 17 March 1812 Stewart sought a cavalry command from Wellington, 'Believing that an increased stimulus, and a wider field, would assist in dispelling the gloomy reflections of my mind' (DRO, D/Lo/C113/13).

23 Stewart had also sat for Lawrence; see 'Recollections of Sir Thomas Lawrence by Miss Croft' in George Somers Layard (ed.), *Sir Thomas Lawrence's Letter-Bag* (London, 1906), p. 254.

24 For an analysis of Alexander's character, see Dominic Lieven, *Russia against Napoleon: The Battle for Europe, 1807 to 1814* (London, 2009), pp. 56–9.

25 Ibid., pp. 60–101.

26 Ibid., pp. 242–84.

27 Castlereagh to Liverpool, 23 January 1813, quoted by Alison, *Lives of Lord Castlereagh*, vol. 3, p. 210. Alison suggests that the post was that of minister to Prussia.

28 Francis Townsend, *Calendar of Knights* (London, 1828), p. 167.

29 D. G. Neville, *History of the Early Orders of Knighthood and Chivalry* (London, 1978), notes that the Order of the Tower and Sword was founded in 1459 and revived in 1808: 'The Order was extensively used to reward military merit in the Peninsular War' (no page number). Townsend notes that he was made a Commander of the Tower and Sword with the Royal Licence to accept given on 27 March 1813 (Townsend, *Calendar of Knights*, p. 99).

30 Wellington also received the Order of the Garter in 1813. Stewart was originally chosen to 'deliver' the insignia of the Garter to the Marquess of Wellington, as outlined in Sir Isaac Heard's letter, dated 10 March 1813 (Charles Vane, third Marquess of Londonderry, *Narrative of the War in Germany and France in 1813 and 1814* (London, 1830), appendix, p. 395). See also second Duke of Wellington (ed.), *Supplementary Despatches and Memoranda of Field Marshal Arthur, Duke of Wellington* (15 vols, London, 1858–72), vol. 7, p. 581. However, the insignia of the

Garter was delivered to Wellington by Sir Thomas Graham (see John Gurwood, *The Dispatches of Field Marshal the Duke of Wellington* (13 vols, London, 1834–9), vol. 10, pp. 370–1).

31 William Schaw Cathcart, first Viscount Cathcart, was appointed as ambassador in 1812. Cathcart had a good knowledge of Russian affairs as his father had also been ambassador to Russia.

4 Roving ambassador

1 Rory Muir, *Britain and the Defeat of Napoleon, 1807–1815* (New Haven, CT, 1996), pp. 248–9; Wendy Hinde, *Castlereagh* (London, 1981), p. 191; John Bew, *Castlereagh: Enlightenment, War and Terror* (London, 2011), p. 316.

2 Lady Jackson (ed.), *The Bath Archives: A Further Selection from the Diaries and Letters of Sir George Jackson, K.C.H., from 1809 to 1816* (2 vols, London, 1873), vol. 2, pp. 26, 28. Jackson also noted 'that Fitzclarence is to go' (p. 26); the military nature of the post was reinforced by Castlereagh's warning to his brother about the use of couriers (see Charles Vane, third Marquess of Londonderry (ed.), *Memoirs of Viscount Castlereagh* (12 vols, London, 1848–53), vol. 9, Third Series, Military and Diplomatic, pp. 5–6). For the Berlin embassy, see Lady Rose Weigall (ed.), *The Letters of Lady Burghersh* (London, 1893), pp. 34–5.

3 BL, Aberdeen Papers, Add. MS 43073, Aberdeen to Castlereagh, f. 289, 6 September 1813. Aberdeen was unsurprisingly horrified by the sight of war, see BL, Aberdeen Papers, Add. MS 43075, f. 102, 5 November 1813.

4 Jackson, *Bath Archives*, vol. 2, p. 27; letter from Mrs Jackson, 25 March 1813, p. 31.

5 Ibid., pp. 53–4.

6 Christopher Clark, *Iron Kingdom: The Rise and Downfall of Prussia 1600–1947* (this edition, London, 2007), p. 314; Dominic Lieven, *Russia against Napoleon: The Battle for Europe, 1807 to 1814* (London, 2009), p. 294; see also Adam Zamoyski, *Rites of Peace: The Fall of Napoleon and the Congress of Vienna* (London, 2007), p. 28.

7 Charles Vane, third Marquess of Londonderry, *Narrative of the War in Germany and France in 1813 and 1814* (London, 1830), p. 3.

8 Lieven, *Russia against Napoleon*, pp. 95–6.

9 Stewart was appointed 'lieutenant general on the Continent of Europe only' dated 8 April 1813, as noted in *The Royal Military Chronicle or British Officers Monthly Register and Mentor for May 1813*, p. 345 (taken from the *London Gazette*, 13 April 1813).

10 TNA, Foreign Office Correspondence, FO 64/87, 19 April 1813: 'Although I have nothing very material to report to Your Lordship, I am anxious by the return of the Nymphon Frigate, to apprize you of my Arrival at Hamburg . . . I had an interview with major Kentzinger off Cuxhaven. – He gave me the most exhilarating Picture of the State of Enthusiasm of the People.'

11 Clark, *Prussia*, p. 278; see also pp. 278–80 on Hardenberg's early career.

12 TNA, FO 64/87, Stewart to Castlereagh, 26 April 1813.

13 TNA, FO 64/87, Stewart to Castlereagh, 27 April 1813; see also Londonderry, *Narrative*, pp. 4–15.

14 Jackson, *Bath Archives*, pp. 82–3.

15 Londonderry, *Narrative*, pp. 24–5; Jackson, *Bath Archives*, vol. 2, p. 85; Stewart's stay in Dresden is found on pp. 82–7.

16 TNA, FO 64/87, 5 May 1813.

17 Ibid.

18 Jackson, *Bath Archives*, vol. 2, pp. 85–6.

19 Henry Kissinger, *A World Restored: Metternich, Castlereagh and the Problems of Peace 1812-1822* (London, 1957), p. 12; Alan Sked, *Metternich and Austria. An Evaluation* (Basingstoke, 2008), p. 1; Zamoyski, *Rites of Peace*, p. 37.

20 Mark Jarrett, *The Congress of Vienna and Its Legacy* (London, 2014), p. 73.

21 Lieven, *Russia against Napoleon*, p. 317; see also pp. 317–20.

22 Jackson, *Bath Archives*, vol. 2, p. 87.

23 Ibid., p. 103. Jackson noted that the conversation 'did not advance matters, beyond enabling me, in the same manner, to place before Sir Charles, the Chancellor's view of the business of the negotiation, at the first favourable opportunity'.

24 TNA, FO 64/87, 17 May 1813.

25 Londonderry, *Castlereagh*, vol. 9, pp. 12–14. In another letter sent from Wurzen on 17 May, Stewart had also advised 'Our Subsidiary Convention proceeds slowly' (TNA, FO 64/87).

26 Herbert Randolph (ed.), *Private Diary of Travels, Personal Services, and Public Events, During Mission and Employment with the European Armies in the Campaigns of 1812, 1813, 1814. From the Invasion of Russia to the Capture of Paris. By General Sir Robert Wilson* (2 vols, London, 1861), vol. 2, p. 17.

27 TNA, FO 64/87, 20 May 1813.

28 BL, Lowe Papers, Add. MS 20111, f. 29; this is an extract from a journal or letter. In a letter to Castlereagh dated 6 May 1813, Napoleon is described as 'the Ruler of France' (Add. MS 20111, f. 21). Lowe obviously looked forward to meeting Stewart, as he wrote to Colonel Henry Bunbury (undersecretary for war and the colonies) on 28 June 1813, Add. MS 20111, f. 42.

29 BL, Lowe Papers, Add. MS 20111, f. 44, Lowe to Colonel Henry Bunbury, 28 June 1813.

30 TNA, FO 64/87, 20 May 1813; the negotiations had involved Armand de Caulaincourt and the senior Russian military commander, General Miloradovich. This letter was presumably written just after Stewart's account of Bautzen; see note 27.

31 See Michael Glover, *A Very Slippery Fellow: The Life of Sir Robert Wilson* (Oxford, 1978), p. 138; see also Ian Samuel, *An Astonishing Fellow: The Life of General Sir Robert Wilson* (Slough, 1995), p. 152, further noting that Wilson saw Stewart as an ally against Cathcart.

32 BL, Wilson Papers, Add. MS 30107, f. 131, 5 June 1813.

33 Londonderry, *Narrative*, p. 59.

34 Londonderry, *Castlereagh*, vol. 9, pp. 22–3.

35 Ibid. In another letter of 6 June, Stewart told Castlereagh of Russian diplomatic moves with Austria, writing that 'Count Nesselrode . . . went to Vienna on a Mission from the Emperor Alexander' (TNA, FO 64/87).

36 TNA, FO 353/62, Convention agreed between the UK and Prussia at Reichenbach, 14 June 1813.

37 TNA, FO 64/87, 16 June 1813.

38 Lieven, *Russia against Napoleon*, pp. 359–62.

39 TNA, FO 64/87, 16 June 1813; George Jackson reported on 28 July 1813, 'I have conversed with Ld. Ct. upon the Subject of the £100,000 Sterling sent in Cash to Colburg, and His Lp. Is decidedly of opinion that nothing sd. for the present be said abt. it. – He seems to consider it also as a joint Aid intended for both Russia & Prussia'

(FO 353/62, Jackson to Stewart, 19 July 1813); see Londonderry Papers, D/Lo/C37/17, Stewart to Castlereagh, 9 March 1814 for the accounts showing the distribution of the £100,000.

40 Londonderry, *Narrative*, p. 76.
41 Stewart advised London of Bernadotte's movements during the peace negotiations; see TNA, FO 64/87, Stewart to Castlereagh, 6 June 1813. Thanks to the Prussians, Stewart was also kept apprised of Bernadotte's attitudes towards the current peace (TNA, FO 64/87, Stewart to Castlereagh, 13 June 1813).
42 Londonderry, *Narrative*, pp. 76–7.
43 Jackson, *Bath Archives*, vol. 2, p. 155, Stewart to Jackson, 10 July 1813. At least Stewart received encouragement from London, as Castlereagh wrote on 14 July (Londonderry, *Castlereagh*, vol. 9, p. 33).
44 Jackson, *Bath Archives*, vol. 2, pp. 163–4; diary entry 14 July 1813.
45 Ibid., vol. 2, pp. 163–4; diary entry 14 July 1813.
46 DRO, D/Lo/C37/10.
47 DRO, Londonderry Papers, D/Lo/C37/13, 16 July 1813; see Londonderry Papers D/Lo/C37/1 and D/Lo/C37/4, [?] July 1813 and 10 July 1813.
48 DRO, D/Lo/C37/13, 16 July 1813.
49 Ibid.
50 BL, Lowe Papers, Add. MS 20111, Lowe to Colonel Bunbury, 25 July 1813.
51 DRO, D/Lo/C37/16, 20 July 1813.
52 Randolph, *Private Diary*, vol. 2, p. 74, 10 August 1813.
53 TNA, FO 353/62, Jackson to Stewart, 19 July 1813; Jackson congratulated Stewart 'on the flattering Testimonies of Approbation' he had received from the Prince Regent.
54 TNA, FO 353/62, Jackson to Stewart, 27 July 1813.
55 TNA, FO 353/62, Jackson to Stewart, 2 August and 12 August 1813. On 6 August, Jackson had reported on the hardening of Austrian attitudes: 'The Emperor & those immediately about His I. My's Person Who till very lately acquiesced most reluctantly in the Idea of War have now unreservedly declared themselves in favor of it as the only Chance the only Alternative left them' (TNA, FO 353/62).
56 TNA, FO 64/89, No. 69, Stewart to Castlereagh, 12 August 1813.
57 Ibid.
58 BL, Aberdeen Papers, Add. MS 43073, Castlereagh to Aberdeen, 6 August 1813. For the Prince Regent's letter, see BL, Aberdeen Papers, Add. MS 43073, f. 11, 6 August 1813. Castlereagh also wrote to Cathcart and Stewart to tell them that Aberdeen 'should have the assistance of one of the Gentlemen of this Office now attached to your respective missions' (Add. MS 43073, f. 265, 7 August 1813).
59 TNA, FO 64/89, Stewart to Castlereagh, 12 August 1813; this is a separate letter to no. 69.

5 *The Brandenburg Hussars*

1 Lady Jackson (ed.), *The Bath Archives: A Further Selection from the Diaries and Letters of Sir George Jackson, K.C.H., from 1809 to 1816* (2 vols, London, 1873), vol. 2, pp. 210–11.
2 TNA, FO 64/89, Stewart to Castlereagh, 14 August 1813.
3 TNA, FO 64/89, Stewart to Castlereagh, 15 August 1813.

4 Ibid.

5 See Michael V. Leggiere, *Napoleon and the Struggle for Germany: The Franco-Prussian War of 1813. Volume II: The Defeat of Napoleon* (Cambridge, 2015), p. 7.

6 TNA, FO 64/89, Stewart to Castlereagh, 18 August 1813.

7 Charles Vane, third Marquess of Londonderry, *Narrative of the War in Germany and France in 1813 and 1814* (London, 1830), pp. 104–5.

8 TNA, FO 64/89, Stewart to Castlereagh, 20 August 1813.

9 TNA, FO 64/89, Stewart to Castlereagh, 22 August 1813.

10 Londonderry, *Narrative*, p. 119; see also Herbert Randolph (ed.), *Private Diary of Travels, Personal Services, and Public Events, During Mission and Employment with the European Armies in the Campaigns of 1812, 1813, 1814. From the Invasion of Russia to the Capture of Paris. By General Sir Robert Wilson* (2 vols, London, 1861), vol. 2, p. 93.

11 Dominic Lieven, *Russia against Napoleon: The Battle for Europe, 1807 to 1814* (London, 2009), p. 408.

12 Ibid., p. 411.

13 Londonderry, *Narrative*, pp. 125, 128; see pp. 123–8.

14 Sir Archibald Alison, *Lives of Lord Castlereagh and Sir Charles Stewart* (3 vols, Edinburgh, 1861), vol. 2, p. 44.

15 BL, Wilson Papers, Add. MS 30107, f. 173.

16 Leggiere, *Struggle for Germany*, p. 355.

17 BL, Lowe Papers, Add. MS 20111, f. 88, 31 August 1813. The Foreign Office subsequently sent Stewart 'the Blank Commissions for the Officers of the different Corps signed by H.R.H. the Prince Regent (which have just been forwarded to this Department) – and I am to desire that you will place your signature upon the Blank space on the left Hand at the Bottom of each Commission, & that you will cause a correct Account to be kept of the Names & Rank of the Persons to whom the same may be granted' (BL, Lowe Papers, Add. MS 20111, f. 119, Castlereagh to Stewart, 14 September 1813).

18 Peter J. Begent and Hubert Chesshyre, *The Most Noble Order of the Garter: 650 Years* (London, 1999), p. 323.

19 Jackson, *Bath Archives*, vol. 2, p. 251.

20 TNA, FO 64/89, 4 September 1813.

21 Ibid.

22 BL, Aberdeen Papers, Add. MS 43073, f. 289, most secret.

23 TNA, FO 64/89, 6 September 1813.

24 TNA, FO 64/89, 17 September 1813; while in Prague, Stewart advised Castlereagh 'that I have not failed to make the necessary Communication in case of the arrival of H.S.H. the Prince of Orange; I should hope the Arrangement for His Serene Highness would be made without Difficulty' (TNA, FO 64/90, 21 September 1813).

25 TNA, FO 64/90, 23 September 1813.

26 Londonderry, *Narrative*, pp. 144–5.

27 Ibid., p. 128; Jackson, *Bath Archives*, vol. 2, p. 288.

28 TNA, FO 64/90, Stewart to Castlereagh, 29 September 1813; Jackson, *Bath Archives*, p. 287. Jackson was unimpressed with the investiture, which he describes in some detail on pp. 287–8. Sir Robert Wilson was present at the dinner to celebrate and noted of the Tsar's Garter: 'The Emperor wore the star of the English Order of the "Garter," recently conferred, and the "Garter" above the knee, as the boot came up to the top of the knee-cap. It was probably the first time that it was ever so worn. I could not help thinking that the place of the "Garter" where I had seen the Legion

of Honour marked a strange revolution.' (Herbert Randolph (ed.), *Private Diary of Travels*, vol. 1, p. 144).

For the details of this Garter mission, see also Begent and Chesshyre, *The Most Noble Order of the Garter: 650 Years*, pp. 241–2. Tyrwhitt is described as 'the other plenipotentiary'. Lord Cathcart received the Order of St Andrew, the highest Order in the Tsar's gift.

29 Alison, *Lives of Lord Castlereagh and Sir Charles Stewart*, vol. 2, p. 88.
30 Lieven, *Russia against Napoleon*, p. 371.
31 Ibid., p. 437.
32 BL, Lowe Papers, Add. MS 20111, f. 164, memorandum of Battle of Leipzig.
33 TNA, FO 64/90, No. 115, 17 October 1813; Stewart never changed his opinion, as can be seen in Londonderry, *Narrative*, pp. 159–66.
34 Ibid., p. 381.
35 TNA, FO 64/90, No. 114, 17 October 1813, Alison, *Lives of Lord Castlereagh and Sir Charles Stewart*, p. 128; for Yorck's losses, see M. V. Leggiere, *The Fall of Napoleon: The Allied Invasion of France* (Cambridge, 2007), p. 12. Stewart's accounts of the battle are also given in FO 64/90, No. 116, Castlereagh to Stewart, 19 October 1813.
36 TNA, FO 64/90, No, 114, 17 October 1813.
37 Londonderry, *Narrative*, p. 172.
38 Ibid., pp. 178–9.
39 See TNA, FO 64/90, No. 120, Stewart to Castlereagh, 21 October 1813.
40 TNA, FO 64/90, No. 117 (Secret), Stewart to Castlereagh, 19 October 1813.
41 BL, Wilson Papers, Add. MS 30107, f. 257, 27 October 1813. This was written some days after the event as an explanation of what had occurred. See also f. 245, Capt Charles to Wilson, and f. 247, Wilson to Aberdeen.
42 BL, Aberdeen Papers, Add. MS 43074, f. 328, Wilson, vol. 2, p. 182.
43 See Londonderry, *Narrative*, pp. 179–80.
44 BL, Lowe Papers, Add. MS 20111, f. 192, Stewart to Lowe, 26 October 1813.
45 BL, Lowe Papers, Add. MS 20111, f. 227, Lowe to Bunbury, 24 November 1813. For Bunbury's importance in intelligence gathering, see Huw J. Davies, *Spying for Wellington: British Military Intelligence in the Peninsular War* (Norman, OK, 2018), p. 41.
46 TNA, FO 64/90, Stewart to Cumberland, 31 October 1813.
47 TNA, FO 64/90, Stewart to Castlereagh, 2 November 1813.
48 BL, Aberdeen Papers, Add. MS 43075, ff. 6, 103. Henry Kissinger notably described the three ambassadors as 'beset by internal rivalry . . . None of the British representatives was really up to his task. Aberdeen was too young, Stewart too vain, Cathcart too phlegmatic.' Henry Kissinger, *A World Restored: Metternich, Castlereagh and the Problems of Peace 1812–1822* (London, 1957), p. 104.
49 BL, Aberdeen Papers, Add. MS 43225, f. 40, 15 November 1813; he had already contrived to annoy the foreign secretary by his repeated attempts to find official employment for Sir Robert Wilson, described by Castlereagh as a 'dangerous coxcomb'; this was also the opinion of Count Münster, and Aberdeen was told 'you will consider it quite Confidential and not let it go beyond Lord Cathcart and my Brother.' BL, Aberdeen Papers, Add. MS 43074, f. 286, 15 October 1813.
50 BL, Aberdeen Papers, Add. MS 43075, f. 166, 12 November 1813.
51 BL, Aberdeen Papers, Add. MS 43075, f. 149, 10 November 1813.
52 TNA, FO 64/91, 28 November 1813.
53 BL, Aberdeen Papers, Add. MS 43075, f. 215, 28 November 1813; Aberdeen further noted that Cathcart 'inform[e]d me that you had in some of your dispatches to him,

objected to its being sent back'; for a detailed account of the Frankfurt negotiations, see, for example, Leggiere, *The Fall of Napoleon*, pp. 42–62.

6 The fall of France

1 BL, Aberdeen Papers, Add. MS 43225, f. 43.
2 Lady Jackson (ed.), *The Bath Archives: A Further Selection from the Diaries and Letters of Sir George Jackson, K.C.H., from 1809 to 1816* (2 vols, London, 1873), vol. 2, p. 379, 3 December 1813. In 1813, new regulations were adopted to address the growing receipt by British subjects of foreign Orders of Chivalry (the regulations were signed by Castlereagh). See Francis Townsend, *Calendar of Knights* (London, 1828), pp. xiv–xviii.
3 Jackson, *Bath Archives*, diary 5 December 1813, p. 382; diary 6 December 1813, pp. 383–4 (the dinner was given by Lord Burghersh).
4 Herbert Randolph (ed.), *Private Diary of Travels, Personal Services, and Public Events, During Mission and Employment with the European Armies in the Campaigns of 1812, 1813, 1814. From the Invasion of Russia to the Capture of Paris. By General Sir Robert Wilson* (2 vols, London, 1861), vol. 2, p. 238.
5 Jackson, *Bath Archives*, vol. 2, p. 383; BL, Aberdeen Papers, Add. MS 43075, f. 315, Aberdeen to Castlereagh, 9 December 1813. Jackson recorded on 8 December that he was leaving for Britain; see Jackson, *Bath Archives*, p. 385.
6 Aberdeen 43075, f. 311, copy of Castlereagh to Stewart, 4 December 1813.
7 Jackson, *Bath Archives*, vol. 2, p. 382, diary 5 December 1813; Jackson wrote that Stewart was expected to leave for Hanover as his 'dissatisfaction with all that is passing here is so great'. Jackson further noted that Bernadotte's 'military movements and political conduct are viewed here with much disfavour'.
8 Stewart was scathing about Bernadotte at this time; see Charles Vane, third Marquess of Londonderry (ed.), *Memoirs of Viscount Castlereagh* (12 vols, London, 1848–53), vol. 9, pp. 109–10.
9 TNA, FO 64/91, Stewart to Castlereagh, 20 December 1813; see also for the liberation of Hanover, Charles Vane, third Marquess of Londonderry, *Narrative of the War in Germany and France in 1813 and 1814* (London, 1830), p. 229.
10 M. V. Leggiere, *The Fall of Napoleon: The Allied Invasion of France* (Cambridge, 2007), p. 40.
11 Munro Price, *Napoleon: The End of Glory* (Oxford, 2014), p. 169; Jackson, *Bath Archives*, pp. 381–2, diary 5 December 1813.
12 Leggiere, *Fall of Napoleon*, pp. 188–9 on the Austrians; for the Russian crossing of the Rhine, see ibid., p. 331; Dominic Lieven, *Russia against Napoleon: The Battle for Europe, 1807 to 1814* (London, 2009), pp. 476–7. The Prussians had launched their own crossing of the Rhine at the beginning of January 1814, as detailed by Leggiere, *Fall of Napoleon*, pp. 226–30.
13 Londonderry, *Narrative*, p. 254.
14 Prince Metternich, *Memoirs of Prince Metternich 1773–1815*. Edited by Prince Richard Metternich, Translated by Mrs. Alexander Napier (5 vols, London, 1880–2), vol. 1, pp. 223–4.
15 Londonderry, *Castlereagh*, vol. 9, p. 217, 31 January 1814.
16 BL, Aberdeen Papers, Add. MS 43225, f. 64.
17 Lady Rose Weigall (ed.), *The Letters of Lady Burghersh* (London, 1893), p. 153.

18 Aberdeen particularly had pressed Castlereagh to let Sir Robert Wilson undertake this role; see BL, Aberdeen Papers, Add. MS 43075, f. 163, Aberdeen to Castlereagh, 11 November 1813). Aberdeen was notified of Burghersh's appointment in a letter dated 11 September 1813 (BL, Aberdeen Papers, Add. MS 43073, f. 299, Castlereagh to Aberdeen).

19 Londonderry, *Narrative*, p. 269.

20 Mark Jarrett, *The Congress of Vienna and Its Legacy* (London, 2014), p. 56.

21 Londonderry, *Narrative*, p. 274.

22 Jarrett, *Congress of Vienna*, p. 55; see also Castlereagh's letter to Liverpool, 30 January 1814, in Londonderry, *Castlereagh*, vol. 9, p. 214.

23 PRONI, Clanwilliam Papers, D3044/F/13, Volume compiled by Lord Clanwilliam, fragmentary, August 1795–June 1850, pp. 25–8.

24 Londonderry, *Narrative*, p. 277.

25 Weigall, *Lady Burghersh*, p. 181.

26 See Floret's Journal of the Congress of Châtillon, 25 February 1814, in August Fornier, *Der Congress Von Châtillon. Die Politik in Kriege von 1814* (Vienna, 1900), p. 384.

27 Jackson, *Bath Archives*, vol. 2, p. 403.

28 BL, Westmorland Papers M/512 Reel 4, microfilm letters of John Fane, 11th Earl of Westmorland 1814–46, ff. 65–7.

29 Ibid.

30 Jarrett, *Congress of Vienna*, p. 58.

31 BL, Aberdeen Papers, Add. MS 43225, f. 77. See also Londonderry, *Castlereagh*, vol. 9, p. 159, Aberdeen to Castlereagh, 9 January 1814.

32 Londonderry, *Narrative*, pp. 277–8.

33 Stewart wrote highly of his ADC, Captain (later Lieutenant Colonel Sir) Thomas Noel Harris in his *Narrative*: 'The cavalry of Marshal Blucher's army was the first to discover this body on their march from Chalons: my aide-de-camp, Captain (now Colonel) Harris, who was, during the whole campaign, most active and intrepid in all his duties, was fortunate enough, looking out with a party of Cossacks, to give the first intelligence to Marshal Blucher of their position' (Londonderry, *Narrative*, pp. 287–8).

34 Ibid., pp. 289–90.

35 Londonderry, *Castlereagh*, vol. 9, p. 413.

36 [T.R. Underwood], *A Narrative of Memorable Events in Paris* (London, 1828), p. 105. For a list of the British present, see John Fane, Lord Burghersh, *Memoir of the Operation of the Allied Armies, under Prince Schwarzenberg and Marshal Blucher during the Latter End of 1813, and the Year 1814* (London, 1822), p. 254.

37 Jackson, *Bath Archives*, vol. 2, pp. 423–5.

38 Londonderry, *Castlereagh*, vol. 9, pp. 418–19.

39 Adam Zamoyski, *Rites of Peace: The Fall of Napoleon and the Congress of Vienna* (London, 2007), p. 180.

40 Jackson, *Bath Archives*, vol. 2, p. 427.

41 Londonderry, *Castlereagh*, vol. 9, p. 442.

42 Ibid., p. 449, 6 April 1814.

43 BL, Aberdeen Papers Add. MS 43225, f. 88, to Marquess of Abercorn. Stewart recalled that his brother's absence 'was to be lamented' as Castlereagh would have afforded 'that invaluable benefit which his presence at this crisis could not have failed to produce'. Londonderry, *Narrative*, pp. 306–7; see Zamoyski, *Rites of Peace*, pp. 169–84.

44 Londonderry, *Narrative*, pp. 326–7. Stewart notes that his apartment was in the 'Hôtel de Montesquieu' (p. 327). This is where Stewart stayed in 1815, and it is possible he was mistaken in recollecting this as his address in 1814.

45 Elizabeth Longford, *Wellington* (this edition, London, 1992), p. 230.

46 Comtesse de Boigne, *Memoirs of the Comtesse de Boigne* (New York, 1907), p. 359.

47 Ibid.

48 Ibid., p. 368.

49 Zamoyski, *Rites of Peace*, p. 213; for the London celebrations, see pp. 204–17.

50 Londonderry, *Narrative*, p. 331.

51 John Bew, *Castlereagh: Enlightenment, War and Terror* (London, 2011), p. 365.

52 Peter J. Begent and Hubert Chesshyre, *The Most Noble Order of the Garter: 650 Years* (London, 1999), p. 323. Prince Metternich had invested the Prince Regent with the Golden Fleece when he was in London. The bestowal of this famous Order of Chivalry was undoubtedly another reason why Metternich was so popular with the Regent.

53 PRONI, Castlereagh Papers, D3030/H/27, Londonderry to Castlereagh, 12 June 1814.

7 The Congress of Vienna

1 BL, Peel Papers Add. MS 40238, f. 65, 19 August 1814. Stewart was seeking an appointment in the Church of Ireland for a family client. He wrote to Peel again on 30 August for another Stewart connection (f. 204). Stewart had not neglected English appointments either and had tried to secure the Crown's patronage in the Church of England for yet another family client, and he wrote to Lord Liverpool accordingly on 13 July (BL, Liverpool Papers Add. MS 38258, ff. 158–9).

2 PRONI, Castlereagh Papers, D3030/P/123, Stewart to Castlereagh, 22 August 1814.

3 Charles Vane, third Marquess of Londonderry, *Narrative of the War in Germany and France in 1813 and 1814* (London, 1830), p. 332; Stewart had received the bedchamber post in June, and had been sworn of the Privy Council in July.

4 Castlereagh led two Garter missions: to the Prince of Orange and, after arriving in Vienna, to the Emperor of Austria. See Peter J. Begent and Hubert Chesshyre, *The Most Noble Order of the Garter: 650 Years* (London, 1999), p. 242.

5 The Earl of Clancarty was replaced temporarily by Sir Charles Stuart, who had been briefly minister in Paris (Stuart would also become accredited to Louis XVIII in Ghent after Napoleon's return to power). See Robert Franklin, *Lord Stuart de Rothesay* (Upton-upon-Severn, 1993), pp. 114–30.

6 Clancarty's hard work was recognized by the British government; he was appointed a Knight Grand Cross of the Bath in 1815 following the enlargement of the Order, although he was reluctant at first to accept the honour; see Charles Vane, third Marquess of Londonderry (ed.), *Memoirs of Viscount Castlereagh* (12 vols, London, 1848–53), Third Series, Military and Diplomatic, vol. 10, Clancarty to Castlereagh, 11 March 1815, pp. 264–9.

7 Mark Jarrett, *The Congress of Vienna and Its Legacy* (London, 2014), p. 28.

8 Pieter M. Judson, *The Habsburg Empire: A New History* (Cambridge, MA, 2016), p. 89; see pp. 89–97.

9 TNA, FO 7/117.

10 Comte de la Garde-Chambonas, *Anecdotal Recollections of the Congress of Vienna* (London, 1902), pp. xv, 90, 267; the comte was also 'the author of a great number of songs', p. xix.

11 Ibid., p. 151.

12 M. H. Weil, *Les Dessous du Congrès de Vienne, d'après les documents originaux des archives de Ministère Impérial et Royal de l'Intérieur à Vienne* (Paris, 2 vols, 1917), vol. 2, p. 517.

13 John Bew, *Castlereagh: Enlightenment, War and Terror* (London, 2011), p. 374; Adam Zamoyski, *Rites of Peace: The Fall of Napoleon and the Congress of Vienna* (London, 2007), p. 345.

14 Frederick Freksa (trans. Harry Hansen), *A Peace Congress of Intrigue* (New York, 1919), p. 31.

15 Ibid.

16 Zamoyski, *Rites of Peace*, pp. 250–1; Weil, *Les Dessous du Congrès de Vienne*, vol. 1, p. 498.

17 For an overview of the attendees, see Jarrett, *Congress of Vienna*, pp. 72–84. See also pp. 96–101 for Poland and Saxony.

18 Kent History and Library Centre, Pratt Manuscripts, U840 C51/2 Hardinge to Marquess Camden, 28 October 1814 (marked as 1813).

19 Robin Harris, *Talleyrand: Betrayer and Saviour of France* (London, 2007), p. 277. The new title came in December 1814.

20 Ibid., pp. 237–8.

21 Freksa, *A Peace Congress of Intrigue*, Talleyrand to Louis XVIII, 19 October 1814, pp. 300–1.

22 W. H. Zawadzki, *Adam Czartoryski as a Statesman of Russia and Poland 1795–1831* (Oxford, 1993), p. 228. Czartoryski 'commented on his isolation among the diplomats gathered in Paris'. For Czartoryski's role at the Congress of Vienna, see pp. 234–58.

23 Lord Castlereagh to Alexander, 12 October 1814; quoted in Sir Charles Webster, *British Diplomacy 1813–1815: Select Documents Dealing with the Reconstruction of Europe* (London, 1921), pp. 208–9.

24 TNA, FO 7/117, Stewart to Castlereagh, 15 October 1814.

25 Ibid.

26 Ibid.

27 Kent History and Library Centre, Pratt Manuscripts, U840 C51/3, Hardinge to Camden, 4 November 1814.

28 TNA, FO 7/117, Stewart to Castlereagh, 3 November 1814.

29 Jarrett, *Congress of Vienna*, p. 109; see pp. 109–10.

30 Christopher Clark, *Iron Kingdom: The Rise and Downfall of Prussia 1600–1947* (this edition, London, 2007), p. 357.

31 TNA, FO 7/117, Stewart to Castlereagh, 6 November 1814.

32 Gregor Dallas, *1815: The Roads to Waterloo* (London, 1996), p. 194.

33 Weil, *Les Dessous du Congrès de Vienne*, vol. 1, Hager to Emperor Francis, 1 November 1814, p. 434; Garde-Chambonas, *Anecdotal Recollections*, pp. 203–4.

34 Hilda Spiel (trans. Richard H. Weber), *The Congress of Vienna: An Eyewitness Account* (London, 1968), p. 222.

35 Garde-Chambonas, *Anecdotal Recollections*, p. 204; Roger Fulford and Lytton Strachey (eds), *The Greville Diaries* (London, 1938), p. 28.

36 Weil, *Les Dessous du Congrès de Vienne*, vol. 1, p. 498, 9 November 1814. Stewart, allegedly drunk, was also reported as disrupting the Emperor of Austria's famous sleigh ride in January 1815. See David King, *Vienna 1814* (New York, 2008), p. 202; the source for the account is given at p. 388.

37 Spiel, *Congress of Vienna*, p. 101, p. 221; the diarist was a Viennese book publisher called Carl Bertuch (dated 11 November 1814).
38 Kent History and Library Centre, Pratt Manuscripts, U840 C51/4, Hardinge to Camden, 11 November 1814.
39 Zamoyski, *Rites of Peace*, p. 343.
40 Webster, *British Diplomacy*, p. 217.
41 Ibid., pp. 244–5.
42 Weil, *Les Dessous du Congrès de Vienne*, vol. 1, p. 724; intercepted letter from Castlereagh to Talleyrand, 24 December 1814.
43 TNA, FO 7/117, Stewart to Castlereagh, 6 and 14 December 1814.
44 The first meeting of the Statistical Committee took place on 24 December.
45 Jarrett, *Congress of Vienna*, pp. 109–11.
46 Freksa, *A Peace Congress of Intrigue*, p. 386.
47 See Jarrett, *Congress of Vienna*, pp. 113–15.
48 Webster, *British Diplomacy*, Castlereagh to Liverpool, pp. 272–3, 278.
49 The agreement was signed between Britain, Austria and France on 3 January 1815. The news of the Treaty of Ghent is described by Bew as a 'timely twist of fate' (Bew, *Castlereagh*, p. 385).
50 Jarrett, *Congress of Vienna*, p. 126.
51 Weil, *Les Dessous du Congrès de Vienne*, vol. 2, p. 123, agent 'oo' to Hager, p. 123.
52 Ibid., p. 19.
53 Webster, *British Diplomacy*, p. 290.
54 Clancarty is nearby leaning over the table next to the Marqués de Labrador, the Spanish representative, while Cathcart is standing at the very right of the picture; Razumovsky's palace, on the outskirts of Vienna, was devastated by fire during the Congress (see Jarrett, *Congress of Vienna*, p. 119).
55 See Jarrett, *Congress of Vienna*, pp. 125–31.
56 PRONI, Castlereagh Papers, D3044/F/18/1 Castlereagh to Stewart, 12 February 1815.
57 Webster, *British Diplomacy*, pp. 306–7. See also Prince Metternich, *Memoirs of Prince Metternich 1773–1815*. Edited by Prince Richard Metternich, Translated by Mrs. Alexander Napier (5 vols, London, 1880–2), vol. 2, pp. 585–6.
58 BL, Westmorland Papers M/512 Reel 4, ff. 69–73.
59 DRO, D/Lo/C20/1. This letter is marked Private, 4 March 1815. The letter was started on this date, but as it is incomplete, it may well have been written over several days. The passages that refer to France indicate that these must post-date the news of Napoleon's escape being known in Vienna.

8 Vive l'Empereur!

1 Comte de la Garde-Chambonas, *Anecdotal Recollections of the Congress of Vienna* (London, 1902), p. 410.
2 DRO, D/Lo/C20/1. This is a continuation of the letter marked Private, 4 March 1815, that is briefly quoted at the end of the previous chapter. Stewart also found time to mention progress over a declaration on Poland. He told his brother that Wellington had informed him 'the Emperor [Alexander] insisted on its being alter'd in all its objectionable passages, & that the Duke succeeded in inducing M[etternich] to suppress them all.' This kind of diplomacy was not to Stewart's taste, and was 'another instance of a disgracefull & miserable weak Transaction'.

3 Munro Price has intriguingly suggested that Napoleon was worried about a possible *coup d'état* by the duc d'Orléans; see Munro Price, *The Perilous Crown: France between Revolutions* (London, 2007), pp. 73–5.

4 TNA, FO 7/117; in his letter of 12 March 1815, Stewart was concerned that a cipher kept under lock and key had been stolen; on 3 April, he advised Castlereagh that the cipher had been taken by one of Clancarty's secretaries.

5 DRO, D/Lo/C20/3; Stewart commented earlier in the letter, 'Metternich, appears to me to have lost his head, and whenever I have seen him, seems to be regulated by the Direction that Talleyrand or the D of Wellington give him, they certainly have him between them.'

6 DRO, D/Lo/C20/4; Stewart praised Clancarty's skill and especially his attention to fine detail, so much so 'he in fact lives upon it and fattens on it, I do not envy the time he dedicates to it that would kill me . . . but I envy the method & Arrangement he has acquird.' For a recent account of Wellington's role at Vienna, as well as the events preceding the military campaign, see Rory Muir, *Wellington: Waterloo and the Fortunes of Peace 1814–1852* (New Haven, CT, 2015), pp. 20–1, 22–35.

7 TNA, FO 7/117, 29 March 1815 (letter 17).

8 TNA, FO 7/117, 29 March 1815 (letter 18).

9 BL, Westmorland Papers M/512 Reel 4, f. 90, 30 March 1815.

10 DRO, D/Lo/C20/7, Stewart to Castlereagh; the letter also relayed news of Clancarty's negotiations and Austrian reactions to Murat's doings.

11 TNA, FO 7/117, 1 April 1815; Taylor's letter to Stewart is dated 26 March 1815. Stewart added in this letter, 'Your Lordship will hear of the arrival of Mr Bombelles from Paris, and the unfortunate mismanagement of General Vincent and ye other Ministers of the Allies remaining. It is difficult in my opinion to exercise such Conduct as it will enable Napoleon to make considerable use of their stay, which he will not fail to avail himself of in point of public effect.'

12 TNA, FO 7/117, 8 April 1815. The allied military headquarters was to leave that day and was expected to arrive in Ulm by 26 April. Stewart had also been involved in organizing the British loan to the Austrian government, writing to Castlereagh on 3 April (TNA, FO 7/117).

13 Rachel Weigall (ed.), *Correspondence of Lord Burghersh Afterwards Eleventh Earl of Westmorland 1808–1840* (London, 1912), p. 111; BL, Westmorland Papers M/512 Reel 4, f. 100.

14 DRO, D/Lo/C20/13; 22 April 1815.

15 DRO, D/Lo/C20/12, 28 April 1815.

16 TNA, FO 7/118, 28 April 1815.

17 See TNA, FO 7/118, 1 May 1815.

18 DRO, D/Lo/C113/19.

19 Ibid.

20 DRO, D/Lo/C53/12.

21 In his letter of appointment to Colonel Church, dated 8 April 1815, Stewart had written, 'You must be aware that I can not appoint You in a more authentick or accredited Shape, nor does it appear to me to be necessary to point out to You, how Your Services can be rendered most available' (TNA, FO 7/117).

22 TNA, FO 7/117, 22 April 1815.

23 DRO, D/Lo/C20/4; D/Lo/C38/1 (2); D/Lo/C38/1 (3).

24 TNA, FO 7/118, Stewart to Castlereagh, 16 May 1815.

25 DRO, D/Lo/C20/17.

26 Ibid.
27 DRO, D/Lo/C58/7, Stewart to Castlereagh, 4 June 1815; D/Lo/C58/18, Stewart to Castlereagh, 27 December 1820. The letter also records a sum of £500 from 1815 which cannot be accounted for, and Stewart assumes 'it must be the 500 drawn by Lord Aberdeen and given to Genz [*sic*] in that Year' (although Aberdeen had ceased to be ambassador to Austria in 1814).
28 DRO, D/Lo/C/C20/18, 2 June 1815.
29 DRO, D/Lo/C58/2 [May 1815]; Sir Charles Stuart's letter of thanks on behalf of Louis XVIII (letter 4) is dated 26 May 1815; see also Stewart's secret and separate letter to Castlereagh on the French embassy of 8 May 1815 (TNA, FO 7/118).
30 DRO, D/Lo/C38/1 (4).
31 DRO, D/Lo/C20/15.
32 Garde-Chambonas, *Anecdotal Recollections*, p. 342.
33 M. H. Weil, *Les Dessous du Congrès de Vienne, d'après les documents originaux des archives de Ministère Impérial et Royal de l'Intérieur à Vienne* (Paris, 2 vols, 1917), vol. 2, pp. 611–42.
34 PRONI, Castlereagh Papers, D3030/4378, Foreign Office draft letter, 9 June 1815.
35 Adam Zamoyski, *Rites of Peace: The Fall of Napoleon and the Congress of Vienna* (London, 2007), pp. 28, 485.
36 They would resume their relationship in Paris. The future Countess Granville wrote in a letter dated 'August 1815' that she had been at 'a great dinner at Lord Stewart's.' At the dinner she met the Duchess 'who has forsaken Frederick Lamb and is now the *régnante* at the court of Prince Charles – for so Lord Stewart is universally called' (F. Leveson-Gower (ed.), *Letters of Harriet, Countess Granville 1810–1845* (2 vols, London, 1894), vol. 1, p. 71).
37 DRO, D/Lo/C20/19.
38 Weil, *Les Dessous du Congrès de Vienne*, vol. 2, p. 611.
39 PRONI Clanwilliam Papers, D3044/F/13, volume compiled by Lord Clanwilliam, fragmentary, August 1795–June 1850, p. 32.
40 Kent History and Library Centre, Pratt Manuscripts, U840 C501/2; Stewart also passed on news of Sir Henry Hardinge, who had 'written in good Spirits . . . I hope in 2 or 3 weeks He may be able to join me, wherever I may be.'
41 DRO, D/Lo/C20/21; for Talleyrand's dismissal, see Robin Harris, *Talleyrand: Betrayer and Saviour of France* (London, 2007), pp. 257–60.

9 *To Paris again*

1 Clanwilliam saw first-hand the continued dangers from the French military after Waterloo: 'Ancram & I remained, Attachés to the Embassy. Immediately after the conclusive battle of Waterloo, Ld. Stewart good naturedly gave us leave to join Headquarters, where Schwarz[enber]g was Commdr in Chief. Off we set. Our last stage was a difficulty: Pflazburg, a strong little fortress, still held by the French, & passed by the Allies. Nothing for it but to drag one's carriage thru a narrow ditch, right under the guns.' PRONI, Clanwilliam Papers, D3044/F/13, volume compiled by Lord Clanwilliam, fragmentary, August 1795–June 1850, p. 33.
2 Munro Price, *The Perilous Crown. France between Revolutions* (London, 2007), p. 83; Gregor Dallas, *1815: The Roads to Waterloo* (London, 1996), pp. 422–3; Robin Harris, *Talleyrand: Betrayer and Saviour of France* (London, 2007), pp. 260–2.

3 DRO, D/Lo/C37/2/6 and D/Lo/C37/2/7; Stewart's full and lengthy report on the meeting is found in D/Lo/C37/2/8, 2 July 1815.

4 DRO, D/Lo/C37/2/10, 6 July 1815; D/Lo/C37/2/14, 8 July 1815. In a secret and separate letter of 6 July, Stewart further advised on irregular French attacks and military disagreements between the Tsar and Prince Schwarzenberg (see TNA, FO 7/117).

5 BL, Aberdeen Papers, Add. MS 43212, f. 3, 9 July 1815.

6 BL, Aberdeen Papers, Add. MS 43212, f. 1, 3 July 1815; Stewart's letter was also personal, as Robert Gordon's brother, Sir Alexander Gordon, had died of wounds received at Waterloo: 'My hopes that You are recovering Your Spirits with that Philosophy which great minds must call forth on such Heavy Calamities.'

7 See TNA, FO 7/117, 12 July 1815.

8 TNA, FO 7/117, 17 July 1815. One of the liaison officers was Sir Henry Hardinge, who was promoted to brigadier general in 1815. The other two officers were General Upton and Colonel Jenkinson. The reports to Stewart from the liaison officers are in FO 7/117, for example letters from Jenkinson dated 18 July and 6 August, and letters from Hardinge dated 19 July and 26 July. Clanwilliam writing many years later stated that they stayed in the Hotel Montmorency; Clanwilliam noted, 'We all took the greatest care of the house.' PRONI, Clanwilliam Papers, D3044/F/13, volume compiled by Lord Clanwilliam, fragmentary, August 1795–June 1850, p. 34.

9 BL, Aberdeen Papers, Add. MS 43212, f. 5, 4 August 1815.

10 Devon Archives and Local Studies Service, Addington Papers, 152M/C/1815/OF40, Earl of Buckinghamshire to Viscount Sidmouth, 28 August 1815. Stewart was reported as having 'arrived yesterday from Paris'.

11 Devon Archives and Local Studies Service, Addington Papers, 152M/C/1815/OF41, Vansittart to Sidmouth, 29 August 1815.

12 Ibid.

13 Adam Zamoyski, *Rites of Peace: The Fall of Napoleon and the Congress of Vienna* (London, 2007), pp. 511–14.

14 Kent History and Library Centre, Pratt Manuscripts, C60/1, 23 September 1815; Stewart was entrusted with Camden's heir, the Earl of Brecknock, while he was in Paris. Stewart was sending regular reports on Brecknock's progress. Camden had been created a marquess in 1812.

15 Harris, *Talleyrand*, pp. 270–2; Zamoyski, *Rites of Peace*, pp. 516–19.

16 BL, Aberdeen Papers, Add. MS 43212, f. 7.

17 DRO, D/Lo/C37/3/2; Robert Gordon also had pressing financial issues to discuss, and he wrote on 3 October 'that it has been determined to place the Hotel Stahremberg [*sic*] in a Lottery which is to drawn at the end of this Year' and wanted to know if Stewart would press Castlereagh to purchase the property for the British embassy as 'the new proprietors may not wish to continue to let the house.' Gordon believed the residence was perfect for the embassy: 'None other is so appropriate for the inhabitance of a British Ambassador.' (TNA, FO 7/117).

18 DRO, D/Lo/C37/3/3–4; D/Lo/C37/3/6.

19 BL, Aberdeen Papers, Add. MS 43212, f. 9, 9 October 1815.

20 See DRO, D/Lo/C37/3/7.

21 W. H. Zawadzki, *Adam Czartoryski as a Statesman of Russia and Poland 1795–1831* (Oxford, 1993), p. 260. Alexander set out from Berlin for the new Kingdom of Poland in November 1815, arriving in Warsaw on 12 November 'wearing a Polish uniform

adorned with the Order of the White Eagle. It was probably on that day that his standing among the Poles reached its zenith.'

22 DRO, D/Lo/C20/27 (i), 26 October 1815. Payments to Sir Sidney Smith can be seen in Stewart's account of secret service monies to Castlereagh, dated 27 December 1820. The total comes to just over £980. Stewart adds later in the letter, 'It remains for me only to add, that as I naturally conceived I should bear a part of the common Loss, with regard to Sir Sidney Smith, I enclose a Bill for £500 – on Coutts' (DRO, D/Lo/C58/18).

23 BL, Westmorland Papers M/512 Reel 4, f. 136, Stewart to Burghersh, 19 November 1815.

24 BL, Aberdeen Papers, Add. MS 43212, f. 13, 23 November 1815. Stewart wrote that 'Brown' had kept him informed of scandals, f. 18, 9 December 1815; f. 20, 26 December 1815; it was later reported that a Mr Griffiths had been arrested in Vienna – see TNA, FO 7/126, Stewart to Castlereagh, 7 February 1816. See also John Bew, *Castlereagh: Enlightenment, War and Terror* (London, 2011), pp. 413–14.

25 PRONI, Clanwilliam Papers, D3044/F/13, volume compiled by Lord Clanwilliam, fragmentary, August 1795–June 1850, pp. 34–5.

26 PRONI Clanwilliam Papers, D3044/F/13, volume compiled by Lord Clanwilliam, fragmentary, August 1795–June 1850, p. 36.

27 BL, Aberdeen Papers, Add. MS 43212, ff. 24, 31.

28 BL, Heytesbury Papers, Add. MS 41531, f. 13.

29 TNA, FO 7/126, 5 January 1816.

30 TNA, FO 7/126, Stewart to Castlereagh, 10 January 1816, and Stewart to Castlereagh, 12 January 1816.

31 DRO, D/Lo/C21/2, 7 January 1816 (?).

32 DRO, D/Lo/C21/15 (i). Sir Charles Stuart clearly saw Lord Stewart as a rival, as reported in a letter by the future Countess Granville of 31 July 1815: 'Sir Charles Stuart is in a fever of mind, which he cannot conceal, from the fear of not remaining Ambassador here, and from all I hear he seems to be the best person, being excessively liked by the French. He has great jealousy of Lord Stewart, who, it is said, is equally anxious to remain' (F. Leveson-Gower (ed.), *Letters of Harriet, Countess Granville 1810–1845* (2 vols, London, 1894, vol. 1, p. 64). An earlier extract from this same letter hints at Lord Stewart's expensive way of life, combined with an insult directed at Lady Castlereagh: 'I called upon Lady Castlereagh and found her in the Villa Borghese, forming the most complete *contraste* to the *locale*, which is all Oriental luxury, she fitter for Wapping. Lord Stewart came in all over stars and tenderness. I hear there never was anything like his vanity and extravagence' (vol. 1, pp. 62–3).

33 TNA, FO 7/126, 24 January 1816.

34 Ibid.

35 TNA, FO 7/126, Stewart to Castlereagh, 25 January 1816.

36 TNA, FO 7/126, Stewart to Castlereagh, 3 February 1816.

37 BL, Aberdeen Papers, Add. MS 43212, f. 33, 1 February 1816.

38 TNA, FO 7/126, Stewart to Castlereagh, 18 January 1816.

39 TNA, FO 7/126, Stewart to Castlereagh, 4 February 1816.

40 TNA, FO 7/126, Stewart to William Hamilton, 6 February 1816 (see also letter from Robert Gordon, dated 24 January 1816, advising that the house was being offered for £30,000 with another £4,000 for furniture. Gordon had then suggested the figure of £20,000 minus deductions for furniture).

41 TNA, FO 7/126, Stewart to Castlereagh, 8 February 1816.

42 TNA, FO 7/126, Stewart to Castlereagh, 12 February 1816.

43 See TNA, FO 7/126, Stewart to Castlereagh, 2 March 1816. Stewart wrote, 'It is known by Austria, that the Court of Turin have applied to Russia for Her Support in their discussions [on defensive alliances].' More intriguingly, Stewart reported that accounts had been received from St Petersburg of a 'Sardinian Courier . . . charged with Dispatches of the utmost importance' who had 'received a special Instruction to avoid touching, in his Route, in any Way on Austrian Territory, for the possibility of Interception and the Mystery and Caution of these Communications have excited the curiosity of this Government'.

44 PRONI, Clanwilliam Papers, D3044/F/13, volume compiled by Lord Clanwilliam, fragmentary, August 1795–June 1850, pp. 36–7. Clanwilliam further reported that Stewart 'was uneasy about his frail friend' (p. 37).

45 TNA, FO 7/127, Stewart to A'Court, 8 April 1816; A'Court's request was dated 31 March. For the news of the Empress of Austria's death, see TNA, FO 7/127, Stewart to Castlereagh, 12 April 1816.

46 TNA, FO 7/127, Stewart to Castlereagh, 23 April 1816.

47 Kent History and Library Centre, Pratt Manuscripts, U840 C501/2.

48 Ibid.; Metternich had joined the Emperor Francis after the peace negotiations had been completed in Paris.

49 See John Frost, *A Translation of the Statutes of the Royal Hanoverian Guelphic Order, Together with a List of the Grand Crosses, Commanders and Knights* (1831).

50 See Andrew Hanham, 'Regency Knights: The Royal Guelphic Order 1815–1837', *The Coat of Arms* 3rd ser., iv (2008), pp. 101–24, who discusses this aspect of the Order in some detail.

51 BL, Westmorland Papers M/512 Reel 4, ff. 163–4, Stewart to Burghersh, 8 May 1816. Clanwilliam wrote that they reached Vienna 'on a fine evening', before recalling an incident involving the Duchess of Sagan: 'At the junction of the road to Baden, espied a string of led horses, some w[ith]. side-saddles, returning to Vienna: evidently from a day's junket. Ld. St. stopt the Carriage & asked each groom. One led the wellknown Grosvenor, his cadeau to the Duchess. The last was a poor V[ienn]a hired hack. "Clanwilliam, ask whose hack that is" – The answer came, "Herr Warrender's". Not another word spoken; and all that evening a constant alleé et venue of billets-doux. The foll[owin]g. week Herr Warrander accepted a bag of dispatches for England.' PRONI, Clanwilliam Papers, D3044/F/13, volume compiled by Lord Clanwilliam, fragmentary, August 1795–June 1850, pp. 37–8.

52 TNA, FO 7/127, Stewart to Castlereagh, 11 May 1816.

53 See TNA FO 7/127, Stewart to Castlereagh, 21 May 1816; TNA FO 7/127, Stewart to Castlereagh, 10 June 1816.

54 TNA, FO 7/127, Castlereagh to Stewart, 23 June 1816.

55 Ibid.

56 Ibid.

57 Stewart's diplomatic correspondence can be found in a number of BL collections, for example: Beauvale Papers Add. MS 60411–14; Heytesbury Papers Add. MS 41531–2; Rose Papers Add. MS 42791; see also DRO, D/Lo/C46 for the relevant correspondence with Clancarty.

10 The Caroline Affair

1 Jane Robins, *Rebel Queen: The Trial of Caroline* (London, 2006), p. 61.

2 Sir Archibald Alison, *Lives of Lord Castlereagh and Sir Charles Stewart* (3 vols, Edinburgh, 1861), vol. 3; H. Montgomery Hyde, *The Londonderrys* (London, 1979), p. 27. Castlereagh's recent biographer has acknowledged Stewart's role in this affair; see John Bew, *Castlereagh: Enlightenment, War and Terror* (London, 2011), pp. 413, 488.

3 DRO, D/Lo/C39/34.

4 Ibid.

5 Robert Huish, *Memoirs of HRH the Princess Charlotte* (London, 1818), p. 475; Huish would also later write Caroline's biography. He states that he is quoting extracts from Anon., *Journal of an English Traveller; or Remarkable Events and Anecdotes of the Princess of Wales, from 1814 to 1816.*

6 E. A. Smith, *George IV* (London, 2003), p. 175; Smith also mentions William Austin in this respect, although the 'Delicate Investigation' of 1806 had confirmed that Austin was not Caroline's illegitimate son.

7 DRO, D/Lo/C39/36, 6 February 1816.

8 Ibid.

9 In his letters to Stewart, he always signs himself as Henry Browne.

10 An account of Browne's career can be found in Norman Buckley (ed.), *The Napoleonic War Journal of Captain Thomas Henry Browne 1807–1816* (London, 1987), pp. 280, 283. A summary of Browne's career under Stewart is given on pp. 34–5. See also Nanora Sweet, '"The Inseparables": Hemans, the Brownes and the Milan Commission', *Forum for Modern Language Studies*, xxxix (2003), pp. 165–77. Professor Sweet also acknowledges the important link between Stewart and Browne in the work of the Milan Commission.

11 DRO, D/Lo/C34/24.

12 Ibid.

13 DRO, D/Lo/C34/24; Prince Metternich held Leopold particularly in regard, and he seemed to think he had moderate abilities.

14 Thomas W. Liqueur, 'The Queen Caroline Affair: Politics as Art in the Reign of George IV', *Journal of Modern History*, liv (September 1982), p. 419.

15 Stewart even referred to him on occasions as 'Bergamo'. Caroline's progress was clearly being relayed to Stewart, as indicated by a letter to George Rose, 12 July 1816; see BL, Rose Papers, Add. MS 42791, f. 14.

16 Robins, *Rebel Queen*, pp. 72–3.

17 DRO, D/Lo/C39/54.

18 DRO, D/Lo/C39/55; a further letter of 23 December states that Ompteda had offered to fight Hownam in London 'as they are prevented from fighting in Italy' (D/Lo/ C39/57).

19 DRO, D/Lo/C39/56, 13 December 1816; the letter also dealt with the various grades of the Order of Caroline for members of Pergami's family, while noting that Pergami himself was Grand Master.

20 DRO, D/Lo/C39/61.

21 DRO, D/Lo/C39/62, 15 March 1817.

22 DRO, D/Lo/C39/63, 25 March 1817.

23 DRO, D/Lo/C55/15, 4 April 1817.

24 DRO, D/Lo/C40/1.

25 DRO, D/Lo/C40/6.

26 DRO, D/Lo/C40/14, n.d., but probably 8 April 1817.

27 DRO, D/Lo/C40/10, 9 April 1817.

28 DRO, D/Lo/C40/13, 10 April 1817.
29 DRO, D/Lo/C40/20 and 21, both dated 10 April 1817; D/Lo/C40/7, 11 April 1817. Stewart also passed on his reasons to other diplomats, for example to George Rose and William A'Court; see BL, Rose Papers, Add. MS 42791, f. 61, 23 April 1817, and BL, Heytesbury Papers, Add. MS 41531, f. 263, 17 April 1817.
30 DRO, D/Lo/C23/13, 13 November 1817 (it is marked as 1819 but its contents means it must be 1817).
31 Sweet, '"The Inseparables"', pp. 169, 170.

11 Vanes and Tempests

1 Diane Urquhart, *The Ladies of Londonderry* (London, 2007), pp. 10–12.
2 PRONI, Castlereagh Papers, D654/G/1/3, Copies of Affidavit in a Chancery Case concerning marriage of Charles William, Lord Stewart and Frances Anne Vane Tempest (1818), f. 3.
3 Castlereagh confirmed that Stewart could request the leave of absence on 7 June 1817; see BL, Aberdeen Papers, Add. MS 43212, f. 58. He was in Carlsbad on his brother's directions, as Castlereagh wrote: 'I only write to say fairly I cannot upon reflection but attach more importance to your being at Carlsbad whilst the Ministers of the three principal Courts are there, especially as our Conferences will soon be renewed in London' (BL, Aberdeen Papers, Add. MS 43212, f. 64, 17 June 1817).
4 TNA, FO 7/151, Stewart to Hamilton, 6 August 1817.
5 See patronage requests sent to Peel by the Ambassador for family clients, BL, Peel Papers, Add. MS 40271, ff. 302–5, 15 November 1817. The letter added: 'And altho' I have not had time to consult my Brother on this letter, I am satisfied I am writing his sentiments as well as my own' (f. 305).
6 See PRONI, Castlereagh Papers, D654/G/1/3, Copies of Affidavit, ff. 13–14; Frances Anne was with Lady Antrim at the Queen's Drawing Room but was accompanied by Mrs Taylor at Almack's. Stewart noted that he had known Frances Taylor since 1802 'or thereabouts'.
7 Urquhart, *Ladies of Londonderry*, p. 13.
8 PRONI, Castlereagh Papers, D654/G/1/3, Copies of Affidavit, ff. 13, 4, 6–8.
9 Ibid., f. 9.
10 Ibid., ff. 4, 9–10.
11 Ibid., ff. 11–13.
12 Ibid., ff. 22–3.
13 Ibid., ff. 27.
14 Urquhart, *Ladies of Londonderry*, p. 16.
15 Mark Jarrett, *The Congress of Vienna and Its Legacy* (London, 2014), p. 179.
16 These were in the form of requests from the Foreign Office. See TNA, FO 7/139, Castlereagh to Stewart, 14 February 1818; 18 February 1818; 11 April 1818.
17 BL, Aberdeen Papers, Add. MS 43212, ff. 52–3, Stewart to Clanwilliam, 9 June 1817.
18 TNA, FO 7/139, Stewart to Castlereagh, 24 August 1818.
19 Ibid.
20 TNA, FO 7/139, Dispatch No. 2, Stewart to Castlereagh, 24 August 1818.
21 TNA, FO 7/139, Stewart to Castlereagh, 24 August 1818.
22 Ibid.

23 DRO, D/Lo/C44/3, 24 August 1818.
24 TNA, FO 7/139, Stewart to Castlereagh, 29 August 1818.
25 TNA, FO 7/139, No. 9, Stewart to Castlereagh, 8 September 1818. The letter was dated
    from Vienna, with Stewart reporting that he had had an audience with the Emperor
    and Empress in Baden the day before. Neipperg was Marie Louise's lover; the two later
    married.
26 Jarrett, *Congress of Vienna*, pp. 180–3.
27 Ibid., p. 182.
28 George Somers Layard (ed.), *Sir Thomas Lawrence's Letter-Bag* (London, 1906), letter
    dated 6 March 1816 (pp. 100–1); the Ambassador was also sure that Lawrence would
    be able to paint the Austrian Empress. For Stewart's possible role in introducing
    Lawrence into the Prince Regent's circle, see p. 96.
29 Ibid., pp. 137–8.
30 PRONI, Clanwilliam Papers, D3044/F/13, volume compiled by Lord Clanwilliam,
    fragmentary, August 1795–June 1850, p. 53 (for Sir Thomas Lawrence, see p. 52).
31 Jarrett, *Congress of Vienna*, p. 185.
32 Ibid., pp. 180–205; John Bew, *Castlereagh: Enlightenment, War and Terror* (London,
    2011), pp. 450–7.
33 TNA, FO 7/139, No. 11, Stewart to Castlereagh, 21 December 1818.
34 Ibid. In a précis to George Rose, Stewart noted, 'The Question in my opinion resolves
    itself into this small Compass. Is it most wise & prudent for the Allies to adhere to the
    Protocol of 20th November, or is it best to decide upon demanding a greater Cession
    of Territory . . . in lieu of the pecuniary payment?' BL, Rose Papers, Add. MS 42791,
    f. 99, 21 December 1818.
35 TNA, FO 7/139, No. 12, Stewart to Castlereagh, 21 December 1818.
36 Philip Mansel, *Louis XVIII* (London, 1981), p. 358.
37 TNA, FO 7/139, No. 17, Stewart to Castlereagh, 21 December 1818.
38 TNA, FO 7/139, No. 18, Stewart to Castlereagh, 21 December 1818.
39 Layard, *Sir Thomas Lawrence's Letter-Bag*, pp. 141–2.
40 Mansel, *Louis XVIII*, p. 361; see also pp. 344–73.

12 The Milan Commission

1 DRO, D/Lo/C39/1, 24 August 1818 (copy of a secret and confidential draft), Stewart
   to Metternich, 24 August 1818; this comment has been pencilled on this letter at a
   later date, as Stewart had written that the official who gave him the verbal response
   had since died: 'So it is clear the Austrian Govt. will deny acting or abetting the
   Enquiry if They are accused of doing so'; DRO, D/Lo/C39/3, 25 August 1818.
2 DRO, D/Lo/C39/4.
3 Robert Huish, *Memoirs of HRH the Princess Charlotte* (London, 1818), p. 475.
4 PRONI, Castlereagh Papers, D3030/P/168, translation from Browne of Pergami's
   letter to the 'Advocate Godazzo', 4 December 1818; see D3030/P/169 translation from
   Browne of letter from the Princess of Wales to the 'Advocate Godazzo', 15 January
   1819 (This is presumably the lawyer Codazzi, see Flora Fraser, *The Unruly Queen: The
   Life of Queen Caroline* (this edition, London 2004), p. 312).
5 Letter from Caroline, 26 October 1819, to unnamed recipient, quoted by Robert Huish,
   Memoirs of Caroline, Queen Consort of England (2 vols, London, 1821), vol. 1, p. 12.

6 See TNA, FO 7/143, Stewart to William Hamilton, 24 April 1819; Stewart to Castlereagh, 1 May 1819.

7 Edith, Marchioness of Londonderry, *Frances Anne, The Life and Times of Frances Anne Marchioness of Londonderry and Her Husband Charles Third Marquess of Londonderry* (London, 1958), pp. 45–6; Diane Urquhart, *The Ladies of Londonderry* (London, 2007), p. 16.

8 DRO, D/Lo/C23/3, 12 August 1819.

9 *A Full Report of the Trial of Major-General Sir Robert Thomas Wilson, Michael Bruce, Esq. and Capt. John Hely Hutchinson, before the Court of Assize at Paris, on the 22d of April 1816, and Two Following Days, for Aiding the Escape of Count Lavalette; Including a Short Memoir of Sir R. T . Wilson* (London, 1816).

10 DRO, D/Lo/C23/4, 14 August 1819. Sir Charles Stuart and the duc de Richelieu had been implicated in the plot. See Robert Franklin, *Lord Stuart de Rothesay* (Upton-upon-Severn 1993), pp. 144–6.

11 TNA, FO 7/143, 1 October 1819.

12 See Urquhart, *Ladies of Londonderry*, pp. 16–17.

13 TNA, FO 7/143, No. 4, 7 October 1819; No. 6, 7 October 1819; FO 7/144, No. 20, 1 November 1819; No. 29, 15 November 1819.

14 TNA, FO 7/144, No. 33, Stewart to Castlereagh, 29 November 1819.

15 TNA FO 7/144, No. 35, Stewart to Castlereagh, 9 December 1819.

16 Minute of Cabinet, 24 July 1819, as detailed in E. A. Smith, *A Queen on Trial: The Affair of Queen Caroline* (London, 1993), pp. 10, 12. For details of these exchanges, see pp. 9–12.

17 Ibid., p. 13.

18 Jane Robins, *Rebel Queen: The Trial of Caroline* (London, 2006), pp. 98–100.

19 DRO, D/Lo/C24/1, 8 March 1820.

20 DRO, D/Lo/C24/12, 12 February 1820.

21 BL, Beauvale Papers, Add. MS 60414, f. 41, to Frederick Lamb, 8 March 1820.

22 Charles Esdaile, *The Peninsular War* (London, 2002), p. 305.

23 For Stewart's reporting on the affair including the views of Marshal Marmont, see TNA, FO 7/150, No. 37, Stewart to Castlereagh, 20 March 1820.

24 Munro Price, *The Perilous Crown: France between Revolutions* (London, 2007), p. 108. See pp. 107–8 for the backlash against Decazes; Louis XVIII made Decazes 'a duke and peer, and found him a prestigious post as ambassador to London' (p. 108).

25 DRO, D/Lo/C24/2.

26 TNA, FO 7/150, 29 March 1820.

27 TNA, FO 7/150, separate, 9 April 1820.

28 Ibid.

29 DRO, D/Lo/C24/5, 20 April 1820. Stewart was also ordered to advise the Emperor, through Metternich, that the queen had shown an 'unbecoming course of Life' surrounded by a 'disgraceful Circle of Attendants'.

30 DRO, D/Lo/C24/5, 24 April 1820; D/Lo/C24/6, copy of Browne's report to Stewart, 27 April 1820; D/Lo/C24/7, Browne to Stewart, 28 April 1820.

31 DRO, D/Lo/C24/14 Dahlberg to Metternich, letter from Stewart to Castlereagh, 24 April 1820.

32 A'Court had succeeded to his father's baronetcy in 1817. On 1 October 1819, Stewart wrote to A'Court, to 'congratulate you on the Red Ribbon' (BL, Heytesbury Papers, Add. MS 41532, f. 14).

33 DRO, D/Lo/C24/18, 8 May 1820.

34 DRO, D/Lo/C24/8.

35 Ibid.

36 Huish, *Caroline*, vol. 2, p. 360.

37 DRO, D/Lo/C42/2, 16 July 1820; Stewart and Maitland had already been in discussion over 'traitrous correspondence and bringing to light the mischief that is brewing in the quarter to which British Interests are now so much attached'; see TNA, FO 7/149, copy of letter from Stewart to Maitland, 7 December 1819 (see also cover letter from Stewart to Castlereagh, 15 January 1820).

38 DRO, D/Lo/C42/3, 23 July 1820.

39 DRO, D/Lo/C42/4, 28 July 1820.

40 DRO, D/Lo/C41/4, 30 July 1820.

41 Ibid.

42 See TNA, FO 7/151. An examination of Stewart's letters shows that he was travelling between Baden and Vienna in July and August 1820.

43 H. Montgomery Hyde and Edith, Marchioness of Londonderry, *More Letters from Martha Wilmot: Impressions of Vienna 1819–1829* (London, 1935), letter to Lady Bloomfield, 1–5 June 1821, pp. 108–9.

44 In retaliation, on New Year's Day 1821, Stewart gave a ball for the sovereigns present in Vienna, on their way to the Congress of Laibach, but 'none of them wd go nor any of the Archdukes of duchesses.' Wellington was clearly unimpressed, 'This is not exactly the position in which our Ambassador ought to stand at the Austrian Court; & it is difficult to account for the extraordinary impertinence & ill breeding of such conduct.' Francis Bamford and the seventh Duke of Wellington (eds), *The Journal of Mrs. Arbuthnot 1820–1832* (2 vols, London, 1950), vol. 1, p. 68, 3 February 1821.

45 Montgomery Hyde and Londonderry, *Martha Wilmot*, letter to Lady Bloomfield, 1 to 5 June 1821, pp. 108–9.

46 Ibid., p. 109.

47 *The Trial at Large of Her Majesty Caroline Amelia Elizabeth, Queen of Great Britain in the House of Lords, on Charges of Adulterous Intercourse* (2 vols, London, 1821), vol. 1, p. 1.

48 [Author of 'The Royal Wanderer'], *The Legislatorial Trial of Her Majesty Caroline Amelia Elizabeth, Queen of England Consort of George the Fourth, For the Alleged Crime of Adultery with Bartolomeo Bergami* (London, 1820) details the cross-examination of Theodore Majocchi on pp. 106–62; also see *Trial at Large*, vol. 1, pp. 203–37.

49 *The Legislatorial Trial of Her Majesty Caroline Amelia Elizabeth*, pp. 130–1; see also *Trial at Large*, vol. 1, p. 232.

50 *The Legislatorial Trial of Her Majesty Caroline Amelia Elizabeth*, pp. 132–3; see also *Trial at Large*, vol. 1, pp. 233–4.

51 *The Legislatorial Trial of Her Majesty Caroline Amelia Elizabeth*, pp. 133–4.

52 *The Legislatorial Trial of Her Majesty Caroline Amelia Elizabeth*, pp. 133–4; see also *Trial at Large*, vol. 1, p. 235.

53 *The Legislatorial Trial of Her Majesty Caroline Amelia Elizabeth*, p. 134.

54 *The Legislatorial Trial of Her Majesty Caroline Amelia Elizabeth*, p. 134; see also *Trial at Large*, vol. 1, p. 236.

55 See Fraser, *The Unruly Queen*, pp. 312 and 338–9.

56 For example, *Curious in Diplomacy, Dealers in Cat's Meat & Home-Bred Leeches. To be SOLD by Auction, by Mr. Crocker, at the Auction Mart, on Monday, the 34th inst. And Following Days, at 12 o'clock, in the Forenoon, by Order of John Bull, the*

Curious and Valuable Effects of Messrs. Muddlepool, Derry-Down, and Co. Bankrupts (London, 1820).

57 ['Milani, Count'], *The Royal Italian Jugglers' Count Milani and Countess Colombier* (London, n.d., but 1820).

58 ['Milani, Count'], *The Royal Italian Jugglers'* (London, n.d., but 1820).

59 *Trial at Large*, vol. 1, p. 325.

60 DRO, D/Lo/C39/6, 18 August 1820; the letter was written at the request of Colonel During.

61 DRO, D/Lo/C39/9, 27 August 1820; an example of Stewart's correspondence with the Queen's defence team can be seen at D/Lo/C/39/7–8, 17.

62 See DRO, D/Lo/C41/5, 6, 10.

63 DRO, D/Lo/C/41/21, 26 September 1820 and D/Lo/C/39/22, 16 September 1820.

64 Stewart's accounts of secret service monies connected with the Caroline Affair show how busy he had been in allocating payments to Browne and During: see DRO, D/Lo/C58/18, Stewart to Castlereagh, 27 December 1820; D/Lo/C58/19, Stewart to Castlereagh, 3 February 1821; D/Lo/C58/23, Joseph Planta to Stewart, 15 May 1821.

65 Charles Greville recalled an interesting anecdote in his diary: 'I may here introduce some anecdotes of Canning told me by Lord George Bentinck, his private secretary: – Some time after they had been in office (after Lord Londonderry's death) they found in a drawer, which apparently had been forgotten or overlooked, some papers, which were despatches and copies of correspondence between Lord Castlereagh and Lord Stewart. These despatches were very curious and more particularly so after his attack last year on Canning for misappropriating the secret service money, for they gave an account of his own employment of the secret service money in getting Italian witnesses for the Queen's trial. There was likewise an account of the discovery Stewart had made of the treachery of an office messenger, who for a long time carried all his despatches to Metternich, before he took them to England, and Lord Stewart says, 'I tremble when I think of the risk which my despatches have incurred of coming before the House of Commons, as there were letters of Lord Londonderry's written expressly "to throw dust in the eyes of the Parliament". These were his own expressions, and he said, 'You will understand this and know what to say to Metternich.' Henry Reeve (ed.), *The Greville Memoirs: A Journal of the Reigns of King George IV, King William IV, and Queen Victoria* (3 vols, 1874), vol. 1, pp. 104–5.

13 A Vane heir

1 DRO, D/Lo/C38/4/39, 26 July 1820.

2 TNA, FO 7/160, Most Private and Confidential, 3 February 1820.

3 BL, Heytesbury Papers, Add. MS 41532, ff. 66–9, 29 July 1820.

4 BL, Heytesbury Papers, Add. MS 41532, ff. 59–60, 14 August 1820.

5 TNA, FO 7/152, No. 98, 25 August 1820.

6 Alan Sked, *Metternich and Austria: An Evaluation* (Basingstoke, 2008), p. 75.

7 TNA, FO 7/152, no. 105, Stewart to Castlereagh, 3 September 1820.

8 DRO, D/Lo/C38/4/57, 20 September 1820; the language was pretty strong as Stewart remarked that Richelieu 'with open mouthd & ill conceal'd dissatisfaction related that the English Ambassr., had shewn him all our Ministers Dispatches from Naples'.

9   DRO, D/Lo/C38/4/62, 2 October 1820.

10 Ibid.

11 TNA, FO 7/160, Castlereagh to Stewart, 16 September 1820; Castlereagh also sent his brother news of diplomatic events in France, TNA, FO 7/160, 28 October 1820.

12 On the proposition to provide British naval protection, see TNA, FO 7/160, No, 105, Secret and Confidential, Stewart to Castlereagh, 3 September 1820. For a summary of the issues and events leading up the Congress, see Mark Jarrett, *The Congress of Vienna and Its Legacy* (London, 2014, pp. 239–47). For a summary of the Congress, see, for example, Paul W. Schroeder, *Metternich's Diplomacy at Its Zenith, 1820–1823* (Austin, TX, 1962), pp. 60–103 and Jarrett, *Congress of Vienna*, pp. 248–69.

13 Sked, *Metternich*, p. 75.

14 TNA, FO 7/152, No. 120, Stewart to Castlereagh, 23 October 1820.

15 W. H. Zawadzki, *Adam Czartoryski as a Statesman of Russia and Poland 1795–1831* (Oxford, 1993), pp. 281–2.

16 TNA, FO 7/152, Separate, Stewart to Castlereagh, 23 October 1820.

17 Ibid.

18 DRO, D/Lo/C38/4/75, 81, 4 and 15 November 1820.

19 Jarrett, *Congress of Vienna*, p. 258.

20 BL, Rose Papers, Add. MS 42791, ff. 153–4, 17 November 1820.

21 BL, Heytesbury Papers, Add. MS 41532, ff. 73–4, 20 November 1820; see also copy in TNA, FO 7/154, 21 November 1820.

22 TNA, FO 7/154, No. 132, 7 December 1820.

23 Jarrett, *Congress of Vienna*, p. 265.

24 TNA, FO 7/154, No. 136, 21 December 1820.

25 TNA, FO 7/154, No. 137, 21 December 1820. Stewart further reported, 'The declining Her mediation, and adopting that by the Pope, has not increased the good Humor in the Quarter of the French Plenipotentiaries.'

26 TNA, FO 7/154, No. 140, 24 December 1820.

27 See DRO, D/Lo/C58/18, 19, 21, 27 December 1820, 3 February, 1821, 9 May 1821.

28 *The Legislatorial Trial of Her Majesty Caroline Amelia Elizabeth, Queen of England* (London, 1820), p. 603; see also *The Trial at Large of Her Majesty Caroline Amelia Elizabeth, Queen of Great Britain in the House of Lords* (2 vols, London, 1821), vol. 2, p. 419.

29 DRO, D/Lo/C38/6/5, 20 January 1821; letter and enclosure. See Nanora Sweet, '"The Inseparables": Hemans, the Brownes and the Milan Commission', *Forum for Modern Language Studies*, xxxix (2003), pp. 173–4.

30 Sweet, '"The Inseparables"', p. 173.

31 L. A. Marchand (ed.), *Byron's Letters and Journals* (13 vols, London, 1973–94), vol. 8, p. 65. See also Sweet, '"The Inseparables"', p. 165.

32 Browne was knighted in 1826 and, among other things, became High Sheriff of Flintshire (in 1824); he also eventually rose to the rank of lieutenant general (*Gentleman's Magazine*, April 1855, p. 421).

33 Edith, Marchioness of Londonderry, *Frances Anne, The Life and Times of Frances Anne Marchioness of Londonderry and Her Husband Charles Third Marquess of Londonderry* (London, 1958), pp. 58–9; see Schroeder, *Metternich's Diplomacy*, p. 112. See, for example, Schroeder, *Metternich's Diplomacy*, pp. 104–28 and Jarrett, *Congress of Vienna*, pp. 270–85.

34 Price, *Perilous Crown*, p. 71.

35 Jarrett, *Congress of Vienna*, p. 272.

36 DRO, D/Lo/C/38/6/6, 27 January 1821 (also found in TNA, FO 7/160). Ruffo was 'an admirer of Metternich' (Jarrett, *Congress of Vienna*, p. 270).
37 Jarrett, *Congress of Vienna*, p. 274; see also pp. 270–4.
38 TNA, FO 7/160, Stewart to A'Court, Private, 28 January 1821.
39 Ibid.
40 TNA, FO 7/160, Stewart to Castlereagh, Secret and Separate, 31 January 1821.
41 TNA, FO 7/160, Most Secret and Confidential, Stewart to Castlereagh, 3 February 1821.
42 Jarrett, *Congress of Vienna*, p. 278.
43 Ibid., p. 279.
44 TNA, FO 120/46.
45 TNA, FO 120/47, Stewart to Londonderry, 30 May 1821.
46 Ibid.
47 TNA, FO 120/47, Stewart to Londonderry, 6 June 1821.
48 BL, Aberdeen Papers, Add. MS 43212, f. 211, 27 February 1821.
49 BL, Aberdeen Papers, Add. MS, 43212, f. 159, 29 November 1820; f. 205, 15 March 1821.
50 For the redecoration, see BL, Westmorland Papers M/512 Reel 4, f. 207, 18 September 1820; for the fire, see BL, Beauvale Papers, Add. MS 60415, Stewart to Frederick Lamb, 11 January 1821; Stewart's absences are detailed in H. Montgomery Hyde, *The Londonderrys* (London, 1979), p. 27.
51 Londonderry, *Frances Anne*, p. 61.
52 Hyde and Londonderry, *Martha Wilmot*, pp. 16–7. Martha Wilmot penned a very obvious hope for their future positions at the embassy.
53 Ibid., p. 107, letter to her sister, Alicia Wilmot, 18 May 1821.
54 Ibid., pp. 107–12.
55 DRO, D/Lo/C58/23, 30 May 1821; D/Lo/C58/24, 30 May 1821.
56 [William Hone], *A Slap at Slop and the Bridge-Street Gang* (second edition, n.d., but 1821).
57 Londonderry, *Frances Anne*, pp. 65–6.
58 John Wilks Jr, *Memoirs of Her Majesty Caroline Amelia Eliz: Consort of George IV King of Great Britain* (2 vols, London, 1822), vol. 1, p. 376.
59 BL, Aberdeen Papers, Add. MS 43212, f. 257, 17 September 1821.
60 John Bew, *Castlereagh: Enlightenment, War and Terror* (London, 2011), p. 522.
61 Londonderry, *Frances Anne*, pp. 66–7.
62 Peter Quennell, *The Private Letters of Princess Lieven to Prince Metternich 1820–1826* (London, 1937), pp. 164–5. The Countess also reported on the Stewarts' marriage, writing that Stewart 'looks bored with his "little wife"; after he had brought her up to me, he took her back to her place, and then returned quite lively and cheerful'.
63 Bew, *Castlereagh*, pp. 515–17, 523–6.

14 *The deplorable event*

1 DRO, D/Lo/C61/8, 18 February 1822.
2 Peter Quennell, *The Private Letters of Princess Lieven to Prince Metternich 1820–1826* (London, 1937), p. 171.
3 Ibid., pp. 173–5.
4 Ibid., pp. 177–8, 10 June 1822.
5 Adam Zamoyski, *Rites of Peace: The Fall of Napoleon and the Congress of Vienna* (London, 2007), p. 548.

6   Quennell, *Princess Lieven*, p. 180, 17 June 1822; p. 192, 6 August 1822.
7   BL, Beauvale Papers, Add. MS 60415, to Frederick Lamb, 13 August 1822.
8   Quennell, *Princess Lieven*, pp. 189–91, 12 August 1822.
9   John Bew, *Castlereagh: Enlightenment, War and Terror* (London, 2011), pp. 545–57; see also especially H. Montgomery Hyde, *The Strange Death of Lord Castlereagh* (London, 1959), pp. 149–80; Wendy Hinde, *Castlereagh* (London, 1981), pp. 277–81; and Giles Hunt, *The Duel; Castlereagh, Canning and Deadly Cabinet Rivalry* (London, 2008), pp. 177–85.
10 Second Duke of Wellington (ed.), *Despatches, Correspondence and Memoranda of Field Marshal Arthur, Duke of Wellington K.G.* (8 vols, London, 1858–72), vol. 1, letter 141, p. 263.
11 Francis Bamford and the seventh Duke of Wellington (eds), *The Journal of Mrs. Arbuthnot 1820–1832* (2 vols, London, 1950), pp. 282–3; 10 June 1829. She recalled, 'At the funeral of the late Lord Londonderry, Lord Liverpool, while they were still in the Abbey, told Ld Castlereagh that he considered he had the greatest claims on the Govt from the name he bore.'
12 See BL, Liverpool Papers, Add. MS 38291, f. 117, Liverpool to Londonderry, 14 October 1822. Liverpool noted that Londonderry's uncle, Lord Camden, had 'consulted' the prime minister about Frederick's 'going out' to Vienna.
13 BL, Liverpool Papers, Add. MS 38291, f. 81.
14 Ibid., ff. 83–5.
15 DRO, D/Lo/C62/1.
16 BL, Liverpool Papers, Add. MS 38291, ff. 116–18, 14 October 1822.
17 DRO, D/Lo/C106/1, 17 September 1822.
18 DRO, D/Lo/C62/4, 3 October 1822.
19 BL, Peel Papers, 28 October 1822; see also BL, Liverpool Papers, Add. MS 38251, f. 152, same date. In the letter to Liverpool, Stewart confirms that he has written to Peel and to Lord Wellesley.
20 Londonderry had one advantage in that he 'knew Metternich better than Wellington did'. Paul W. Schroeder, *Metternich's Diplomacy at Its Zenith, 1820–1823* (Austin, TX, 1962), p. 214. For a summary of the Congress of Verona, see, for example, Schroeder, *Metternich's Diplomacy*, pp. 195–236 and Mark Jarrett, *The Congress of Vienna and Its Legacy* (London, 2014), pp. 319–43.
21 Frances Anne and Alexander I became close friends at the Congress of Verona. The warmth of their relationship can be seen in letters held at DRO from Alexander; see DRO, D/Lo/C523/2–11. Letters 2–9 are not dated, letter 10 is dated 14 June 1823 and letter 11 is dated 29 February 1824. See also Edith, Marchioness of Londonderry, *Frances Anne, The Life and Times of Frances Anne Marchioness of Londonderry and Her Husband Charles Third Marquess of Londonderry* (London, 1958), pp. 87–113; H. Montgomery Hyde, *The Londonderrys* (London, 1979), pp. 26, 31–2; Diane Urquhart, *The Ladies of Londonderry* (London, 2007), pp. 20–7.
22 Wendy Hinde, *George Canning* (London, 1973), pp. 321–44, and Zamoyski, *Rites of Peace*, p. 548.
23 Memoranda of Lord Londonderry regarding Verona, 2 and 3 November 1822, from Wellington, *Despatches*, vol. 1, pp. 484–8.
24 BL, Liverpool Papers, Add. MS 38291, f. 152.
25 Ibid., ff. 321–5, 10 December 1822.

26 For these letters on the UK earldom, see Kent History and Library Centre, Pratt Manuscripts, C528/2, 8 November 1822 to C528/6, 18 December 1822; see BL, Liverpool Papers, Add. MS 38291, f. 320, 5 January 1823.

27 Kent History and Library Centre, Pratt Manuscripts, C60/6, 29 December 1822.

28 BL, Liverpool Papers, Add. MS 38293, f. 77, 12 March 1823.

29 DRO, Londonderry Papers, D/Lo/C63/12 (copies of FO papers), Planta to Londonderry, 6 June 1823.

30 Ibid.; Liverpool to Planta 4 June 1823; the request for the pension was dated Paris, 23 May 1823, Londonderry to Planta.

31 DRO, D/Lo/C63/12.

32 DRO, D/Lo/C112/5 and D/Lo/C112/5/7, Londonderry to Dudley, 14 May 1827; Dudley to Londonderry, 22 May 1827. Dudley denied that the 'leak' had come from the Foreign Office; see D/Lo/C112/5/6, 15 May 1827.

33 The sinecure appointment as governor of Fort Charles in Jamaica was resigned in favour of Londonderry's friend Benjamin Bloomfield, who had fallen foul of the prevailing influences at court. Bloomfield had been eased from his post in the Royal Household with the promises of a peerage and emoluments to ensure his financial security. One of those was the Jamaica appointment.

34 DRO, D/Lo/C113/40.

35 DRO, D/Lo/C113/44, 17 July 1823; the correspondence continues over the course of July and August 1823.

36 BL, Westmorland Papers M/512 Reel 4, f. 241, 12 July 1823.

37 Sir Archibald Alison, *Lives of Lord Castlereagh and Sir Charles Stewart* (3 vols, Edinburgh, 1861), vol. 3, p. 239.

38 See BL, Ripon Papers, Add. MS 40862, ff. 176–9, Londonderry to first Earl of Ripon, 13 July 1839. Lord Ripon (the former Viscount Goderich) had been a political opponent. Londonderry, now reconciled to the Earl of Ripon, was writing of his dispute with Lord Brougham.

15 Gentlemanly conduct

1 Sir Archibald Alison, *Lives of Lord Castlereagh and Sir Charles Stewart* (3 vols, Edinburgh, 1861), vol. 3, pp. 268–9.

2 J. G. Millingen, *The History of Duelling* (2 vols, London, 1841), vol. 1, pp. 281–3. See second Duke of Wellington (ed.), *Supplementary Despatches and Memoranda of Field Marshal Arthur, Duke of Wellington* (15 vols, London, 1858–72), vol. 2, Londonderry to Wellington, 9 May 1824; Wellington to Earl Bathurst, 13 May 1824 (pp. 266–71).

3 DRO, D/Lo/C113/52a, 4 January 1826.

4 Kent History and Library Centre, Pratt Manuscripts, U840 C39/13, copy of *Belfast News Letter*, 30 December 1825.

5 Wellington, *Despatches*, vol. 3, p. 636, Londonderry to George IV, 12 April 1827. The account of the meeting is contained in a memorandum to Wellington, dated 13 April 1827 (pp. 633–5).

6 Ibid., p. 657, Londonderry to Wellington, 22 April 1827.

7 BL, Westmorland Papers M/512 Reel 4, 20 October 1827.

8 DRO, D/Lo/C86/1, 19 May 1828.

9   Wellington, *Despatches*, vol. 4, p. 84, Londonderry to Wellington, 12 August 1827; pp. 120–1, Londonderry to Wellington, 28 August 1827.

10 *New Monthly Magazine and Literary Journal*, 1 January 1828 (London, 1828), p. 568.

11 DRO, D/Lo/C83, letter 13, Hardinge to Londonderry, 22 January 1828; letter 14, Londonderry to Hardinge, n.d.; see also letters 15–17; letter 18, Hardinge to Londonderry, 24 January 1828; the letter continued '& I wish you wd. let me read that paragraph of yr. letter to the Duke where you use such kind expressions to him'.

12 Wellington, *Despatches*, vol. 4, pp. 340–409; 6–28 April 1828; the newspaper article described Londonderry as the possible successor to the current British ambassador, Lord Granville. See p. 379, extract from *Journal des Débats*, 12 April 1828.

13 Wellington, *Despatches*, vol. 4, p. 409, 21 April 1828; pp. 436–8, 10 May 1828.

14 Ibid., vol. 4, p. 475.

15 See Alison, *Lives of Lord Castlereagh*, vol. 3, pp. 253–4.

16 Francis Bamford and the Duke of Wellington (eds), *The Journal of Mrs. Arbuthnot 1820–1832* (2 vols, London, 1950), vol. 2, pp. 280; see also pp. 192–3, 282–5 and H. Montgomery Hyde, *The Londonderrys* (London, 1979), pp. 44–5.

17 Bamford and Wellington, *Mrs. Arbuthnot*, vol. 2, pp. 282–3.

18 Ibid., pp. 284–5.

19 E. A. Smith, *George IV* (New Haven, CT, 1999), pp. 268–70.

20 Bamford and Wellington, *Mrs. Arbuthnot*, vol. 2, pp. 359–60, 361–2.

21 Smith, *George IV*, pp. 270–2.

22 Munro Price, *The Perilous Crown: France between Revolutions* (London, 2007), pp. 126–50, 151–88.

23 DRO, D/Lo/C124, 12 October 1830.

24 See DRO, D/Lo/C81/3–11, Buckingham to Londonderry, 14 July to 2 October 1830.

25 DRO, D/Lo/C86/16.

26 W. H. Zawadzki, *Adam Czartoryski as a Statesman of Russia and Poland 1795–1831* (Oxford, 1993), pp. 300–21.

27 Charles Vane, third Marquess of Londonderry, *Recollections of a Tour in the North of Europe 1836–1837* (2 vols, London, 1838), vol. 1, pp. 169–75 and vol. 2, pp. 27–8.

28 BL, Peel Papers, Add. MS 40405, ff. 306–7, 16 December 1834.

29 BL, Peel Papers, Add. MS 40415, f. 185, 25 February 1835.

30 Henry Reeve (ed.), *The Greville Memoirs: A Journal of the Reigns of King George IV, King William IV, and Queen Victoria* (3 vols, 1874), vol. 3, pp. 225–7, 14 and 15 March 1835.

31 BL, Peel Papers, Add. MS 40417, f. 141; for the resignation letter to Wellington, see DRO, D/Lo/C96/16.

32 For Browne's assistance see DRO, D/Lo/C65/1–7, 1 August–October 1837. For Browne and Lady Londonderry's journal, see DRO, D/Lo/65/8, 12 December 1837. The trip to Russia also provided the opportunity for the Londonderrys to enjoy the hospitality of their county neighbour, the first Earl of Durham, British ambassador since 1835.

33 Londonderry, *Recollections*, vol. 1, p. 165.

34 Ibid., vol. 2, pp. 27–8.

35 Ibid., p. 31.

36 See, for example, Lord Londonderry's recommendation of Dr (later Sir) Charles Forbes's promotion from a Knight of the Royal Guelphic Order to that of a Knight Commander. This caused headaches for Forbes as the government of the day was less than keen to give

permission for British subjects to receive what was now the order of a foreign sovereign; see D/Lo/C452/3–5, 7, Forbes to Londonderry, 10 August–25 November 1837.

37   Edith, Marchioness of Londonderry (ed.), *Letters from Benjamin Disraeli to Frances Anne Marchioness of Londonderry 1837–61* (London, 1938), p. xv.

38   Ibid., pp. 3, xiv.

39   Ibid., pp. xv–xvi.

40   Ian Anstruther, *The Knight and the Umbrella: An Account of the Eglinton Tournament 1839* (London, 1963), pp. 147–8, 197.

41   D/Lo/C130/1, Londonderry to Knights of the Tournament, circular letter, 4 September 1839; the last letter is dated 13 June 1840 (letter 32); see also Anstruther, *Knight and the Umbrella*, p. 232.

42   Alison, *Lives of Lord Castlereagh*, vol. 3, pp. 269–73.

43   Charles Vane, third Marquess of Londonderry, *A Steam Voyage to Constantinople, by The Rhine and the Danube in 1840–41, and to Portugal and Spain, &c in 1839* (2 vols, London, 1842), vol. 1, pp. 55, 59.

44   Ibid., pp. 184 and 203–8.

45   See DRO, D/Lo/C72 book 2, letters 53–132.

46   DRO, D/Lo/C83/78(2), Londonderry to Hardinge, 15 May 1841. There had also been personal tragedy for the Londonderrys just before this, when Wynyard was severely damaged in a fire. This brought a heartfelt letter from Lord Londonderry, then in Naples, to Lord Burghersh on 21 March 1841. See BL, Westmorland Papers M/512 Reel 4, ff. 297–8. Castlereagh would soon be travelling abroad; for an example of his travel accounts to his father, see DRO, D/Lo/C104/2, 2 August 1842, dated from Beirut.

47   BL, Westmorland Papers M/512 Reel 4, ff. 303–4.

48   BL Aberdeen Papers, Add. MS 43238, f. 30, 6 October 1841.

49   DRO, D/Lo/C79/2, Aberdeen to Londonderry, 8 October 1841.

50   BL, Aberdeen Papers, Add. MS 43238, f. 247, 29 June 1842.

51   BL, Aberdeen Papers, Add. MS 43238, f. 248, 1 July 1842.

52   DRO, D/Lo/C110/1, 12 February 1842; the Duke had expected to be nominated himself to the post, as his response of 17 February (letter 2) makes clear.

53   For Londonderry's letters as Gold Stick see DRO, D/Lo/C136.

54   DRO, D/Lo/C65/26, 21 May 1845.

55   BL, Aberdeen Papers, Add. MS 43244, 28 July 1845.

56   Hardinge's very warm letter to Londonderry was written at the end of the campaign, dated from Simla, 24 June 1846 (DRO, D/Lo/C456).

57   DRO, D/Lo/C83/109, 21 November 1847; for examples of Adolphus's letters to his father in India, see DRO, D/Lo/C109/47 and 48, dated from Bombay (Mumbai), 20 May and 28 August 1847.

58   Anne Casement 'The Management of the Londonderry Estates in Ulster during the Great Famine in *Familia*', *Ulster Genealogical Review* xxi (2005), pp. 19–68; Trevor Parkhill, '"Chivalrous Rather Than Administrative": The Career of the Third Marquess of Londonderry, Soldier, Diplomat, Landlord', in Alan Blackstock and Eoin Magennis (eds), *Politics and Political Culture in Britain and Ireland* (Belfast, 2005), pp. 157–72.

59   Parkhill, '"Chivalrous Rather Than Administrative"', p. 164.

60   DRO, D/Lo/C65/33, 14 September 1850.

61   Parkhill, '"Chivalrous Rather Than Administrative"', p. 172; for details of the election, see pp. 170–1.

62 Frederick Stewart, Viscount Castlereagh, *A Journey to Damascus through Egypt, Nubia, Arabia, Petraea, Palestine and Syria* (2 vols, London, 1847), vol. 1, p. iii.

63 Henry Brougham, first Lord Brougham, *Historical Sketches of Statesmen Who Flourished in the Time of George III* (London, 1845), p. 156; Londonderry's initial response was a pamphlet reproduced in volume 1; see Charles Vane, third Marquess of Londonderry (ed.), *Memoirs of Viscount Castlereagh* (12 vols, London, 1848–53), vol. 1, pp. 89–124.

64 PRONI, Clanwilliam Papers, D3044/F/13, volume compiled by Lord Clanwilliam, fragmentary, August 1795–June 1850, pp. 29–30.

65 PRONI, Clanwilliam Papers, D3044/F/13, volume compiled by Lord Clanwilliam, fragmentary, August 1795–June 1850, pp. 320–1. The past was clearly much in Londonderry's thoughts during this time; see DRO, D/Lo/C65/49, Browne to Londonderry, 28 January 1851.

66 Pieter M. Judson, *The Habsburg Empire: A New History* (Cambridge, MA, 2016), pp. 155–217.

67 *Speeches of the Marquess of Londonderry and the Duke of Wellington on the Presentation of Petitions against the Bill for the Abolition of the Lord Lieutenancy of Ireland House of Lords Thursday 27 June 1850* (Dublin, 1850). See also DRO, D/Lo/C67/1, Earl of Glengall to Londonderry, 2 January 1851.

68 DRO, D/Lo/C65/34, Browne to Londonderry, 24 March 1851.

69 Alison, *Lives of Lord Castlereagh*, vol. 3, pp. 285–6. It was reported that Londonderry was to receive a 'Black Arab horse' from Abd-el-Kader; see D/Lo/C137/7, Lord Stratford de Redcliffe to Londonderry, 2 October 1853. This file also contains other letters concerning the case, including one from Lord Brougham, who by this time was on more friendly terms (D/Lo/C137/1, 23 April 1851).

70 See DRO, D/Lo/C93/1, Eglinton to Londonderry, 3 March 1852. Londonderry was 'too tired' to give Eglinton an interview, and so the offers were made via Lady Londonderry.

71 DRO, D/Lo/C83/152, Hardinge to Londonderry, 16 March 1852.

72 DRO, D/Lo/C83/153, Hardinge to Londonderry, 16 March 1852; DRO, D/Lo/C83/169, Lady Hardinge to Londonderry, n.d. For Londonderry's reply to Hardinge's letter no. 153, see D/Lo/C83/156. Londonderry also wrote to his sister on 14 March – see D/Lo/C83/170; while there is another undated letter from Lady Hardinge on the quarrel at D/Lo/C83/171.

73 *The Letters of Queen Victoria: A Selection from Her Majesty's Correspondence between the Years 1837 and 1861*, ed. Arthur Benson and second Viscount Esher (3 vols, 1907), vol. 2, Victoria to Derby, 26 August 1852 (p. 475) and Memorandum of Prince Albert, 17 September 1852 (pp. 476–7). For Derby's letter, see Alison, *Lives of Lord Castlereagh*, vol. 3, pp. 289–90.

74 DRO, D/Lo/C785/9, Londonderry to Derby, 23 September 1852. In a symbolic gesture, the second Duke of Wellington sent his father's blue ribbon (DRO, D/Lo/C114). That it was Wellington's Garter was seen as an extra mark of honour, as Lord Strangford (a former ambassador to the Portuguese court in Brazil) wrote: 'I am very glad, (very very glad) that it should be Wellington's Garter – and not that of the silly old Pomposo Hamilton' (DRO, D/Lo/C100/363, 24 September 1852). As an addition to this letter, Strangford added a strange newspaper cutting which stated that Londonderry had been arrested in Paris for an unpaid debt.

75 BL, Aberdeen Papers, Add. MS 43248, Londonderry to Aberdeen, 15 January 1853.

76 DRO, D/Lo/C110/60, 16 January 1853; the Bishop of Oxford was chancellor of the
    Order of the Garter. Londonderry was nominated a Knight of the Garter on 19
    January 1853 (see Peter J. begent and Hubert Chesshyre, *The Most Noble Order of the
    Garter: 650 Years* (London, 1999), p. 324).

77 Hyde, *The Londonderrys*, pp. 45, 49.

78 BL, Aberdeen Papers, Add. MS 43248, Aberdeen to Londonderry, 22 January 1853;
    the rumour was obviously widely circulated, as noted by Strangford on 1 February
    1853 (DRO, D/Lo/C100/373). For relations between Castlereagh and Londonderry,
    see DRO, D/Lo/C104.

79 See Alison, *Lives of Lord Castlereagh*, vol. 3, pp. 294–6.

80 DRO, D/Lo/C/Acc. 451 (D) file 5, letter 6 Disraeli to Londonderry, 30 January 1854.
    Browne wrote of accounts that the Marquess had an attack of 'Neuralgia – which was
    made in the papers of the 18th' (DRO, D/Lo/C65/52, Browne to Londonderry, 22
    January 1854).

81 Alison, *Lives of Lord Castlereagh*, vol. 3, pp. 296–7.

82 *Gentleman's Magazine*, April 1854, p. 417.

83 Ibid., pp. 415–18.

SELECT BIBLIOGRAPHY

Archives

British Library

Aberdeen Papers
Beauvale Papers
Heytesbury Papers
Liverpool Papers
Lowe Papers
Moore Papers
Peel Papers
Ripon Papers
Rose Papers
Wilson Papers
Microfilm of letters of John Fane, 11th Earl of Westmorland 1814–46

The National Archives

Foreign Office: Correspondence and Jackson Papers

Public Record Office of Northern Ireland

Castlereagh Papers
Clanwilliam Papers

Devon Archives and Local Studies Service

Addington Papers

Durham Record Office

Londonderry Estates Papers

Kent History and Library Centre

Pratt Manuscripts

Books and articles

Books in English are published in London except where otherwise noted.

Aiken, Arthur (ed.), *The Annual Review and History of Literature for 1805* (1806).

A Full Report of the Trial of Major-General Sir Robert Thomas Wilson, Michael Bruce, Esq. and Capt. John Hely Hutchinson, before the Court of Assize at Paris, on the 22d of April 1816, and Two Following Days, for Aiding the Escape of Count Lavalette; Including a Short Memoir of Sir R. T .Wilson (1816).

Alison, Sir Archibald, *Lives of Lord Castlereagh and Sir Charles Stewart* (3 vols, Edinburgh, 1861).

Anstruther, Ian, *The Knight and the Umbrella: An Account of the Eglinton Tournament 1839* (1963).

Bamford, Andrew, *A Bold and Ambitious Enterprise: The British Army in the Low Countries, 1813–1814* (Barnsley, 2013).

Bamford, Francis, and Wellesley, Gerald, seventh Duke of Wellington (eds), *The Journal of Mrs. Arbuthnot 1820–1832* (2 vols, 1950).

Bassett, Richard, *For God and Kaiser: The Imperial Austrian Army* (New Haven, CT, 2015).

Begent, Peter J., and Chesshyre, Hubert, *The Most Noble Order of the Garter: 650 Years* (1999).

Benson, Arthur, and Brett, Reginald, second Viscount Esher (eds), *The Letters of Queen Victoria: A Selection from Her Majesty's Correspondence between the Years 1837 and 1861* (3 vols, 1907).

Bew, John, *Castlereagh: Enlightenment, War and Terror* (2011).

Boigne, Adèle, comtesse de, *Memoirs of the Comtesse de Boigne* (1907).

Broers, Michael, *Europe under Napoleon* (this edition, 2015).

Brougham, Henry, first Lord Brougham, *Historical Sketches of Statesmen Who Flourished in the Time of George III* (1845).

Buckley, Norman (ed.), *The Napoleonic War Journal of Captain Thomas Henry Browne 1807–1816* (1987).

Casement, Anne, 'The Management of the Londonderry Estates in Ulster during the Great Famine in *Familia*'. *Ulster Genealogical Review*, xxi (Belfast, 2005), pp. 19–68.

Chamberlain, Muriel E., *Lord Aberdeen: A Political Biography* (1983).

Clark, Christopher, *Iron Kingdom: The Rise and Downfall of Prussia 1600–1947* (this edition, 2007).

Curious in Diplomacy, Dealers in Cat's Meat & Home-Bred Leeches. To Be SOLD by Auction, by Mr. Crocker, at the Auction Mart, on Monday, the 34th inst. And Following Days, at 12 o'clock, in the Forenoon, by Order of John Bull, the Curious and Valuable Effects of Messrs. Muddlepool, Derry-Down, and Co. Bankrupts (1820).

Dallas, Gregor, *1815: The Roads to Waterloo* (1996).

Davies, Hugh J., *Spying for Wellington: British Military Intelligence in the Peninsular War* (Norman, OK, 2018).

Davies, Hugh J., *Wellington's Wars: The Making of a Military Genius* (New Haven, CT, 2012).

Debrett, John, *Debrett's Peerage of the United Kingdom of Great Britain and Ireland* (2 vols, 1828).

Esdaile, Charles, *Napoleon's Wars: An International History 1803–1815* (this edition, 2008).

Esdaile, Charles, *The Peninsular War* (2002).

Fane, John, Lord Burghersh, *Memoir of the Operations of the Allied Armies under Prince Schwarzenberg and Marshal Blucher During the Latter End of 1813, and the Year 1814* (1822).

FitzClarence, George, first Earl of Munster, *An Account of the British Campaign in 1809 under Sir A. Wellesley in Spain and Portugal* (1831).

Fordyce, William, *The History and Antiquities of the County Palatine of Durham* (2 vols, Newcastle, 1857).

Fornier, August, *Der Congress Von Châtillon. Die Politik in Kriege von 1814* (Vienna, 1900).

Fortescue, Sir John, *A History of the British Army* (20 vols, 1899–1930).

Franklin, Robert, *Lord Stuart de Rothesay* (Upton-upon-Severn, 1993).

Fraser, Flora, *The Unruly Queen: The Life of Queen Caroline* (1996).

Freksa, Frederick (trans. Harry Hansen), *A Peace Congress of Intrigue* (New York, 1919).

Frost, John, *A Translation of the Statutes of the Royal Hanoverian Guelphic Order, Together with a List of the Grand Crosses, Commanders and Knights* (1831).

Fulford, Roger, and Strachey, Lytton (eds), *The Greville Diaries* (1938).

Glover, Michael, *A Very Slippery Fellow: The Life of Sir Robert Wilson* (Oxford, 1978).

Gurwood, John, *The Dispatches of Field Marshal the Duke of Wellington* (13 vols, 1834–9).

Hanham, Andrew, 'Regency Knights: The Royal Guelphic Order 1815–1837', *The Coat of Arms* 3rd ser., iv (2008), pp. 101–24.

Harris, Robin, *Talleyrand. Betrayer and Saviour of France* (2007).

Hart, H. G., *The New Annual Army List, Corrected to 7 February 1840* (1840).

[Hawker, P], *Journal of a Regimental Officer during the Recent Campaign in Portugal and Spain under Lord Viscount Wellington. With a Correct Plan of the Battle of Talavera* (1810).

Hinde, Wendy, *Castlereagh* (1981).

Hinde, Wendy, *George Canning* (1973).

[Hone, William], *A Slap at Slop and the Bridge-Street Gang* (second edition, n.d., but 1821).

Huish, Robert, *Memoirs of Caroline, Queen Consort of England* (2 vols, 1821).

Huish, Robert, *Memoirs of HRH the Princess Charlotte* (1818).

Hunt, Giles, *The Duel; Castlereagh, Canning and Deadly Cabinet Rivalry* (2008).

Jackson, Lady (ed.), *The Bath Archives: A Further Selection from the Diaries and Letters of Sir George Jackson, K.C.H., from 1809 to 1816* (2 vols, 1873).

Jarrett, Mark, *The Congress of Vienna and its Legacy* (2014).

Jennings, Louis J. (ed.), *The Croker Papers* (3 vols, 1884).

Judson, Pieter M., *The Habsburg Empire: A New History* (Cambridge, MA, 2016).

King, David, *Vienna 1814* (New York, 2008).

Kissinger, Henry, *A World Restored: Metternich, Castlereagh and the Problems of Peace 1812–1822* (1957).

Knight, Roger, *Britain against Napoleon: The Organization of Victory 1793–1815* (2013).

La Garde-Chambonas, Auguste Louis Charles, comte de, *Anecdotal Recollections of the Congress of Vienna* (1902).

Layard, George Somers (ed.), *Sir Thomas Lawrence's Letter-Bag* (1906).

Leggiere, Michael V., *The Fall of Napoleon: The Allied Invasion of France* (Cambridge, 2007)

Leggiere, Michael V., *Napoleon and the Struggle for Germany: The Franco-Prussian War of 1813. Volume II: The Defeat of Napoleon* (Cambridge, 2015).

[Author of 'The Royal Wanderer'], *The Legislatorial Trial of Her Majesty Caroline Amelia Elizabeth, Queen of England Consort of George the Fourth, For the Alleged Crime of Adultery with Bartolomeo Bergami* (1820).

Leigh, Ione, *Castlereagh* (1951).

Leveson-Gower, F. (ed.), *Letters of Harriet, Countess Granville 1810–1845* (2 vols, 1894).

Lieven, Dominic, *Russia against Napoleon: The Battle for Europe, 1807 to 1814* (2009).

Liqueur, Thomas W., 'The Queen Caroline Affair: Politics as Art in the Reign of George IV', *Journal of Modern History*, liv (September 1982), pp. 417–66.

Lodge, Edmund, *The Peerage of the British Empire* (1832).

Longford, Elizabeth, *Wellington* (this edition, 1992).

Mansel, Philip, *The Eagle in Splendour: Inside the Court of Napoleon* (this edition, 2015).

Mansel, Philip, *Louis XVIII* (1981).

Marchand, L. A. (ed.), *Byron's Letters and Journals* (13 vols, 1973–94).

Metternich, Prince, *Memoirs of Prince Metternich 1773–1815, Edited by Prince Richard Metternich, Translated by Mrs Alexander Napier* (5 vols, 1880–2).

['Milani, Count'], *'The Royal Italian Jugglers' Count Milani and Countess Colombier* (n.d., but 1820).

Millingen, J. G., *The History of Duelling* (2 vols, 1841).

Montgomery Hyde, H., *The Londonderrys* (1979).

Montgomery Hyde, H., *The Strange Death of Lord Castlereagh* (1959).

Montgomery Hyde, H., and Vane-Tempest-Stewart, Edith, Marchioness of Londonderry (eds), *More Letters from Martha Wilmot: Impressions of Vienna 1819–1829* (1935).

Muir, Rory, *Britain and the Defeat of Napoleon, 1807–1815* (New Haven, CT, 1996).

Muir, Rory, *Wellington: The Path to Victory 1769–1814* (New Haven, CT, 2013).

Muir, Rory, *Wellington: Waterloo and the Fortunes of Peace 1814–1852* (New Haven, CT, 2015).

Napier, Sir William, *History of the War in the Peninsula* (Oxford, 1836).

[Underwood, T. R.], *A Narrative of Memorable Events in Paris* (1828).

Neville, D. G., *History of the Early Orders of Knighthood and Chivalry* (1978).

Oman, Sir Charles, *A History of the Peninsular War* (7 vols, this edition, 1995).

Oman, Sir Charles, *Wellington's Army, 1809–1814* (this edition, 1986).

Parkhill, Trevor, '"Chivalrous Rather Than Administrative": The Career of the Third Marquess of Londonderry, Soldier, Diplomat, Landlord', in Blackstock, Alan, and Magennis, Eoin (eds), *Politics and Political Culture in Britain and Ireland* (Belfast, 2007), pp. 157–72.

Price, Munro, *Napoleon: The End of Glory* (Oxford, 2014).

Price, Munro, *The Perilous Crown: France between Revolutions* (2007).

Quennell, Peter, *The Private Letters of Princess Lieven to Prince Metternich 1820–1826* (1937).

Randolph, Herbert (ed.), *Private Diary of Travels, Personal Services, and Public Events, during Mission and Employment with the European Armies in the Campaigns of 1812, 1813, 1814. From the Invasion of Russia to the Capture of Paris. By General Sir Robert Wilson* (2 vols, 1861).

Reeve, Henry (ed.), *The Greville Memoirs: A Journal of the Reigns of King George IV, King William IV, and Queen Victoria* (3 vols, 1874).

Robins, Jane, *Rebel Queen: The Trial of Caroline* (2006).

Royal Military Calendar, or Army Service and Commission Book (third edition, 5 vols, 1820).

The Royal Military Chronicle or British Officers Monthly Register and Mentor for May 1813 (1813).

Samuel, Ian, *An Astonishing Fellow: The Life of General Sir Robert Wilson* (Slough, 1995).

Schroeder, Paul W., *Metternich's Diplomacy at its Zenith, 1820–1823* (Austin, TX, 1962).

Schroeder, Paul W., *The Transformation of European Politics 1763–1848* (this edition, Oxford, 1996).

Seaman, W. A. L., and Sewell, J. R. (eds), *Russian Journal of Lady Londonderry 1836–7* (1973).

Sked, Alan, *Metternich and Austria: An Evaluation* (Basingstoke, 2008).

Smith, E. A., *George IV* (2003).

Smith, E. A., *A Queen on Trial: The Affair of Queen Caroline* (1993).

Speeches of the Marquess of Londonderry and the Duke of Wellington on the presentation of Petitions against the Bill for the Abolition of the Lord Lieutenancy of Ireland House of Lords Thursday 27 June 1850 (Dublin, 1850).

Spiel, Hilda (trans. Richard H. Weber), *The Congress of Vienna: An Eyewitness Account* (1968).

Stewart, Frederick, Viscount Castlereagh, *A Journey to Damascus through Egypt, Nubia, Arabia, Petraea, Palestine and Syria* (2 vols, 1847).

Sweet, Nanora, '"The Inseparables": Hemans, the Brownes and the Milan Commission', *Forum for Modern Language Studies*, xxxix (2003), pp. 165–77.

Tomkinson, James (ed.), *The Diary of a Cavalry Officer* (this edition, 1895).

Townsend, Francis, *Calendar of Knights* (1828).

The Trial at Large of Her Majesty Caroline Amelia Elizabeth, Queen of Great Britain in the House of Lords, on Charges of Adulterous Intercourse (2 vols, 1821).

Urquhart, Diane, *The Ladies of Londonderry* (2007).

Vane, Charles, third Marquess of Londonderry (ed.), *Memoirs of Viscount Castlereagh* (12 vols, 1848–53)

Vane, Charles, third Marquess of Londonderry, *Narrative of the War in Germany and France in 1813 and 1814* (1830).

Vane, Charles, third Marquess of Londonderry, *Recollections of a Tour in the North of Europe 1836–1837* (2 vols, 1838).

Vane, Charles, third Marquess of Londonderry, *A Steam Voyage to Constantinople, By the Rhine and the Danube in 1840–41, and to Portugal and Spain, &c in 1839* (2 vols, 1842).

Vane, Charles, third Marquess of Londonderry, *Story of the Peninsular War* (this edition, 1856).

Vane-Tempest-Stewart, Edith, Marchioness of Londonderry, *Frances Anne, The Life and Times of Frances Anne Marchioness of Londonderry and Her Husband Charles Third Marquess of Londonderry* (1958).

Vane-Tempest-Stewart, Edith, Marchioness of Londonderry (ed.), *Letters from Benjamin Disraeli to Frances Anne Marchioness of Londonderry 1837–61* (1938).

Vane-Tempest-Stewart, Theresa, Marchioness of Londonderry, *Robert Stewart, Viscount Castlereagh* (1904).

Vick, Brian E., *The Congress of Vienna: Power and Politics after Napoleon* (Cambridge, MA, 2014).

Webster, Sir Charles, *British Diplomacy 1813–1815: Select Documents Dealing with the Reconstruction of Europe* (1921).

Webster, Sir Charles, *Foreign Policy of Castlereagh 1815–1822* (1925).

Webster, Sir Charles, *Foreign Policy of Castlereagh 1812–1815* (1931).

Weigall, Lady Rose (ed.), *The Letters of Lady Burghersh* (1893).

Weigall, Rachel (ed.), *Correspondence of Lord Burghersh Afterwards Eleventh Earl of Westmorland 1808–1840* (1912).

Weil, M. H., *Les Dessous du Congrès de Vienne, d'après les documents originaux des archives de Ministère Impérial et Royal de l'Intérieur a` Vienne* (2 vols, Paris 1917).

Weller, Jac, *Wellington in the Peninsula* (this edition, Barnsley, 2012).

Wellesley, Arthur, second Duke of Wellington (ed.), *Despatches, Correspondence and Memoranda of Field Marshal Arthur, Duke of Wellington K.G.* (8 vols, 1858–72).

Wellesley, Arthur, second Duke of Wellington (ed.), *Despatches, Correspondence and Memoranda of Field Marshal Arthur, Duke of Wellington K.G.* (3 vols, 1867–8).

Wilks, John junior, *Memoirs of Her Majesty Caroline Amelia Eliz. Consort of George IV King of Great Britain* (2 vols, 1822).

Zamoyski, Adam, *Rites of Peace: The Fall of Napoleon and the Congress of Vienna* (2007).

Zawadzki, W. H., *Adam Czartoryski as a Statesman of Russia and Poland 1795–1831* (Oxford, 1993).

Periodicals

Gentleman's Magazine

New Monthly Magazine and Literary Journal

Online sources

History of Parliament

http://www.historyofparliamentonline.org.

Oxford Dictionary of National Biography

http://www.oxforddnb.com.

INDEX